Becoming a
CRITICAL THINKER

A Guide for the New Millennium

SECOND EDITION

Robert Todd Carroll, Ph.D.
Sacramento City College

PEARSON
Custom
Publishing

Cover Art: *Excavations,* by Brian Stevens

Printed in the United States of America

10 9 8 7 6 5

ISBN 0-536-85934-5

2004440041

LW

Please visit our web site at *www.pearsoncustom.com*

PEARSON CUSTOM PUBLISHING
75 Arlington Street, Suite 300, Boston, MA 02116
A Pearson Education Company

Table of Contents

Website for Becoming a Critical Thinker   *http://lscc.losrios.edu/~carrolb/logic.html*
For updates and corrections, go to the website.

Preface

Becoming a Critical Thinker - A Guide for the New Millennium is intended as a text for a course in introductory logic or critical thinking. As we enter a new millennium, a kind of madness in the media and the marketplace caters to our uncritical desire for more exciting and mysterious entertainment. The need for critical thinking skills has never been greater, as the power of the mass media to influence us has never been greater. Our television programs and films get wilder in their speculations and claims that most scientists would scoff at. Scientific illiteracy grows despite compulsory education and much advancement in science.

Becoming a critical thinker in the new millennium will require the development of some fundamental skills, as it has in every age. However, the skills needed for our particular time must focus on the kinds of issues and obstacles peculiar to our age.

Thus, much of this book aims at honing skills useful for separating the probable from the improbable in the daily barrage of claims hurled at us from our newspapers, magazines, televisions, our movie screens, our radios and CD players, and, of course, from our computers. The entry of the Internet into our lives means there is one more source we must be skilled at critically evaluating. The Internet has also provided opportunities for communication heretofore undreamed of. There is a website for this text. At *scc.losrios.edu/~carrolb/logic.htm,* I will list links to supplementary material. I will also list on the website any errors discovered in the text after publication.

Robert T. Carroll
June 16, 1999

Preface to the Second Edition

Chapters one, two, and three have been updated and rewritten. Chapters four, five, and six have been moderately revised. Chapters seven and eight have been significantly revised. Analogical reasoning is now covered in chapter seven, along with sampling. Chapter eight is now devoted only to causal reasoning. Chapter nine has been updated.

Robert T. Carroll
September 6, 2004

Chapter One - Critical Thinking

*"... intelligence ... is in plentiful supply
... the scarce commodity is systematic training
in critical thinking." --Carl Sagan*

*"The true critical thinker accepts what few
people ever accept -- that one cannot routinely
trust perceptions and memories." –James Alcock*

*"Truth gains more ... by the errors of one who,
with due study and preparation, thinks for himself
than by the true opinions of those who only hold them because
they do not suffer themselves to think." --John Stuart Mill*

A Problem

Imagine you are in charge of airport security at an international airport in Florida. An American Airlines counter-clerk calls to inform you that a person scheduled to get on Flight 1304 to Dallas has refused to board the plane, claiming that she is psychic and she senses that there is a bomb on board. You meet with the psychic and recognize her from the Larry King and Montel Williams shows. You vaguely remember her claiming to have used her psychic ability to solve several important criminal investigations. Aside from being agitated about the bomb, she seems normal. You order everyone off the plane and call in a crew to do a bomb search. No bomb is found but the flight has to be cancelled because some crew members have exceeded their work hours by the time the search is finished. Your action causes hundreds of people to miss their flights. The airline loses money because it has to arrange other flights for the passengers, including one for the psychic. Did you do the right thing? In your defense you claim, "In these times, we can't ignore anything." Your boss disagrees. She tells you that to her knowledge no psychic anywhere has ever discovered a bomb using psychic powers. She says that you should not have been impressed that the psychic seemed normal or was famous and had appeared on entertainment programs. She tells you that you should have had the psychic detained and questioned. Your boss considers firing you and sending word to Dallas to have the psychic arrested for making threats against a flight. Who is the better critical thinker, you or your boss? Why?

1. What does it mean to think critically?

Why are some people better than others at solving problems and making decisions? The answer seems obvious: Some people are smarter than others. But being smart isn't enough. People who follow broad rules like "We can't ignore anything" are playing it too safe. We should ignore some things because they are improbable. It is unreasonable to do a bomb search on the advice of a psychic tip because there is no evidence that psychic tips are any more reliable than flipping a coin or throwing darts at a board. What if the psychic said that her parrot told her—telepathically—that there was a bomb on the plane? Would you do a search on such evidence? If you would, you are not thinking very critically. Had you detained the psychic, you might have interrogated her while having her investigated. Has she made these kinds of claims before? What about her claim to have solved crimes using only her psychic powers? Do you think that Larry King or Montel Williams had her claims investigated?   (In fact, your boss gets on the Internet and within five minutes finds a Web site that notes that a reputable

1

investigative journalist has dug into the psychic's claims about solving crimes and found that none of her claims were true.)

Why are some people better than others at supporting their beliefs and actions with good reasons? Again, the answer seems obvious: Some people have more knowledge or are more eloquent than others. Still, two equally intelligent people can be equally articulate and knowledgeable, but not be equally good thinkers. If only one of them is thinking critically, that one will be better at analyzing and evaluating facts and opinions, sources and claims, options and alternatives. The critical thinker will be a better problem-solver and better decision-maker.

When we're thinking critically, we're using our knowledge and intelligence effectively to arrive at the most reasonable and justifiable position possible. When we're thinking uncritically--no matter how intelligent or knowledgeable we are--we'll make unreasonable decisions and arrive at unreasonable beliefs or take unjustifiable actions, *unless we are lucky and end up making the right choice for the wrong reasons!* For example, imagine that the search crew finds a bomb. You're vindicated, right? Not necessarily. If it turns out that the psychic planted the bomb herself in order to make it look like she really had psychic powers so she could advance her career, but you had the plane searched because you thought a psychic might actually be able to know such things by paranormal means, then you made the right decision by pure luck. You should have had the plane searched, but you should have held and interrogated the psychic. If a bomb is found, it would be reasonable to infer that the psychic had non-psychic information about the bomb and might even have been involved in planting it. It would not be reasonable to infer that the "psychic" is really psychic. As your boss said, there is little, if any, evidence that any psychic anywhere has ever correctly predicted when a bomb had been placed on a plane. On the other hand, there are plenty of examples where people have lied and deceived in order to advance their careers or to get attention.

The goal of thinking critically is simple: to guarantee, as far as possible, that one's beliefs and actions are justifiable and can withstand the test of rational analysis. Just what do we do when we're thinking *critically?* In general terms, we can say that *to think critically is to think clearly, accurately, knowledgeably, and fairly while evaluating the reasons for a belief or for taking some action.* This is sometimes easier said than done. Later in this chapter we will review some of the main factors that will limit or hinder even the most diligent and intelligent among us from being successful critical thinkers. But first, let's look at the standards that guide a critical thinker.

2. Standards of critical evaluation

From its beginnings in Greece over 2,500 years ago, Western philosophy and science have been primarily public activities. Some of the best minds of each generation have presented their views on important issues for their fellow citizens to accept or reject. Using only the forces of reason and eloquence to persuade, rather than torture or threats of death or damnation, the critical thinkers of the past developed rules and guidelines for determining beliefs and actions. Their predecessors or contemporaries relied on the authority of ancient texts and customs, or on the power granted them by their social position, to coerce agreement. Critically thinking philosophers and scientists used evidence available to all as they sought to discover the truth and to persuade others to accept their discoveries.

It is true that often the arguments and disputations of philosophers have been over questions that are unanswerable in any final sense. It is also true that there is no universal agreement about the methods and standards of evaluation used in these disputes. Nevertheless, much progress has been made in understanding not only the scope and limits of possible knowledge, but also the bases for reasonable belief. Three of the most important areas of philosophy relevant to critical thinking are *logic, epistemology,* and *ethics.* The first two have long and important histories of making significant contributions to the methods and standards of evaluation now prevalent in science, law, and philosophy. *Ethics* is most important for its contributions to the standards for evaluating the morality of actions. *Logic* studies the *principles of valid and invalid reasoning.* The domain of logic is narrower than the domain of critical thinking, which is concerned with evaluating the justification of beliefs and actions. *Epistemology* studies the *origin, nature, and limits of knowledge.*

2.1 Socrates

One philosopher stands out as having had the greatest influence on our critical thinking standards: the Socrates (469?–399 BCE) of Plato (470-347 BCE). "The unexamined life is not worth living," says the Socrates of Plato's *Apology*. The Socrates known to us is a figure from Plato's dialogues. For centuries, Socrates has stood as a model of intellectual integrity and inquiry: the ideal critical thinker. It is not any particular *idea* that earned him this reputation. It is his *method of questioning and cross-examination of positions* that is taken as an ideal for critical thinking. The technique is known as the Socratic Method--named after the technique he used in Plato's earliest dialogues such as *Gorgias, Euthyphro, Apology*, and the first part of the *Republic*. In those dia- logues, Socrates takes up such issues as the nature of virtue, piety, or justice, and through a series of questions examines the meanings and implications of various views expressed by others. In each case, Socrates is depicted as confronting someone who claims to be an expert. Each expert is depicted as arrogant and self-righteous, without the slightest self-doubt. Socrates leads his antagonists not to the answer but to confusion. What Plato seemed to admire about Socrates was not only his method of cross-examination, but also his humble and skeptical attitude. That attitude was in stark contrast to the arrogance of the priest Euthyphro or the sophist Thrasymachus. Socrates' meaning is clear. *The arrogant do not examine their views. They are not worth imitating.*

Of all Plato's works, perhaps the best known is his *Apology*, the account of Socrates' trial for impiety and corrupting the youth of Athens. Nothing else Plato wrote has had a more profound effect on the intellectual attitude of philosophers who came after him. In the *Apology*, Socrates is depicted as defending his way of life, rather than defending himself against the charges against him. In one of the most eloquent works in Western literature, Socrates defends a life of constant inquiry and examination of beliefs and actions. Finally, Socrates assures his accusers that the death sentence handed down to him would guarantee that he would be known to history as a heroic figure, one who died for the "crime" of thinking for himself and for encouraging others to do likewise.

Socrates may have been put to death over two thousand years ago, but his spirit of critical inquiry lives on. One of Socrates' main critical concerns was *clarity*. Of course, standards of clarity change. As we have become more aware of the power and functions of language, we have become both more demanding in our quest for clarity and more understanding of the limits of language. Simultaneously, those who would like to manipulate the thoughts and deeds of others (advertisers, politicians, con artists, evangelists, talk show hosts, lawyers, cult recruiters, and the like) continue to use their creative powers to persuade us to believe or do things that remain unclear to us. Today, the study of clarity requires a companion study of the persuasive techniques of modern propagandists, especially their attempts to manipulate thought and action through the clever use and abuse of language. Chapter Two will examine these and other issues concerning language and critical thinking.

Socrates was not concerned with clarity for its own sake, however. He knew that without clarity we couldn't understand what it is we are being asked to believe or to do. But he also recognized that clarity is not enough to base any belief or action on. Today we recognize that in addition to being based on clear claims, a critical thinker's beliefs and actions should be based on *accurate* information. Information can only be as accurate as the source from which it comes. Chapter Three examines the issue of *sources*. If we can't discover something for ourselves, what criteria should we use to determine the accuracy and reliability of sources, especially sources who claim some sort of special expertise or knowledge? How accurate is the mass media, one of the main sources of information for many of us?

Other chapters will concern such questions as what makes a reason a *good* reason for believing something or for taking some action. Or, what makes any reason or set of reasons *adequate* to justify believing something or taking some action. Since, at the very least, a good reason must be *relevant* to justifying a belief or action, the issue of relevance is one we must take up. Good reasons must also be *sufficient* to warrant accepting a belief or taking some action. Hence, the criteria by which we judge the sufficiency of evidence are going to be examined in detail, including how much weight should be given to each piece of evidence. We'll also consider the *completeness* requirement: that pertinent evidence not be suppressed or ignored, that everything relevant to the issue be presented. It was good that you, as our hypothetical airport safety manager, took every bomb threat seriously. But you should have considered *all* the relevant evidence, including the fact that people sometimes lie to further their own ends. You should have made some effort to get more information about the source of the tip. Relying on the psychic's self-proclaimed talent on a television show is not sufficient.

Knowing and adhering to the standards of critical thinking will take us a long way toward becoming a critical thinker. But if we don't have the right *attitude*, we may fail despite our knowledge of the standards.

3. Attitude of a critical thinker: open-minded, skeptical, and tentative

A critical thinker is neither dogmatic nor gullible. The most distinctive features of the critical thinker's attitude are *open-mindedness* and *skepticism*. These characteristics may seem contradictory rather than complementary. On the one hand, a critical thinker is expected to consider viewpoints different from his or her own. On the other hand, a critical thinker is expected to recognize which claims do not merit investigation. Also, sometimes what looks like open-mindedness is simply gullibility and what looks like skepticism is really closed-mindedness. To you, you are being open-minded when you take at face value the psychic's tip about a bomb on the plane. To your boss, you are being gullible. On the other hand, if you had dismissed the psychic's claim out-of-hand and written her off as deluded despite her offering to prove her psychic ability by reading your mind, then you would have crossed over from a healthy skepticism to closed-mindedness.

> "A broad mind is no substitute for hard work."
> --Nelson Goodman

To be skillful and fair in evaluating beliefs and actions, we need to seek out various views and positions on the issues we intend to judge. Being open-minded means being willing to examine issues from as many sides as possible, looking for the good and bad points of the various sides examined.[1]

One's goal in examining the positions and reasoning of others must be to get at the truth rather than to find fault. To be open-minded doesn't mean simply listening to or reading viewpoints that differ from one's own. It means accepting that someone else might have thought of something we've overlooked or that we could be in error ourselves. It may be painful, but you must admit that your boss has brought up a good point when she reminded you that there is no evidence for psychics using paranormal powers to discover bombs planes. You must admit that you were wrong in not considering this fact.

Most of us have little difficulty in being open-minded about matters that are unimportant to us. In such cases, the possibility that we may be wrong is not very threatening. If we're wrong, we can change our minds without feeling embarrassed or humiliated. But if the issue is ingrained in us or is one we feel strongly about, it becomes more difficult to be open-minded. It becomes harder to accept the fact that we might be wrong or that other views might be more reasonable than our own.

How can we overcome the tendency to be closed-minded on important issues? First, we must overcome the feeling of being threatened when a cherished belief is opposed. One way to overcome this feeling is to *commit oneself to search for the most reasonable beliefs and the most reasonable ways to act.*

> "Both teachers and learners go to sleep at their post as soon as there is no enemy in the field." --John Stuart Mill, *On Liberty*

Approaching all-important issues with a view to improving your beliefs does *not* mean that you must think that your views are wrong. It does imply that you must be able to step back from your beliefs to evaluate them along with other views. Certainly, everyone needs a basic set of beliefs in order to live a meaningful life. Yet, if those beliefs are inflexible and unchangeable, their very rigidity may work against you when you need them most, namely, in times of personal crisis. Becoming a critical thinker, in other words, requires more than mastering a set of skills; it requires a certain spirit or attitude. Sometimes this spirit is mistakenly thought to be negative only. Indeed, the primary use of the word 'critical' is to note an inclination to find fault or to judge severely. But uncovering faults and errors in one's own and other's reasoning is only a part of critical thinking. One must cultivate a *healthy skepticism* along with an ability to be open-minded, especially when considering viewpoints contrary to one's own. Too much skepticism leads to doubting everything and committing oneself to nothing; too little skepticism leads to gullibility. We need not be so demanding that we will commit ourselves to a belief or action only if we can be absolutely certain we are right. On the other hand, we should not accept claims simply because the person making the claim seems "normal" or because the majority or the experts or some witty talk-show host makes them.

On the other hand, being open-minded does not mean that one has an obligation to examine every crackpot idea or claim made. For example, I have studied occult and supernatural claims for many years. When someone says aliens have abducted him, but he has no physical evidence of his abduction, I feel no need to investigate the issue further. If someone claims to have alien body parts or vehicle parts, by all means let's examine the stuff. But if the only proof for the abduction is that the alleged abductee can't remember what happened to him for a few hours or days and he has some marks on his body he can't account for--common claims by alleged abductees-- then my hunch is that there is a natural explanation for the memory loss and the marks. He may be lying because he doesn't want anyone to know where he really was; or he passed out from natural or self-induced causes and then dreamt or hallucinated. Many of us have scrapes and bruises we can't account for. Am I closed-minded? I don't think so. However, many years ago, when I heard about UFOs and alien abductions for the first time, I would have been closed-minded had I not investigated. Once a person has studied an issue in depth, to be open-minded does not mean you must leave the door open and let in any idea that blows your way. Your only obligation is not to lock the door behind you.

An open-minded person who is inexperienced and uninformed will need to be willing to investigate issues that an experienced and informed person need not pursue. A critical thinker must find things out for herself, but once she has found

> "...if opponents of all-important truths do not exist, it is indispensable to imagine them and supply them with the strongest arguments which the most skillful devil's advocate can conjure up." --John Stuart Mill, *On Liberty*

them out she does not become closed-minded simply because her opinion is now informed! So, the next time you hear some defender of astral projection, past-life regression, or alien abductions accuse a skeptic of being "closed-minded," give thought to the possibility that the skeptic isn't closed-minded. Perhaps she has arrived at an informed belief. It is also possible that the accuser is a clever arguer who knows that charging an opponent with being closed-minded is often a successful tactic in the art of persuasion.

There are some issues about which it is not possible for a given person to be open-minded. I am thinking of issues that are not, in the words of William James, *living options.*[2] It is not possible for me to seriously consider that Muhhamad was a prophet of God, any more than it is possible for a devout Muslim to consider that Siddhartha Gautama was a divine incarnation. Before anyone can be open-minded in the sense we are talking about here, an issue must be *alive* for that person. It must be within the realm of possible belief for that person. Nevertheless, even if a belief is not a living option for you, it should be possible to be open-minded enough to try to understand what it is for someone to have that belief. It may not be possible for me to believe that Muhhamad was a prophet of God, but it is possible for me to understand what such a belief consists of. I can study Islam, listen to Muslims, and try to understand their beliefs.

I'll try to clarify this complex relationship between open-mindedness and skepticism with one more example, taken from a teacher of critical thinking, Connie Misimer. She told this story at a critical thinking conference. A student believed that chanting a

> "Be open-minded, but not so open-minded that your brains fall out." --Jacob Needleman

6

mantra (repeating some phrase, e.g., "Gopaugovinda, Gopaugovinda....") as she drove around looking for a parking space always resulted in her finding a parking space. Most teachers of critical thinking would be skeptical of the claim that a chant would have any effect on traffic or parking spaces. We would not investigate such a claim because we would consider it absurd or trivial on its face: absurd if the claim is that chanting causes parking spaces to open up; trivial if it means that she always finds a place to park her car. Some teachers might ridicule the student for being so gullible. Ms. Misimer, however, took another approach. She advised the student to set up a controlled experiment to test the claim. The student might, for example, chant every other day and keep a record of whether she is more successful on the days she chants. She might get several other students to do the same thing. They can compare notes after a few weeks and see if there is any difference in success rates. I need not go into all the details here about how this leads the student to clarify her claim, critically examine it, and find out for herself why the claim is either false or trivial. The key point is that the student needs to be open-minded enough to be willing to test her belief. Others with more experience and knowledge are not closed-minded, however, simply because they don't test her claim themselves. Furthermore, to simply impose one's views on others by fiat or ridicule, no matter how correct those views are, would hinder the development of critical thinking.

One must be careful, however, that one does not become so in love with one's own beliefs that one becomes incapable of recognizing when it is time to change. Remember that it was the Swiss who invented the quartz watch but failed to patent it because they were sure the world would always want only the traditional mechanical devices the Swiss were so expert at producing. The failure to be open-minded enough to consider the possibility that the quartz watch would become popular cost the Swiss billions of dollars and thousands of jobs.

Finally, the attitude of the critical thinker should be characterized by *intellectual humility*. Whatever we come to believe must be adhered to *tentatively*. We must always be ready to examine new evidence and arguments, even if our examination leads us to discover that a cherished belief is in error. In short, arrogance, as Socrates noted, does not befit the critical thinker. However, as we shall see, having the right attitude is not sufficient. There are many factors that can limit and hinder our desire to be a critical thinker.

Exercises 1-1

1. Define critical thinking and describe how it is related to intelligence and knowledge.
2. List the standards of evaluation used by the critical thinker. Where did they originate?
3. What are the main characteristics of the critical thinking attitude? Why is this kind of attitude important in critical thinking?
4. What does it mean to be open-minded, and why is open-mindedness essential to critical thinking? How does open-mindedness differ from being gullible?
5. What is meant by 'healthy skepticism,' and why is having a healthy skepticism important to critical thinking? How does having a healthy skepticism differ from being closed-minded?

4. Sense perception

Having the right attitude and knowing the standards of evaluation are not enough to guarantee that one will always succeed at critical thinking. Human beings are subject to a number of limitations and hindrances that forever get in the way of our best intentions.

"To doubt everything or to believe everything are two equally convenient solutions; both dispense with the necessity of reflection." --Jules Henri Poincaré

Aristotle advised that we should not demand more certainty than the subject allows (*Nichomachean Ethics,* I, iii.). That was good advice 2,500 years ago and it's good advice today. Most of the subjects that concern us in our daily lives are incapable of absolute certainty. The most we can hope for is a reasonable certainty that we've arrived at the best possible beliefs. Infallibility and absolute certainty are beyond our reach. Think, for example, about the source of most of our beliefs: *sense perception*. Each of the senses is limited in extent: Each sense has a threshold beyond which we cannot perceive. We can extend those thresholds by using instruments such as telescopes and microscopes. But those instruments have thresholds, too. Our instruments enhance our knowledge but they, too, are limited.

Furthermore, each perception must also be interpreted. With each interpretation there is the possibility of error. Each of us has been mistaken about something we thought we saw or heard. Although we often treat *facts* as if they were infallibly certain, they aren't. Facts are those things we don't have any doubts about. We call something a fact if we consider it grossly unreasonable to deny it. But, since our grasp of facts is based on sense perception, we should not claim to know any facts with infallible certainty.

4.1 Apophenia and pareidolia

In statistics, *apophenia* is called a Type I error, perceiving patterns where there are none. Some people do not just see birth marks on a lamb; they see the word "Allah" spelled out in Arabic and interpret this as a sign. They spontaneously perceive connections and meaningfulness in unrelated phenomena. They see a mark on a pizza box and are sure it is a pentagram, signifying that the pizza parlor is run by worshippers of Satan. According to neuroscientist Peter Brugger, "The propensity to see connections between seemingly unrelated objects or ideas most closely links psychosis to creativity ... apophenia and creativity may even be seen as two sides of the same coin" (Brugger 2001).[3]

While such creativity may be desired sometimes, it can also lead us astray. Some people see patterns in such things as the entrails of animals, the stars, thrown dirt or sticks, folded paper, the lines on the palm of the hand, and so on. They believe that the patterns they perceive are magically connected to the empirical world past, present and future. This belief is known as *sympathetic magic* and is the basis for most forms of divination. It is also the basis for such practices as sticking needles into figurines representing enemies, as is done in voodoo. The pins and needles stuck in a doll are supposed to magically cause pain and suffering in the person the doll represents.

Apophenia and magical thinking at one time may have represented a significant improvement in human evolution, but these pre-scientific ways of seeing and responding to the world of perception can be major hindrances to critical thinking and lead us to many illusory beliefs.

Pareidolia is a type of illusion or misperception involving a vague or obscure stimulus being perceived as something clear and distinct (Schick and Vaughn 2001). For example, a water stain on a window or the discoloration in tree bark is clearly perceived to be the Virgin Mary. While it is useful for any perceiving animal to be able to quickly interpret vague or obscure stimuli, we must be careful or we will delude ourselves with our interpretations, especially if others confirm them (see *communal reinforcement*, below). Pareidolia helps explain such things as sightings of Elvis, Bigfoot, or the Loch Ness Monster. And it may explain many religious apparitions and visions.

4.2 Autokinetic effect

The autokinetic effect refers to perceiving a stationary point of light in the dark as moving. Psychologists attribute the perception of movement where there is none to "small, involuntary movements of the eyeball" (Schick and Vaughn 2001). The autokinetic effect can be enhanced by the power of suggestion: If one person reports that a

8

light is moving, others will be more likely to report the same thing (Zusne and Jones). Some, but not all, UFO sightings are attributable to the autokinetic effect while perceiving bright stars or planets such as Venus (Schick and Vaughn 2001).

4.3 Hypersensory perception, the Clever Hans phenomenon, and ideomotor action

Hypersensory perception (HSP) is what some people call intuition (Schick and Vaughn 2001). A person with HSP is very observant and perceptive. She may be adept at reading body language or simply be more attentive to detail than most people. She may pick up subtle behavioral cues unconsciously, cues that are also unconsciously given. Because others are not so adept at reading such signs, someone with hypersensory perception may seem psychic.

Nonverbal influence can be quite profound and has been demonstrated in a number of psychological experiments (Rosenthal 1998). One of the more interesting examples of nonverbal influence is the *Clever Hans phenomenon*, named after a horse that responded to subtle visual cues when asked questions such as "What is 3 plus 2?" The horse would respond by tapping his hoof five times. He appeared to be capable of understanding human language and doing simple mathematics. However, "Hans was responding to a simple, involuntary postural adjustment by the questioner, which was his cue to start tapping, and an unconscious, almost imperceptible head movement, which was his cue to stop" (Hyman 1989: 425). Hans's master, William Von Osten, was unaware of his own movements that were signaling the horse. Such unconscious movements are known as *ideomotor action*. The term was coined by William B. Carpenter in 1852 in his explanation for the movements of rods and pendulums by dowsers, and some table turning or lifting by spirit mediums (the ones that weren't accomplished by cheating). "Carpenter argued that muscular movement can be initiated by the mind independently of volition or emotions. We may not be aware of it, but suggestions can be made to the mind by others or by observations. Those suggestions can influence the mind and affect motor behavior" (Carroll 2003: 172). "The movement of pointers on Ouija boards is also due to the ideomotor effect" (Carroll 2003: 172).

4.4 Inattentional blindness

So, we sometimes perceive things that are not there and sometimes we perceive things that *are* there, but we are unaware of them. It may seem surprising, but we sometimes do not perceive things that are there right before our eyes. Psychologists call this *inattentional blindness*. A number of studies have shown that if we are focusing our attention on one thing, we may completely miss other things that are present. For example, a pilot has flown to see a recently discovered crop circle near Stonehenge. After visiting the site, he flies back to the airport to refuel before setting off on a trip that will take him back over the site he had just visited. On the return flight he notices another crop circle near the one he had visited and swears that the new circle was not there just forty-five minutes earlier. The new circle is very elaborate and could not have been produced by human hoaxers in such a short time. He concludes that some mysterious force is at work. Perhaps, but it seems more likely that the pilot experienced inattentional blindness when he was flying to the airport. He was focused on other tasks when he flew over the site and didn't notice what was right beneath him all the time.

5. Worldviews

We each have a set of basic values and beliefs about the world. These values and beliefs are filters though which we perceive the world and interpret experience. A person's values may affect not only how much importance she gives to facts, but also what she takes to be the facts. Moral and religious beliefs are part of a person's worldview

9

and they often clash with the views of others.

Some worldviews include the notion that other worldviews must be extinguished and that theirs should become the dominant worldview. Such worldviews do not accept compromise and view those who would plead for tolerance of other worldviews as being part of a conspiracy to undermine them by encouraging free thinking. Ultra-conservative religious groups are characterized by such a worldview.

You may think that encouraging self-esteem is a proper value for education and raising children. Someone else might consider this the work of Satan and consider you a threat. Some, like the worldview advanced by Christian evangelists Jerry Falwell and Pat Robertson (*The New Millennium,* 1990), would consider the encouragement to become a critical thinker to be part of a liberal conspiracy. Some worldviews think diversity and tolerance are virtues; others consider them vices. Some worldviews are purely secular. As they do not include religious values, such worldviews hinder the ability to understand the motivations and behaviors of those whose worldviews are primarily religious. Most Americans, whether their worldviews are religious or secular, have a difficult time understanding the motivations of terrorists who intentionally kill civilians, especially if the acts are carried out by suicide bombers. To us, such behavior seems insane and we are apt to think that only deranged people could commit such atrocities. But to many people such acts are considered heroic and virtuous.

Sometimes people with clashing worldviews, like ultra-conservative Christians and ultra-liberal atheists, might use the same words to mean something quite different. Both might claim to value *freedom*, but the one may mean freedom from sinful and wicked influences, while the other may mean freedom to do what the other thinks is sinful or wicked. When some worldviews clash, there may be no middle ground; agreement may be impossible. The best one can hope for in such cases is that each side will try to understand where the other is coming from.

Our fallibility and bias, as well as our disagreements about fundamental values and principles, must limit the expectation that critical thinking will resolve all our disputes. This should be obvious since some worldviews are contradictory and some discourage critical thinking in favor of mindless obedience to some ancient text or modern guru.

6. Memory

If you're not convinced that absolute certainty and universal agreement on what to believe and do are impossible goals for critical thinking, consider *memory*. How accurate and reliable is memory? We're often wrong about how accurately we've remembered things. Studies on memory have shown that we often construct our memories after the fact and that our memories are susceptible to suggestions from others (Loftus 1980b, 1987; Schacter 1996). Those suggestions blend with our memories of events and fill in memory-gaps. That is why, for example, a police officer investigating a crime should not show a picture of a single individual to a victim and ask if the victim recognizes the assailant. If the victim is then presented with a lineup and picks out the individual whose picture the victim had been shown, there is no way of knowing whether the victim is remembering the assailant or the picture.

> "There is no such thing as absolute certainty, but there is assurance sufficient for the purposes of human life." -- John Stuart Mill

Furthermore, studies have shown that there is no significant correlation between the accuracy of a memory and the subjective feeling of certainty a person has about the memory. Child psychologist Jean Piaget, for example, claimed that his earliest memory was of nearly being kidnapped at the age of two. He remembered details such as sitting in his baby carriage, watching the nurse defend herself against the kidnapper, scratches on the nurse's face, and a police officer with a short cloak and a white baton chasing the kidnapper away. The nurse, the family, and others who had heard it reinforced the story. Piaget was convinced that he remembered the event. However, it never happened. Thirteen years after the alleged kidnapping attempt, Piaget's former nurse wrote to his parents to confess that she had made up the entire story. Piaget later wrote: "I therefore must have heard, as a child, the account of this story...and projected it into the past in the form of a visual memory, which was a memory of a memory, but false."

6.1 Confabulation

A confabulation is a fantasy that has unconsciously replaced events in memory. A confabulation may be based partly on fact or be a complete construction of the imagination. The term is often used to describe the "memories" of mentally ill persons, memories of alien abduction, and false memories induced by careless therapists or interviewers (Carroll 2003: 81).

6.2 Hypnosis and repressed memory

Contrary to what many people believe, hypnosis does not significantly aid memory's accuracy. Because subjects are extremely suggestible while hypnotized, some states do not allow as evidence in a court of law testimony made while under hypnosis (Loftus 1980a).[4] Minnesota's Supreme Court was the first state court to rule that recollections under hypnosis would not be admissible as evidence in court. The American Medical Association (AMA) agrees. An AMA committee reported that there was "no evidence to indicate that there is an increase of only accurate memory during hypnosis." Martin Reiser, director of behavioral science services for the Los Angeles Police Department, disagrees. He thinks that hypnosis is a natural human ability anyone can use to improve memory. Defenders of hypnosis cite cases such as the bus driver who, while under hypnosis, recalled most of the license plate number of a van he saw. This helped break the Chowchilla kidnapping case. (On July 15, 1976, a busload of school children and their bus driver were abducted on their way back from a swim outing.) Opponents point to the fact that people can have vivid memories under hypnosis that are false and that a hypnotized person, because of being very suggestible, runs a great risk of using the imagination to fill in memory-gaps. But even if some hypnotic memories are accurate, there is no significant probability that a memory is any more reliable simply because it has been hypnotically induced.

Even more controversial is the case of *repressed memory*. Some psychologists believe that a person can experience something extremely unpleasant and then almost immediately forget it. Many years later another experience may trigger a recollection of the horrible event. Many people forget things and *intentionally* repress memories of unpleasant experiences. But all the evidence on memory supports the notion that the more traumatic an event, the more likely one is to remember it. The only exceptions are when one is rendered unconscious and when one is too young to process the experience in terms of language (Schacter 1996).

What is the evidence, then, that repressed memories are *accurate*? San Francisco psychiatrist Lenore Terr believes that traumatic memories can be "far clearer, more detailed and more long-lasting" than ordinary memory.[5] That may be true but the real issue is the *accuracy* of the memory. Being clearer or more detailed does not mean the memory is more accurate.

> We should not expect critical thinking to lead to universal agreement on all issues, even on important issues about which there is abundant information and general agreement about the facts. We should reflect on the limitations imposed by perception, memory, our worldviews, and the testimony of others. But we need not become *entirely* skeptical regarding beliefs based on observation, memory, and testimony. Such reflection ought to encourage us to cultivate a healthy skepticism toward our pet theories and ideas. As long as we stand ready to argue for and defend our beliefs publicly, and are open-minded enough to hear out contrary arguments and change our position if need be, we will stand a good chance of avoiding unreasonable and unjustified beliefs.

The myth of the accuracy of vivid repressed memories is the basis for a number of popular works on child abuse by self-proclaimed experts such as Ellen Bass, Laura Davis, Wendy Maltz, Beverly Holman, Beverly Engel, Mary Jan Williams and E. Sue Blume.[6] A whole industry has been built up out of the hysteria that inevitably accompanies charges of the sexual abuse of children. Therapists who are supposed to help children recover from the trauma of child abuse are hired to interrogate children to find out if they've been abused. All too often the therapist suggests the abuse to the child and then the child has "memories" of being abused. No rational person should find a parent or caretaker guilty on the basis of such tainted testimony.[7] Since March 1992, the False Memory Syndrome (FMS) Foundation in Philadelphia has collected 2,700 cases of parents who report false accusations that were the result of "memories" recovered in therapy.[8] The FMS Foundation claims that these cases include about 400 families who have been sued or threatened with suits for child abuse.[9]

A variant of the memory of non-experiences is the notion that a person can remember experiences from past lives. This myth has been perpetuated primarily by accounts of people who in dreams or under hypnosis recall experiences of people who lived in earlier times. A classic example of a false memory of a past life is the case of Bridey Murphy. In 1952, Morey Bernstein hypnotized Virginia Tighe, who then began speaking in an Irish brogue and claimed that she had been Bridey Murphy from Cork, Ireland, in a previous incarnation. While under hypnosis, Tighe sang Irish songs and told Irish stories, always as Bridey Murphy. *The Search for Bridey Murphy* (Tighe is called Ruth Simmons in the book) was a best seller. Recordings of the hypnotic sessions were translated into more than a dozen languages. The recordings sold well, too. The reincarnation boom in America had begun. Never again would an American publisher lose money on a book dealing with reincarnation, past life regression, channeling, life after life, or any occult topic appealing to the human desire to live forever.

Newspapers sent reporters to Ireland to investigate. Was there a redheaded Bridey Murphy who lived in Ireland in the nineteenth century? Who knows, but one paper--the *Chicago American*--found her in Chicago in the 20th century. Bridie Murphey Corkell lived in the house across the street from where Elizabeth Tighe grew up. What Elizabeth reported while hypnotized were not memories of a previous life but memories from her early childhood. Many people were impressed with the vivid details of her memories, but details are not evidence of authenticity. Tighe engaged in *confabulation*

As Martin Gardner says, "Almost any hypnotic subject capable of going into a deep trance will babble about a previous incarnation if the hypnotist asks him to. He will babble just as freely about his future incarnations....In every case of this sort where there has been adequate checking on the subject's past, it has been found that the subject's unconscious mind was weaving together long-forgotten bits of information acquired during his early years" (Gardner 1977).[10]

7. Testimony

For much of what we believe, we have to rely on what other people tell us. Their reports are as liable to error as our own. Still, we can be reasonably certain of some people's reports and reasonably doubtful of others. In chapter three, we'll present some rules for deciding which reports are trustworthy. Here we will simply raise a few cautionary concerns about relying on testimonials.

Testimonials are often very vivid and detailed, making them appear very believable. They are often made by enthusiastic people who seem trustworthy and honest and who lack any reason to deceive us. They are often made by people with some semblance of authority, such as those who hold a Ph.D. in psychology or physics.

To some extent, testimonials are believable because people *want* to believe them [See *wishful thinking*, below.]. Often, one anticipates with hope some new treatment or instruction. One's testimonial is given soon after the experience while one's mood is still elevated from the desire for a positive outcome. The experience and the testimonial it elicits are given more significance than they deserve. (Carroll 2003: 375).

Because it is easy for people to deceive themselves (see *self-deception*, below), scientists do not usually rely on testimonials or anecdotes, except perhaps to stimulate them to design controlled experiments to test hypotheses. (Designing controlled experiments is discussed below in the chapter on causal reasoning.)

The testimonial of personal experience in paranormal or supernatural matters has no scientific value. If others cannot experience the same thing under the same conditions, then there will be no way to verify the experience. If there is no way to test the claims made, then there will be no way to tell if the experience was a delusion or was interpreted correctly. If others can experience the same thing, then it is possible to make a test of the testimonial and determine whether the claim based on it is worthy of belief.

Testimonials regarding paranormal experiences are scientifically worthless because selective thinking and self-deception must be controlled for. Most psychics do not even realize that they need to do a controlled test of their powers to rule out the possibility that they are deceiving themselves. They are satisfied with their experience as psychics. Controlled tests of psychics will prove once and for all that they are not being selective in their evidence gathering, that is, that they are counting only the apparent successes and conveniently ignoring or underplaying the misses. Controlled tests can also determine whether other factors, such as cheating might be involved. (Carroll 2003: 375).

Thus, while testimonial evidence is sometimes essential—as in telling your physician your symptoms—it is easy to overvalue other people's experiences, especially if they are put forth enthusiastically and authoritatively.

8. Ignorance

Perhaps the greatest hindrance to thinking critically is ignorance: the lack of essential background knowledge on the subject at hand. Ignorance is not the same as stupidity, which has to do with lack of, or incompetent application of, *intelligence*. Ignorance has to do with lack of *knowledge* or *information*. Perhaps nothing hinders critical thinking more than lack of adequate vocabulary. Using a good dictionary is often a quick and efficient way to overcome one of the main hindrances to critical thinking. After all, if you don't understand what a person means, you can't very well evaluate that person's claims or arguments.

Without a firm understanding of the basic principles and accepted beliefs in a particular field, it is impossible to judge the truth, relevance, or sufficiency of evidence put forth to support positions in that field. Without adequate background knowledge of a subject, one can't tell whether claims are clear enough or whether relevant material has been omitted. In short, one can be a master of critical thinking skills, but without knowledge those skills won't do you much good.

A good critical thinker knows that conclusions, decisions, or actions should be knowledgeable ones. He or she knows that the best thinking is done when *all* pertinent data is presented. Critical thinking requires the ability to do skillful reading and research. This will require hard work, and, as the saying goes, there really is no substitute for it. A critical thinker must know how to use the library and computer data banks to get needed information. And since it is often impossible to do one's own research, a critical thinker must be skilled at evaluating the claims of experts and authorities in various fields. These are topics we will take up in chapter three.

> **Exercise 1-2**
>
> As you read the material on limitations and hindrances to critical thinking, keep a notebook and list each hindrance. Later, review your list and select one or more areas that you believe you need to work on most. Commit yourself to conquering at least one hindrance you think is likely to prevent you from becoming a better critical thinker. Suggestions on ways to overcome the hindrances to critical thinking are discussed in section 6 of this chapter.

9. Beliefs

Some beliefs can hinder critical thinking. If you believe you will fail at trying to solve a problem, you probably won't try. If you don't try, you won't avail yourself of the opportunity to learn and develop your talents, including your critical thinking talents. Surprisingly, much research has found that believing that intelligence is something you are born with, and is fixed for life by your genes, hinders people in several ways that might affect their ability to think critically. "One of the dumbest things people do with the fixed view of intelligence is to sacrifice important learning opportunities when those opportunities contain a risk of revealing ignorance or making errors" (Dweck 2002: 29). Why? Because people who believe intelligence is completely fixed tend to fear failure more than people who view intelligence as largely a potential that can be developed. They seem to fear failure because they tend to measure their self-worth by their intelligence. They interpret any failure as a sign that they lack intelligence. They thus tend to play it safe. People who believe intelligence is malleable tend to interpret any given failure as a sign that they lack a specific skill or bit of knowledge. Instead of being put off by failure, they are often inspired by it to take action and even take more risks. Without risks, learning is impossible. Dweck puts it this way: "Students who hold a fixed view of their intelligence care so much about looking smart that they act dumb…."(2002: 31).

Another belief that can hinder critical thinking is the belief that only dumb people have to work hard or that intelligent people learn effortlessly (Dweck 2002: 31). This phenomenon is called self-handicapping (Berglas 1990), and it is the tendency to do things that will prevent you from looking like you have low ability, even if these are things that will jeopardize your performance. When people self-handicap, it means that they care more about looking smart (or avoiding looking dumb) than about accomplishing something (Dweck 2002: 32). Unfortunately, self-handicapping is something intelligent people who believe in fixed intelligence tend to do because they tend to believe things should come easy to them. The moral of the story seems to be: Even if there is some limit to intelligence imposed by biology, believing that intelligence is largely a potential to be developed, will often be the main difference between two equally intelligent people who are unequal critical thinkers.

> **Exercise 1-3**
>
> There are many beliefs that could hinder the development of critical thinking. Create a list of five beliefs that you believe would hinder critical thinking and explain why you think so.

10. Wishful thinking and self-deception

Wishful thinking is interpreting facts, reports, events, perceptions, etc., according to what one would like to be the case rather than according to the actual evidence. For example, I am convinced that my girlfriend is faithful even though several of my friends have told me they've seen her being intimate with another guy. *Self-deception* is the process or fact of misleading ourselves to accept as true or valid what is false or invalid. Self-deception, in short, is a way we justify false beliefs to ourselves. When I convince myself that my girlfriend is unfaithful to me because she loves me and is just trying to make me jealous, I'm deceiving myself.

> **Ninety-four percent of university professors think they are better at their jobs than their colleagues.**
>
> **Twenty-five percent of college students believe they are in the top 1% in terms of their ability to get along with others.**
>
> **Seventy percent of college students think they are above average in leadership ability. Only two percent think they are below average.**
> ---Thomas Gilovich *How We Know What Isn't So*

We often believe things not because we have good evidence for them but because we *want* to believe them. We tend to construe things in our own favor, to look for evidence that fits with what we already believe or want to believe. Too often, we are easily deceived when it suits our purposes. We allow loyalty or hostility to control how we think about those we love and hate. Too often, we see only what we want to see and believe only what we want to believe. For example, when mail with money for our daughter is found opened and empty or when money is stolen from our house, we don't want to believe that it is our own son who is doing the stealing, so we accept his claims of innocence at face value. When he suggests that it might have been one of his friends or a friend of a friend, we are all too ready to put the blame elsewhere. We don't need any evidence of guilt; our wish not to believe our own son is a thief is sufficient to deceive us into thinking we know who the guilty party really is.

> **"We are never deceived; we deceive ourselves."** --Goethe
>
> **"We like to be deceived."** --Blaise Pascal
>
> **"....delusions are always more alluring than facts."**
> --Clarence Darrow

Our desire to succeed at some task may make us blind to our faults or inadequacies, resulting in our putting blame for our own lack of ability on others. The most perverted form of this type of self-deception occurs in those who refuse to face facts about their own lack of intelligence, ambition, or skill, and so blame other races, ethnic groups or religions for their own troubles. No failure in their lives is due to any action or inaction on their own part. The fault is always with some other group: Catholics, Jews, Muslims; Protestants, Republicans, Democrats; Africans, Asians, Mexicans; Serbs, Croatians, Americans; Arabs, Iranians, Israelis, or dead white European males.

10.1 The Forer Effect

People have a tendency to accept a vague and general personality description as uniquely applicable to themselves without realizing that the same description could be applied to just about anyone. Psychologist B. R. Forer gave a personality test to his students, ignored their answers, and gave the same assessment to each student. He asked them to grade their assessment on a scale of 0 to 5, with 5 being *very accurate*. The evaluation average was 4.26. The test has been repeated hundreds of time and the average remains around 4.2.

The Forer effect may be why many people believe in astrology, biorhythms, fortune telling, graphology, palm reading, and other such methods of character analysis. Forer thought that *gullibility* could account for the customers' tendency to accept identical personality assessments. It seems more complicated than that and may involve not only gullibility, but self-deception, wishful thinking, and confirmation bias (see below).

> People tend to accept claims about themselves in proportion to their desire that the claims be true rather than in proportion to the empirical accuracy of the claims as measured by some nonsubjective standard. We tend to accept questionable, even false statements about ourselves, if we deem them positive or flattering enough. We often give very liberal interpretations to vague or inconsistent claims about ourselves in order to make sense out of the claims. (Carroll 2003: 147).

The Forer effect is sometimes referred to as *the Barnum effect*, after P.T. Barnum who claimed to have something for everybody.

11. Suggestibility, conformity, and admiration for experts and authorities

In many areas of inquiry, having an open mind and possessing a healthy skepticism won't be sufficient to produce the most reasonable beliefs. In areas where we are not competent to make reasonable judgments, we must rely on experts and authorities. It is essential, therefore, that we learn how to use intelligently the claims of authorities and

> *"The despotism of custom is everywhere the standing hindrance to human advancement...."*
> —John Stuart Mill, On Liberty

experts. This may be difficult since we may be vulnerable to certain tricks of persuasion. Psychologist Robert Thouless writes:

> The psychological fact of suggestion is the fact that if statements are made again and again in a confident manner, without argument or proof, then their hearers will tend to believe them independently of their soundness and of the presence or absence of evidence for their truth. More particularly will his hearers tend to accept the suggestions of a speaker if he has what we may call 'prestige'--the acknowledged dignity of authority possessed by senators, bishops, prize fighters, successful authors, and other famous men (Thouless 1950: 57-58).

> If I said in an impressive tone of voice, on my authority as a psychologist, that there are or are not such things as ghosts, or that our souls are or are not immortal, I could succeed in influencing a great many suggestible people, although a moment's reflection should convince them that I have exactly the same right to an opinion on such subjects as they have themselves and no more (Thouless 1950: 70-71).

Authorities themselves do much to perpetuate their power and convince the rest of us that it is a good thing to accept their claims uncritically. One reason we tend to accept claims solely on the authority of experts is that the experts themselves have repeatedly asserted that it is good for us to do so.

Another writer on the subject of the mind's susceptibility to suggestion, Giles St. Aubyn, writes

> Susceptibility to suggestion is one of the consequences of man's gregariousness. He tends to accept statements and opinions that are constantly repeated, whether there are grounds for believing them or not . . . .Our suggestibility involves us in a great deal of illogical thinking because it encourages us to accept ideas and opinions uncritically, without examining the evidence for or against them. Human suggestibility arises from a deeply rooted instinct to respond to the herd. If several wolves are to maneuver as one, every wolf must instantly conform to the needs of the pack. The individual's sensitivity to such requirements is the essence of gregariousness. But man's instinctive desire to conform is fundamentally unreasonable, because it encourages him to accept as self-evident ideas prevalent in the community in which he happens to live (St. Aubyn 1962: 57).

If we have a strong inclination to conform, then we would tend to desire agreement rather than disagreement with others. Desiring agreement with others, we would be less likely to challenge them than if we had a stronger inclination to get at the truth. On the other hand, desiring agreement would also lead us to devise ways to keep others from disagreeing with us. There seems to be a strong connection between the tendency to conform and the tendency of authorities and those with power to encourage us to think and act uncritically. We're all aware of how parents, teachers, and friends, use fear and guilt to persuade and manipulate us when reason and evidence are lacking. We've all seen the effects of stating publicly a viewpoint that is not popular.

Still, despite St. Aubyn's claim that the desire to conform is fundamentally unreasonable, conformity is essential for social creatures to co-exist peacefully. As children, for example, we had to put our trust in our parents, teachers, and leaders in order to survive and grow into mature adults. The problem, in other words, is not suggestibility, authority, prestige, or conformity. The problem is in the *perversion* of the need to trust authorities and to conform. The problem is finding the right point at which we should become an independent thinker.

The natural and usually beneficial tendency to conform can, when misdirected or unreflectively applied, lead us to accept uncritically the ideas of friends, colleagues and relatives. Accepting their views makes us acceptable to them: *to believe is to belong.* Accepting their views makes us one of them: *to believe is to become more prestigious in our own eyes.* Accepting their views means we can stop thinking or worrying about one more thing: *to believe is to be more comfortable.*

Exercise 1-4

List several ways that each of the following professionals use their authority to keep us in an uncritical state: *scientists, physicians, teachers, lawyers, military and religious leaders, journalists and politicians.*

12. Laziness and pride

Laziness plays a role in encouraging us to conform and to kowtow to authority. Combined with the common desire for quick results and simplicity, laziness also leads to the tendency to think in terms of stereotypes and slogans. A stereotype (e.g., "the woman driver," "the redneck," "the teenager," "the liberal") is a classification, and a slogan is a generalization ("Love it or leave it;" "Make love not war," "Skepticism is a virtue") or an oversimplification ("Darwin's theory is that we all come from monkeys;" "Freud said everything is sex," "Atheists believe life is meaningless") based not on evidence but on prejudice or unexamined beliefs. Gordon Allport called stereotyping "the principle of least effort" (1954: 173). Thouless calls it "tabloid thinking" (1950: 91-101).

Pride, too, plays a part in hindering us from thinking critically. Most of us want to appear knowledgeable and right, rather than ignorant or wrong, so we don't object to or challenge claims made by others, especially authorities. We pretend we understand things for fear of appearing foolish. Or we let false or stupid remarks go by without saying anything because we don't want to cause a scene.

13. Communal reinforcement

Communal reinforcement is the process by which a claim becomes a strong belief through repeated assertion by members of a community. The process is independent of whether or not the claim has been properly researched or is supported by empirical data significant enough to warrant belief by reasonable people.

Communal reinforcement accounts for the popularity of unsupported claims regarding repressed memory and child abuse, which was discussed above. It accounts for such beliefs that children have memories that are completely accurate, that children rarely says things that aren't true, that you can rid yourself of cancer by visualization or humor, that Jews control all the power and money of the world, and so on.

Communal reinforcement explains how entire nations can believe in such things as witchcraft or demonic possession. It also explains how testimonials reinforced by other testimonials within the community of therapists, sociologists, psychologists, theologians, politicians, talk show aficionados, and so on, can be more powerful than scientific studies or accurate gathering of data by unbiased parties.

14. Bias or prejudice

Bias is a predisposition to tackle a problem or react to people or situations in a certain way. Referring to the "liberal bias" of the media means one thinks the media has a predisposition to present stories and information in ways that favor the liberal, as opposed to a conservative, viewpoint. Whether this is a fair charge is something we will examine in chapter three.

Prejudice refers to judgments that are not based on evidence or study, but are preformed opinions about a person, group, or issue. Prejudicial views can be either favorable or unfavorable.

Everybody's worldview includes some biases and prejudices, not the least of which is the general tendency to see oneself as the center of the universe and one's culture as the standard by which to measure all others. We interpret new experiences through our worldviews and if they are in error, it seems we will be hopelessly locked into a lifetime of more error. The only way out seems to be to make a conscious effort to be open-minded, to reflect

> *The unexamined life is not worth living.*
> *—Socrates*

on our experience and use our intelligence as best we can to correct our errors and overcome our biases and prejudices.

Overcoming the effects of preconceived notions is very difficult. The philosopher René Descartes (1596-1650) believed that the only way to be successful with this hindrance would be to doubt everything one believes and start over by developing a method that would guarantee absolute certainty. While there have been attempts since to realize Descartes' ideal,[11] we are more likely to be successful if we abandon the goal of absolute certainty in most matters and settle for reasonable probabilities. The idea of doing an inventory of one's beliefs, trying to identify personal prejudices, is certainly a good one. Awareness of one's prejudices will not guarantee over-coming them, but ignoring them will guarantee not making any progress in this area. The best advice may well be that given by Socrates at his trial over two thousand years ago: always be willing to examine your beliefs and actions. The unexamined life is not worth living.

If we cannot master our *egocentrism* and our *ethnocentrism*--the tendency to think that oneself and one's culture are the standards of truth and reality--we will never become critical thinkers. Every society, however, promotes ethnocentrism and discourages the disputing of traditional beliefs and values. Thus, critical thinking is likely to be more rare than common, more difficult than easy to achieve.

15. Confirmation Bias

Confirmation bias refers to a type of selective thinking whereby one tends to notice and look for what confirms one's beliefs, and to ignore, not look for, or undervalue the relevance of what contradicts one's beliefs. For example, if someone who works in a hospital emergency room believes that during a full moon there is an increase in admissions, she will take notice of admissions during a full moon. However, she will be inattentive to the phase of the moon when accidents occur during other times of the month. A tendency to do this over time unjustifiably strengthens one's belief in the relationship between the full moon and emergency room admissions.

Most people don't seem to realize how easy it is to find supportive evidence for almost any belief. By ignoring contrary evidence or by making no effort to find such evidence, one can convince oneself of almost anything. For example, when

> *"It is the peculiar and perpetual error of the human understanding to be more moved and excited by affirmatives than by negatives."*
> *—Francis Bacon*

Joseph Banks Rhine, one of the pioneers in ESP research, found that some test subjects failed to do better than would be expected by chance, he explained the data away as being due to unconscious direction to avoid the target. Parapsychologists have even given this alleged phenomenon a name: *psi-missing*. (*Psi* is a word used in parapsychology to refer to any kind of paranormal phenomena.) Rhine even claimed that subjects who weren't performing in such a way as to support his ESP hypothesis didn't like him and were consciously guessing incorrectly to spite him (Park 2000: 42). When skeptics could not replicate ESP experiments, parapsychologists attributed this to *the experimenter effect*, which they defined to mean that believers in ESP got positive results, while non-believers get negative results because their *telepathic effect is different on the subjects*. When the laws of chance predict that over a long period of time a person will guess at something at a chance rate, parapsychologists take doing better than chance over a short period as a time when ESP was working. If a psychic is caught cheating, the defender of the paranormal will say that that doesn't mean she *always* cheats and that some of her feats may still be genuinely psychic. If you are clever enough, you will be able to rationalize any data that seem to contradict your belief and find *more* support in the data rather than less.

This tendency to give more attention and weight to data that support our preconceptions and beliefs than we do to contrary data is especially pernicious when our beliefs are little more than prejudices. If our beliefs are firmly established upon solid evidence and valid confirmatory experiments, the tendency to give more attention and weight to data that fits with our beliefs should not lead us astray. Of course, if we become blinded to evidence truly refuting a favored hypothesis, we have crossed the line from reasonableness to closed-mindedness.

Numerous studies have demonstrated that people generally give an excessive amount of value to confirmatory information, i.e., data which is positive or which supports a position (Gilovich 1993). Thomas Gilovich speculates that the "most likely reason for the excessive influence of confirmatory information is that it is easier to deal with cognitively." It is much easier to see how a piece of data supports a position than it is to see how it might count against the position. Consider how dowsers are convinced that they have paranormal powers that guide them in finding water with a bent stick. The belief in their power is based upon remembering the times they found water. However, dowsers and their advocates don't keep track of failures. When tested under controlled conditions, they have failed to perform at anything better than a chance rate. (Controlled experiments are discussed in chapter eight.)

This tendency to give more attention and weight to the positive and the confirmatory has been shown to influence memory. When digging into our memories for data relevant to a position, we are more likely to recall data that confirm the position (Gilovich).

Researchers are sometimes guilty of confirmation bias by setting up experiments or framing their data in ways that will tend to confirm their hypotheses. They compound the problem by proceeding in ways that avoid dealing with data that would contradict their hypotheses. For example, American anthropologists generally accept what is known as the "Clovis model." Some 11,000 years ago, according to this model, people from Northeast Asia entered the Americas and spread across the Great Plains, the Southwest, and eventually to the East. These peoples are considered to be the ancestors of today's Native Americans. Anthropologists had no problem piling up the evidence in support of the Clovis model. However, few bothered to look for anything older and did not excavate for sites beneath the Clovis limit. Recently, excavations at Monte Verde in Chile and Meadowcroft Rockshelter in Avella, Pennsylvania, have led to discoveries that may set back the time of the earliest settlers from one to several thousand years. Even more interesting is that skulls that had been assumed to be of the stock from which Native American descended are being re-examined and there is now some doubt as to the racial origins of the skulls.[12]

Experimenters might avoid or reduce confirmation bias by collaborating with colleagues who hold contrary hypotheses. By jointly working on the design of an experiment and on the analysis of the resulting data, the experimenters might keep each other from inadvertently biasing the study. For example, Peter Brugger, a neuroscientist who is skeptical of ESP claims, joined with noted parapsychologist John Palmer to conduct a series of studies to test, among other things, Brugger's hypothesis that some individuals who seem to show paranormal abilities in experiments on telepathy are actually subconsciously recognizing hidden patterns. The two-year project was funded by the Cogito Foundation on condition that both a parapsychologist and a skeptic be involved. (Results will not be available until after 2006.)

16. Physical and emotional hindrances

Physical or emotional stress, fatigue, and certain drugs can severely affect our ability to think clearly and critically. Hospital interns complain of the inability to do their medical duties to the best of their ability because they are required to serve thirty-six hour or longer shifts. Air traffic controllers and airline pilots complain of the inability to make good judgments when they are fatigued after long hours on duty. Add the stress of immense responsibility and it is easy to see why we make bad judgments when we are fatigued.

How often have you stayed up all night studying for an exam? Usually, however, you can think well if you are rested. Any benefit from all-night cramming will be more than offset by the disadvantages of being tired. The problem can be compounded if the student is ingesting copious quantities of caffeine and nicotine, or other more potent stimulants as well. It should be obvious that drugs, even certain medically prescribed and legal ones, can severely hamper an individual's ability to reason well. (Of course, not all drugs are hindrances to critical thinking. Some drugs have a calming or healing effect, and are necessary for some people to enable them to think critically.)

And just as stress or drugs can adversely affect our ability to think critically, so too can being under the influence of any strong emotion. It is true that some people do their best thinking under pressure, but usually we can neither perceive clearly nor make good judgments while terrified, angry, jealous, etc. If we cannot learn to control our emotions, we might at least try to avoid making any decisions while emotionally upset. Wait, if possible, until a calmer moment arrives.

17. Censorship

Certain political liberties are essential to the development of critical thinking. The repression of free speech is a major hindrance to critical thinking. Without adequate information, judgments and evaluations of issues will be slanted and biased. The main reason for censorship is to control the thoughts and actions of people. When information is controlled, thought is controlled. When thought is controlled, actions are controlled.

Every parent knows that there are times when censorship is justified for the good of one's child. Graphic violence or sex, depictions of cruelty and the like, are reasonably excluded from children's books and television programming. However, no child will ever learn to think for herself if

> "Give me the liberty to know, to utter, and to argue freely according to conscience, above all liberties."
> **John Milton (1608-1674),** *Areopagitica.*

she is only allowed to see or hear what her parents want her to see or hear. Some nations treat their adult citizens as children and prohibit such material to everybody. They assume their citizens not only *should not* but *cannot* think and act for themselves.

Freedom of speech, however, is sometimes repressed in "free" countries. Three examples should suffice: the censoring of books in our public schools; the censoring of art by public programs such as the National Endowment for the Arts; and the censoring of information by the military.

Each year in hundreds of school districts around the country, there are attempts to ban certain books from the public schools. In 1990-1991 there were over 200 such book-banning confrontations between the "protectors of decency and truth" and "the defenders of liberty." Some of the works the protectors wanted to ban were *The Grapes of Wrath, One Hundred Years of Solitude, Huckleberry Finn, Lord of the Flies*, and *Webster's Ninth Collegiate Dictionary*. The justification for banning the books varied, but usually the protectors cited items such as offensive language, pictures, or ideas. The would-be censors range from religious conservatives wanting to ban stories about witches, to political liberals wanting to ban stories that depict women or minorities in "demeaning" ways. Some found offense with Bible stories; others were offended by scientific theories. Some wanted to censor anything sexual; others wanted to censor sexual material that reflected disdain for homosexuality.

Another group of censors, led by Sen. Jesse Helms of North Carolina, wanted to ban public funding of "indecent" art. The National Endowment for the Arts agreed to require the signing of a "decency document" by any person or group applying for funds. Some prior beneficiaries, such as the Ashland Shakespeare Festival, refused to sign the document and became ineligible for a grant. Those who refused to be censored did so not out of a desire to be indecent, but out of concern for the loss of liberty. Those who defended the censorship did so out of concern for spending public money on art that offended certain Christians. The American censors reminded the art community that things could be worse. Irate Muslims, led by the Iranian Ayatollah Khomeini, were calling for the execution *by anyone at anytime* of Salman Rushdie for having written *Satanic Verses*, a book that is said to blaspheme Muhammad.

Finally, the United States military has become more and more controlling of information regarding its invasions of such countries as Grenada, Panama, and Iraq. Military censorship and control of information reached unprecedented heights during the Gulf War. The Gulf War was a television war, but not in the sense that many journalists and much of the public had hoped for. It was a Nintendo War for the deaf. We did not get to see and hear live coverage of bloody battles. We never got a ground level video of bombs being dropped, of explosions in our ears. What we got instead were soundless videos taken from airplanes or from bombs as they entered buildings. No loud explosions. No screams. No dead bodies. We did see a few thousand burned out vehicles.

We didn't see many pictures taken from the ground. Many of those we did see were censored by the Iraqis. Especially dramatic was the film of the bombed out building that became the tomb for hundreds of Iraqi women and children. U.S. officials called the building a military headquarters; Iraqi officials called it a bomb shelter. There was also the video of the bombed out factory which Iraqi officials say was a baby formula factory, while U.S. officials insist it was a chemical warfare plant.

The first video of ground damage, including pictures of charred and dismembered Iraqi soldiers, was released on March 27, 1991, long after the war had ended. The U.S. military released the videos to the mass media, not the other way around. Other videos of damage done by bombs dropped on Iraq, such as the one narrated by former U.S. attorney general Ramsey Clark, have not been shown by the major networks.

What television brought us was a highly censored view of war. What wasn't censored by the military was censored by the networks themselves. We saw, for the most part, only what the U.S. government wanted us to see. There were a few dramatic exceptions. There was the reporter in Israel showing us a map of Tel Aviv with a clear marking where a Scud missile had landed. Back in Baghdad they might have thought this report interesting, if not valuable, from a military perspective. However, it doesn't appear that the Iraqi military leaders were watching too much television. After the ground fighting ceased, we were informed by the Pentagon that the only information that might have been vital to the enemy had passed through the

> "If kids don't run up against ideas that are disquieting, or challenging, or different from what they've always believed, or different from what their parents believe, how will they ever grow as human beings?...Banning books shows you don't trust your kids to think and you don't trust yourself to be able to talk with them."
> --Anna Quindlen

military censors' hands and was reported on television. Several of our reporters figured out General Schwarzkopf's plan from a piece of information about engineers working in the western Saudi Arabian town of

Rahra. The reporters voluntarily kept silent about it. They even encouraged their bosses to keep silent about it. So, it was self-censorship, rather than military censorship, which proved more important in the end at keeping vital information from the enemy.[13]

What television brought us during the Gulf War was what the U.S. Military information managers wanted us to see. The military set up a pool system whereby a select number of reporters were taken by the military to designated places in the war zone. What they saw and who they had contact with was strictly controlled by the military. But the reporters were then free to pass out what information they had garnered to other reporters waiting at the home base. The military flew reporters with cameras out to sea so they could make stunning visuals of the preparation for the massive amphibious landing. The assault from the sea never took place, of course. That was a ruse, a feint. Television was used to help dupe Hussein into thinking we were planning a massive attack from the sea. (See how busy we are sweeping those Iraqi mines in the harbors. See how concerned we are about all that oil which might be ignited and burn to death our marines as they try to make their way through heavy seas to the coast of Kuwait.)[14]

Despite the furor such debates cause, much of the debate over books in the schools, government-supported artists, and press coverage of military operations is not about censorship per se. It is about the *appropriateness* of certain materials for certain age groups, or the *appropriateness* of government-funded art that is irreligious or unpatriotic, or the *appropriateness* of releasing information which might prove harmful to the national interest. Still, a good part of the debates is about censorship per se. There are many people in our society who do not want anyone to be allowed to express certain ideas or use certain language. Such people, whether they are conservative or liberal, are always a danger to critical thinking. They are a danger not because of the ideas they defend or express, including the idea of censorship. They are a danger because often what they want to suppress is offensive to many of us and, as a result, we will be less likely to challenge them. Unchallenged, the censors will get their way and the result will be stifling. It is inevitable that freedom of speech will be abused. The price of preventing abusive speech is to censor it; the additional cost will be a severe reduction in critical and creative thinking.

There is, however, a benefit to the existence of would-be censors: they can serve as a stimulus to the defenders of liberty and critical thinking. They make us reflect on our beliefs and argue to defend them. That is always valuable. Furthermore, sometimes the censors make us aware of what is happening in the schools or in the world of art or on the battlefield. Maybe we are introducing children to inappropriate materials. Such dialogue can be healthy. Maybe the government is too influential in the content of the art it supports. Maybe the military is censoring information because they have a lot to hide about their own incompetence or evil. The censors, at least, initiate a dialogue on the issue.

17.1 Lawsuits and the law as forms of censorship

One way to stifle speech is to frighten people into silence by threatening to sue them for millions of dollars if they speak up. That is what happened to James Randi when he wrote that Uri Geller, who claims to have psychic powers, is a fraud, a magician, and con artist. That is what happened to several people who have publicly criticized Scientology. That is what happened to journalist Andrew Skolnick for his investigative report on health fraud by the Maharishi Mahesh Yogi and his Transcendental Meditation Movement. The purpose of the lawsuits is to harass and intimidate critics.

Shortly after the ratification of the first amendment, Congress passed a sedition act that made it illegal to criticize the government. Such uses of the law continue in our own day. Florida made it illegal to criticize their citrus crops. Presumably this was done to protect a vital economic interest, but environmentalists fear they can be sued or arrested for writing about pesticides in foods. Whatever the goal of such legislation, it has the effect of censorship. Several states have followed Florida's example, including Texas, which has a "perishable food disparagement law." Celebrity Oprah Winfrey was sued by some cattle ranchers for libeling beef on her television program. She had said that she'd eaten her last burger after a guest on her show stated that American cattle could be infected with bovine spongiform encephalopathy (BSE), the so-called mad cow disease. Winfrey won the lawsuit, but one wonders what chilling effect on free speech such suits will have on others.

Harassment lawsuits have led the Committee for the Scientific Investigation of Claims of the Paranormal (CSICOP) to form a Legal Defense Foundation. What does that say to us? We pride ourselves in being the freest country in the world. Yet, the expression of skeptical opinions or truthful observations critical of psychics, occultists, and paranormals are in danger of being stifled. The Legal Defense Foundation, says CSICOP, is "the best way to blunt this frightening new weapon of the apostles of nonsense."[15] I'm not so sure. California and New York have passed laws to provide relief for victims of harassment lawsuits. That seems to me to be a better way to deal with this type of censorship. Make the plaintiffs in frivolous defamation suits pay all the legal costs and make it easy for defendants in such cases to collect their legal expenses. I would also like to see the defendants awarded damages in the amount of the original suit, should it be declared to be frivolous. So, if the scientologists sue me for $20,000,000 for calling Scientology the rankest pseudoscience of the twentieth century, and the court decides their suit is frivolous, intended to harass and intimidate me, then the scientologists pay me $20,000,000. Sounds fair to me.

18. Overcoming limitations and hindrances to critical thinking

The only way to overcome the lack of essential background knowledge in a field is to do the necessary reading and studying in that field.

Overcoming the social pressure to conform is difficult. The first step toward conquering this hindrance is to recognize that it is a problem. Ask yourself if it is conformity that is motivating you to believe something. Awareness of the problem won't eliminate it and challenging one's friends (or one's boss, etc.) is not always to one's advantage. You must know your priorities. If challenging the boss might mean the loss of a job you desperately need, then it may be wise to keep your ideas to yourself. The critical thinker must ask "do I believe this only because of fear of being rebuked or of being thought disagreeable?" The question itself (or one like it) shows an awareness of the power of the desire to conform. It is difficult to know, however, whether one's answer to the question is honest or reflects self-deception and wishful thinking. One thing is certain, though; if you're not aware of this hindrance and don't remind yourself of it, you will never overcome it to any degree.

> "Men are disturbed not by things, but by the views they take of things." --Epictetus

The tendency to be uncritical of claims made by authorities, experts, and people we admire is also difficult to overcome. One method professional journals use to prevent prejudice from clouding a referee's judgment is to send out a paper for evaluation without letting the referees know who wrote the paper. Some teachers have their students use codes rather than their names on their essays. We will return to this subject in detail in chapter three, so here we will only say that awareness of the problem is a necessary step toward overcoming it.

Overcoming laziness and the desire for quick results, and thinking in terms of slogans and stereotypes, can only occur if one makes a conscientious effort to do so. This is true also of those physical hindrances that are in our power to control, such as the use of brain-altering drugs. Controlling the stress in one's life, however, is more complex. Stress-causing events are often beyond one's control, e.g., the death or serious injury or illness of a loved one. Other stressful events are partly in one's control, but may be necessary, e.g., a divorce or separation, or caring for an elderly parent. In any case, whatever the source of the stress, what is important is how one deals with it. You may not be able to change yourself or an external source of stress, but you may be able to change how you respond to the stress. Instead of seeing obstacles and troubles, you might force yourself to see challenges and opportunities.

While it would be unreasonable to expect us to control our emotions all of the time, we should be able to control ourselves enough so that we do not make important decisions while angry, upset, jealous, etc. For example, you might leave the room to avoid saying something you might later regret.

Overcoming social or political repression of information and ideas is often difficult because we may find the repressed ideas repulsive. Since we don't like the ideas being repressed, we don't object to the repression. We may regret our inaction later, when it is *our* ideas that are being repressed.

19. Personal benefits of critical thinking

Self-confidence and a sense of control over one's life are the two main personal benefits of being a critical thinker. Once one commits oneself to a lifelong search for the most reasonable beliefs and actions, and one learns how to conduct that search properly, self-confidence and self-respect begin to flourish. Also, the better one is at evaluating and constructing arguments, the more likely one will be in control of situations where decisions need to be made or problems solved.

Another benefit of critical thinking is that one should notice an improvement in one's studying and course work. It is possible--perhaps even likely--that many students will become more efficient at using their intelligence because of becoming more critical in their thinking. Whatever benefits accrue to you because of using this text, the benefits will be due mainly to your efforts. The text is merely a guide. It points you in the right direction. Where you arrive is largely up to you. What a critical thinker hopes for is to become free from the tyranny of those who would rather see obedient servants than thoughtful, independent thinkers. We should also hope to become free from our own tyranny--the tyranny of self-deception and wishful thinking. Only by becoming free from these tyrannies can we hope to think clearly and accurately so that we might judge fairly what we ought to believe and do. We will still make mistakes, but they will be *our* mistakes.

20. Drawbacks to Critical Thinking

There can be drawbacks to being a critical thinker. Some people are offended by being challenged. They do not like being questioned or they can't tolerate people who disagree with them. Some people's worldviews are antithetical to critical thinking. Such people may be friends or family members, and critical thinking may alienate you from them. People who love you may think you are being corrupted by critical thinking. The more critically you think, the more likely it is that you will change your views on many important issues. These changes may not only cause friction with others; they may cause some discomfort in your own life as you try to adjust to giving up attitudes and beliefs you've held since childhood. You may even find yourself coming to believe things that once seemed obviously false to you. Many of you will have been encouraged to think critically all of your lives and there will be few drawbacks to developing your skills even further. Others, however, may have a more difficult time of it. You will have to decide for yourself what you value more: being an independent thinker or having the approval of people who do not value independent thinking.

Exercises 1-5

1. Describe each of the following hindrances to critical thinking and suggest ways to overcome them: the pressure to conform; prejudice or bias; lack of adequate background knowledge (ignorance); the tendency to accept claims made by experts and authorities; fatigue or stress; confirmation bias; communal reinforcement; anger; laziness; pride; self-deception and wishful thinking; censorship.

24

2. Pick one of the professions mentioned by Thouless in the passage quoted on page 15 and discuss how the members of that profession exercise their power in ways that encourage us to be uncritical, passive recipients of their claims. Do these professions have the same influence today that they had in Thouless' day (ca. 1950)? What professions, if any, would you add to this list today?

3. Imagine that you are on the local Library Board and some citizens have complained that a newspaper which you allow to be distributed in the lobby of the library often contains material with graphic sexual descriptions. They say that they are concerned that the material can be easily obtained by children. You must vote on whether or not to allow the paper to continue to be distributed in the library lobby. How would you vote and what arguments would you make to persuade the other board members to agree with you?

4. Write a short essay, describing what you hope to gain by becoming a more critical thinker.

Chapter One Self-test: true or false? (Check your answers in Answers to Selected Exercises.)

1. Critical thinking is clear and accurate thinking which aims at evaluating the justification of beliefs and actions.
2. Two equally intelligent people can be equally articulate and informed, but not be equally critical thinkers.
3. The standards of evaluation used by critical thinkers originated at the First International Conference on Critical Thinking at Sonoma State University.
4. Self-confidence and a sense of being in control of one's beliefs are the two main personal benefits of being a critical thinker.
5. Having the proper attitude is sufficient to guarantee the development of critical thinking.
6. To be open-minded means accepting that we could be in error.
7. Studies on memory have shown that we often construct our memories after the fact.
8. Authorities themselves, in all areas, do much to perpetuate their power and convince the rest of us that it is a good thing to accept their claims uncritically.
9. Facts are those things that are infallibly certain.
10. Being open-minded means believing that all ideas are equally reasonable: there can be no justification for believing one idea over another.
11. *Confirmation bias* is a kind of prejudice one develops from seeking to confirm beliefs one knows to be false.
12. Developing the proper attitude toward experts and authorities comes naturally to most people.
13. A person's skepticism is healthy if it leads him or her to doubt everything said by anyone who is an expert or authority in some field.
14. An option is a *living option*, in William James's sense of the expression, when it is possible to seriously consider believing that option.
15. Because scientists are trained in scientific methods, they are not subject to *confirmation bias*.
16. We should expect critical thinking to lead to universal agreement on important issues.
17. Studies have shown that under hypnosis a person's memory accuracy increases 100%.
18. The fact that a person remembers something very vividly in clear detail is sufficient proof that the memory is accurate.
19. Critical thinking demonstrates that ultimately no viewpoint is better than any other; all viewpoints are equally reasonable and justifiable.
20. There are many sets of values and principles by which reasonable people can and do live.
21. Ethnocentrism is the belief that our own culture is the standard of truth and reality.
22. Every society discourages ethnocentrism and encourages challenging traditional beliefs and values.
23. Critical thinking is not concerned with evaluating the justification of beliefs and actions.
24. Most people can usually perceive clearly and make good judgments while terrified, angry or jealous.
25. Overcoming the social pressure to conform is easy for most people.
26. A person's worldview is his or her basic view about the state of the world.
27. *Communal reinforcement* is support given to a community for its unpopular views.
28. Every observation is an interpretation of one's perceptions.
29. The psychological fact of suggestion is the fact that if statements are made again and again in a confident manner, without argument or proof, then their hearers will tend to believe them quite independently of their soundness and of the presence or absence of evidence for their truth.

30. The Socratic Method refers to a method of questioning and cross-examination of positions.
31. According to Giles St. Aubyn, human beings have an instinctive desire to conform.
32. Perhaps the greatest hindrance to the ability to think critically is ignorance, the lack of essential background knowledge.
33. The better one is at critically evaluating arguments, the less self-confidence one will have.
34. The philosopher Descartes believed that the only way to overcome personal prejudices and preconceived notions would be to doubt everything one believes and start over by developing a method that would guarantee absolute certainty.
35. A critical thinker is able to solve all problems and arrive at absolute certainty in all matters.

Further Reading – Chapter One

Alcock, J. (1995). "The Belief Engine," *Skeptical Inquirer*. 19(3): 255-263.

Allport, Gordon. (1954). *The Nature of Prejudice.* Addison Wesley Publishing Co.

Berglas, S. (1990). Self-handicapping: Etiological and diagnostic considerations. In R. L. Higgins (Ed.), *Self-handicapping: The paradox that isn't.* Plenum.

Brugger, Peter. (2001). "From Haunted Brain to Haunted Science: A Cognitive Neuroscience View of Paranormal and Pseudoscientific Thought,' in *Hauntings and Poltergeists: Multidisciplinary Perspectives*, edited by J. Houran and R. Lange. McFarland & Company, Inc. Publishers.

Carroll, Robert Todd. (2003). *The Skeptic's Dictionary: A Collection of Strange Beliefs, Amusing Deceptions & Dangerous Delusions.* Wiley & Sons.

Dweck, Carol S. (2002). "Beliefs That Make Smart People Dumb." In *Why Smart People Can Be So Stupid*, ed. Robert J. Sternberg. Yale University Press.

Gardner, Martin. (1957). *Fads and Fallacies in the Name of Science.* Dover Publications, Inc..

Gilovich, Thomas. (1993). *How We Know What Isn't So: The Fallibility of Human Reason in Everyday Life.* The Free Press.

Hyman, Ray. (1989). *The Elusive Quarry: a Scientific Appraisal of Psychical Research.* Prometheus Books.

Loftus, Elizabeth. (1980a). *Eyewitness Testimony.* Harvard University Press.

Loftus, Elizabeth F. (1980b). *Memory, Surprising New Insights Into How We Remember and Why We Forget.* Addison-Wesley Pub. Co.

Park, Robert L. (2000). *Voodoo Science: The Road from Foolishness to Fraud.* Oxford U. Press.

Rosenthal, Robert. (1998). "Covert Communication in Classrooms, Clinics, and Courtrooms," *Eye on Psi Chi.* Vol. 3, No. 1, pp. 18-22.

Schacter, Daniel L. (1996). *Searching for Memory - The Brain, The Mind, and The Past.* Basic Books.

Schick, Theodore, Jr. and Lewis Vaughn. (2001). *How to Think About Weird Things: Critical Thinking for a New Age.* McGraw-Hill.

St. Aubyn, Giles. (1962). *The Art of Argument.* Emerson Books.

Thouless, Robert H. (1950). *How to Think Straight.* Simon and Schuster.

Zusne, Leonard and Warren Jones. (1990). Eds. *Anomalistic Psychology: A Study of Magical Thinking.* 2nd ed. Lawrence Erlbaum Assoc.

Notes - Chapter One

[1]Many bad decisions are made because leaders surround themselves with clones who all think alike or who are afraid to rock the boat by offering viewpoints that differ from the leader's or the majority's position. Another major cause of poor decision-making is the practice of not consulting people who will be affected by the decision.

Remember when Congress had to rescind its legislation on Social Security catastrophic health insurance after millions of dollars and countless hours had been spent by advocates--particularly by the American Association of Retired Persons--for a policy that was supposed to benefit the elderly. The people who were to be 'helped' most by this legislation weren't adequately consulted, and they let their representatives know how they felt *after* the bill was passed!

On our campus, a few years ago the administration put in a system which was supposed to make all buildings accessible to the handicapped. To get into a building, a person had to punch a large rubber box, which then activated the door. If you had the strength or agility needed to punch the box, but were in a wheelchair, you then had to wheel back so the door wouldn't knock you over. Then, you had to wheel forward quickly to get through before the door closed. Apparently, no handicapped person was consulted before the decision was made to install this particular system which, of course, had to be replaced at no expense to the decision-makers.

[2]See his famous essay, "The Will to Believe." The essay has been reprinted many times and is available in many editions. *The Will to Believe and Other Essays in Popular Philosophy* (New York: Longmans Green, 1896).

[3] Brugger's research indicates that high levels of dopamine affect the propensity to find meaning, patterns, and significance where there is none, and that this propensity is related to a tendency to believe in the paranormal. According to Franýoise Schenk from the University of Lausanne in Switzerland, dopamine "is an important chemical involved in the brain's reward and motivation system, and in addiction. Its role in the reward system may be to help us decide whether information is relevant or irrelevant." See "Paranormal beliefs linked to brain chemistry," *New Scientist*, July 27, 2002.

[4]See also two articles in the *Skeptical Inquirer*, Vol. XII No. 2, Winter 1987-88: "The Power of Suggestion on Memory" by Robert A. Baker and "Fantasizing Under Hypnosis: Some Experimental Evidence" by Peter J. Reveen. Three witnesses to a staged armed robbery were hypnotized by Reveen. Their accounts were very detailed, but neither agreed with the other and none was close to the actual facts of the event.

[5]*Newsweek*, February 11, 1991, p. 58. Dr. Terr was the prosecution's expert witness in the trial of George Franklin Sr. who was found guilty of murdering a child twenty years earlier. The only witness against him was his 30-year-old daughter who says she repressed the memory of the murder until one day when she looked into her own daughter's eyes. Suddenly, she remembered her father molesting her 8-year-old girl friend and smashing the child's skull with a rock. Eileen Franklin-Lipsker also says she remembers her father threatening to kill her if she told anyone. She now remembers that her father sexually abused her numerous times. She says that she learned to protect herself by "forgetting" what had happened. Maybe. Or maybe the idea of being abused and forgetting it were suggested to her by her therapist. Defense lawyers argued that the daughter could have unconsciously fabricated the whole story out of anger and fear of her father. They even suggested she may have made up everything for the $500,000 book and movie deal she's signed. Maybe. However, it is possible that the daughter's account is accurate. Still, I would hope that a jury would require some corroborating evidence that would prove beyond a reasonable doubt that the repressed memory was accurate.

[6]Carol Tavris, "Hysteria and the incest-survivor machine," *Sacramento Bee*, Forum section, January 17, 1993, p. 1. Tavris is the author of several works in psychology, including *The Mismeasure of Woman* (New York: Simon & Shuster, 1992). She is also the editor of *Every Woman's Emotional Well-being* (Garden city, N.Y.: Doubleday, 1986).

[7]Yet, it has happened. In a modern version of the Salem witch hunts, the McMartin pre-school case exemplifies the very worst in institutionalized injustice in the hunt for child molesters. See Mary Ann Mason, "The McMartin case revisited: the conflict between social work and criminal justice," [on evaluating the credibility of children as witnesses in sexual abuse cases] *Social*

Work, v. 36, no. 5 (Sept, 1991), pp. 391-396, and Marion Zenn Goldberg, "Child witnesses: lessons learned from the McMartin trials," *Trial,* v. 26, no. 10 (Oct, 1990), pp. 86-88. See also Richard Lacayo, "The longest mistrial; the McMartin Pre-School case ends at last," *Time* (August 6, 1990), p. 28; Frank McConnell, "The trials of television: the McMartin case," *Commonweal* (March 23, 1990), pp. 189-190; Douglas J. Besharov, "Protecting the innocent," *National Review* (Feb 19, 1990), pp. 44-46; Margaret Carlson, "Six years of trial by torture: children, defendants, jurors and judge were all abused in the wasteful McMartin case," *Time* (Jan 29, 1990), pp. 26-28; and "The child-abuse trial that left a national legacy," *U.S. News & World Report* (Jan 29, 1990), p. 8.

[8]"'Trauma searches' plant the seed of imagined misery," Joseph de Rivera, *The Sacramento Bee*, May 18, 1993. De Rivera is a professor of psychology at Clark University in Worcester, Massachusetts, and is a consultant to the False Memory Syndrome Foundation.

[9]*The Sacramento Bee*, March 18, 1993, p. B4. The article, "Repressed-memory lawsuits spur backlash from accused," by Claire Cooper outlines the legal battleground where son and daughter sue mother and father who in turn sue their children and their children's' therapists.

[10]The reader should understand that I am not claiming that reincarnation does not occur or that Martin Gardner's say-so on an issue proves anything. My claim is narrower. I am saying that in those cases which have been examined by people such as Gardner the evidence points more to fraud or error than to genuine reincarnation or past-life regression.

[11]The attempt to find absolute certainty is notable in the development of phenomenology by Edmund Husserl (1859-1938) and his collaborators. Husserl's link to Descartes is obvious in his *Cartesian Meditations* (1929).

[12]See "The First Americans," *Newsweek*, April 26, 1999, pp. 50-57.

[13]See "How press kept lid on military's plan," by Thomas B. Rosensteil, *Los Angeles Times,* reprinted in *The Sacramento Bee*, March 2, 1991. The account of the engineer's activity was in a pool account by a *Los Angeles Times* reporter which had the approval of military censors. CBS Pentagon correspondent David Martin recognized that allied troops were secretly moving much farther west than anyone had thought. Most experts expected the allied assault to occur about 200 miles east of Rahfa. NBC correspondent Fred Francis also figured out Schwarzkopf's plan. Military officials pleaded with Francis "to not emphasize the activity you are seeing in the west." The dutiful Francis even warned his network against inadvertently disclosing the plan after one of NBC's expert military commentators speculated about cutting off the enemy near Nasiriyah.

[14]Of course, censorship in wartime is justified. We must censor information to protect our troops, journalists and civilians. Remember Bob Simon and his camera crew who went off on their own and were captured by the Iraqis and treated as spies. Remember Tel Aviv. The issue here, however, is not censorship *per se*, but the *kind* and *extent* of censorship.

[15]See *Skeptical Inquirer*, vol. 17, No. 3, Spring 1993, p. 226 and the article by Andrew Skolnick, "Free Speech and SLAPP Suits," pp. 244-246. SLAPP is an acronym for *strategic lawsuits against public participation.*

Chapter Two - Language and Critical Thinking

> *"... in our time,*
> *political speech and writing*
> *are largely the defense of the indefensible."*
> —George Orwell

> *"As people do better, they start voting like Republicans...*
> *...unless they have too much education and vote Democratic,*
> *which proves there can be too much of a good thing."*
> --Karl Rove

> *"If I turn out to be particularly clear,*
> *you've probably misunderstood what I've said."*
> --Alan Greenspan

___

Human beings have been using language for thousands of years. One would think that by now we would have no trouble communicating clearly. Experience demonstrates otherwise. What's worse, some people are often intentionally unclear. They use language to conceal the truth, to mislead, confuse, or deceive us. They do not use language to communicate ideas or feelings; they use it to control thought and behavior. Manipulation, not communication, is their goal. In this chapter, we will explore several common verbal tricks and deceptions used by an array of manipulators; including advertisers, politicians, evangelists, sales persons, and talk show hosts. We will also describe several key features of clear and effective communication.

We'll begin by examining two of the more interesting features of language: how words can *stimulate* thought and action by *arousing* feelings, and how words can *fail* to arouse thought or action by *failing* to arouse any feelings.

1. Emotive and cognitive meanings

Detergents are called *Joy* or *Cheer,* not *Dreary, Tedious,* or *Boring.* Consumer products are touted as being *new, improved, new* **and** *improved, fresh, clean, pure, better, great, light, natural, healthy,* etc. Why? Because of the positive feeling conveyed by those terms.

When one wants to arouse disgust and displeasure with another person's ideas, one calls him a "Nazi" or a "murderer of innocent babies." Why? Because of the negative feeling conveyed by those terms.

What is the difference between an *erotic film* and a *pornographic movie?* Or between *ethnic cleansing* and *genocide,* or between *murdering* and *terminating with extreme prejudice?* What is the difference between a *domestic dispute* and *wife battering* or between a *pro-life activist* and an *anti-abortion terrorist?* The difference is primarily in the *emotive meanings* of the different terms in each pair.

When I studied history, I learned about the *Holy Crusades*. Muslims in Saudi Arabia probably studied the *Infidel Invasions*. For over a quarter of a century, murders, bombings, and assassinations in Northern Ireland were referred to as *The Troubles,* an expression with little emotive content.

If you are hired to come up with the name of a new automobile, you will not keep your job for long if you suggest *Ford Tortoise* or *Dodge Snail*. Your golf ball company will go bankrupt if you name your ball the *Titleist Slice* or the *Prostaff Shank*. The names must suggest something positive, not negative. In the case of autos, the names must suggest speed or power or status, not slowness or sluggishness. In the case of golf balls, the name should suggest distance or accuracy or success.

The cognitive content is the literal sense or reference of a word or expression. One news reporter referred to "female circumcision" when describing a practice a woman from West Africa did not want to undergo. Another reporter described the practice as "genital mutilation." Who was right? Cognitively, both were. Emotively? Well, that depends on your attitude toward the practice.

Why did President Jimmy Carter refer to the failed mission to rescue American hostages in Iran as "an incomplete success?" Why do government agents refer to civilians killed by military bombs as "collateral damage" or to murders and assassinations as "unlawful deprivation of life?" *Because these terms express very little feeling.* Why use words that have little emotive content? Because you and I generally respond only to things we care about. If words or images or actions arouse no feelings in us, we are not likely to respond to them. If we do not respond to them, we will not think about them. If we do not think about them, we will not do anything about them. If we do not do anything about them, then those in power can continue doing whatever they wish to. Even if they do not have our consent, they do not arouse our opposition, either.

At the other extreme from using dull, non-emotive language to prevent us from responding and thinking about unpleasant realities are those who use language primarily for its emotive power. They use words that function like the names of detergents or mass murderers: words that primarily or exclusively convey feelings, words that have little or no *cognitive content.* For example, a letter I received from the National Right to Life Committee uses several references to *killing* "innocent" or "defenseless" *unborn babies.*" The letter refers to the National Abortion Rights Action League, Planned Parenthood, and the National Organization of Women (NOW) as "pro-death groups."

Many words and expressions convey nothing more than a positive or negative attitude. Words such as *lovely, wonderful, good, great*, and *beautiful* are usually used to express approval. Such words are said to have positive emotive content. Words such as *disgusting, despicable, bad, stupid*, and *ugly* usually are used to express disapproval. Such words are said to have a negative emotive content. Some words, such as *tangent* and *neutrino*, have little or no emotive content; they are not used to express an attitude, but are used for their descriptive or cognitive content.

HOW TO TELL A BUSINESSMAN FROM A BUSINESSWOMAN

A businessman is assertive; a businesswoman is pushy.
A businessman is meticulous; she is picky.
He loses his temper; she's bitchy.
He gets depressed; she's moody.
He's persistent; she's hysterical.
He's confident or self-assured; she's arrogant.
He's a loner; she's aloof.
He's firm; she's stubborn.
He's assertive; she's mouthy.
He's a private person; she's secretive.
He makes quick decisions; she's impulsive.
He's only human; she's emotional.

A difference in attitude explains why different terms are used to describe the same behavior of men and women, a difference usually described by the highly emotive term 'sexism.'

Many words, however, are used to express both a cognitive and an emotive meaning; their function is not only to describe something or convey information, but to express an attitude about it as well. For example, what one person might call "a barbaric and savage slaying," another might refer to simply as "a homicide." Their different attitudes are expressed by their different choice of words; though their cognitive meaning is identical (both expressions describe the murder of a human being).

Those in the business of persuading others to accept ideas or values, or to buy products or vote for candidates, must know how to select words and pictures that are likely to evoke emotional responses. They know the power of *loaded language,* i.e., highly emotive language aimed at evoking a response through emotions such as fear and hope, rather than through thought. As one anti-abortion advocate put it: just put together the words "baby" and "kill"--no one can resist that!

Exercises 2-1

A. The following words are likely to have no emotive content in most contexts. For each word, find two synonyms, one with a negative and one with a positive emotive content. (A thesaurus would be useful in doing this exercise.) See Answers to Selected Exercises at the back of the book for answers to those with asterisks (*).

1. arbitrary	*2. old	3. indelicacy	
4. detain	5. review	6. undisturbed	
*7. plan	8. altercation	9. move (someone)	*10.take

B. The following words are usually used with positive or negative emotive content. For each word, find a synonym that would probably have no little or no emotive content in most contexts.

*1. stink	2. remarkable	3. pitiless	
*4. shy	5. chastise	*6. murder	
7. pathetic	8. incoherent	9. inspire	10. inadequacy

C. Bertrand Russell devised what he called "irregular conjugations" of words. The idea is to find three words with nearly the same cognitive meaning, but with emotive contents that get increasingly negative or positive. For example, "I am firm, you are obstinate, he is pig-headed." Or, "She is introverted, he is shy, and I am the strong, silent type.

Invent three irregular conjugations of your own, using words other than those in exercises A and B above.

D. Write a short commercial, advertisement or political speech in which you select at least six words or expressions primarily for their emotive content, disregarding any vagueness in their cognitive contents.

E. Rewrite a newspaper article, giving it a different slant and tone by replacing several words with synonyms which convey a more negative or more positive emotive meaning.

2. Doublespeak

In his essay "Politics and the English Language," George Orwell claimed that the "mixture of vagueness and sheer incompetence is the most marked characteristic of modern English prose, and especially of any kind of political writing." People have to think less if they use vague or stale language, he said, and "this reduced state of consciousness, if not indispensable, is at any rate favorable to political conformity." According to Orwell, political speech is "largely the defense of the indefensible" and thus "political language has to consist largely of euphemism, question-begging and sheer cloudy vagueness." As examples, Orwell cited the following terms and their real meanings: *pacification* really meant bombarding defenseless villages and machine-gunning cattle; *transfer of population* really meant the forcing of millions of peasants to take to the roads while their farms were confiscated; and, *elimination of unreliable elements* really meant that people would be imprisoned for years without trial, or shot in the back of the neck.

Orwell reminds us that a critical thinker must be on guard not only against language that intentionally obscures thought by arousing emotions, but also against more subtle abuses of language: using *euphemisms, jargon*, and *obscure language* to deceive and mislead. Such language is called *doublespeak*.[1] It is described by William Lutz as language which "makes the bad seem good, the negative appear positive, the unpleasant appear attractive or at least tolerable . . . .It is language that conceals or prevents thought" (Lutz 1989, 1). Lutz identifies several kinds of doublespeak. One type uses euphemisms to mislead or deceive us about an ugly reality or embarrassing situation. Another uses pretentious, inflated, obscure, or esoteric jargon to give an air of prestige, profundity, or authority to one's speech or to hide ugly realities or embarrassing matters.[2]

Another kind of doublespeak which Lutz does not label, but which ought to be mentioned, is the *false implication*: clear and accurate language that implies something false. For example, there is a false implication in the expression "no cholesterol" on the front of a potato chip package whose ingredients (clearly listed on the back of the package) include saturated fats, which are converted to cholesterol when eaten. You will not be ingesting cholesterol when you eat the chips, but you will be increasing the cholesterol in your body nevertheless.

2.1 Euphemisms

Euphemisms are inoffensive or dull terms used in place of more blunt cognitive synonyms. Euphemisms have a perfectly acceptable social function. We use euphemisms to be polite or to avoid offending people. We talk about "passing away" or "using the rest room" instead of being blunt and saying that someone died or is excreting bodily waste.

> In defending Richard Loeb, a kidnapper and murderer, Clarence Darrow said to the jury: "where is the man who has not been guilty of delinquencies in youth?"

Euphemisms become doublespeak when the inoffensive, less emotive word or expression is used to mislead or deceive us about unpleasant realities, e.g., referring to a policy of mass murder and rape as "ethnic cleansing."

When the United States attacked Libya on April 14, 1986, bombs were dropped on the city of Tripoli, killing civilians, including several children. Such deaths were referred to by White House press secretary Larry Speakes as "collateral damage." Why? Because "collateral damage" does not hit home as hard as "killed innocent children and other noncombatants." We might not be so willing to support our government's actions if we put it bluntly that in retaliation for killing innocent Americans we killed innocent Libyans. A murder for a murder is the truth, but the truth is too ugly to face. We use language to soften the truth, to reshape it to a form we can stomach or even be proud of. Instead of saying that a person failed, one says that the person "did not respond to training." Instead of "Death Insurance," we're sold "Life Insurance." Cemeteries are called "Memorial Gardens." The Air Force refers to a lost plane as being "temporarily geographically misplaced." The Army refers to caskets or body bags as "transfer tubes." Spying is "covert activity." Retreating is "exfiltrating." When an ally betrays us by revealing our plans to the enemy it is referred to as an "unintentional leak." People who sneak into a country illegally are said to be "infiltrating." When we surrender we don't call it surrender; we call it "peace with honor." A recent memo from my dean gave advice on what to do with students who were "psychologically challenged," not emotionally disturbed. A member of Earth First! says on the radio that he had "decommissioned a bulldozer." The President of the United States recently announced that the topic of discussion at a meeting had been "cultural issues." Others at the meeting said the topic was "racism." A singer recently told the world in her autobiography that her daughter was a "love-child." The person the child had learned to call *daddy* was not her biological father.

Pornographic bookstores and theaters refer to themselves as "adult." People who engage in sexual relations with each other say they are "sleeping together." "Adultery" seems to have given way to "extramarital affairs." A "drug addict" is now said to have a "chemical dependency." When Janis Jackson exposed a breast during a Super Bowl halftime dance, she was said to have suffered a "wardrobe malfunction."
If the media are sympathetic to your cause you are "homeless"; otherwise you are just another transient.

There are several euphemisms for *tax increases*: *revenue enhancement, rate adjustment, benefit reduction, service charge, user fee, licensing fee, impost, tariff,* and *toll,* just to name a few. When the US Department of Agriculture ordered the slaughtering of 450 cattle because of mad cow disease, it said it was *depopulating* the animal farm.

A Planned Parenthood booklet mentions a contraceptive which *kills* sperm, but an abortion is not said to kill a fetus or embryo. In fact, abortion is described without mentioning the fetus at all; it is simply called "terminating a pregnancy." Some school districts want *evolution* to go away, so they call it "biological changes over time." *Religious* might be too emotive a term in some contexts, so it has been replaced by the euphemism *faith-based.*

32

When a local newspaper fired people and reduced the salaries of other employees the paper referred to "work force adjustments" and "job reclassifications." A Houston judge and minister was rejected for the post of George Bush's Ethic's Czar because an FBI check revealed "a personal situation."

Doublespeak euphemisms are used to make a bad action seem good or at least seem not too bad. Dull or weakly emotive language is often used so that we will not be stimulated to think about or act on what is said.

> *"A good catchword can obscure analysis for fifty years." —Wendell L. Wilkie*

For example, during World War II the Japanese Imperial Army instituted a policy that involved kidnapping young women in conquered areas such as Korea or the Philippines. The women were forced to have sex with Japanese soldiers in army run "brothels." The kidnapped sex slaves were referred to as *comfort girls*. The Nazis called their comfort girls the *Joy Division*.

During the Vietnam War era, the term *friendly fire* meant shelling and killing your own troops or allies by mistake. During the second war on Iraq, *friendly fire* was used interchangeably with *fratricide*, and both were used to describe not only the killing of American troops by their own but also to describe the rape of American soldiers by other American soldiers. The former president of Uganda, Idi Amin, called his murder squad the PUBLIC SAFETY UNIT (Kahane 1997: 137).

> The opposite of a euphemism is a *dysphemism*: using an offensive term for an inoffensive one., e.g., referring to a homosexual as a *faggot*, a woman as a *bitch*, or an incentive as a *bribe*.

The euphemisms used by government officials are often put forth in an attempt to dull the force of what the expressions mean and to make acceptable what otherwise might be repulsive; for example, referring to nuclear war as "ultimate high intensity warfare" or to any one of a number of illegal or immoral activities as "covert operations" or "inappropriate actions"—President Nixon's description of the Watergate burglary.

According to William, poor people are "fiscal underachievers" and a bank robbery is an "unauthorized withdrawal." To kill is "to terminate with extreme prejudice." Medical malpractice that either kills or maims is a "therapeutic misadventure" or "a diagnostic misadventure of a very high magnitude." "Negative patient care outcome" means the patient died. "Peacekeeping forces" aren't trained to kill the enemy anymore; they are now "servicing the target" with the deployment of missiles called "Peacemakers."

A prison that I taught at was called a "conservation center." Other prisons in California are called "correctional institutions" and the armed guards who run them are called "correctional officers."

When a nuclear reactor malfunctioned at Three Mile Island in Pennsylvania in 1979, officials at the facility spoke of "energetic disassembly" rather than of an explosion. A fire was called "rapid oxidation" and the reactor accident was described as an "event" or a "normal aberration." Plutonium contamination was called "infiltration" or described as "plutonium has taken up residence." The governor of California, which had an identical nuclear plant to the one at Three Mile Island, was told by Joseph Hendrie, the director of the Nuclear Regulatory Commission, that the sister plant was "within an acceptable flat band of risk." That euphemism is also a nice bit of *jargon*, the topic of the following section.

Exercises 2-2

A. Find or invent three examples of euphemisms used to obscure the truth or deceive others. Advertisements and the discourse of politicians ought to provide you with plenty of examples. Here is an example from *The New Yorker*: Dr. Don Laub, a surgeon specializing in transsexual surgery, does not do *sex-change operations*; he prefers to say that he does *sex confirmation surgeries*. ("The Body Lies," by Amy Bloom, July 18, 1994, p. 43.) Here is another example from a letter to the editor of *The Sacramento Bee*: "...characterizing a Planned Parenthood facility as a *reproductive-health clinic*...is like describing a slaughterhouse as an *animal-euthanizing chamber*.

B. Rewrite a polemical diatribe or news story about some terrible disaster or event, replacing highly emotive terms with euphemisms. (This is good practice for those of you going into advertising, journalism, or politics.)

2.2 Jargon

Jargon is the technical language of an art or science, trade or profession. When used properly, jargon facilitates communication among members of the same field. The special terminology of computer programmers, for example, is not confusing or deceptive when used amongst themselves. Jargon becomes doublespeak when pretentious, obscure, or esoteric terminology is used to give an air of profundity, authority, or prestige to one's claims. If the doublespeak jargon is typical of some class of people such as bureaucrats, politicians, academics, lawyers, etc., it is called "bureaucratese," "politicalese," "academese," "legalese," etc.

Doublespeak jargon has the effect of making the simple seem complex, the trivial seem profound, or the insignificant seem important. According to Edwin Newman, "Sociologists are people who pretend to advance the cause of knowledge by calling a family a 'microcluster of structured role expectations' or 'a bounded plurality of role-playing individuals'" (Newman 1975: 13). George Orwell ridiculed misleading jargon in his famous "translation" of a well-known verse from Ecclesiastes. The King James version of this passage reads

> I returned and saw under the sun, that the race is not to the swift, nor yet riches to men of understanding, nor yet favour to men of skill; but time and chance happeneth to them all.

Orwell's version:

> Objective considerations of contemporary phenomena compel the conclusion that success or failure in competitive activities exhibits no tendency to be commensurate with innate capacity, but that a considerable element of the unpredictable must invariably be taken into account.

People hired to sell things over the telephone are called "telemarketers" and grocery store cashiers are referred to as "career associate scanning professionals." Baggers are "courtesy clerks." The garbage collector is a "sanitation engineer" and the dump where the garbage is delivered is a "sanitary landfill." A pothole is a "pavement deficiency" and a bum is a "non-goal oriented member of society." A thermometer is a "digital fever computer." Poor people are "economically non-affluent." Cloths to clean compact discs do not pick up dirt but "micro-dust," and dust becomes "airborne particulates." That was not a bomb that inadvertently departed an airplane over a campground; it was a "vertically deployed anti-personnel device."

A popular form of doublespeak jargon is to add the term *officer*, *specialist*, or *technician* to a job title. A public relations person is "public information officer" or a "public services specialist." A person who picks up the trash from the city beach or playground is an "environmental technician." The one who cleans the toilets is an "environmental officer."

Jargon can also be used to create technical sounding euphemisms that try to hide ugly realities or make bad or indifferent things seems good or fantastic. Such jargon can have the effect of deceiving us about things that are dangerous, harmful, or wasteful. Why does the CIA refer to a poison dart gun as a "nondiscernible microbionoculator?" To keep us from knowing what they are doing or why they spend so much money? To American military troops "airborne vector" refers to germ warfare by air and "employment of incapacitory agents" means using nerve gas. Why does a psychiatry manual refer to making obscene phone calls as "telephone scatologia?" To suggest that the one making the calls is sick and in need of treatment rather than wicked and in need of punishment? The chemically dependent don't go to drug rehab; they are sent to the nearest "Opiate Detoxification Unit."

When the United States invades a foreign country, we refer to the forces we support as "freedom fighters;" those we oppose are "terrorists" or "guerrillas." Even "invade" is avoided in favor of misleading jargon. When we invaded Grenada during the night, reporters were not allowed in and the government reported that there was "a pre-dawn vertical insertion." That did not sound like we were sending paratroopers in under the cover of darkness. It sounded more like we were digging holes or performing surgery early in the morning.

When United States armed forces initiated their pre-dawn vertical insertion of Panama, the raid to kidnap Manuel Noriega was called *Operation Just Cause*! After we invaded Iraq and found neither weapons of mass destruction nor evidence Sadaam Hussein had links with Al Queda, we began calling the invasion *Operation Iraqi Freedom.*

The government is not the only one concerned with using language to keep us from knowing the truth. Businesses are just as concerned that their stockholders do not know the whole truth about many of their dealings. In a footnote in National Airlines' annual report for 1978, National explained that revenues of $1.7 million came from "the involuntary conversion of a 727" (Lutz 1989: 4). Three of the fifty-two people aboard the involuntarily converted airplane were killed in the crash. What stockholder wants to be reminded that profits were made from an after-tax insurance benefit from the accident? If straight talk were used, somebody might figure out that the company's profits weren't due to good business but to accidents in which people were killed. If the company lost money, however, the annual report might have made mention of some "deficit enhancement" or "negative earnings." A company with increased profits may have decreased revenues or earnings. Maybe this is why executives of companies that are losing billions of dollars a year can justify huge bonuses: they are based on *profits* not *revenues.* Profits can be increased by closing down plants, laying-off workers, collecting insurance, and a host of other ways that have nothing to do with increased sales or earnings.

Public television stations use deceptive language when they refer to commercial messages from Mobil Oil or Exxon as "enhancement underwriting" rather than as commercials. The corporate benefactors of public television cannot legally buy commercial time, but they can make contributions in exchange for broadcasting messages that seem like commercials. In 2001, the Public Broadcasting System (PBS) and producers of PBS programs received more than $220 million dollars in corporate contributions. Since the money is not income but a *gift* to non-profit organizations, PBS saves money that would otherwise go to the U.S. government for taxes.[3]

When is a hammer a "manually powered fastener-driving impact device?" hen is a steel nut a "hexiform rotatable surface compression unit?" When you are a contractor doing business with the Department of Defense and wand to charge exorbitant fees for your wares.

Finally, businesses and companies seem to think that they can take the sting out of laying off people by referring to "downsizing," "dehiring," "right-sizing," "repositioning," "reshaping," "decruiting," "de-selection," "furloughing," "reducing duplication," "focused reduction," "normal involuntary attrition," "census reduction," or "involuntary separation from payroll." The fact that so many terms have been used to replace "fired," "reducing the head count," or "getting the ax" may not indicate that corporations are developing bigger hearts, but that they recognize the value of euphemistic jargon in manipulating our perception of reality.

Exercise 2-3

Find three examples of doublespeak jargon in newspaper or magazine articles. (E.g., calling a shovel an "emplacement evacuator," using "incontinent ordnance" to describe the mistaken shelling of one's own troops, or calling a parachute an "aerodynamic personnel decelerator.")

2.3 Obscure and confusing language: gobbledygook

Gobbledygook is confusing non-technical language that misleads or deceives. For example:

> The Undersecretary of the Treasury, Edwin H. Yeo III, is asked about additional loans to New York City: "If we find the reasonable probability of repayment is slipping away from us, then we'll have to respond in terms of extension of future credit." If they don't pay what they owe, we won't lend them any more (Newman, 5).

> Late in 1974 the Secretary of Commerce, Frederick Dent, said that the rate of inflation in the second quarter of the year was 9.6 percent, and this "validated the essentiality of President Ford's struggle to cut the inflation rate." A civil tongue would have said justified, but that would have cost Dent three words and nine syllables

and, in the way of Washington, which would never say satellite photography when it could say technical over-head reconnaissance, commensurate self-respect. (Newman 1975: 10)

When Nelson Rockefeller was asked whether he would be nominated for President at the 1976 convention, he replied, "I cannot conceive of any scenario in which that could eventuate (Newman 1975: 10)."

Often, obscure language is used in the attempt to make the necessarily vague appear to be scientific, to make the ordinary seem extraordinary, the simple seem complex, or the mundane seem profound. Sometimes obscure language is used to confuse the public or conceal the truth.

On the other hand, sometimes the intentions of those who purposely obscure matters are understandable, if not acceptable. For example, some obscurity results from the attempt to eliminate ambiguity and vagueness in legal contracts. Also, many people consider obscure anything which they do not immediately understand. It is true that what is clear to one person may be obscure to another. Obscurity is often a function of the lack of necessary background knowledge, especially the lack of necessary vocabulary.

Finally, for some people obscure language is simply a reflection of a confused mind and should not be considered doublespeak. For example, one of my students wrote that "The Bible is not a single book; it is the copulation of many books." Such unintentional misuses of language should not be considered doublespeak any more than the linguistic gems provided by people attempting a language other than their own. For example, when Coca-Cola was introduced to China a multimillion-dollar campaign was introduced that proudly proclaimed its slogan: *Bite the wax tadpole*. No doubt, something was lost in the translation.

> "Half the game is 90 percent mental."
> ---Danny Ozark
>
> "A nickel aint worth a dime anymore."
> --Yogi Berra

In order to avoid being obscure, good writers and speakers define expressions that their readers and listeners are likely to be unfamiliar with. Bad writers use definitions to make things even more confusing, as in this attempt to define "pattern of criminal profiteering":

> . . . engaging in at least two incidents of criminal profiteering that have the same or similar intents, results, accomplices, victims or methods of commission or otherwise are interrelated by distinguishing characteristics, including a nexus to the same enterprise, and are not isolated incidents, provided at least one of such incidents occurred after the effective date of this chapter and that the last of such incidents occurred within five years after a prior incident of criminal profiteering.[4]

This example of gobbledygook is about one notch less confusing than the following attempt to say "If your check bounces, our receipt is void":

> Any receipt for payment made is subject to the condition that it shall be void if any check or draft, to whomsoever payable, taken for or on account of the amount specified herein is dishonored for any reason and that no such check or draft shall constitute a payment to the Company, whether or not the amount due, or any part thereof, has been advanced or credited to the Company by any of its representatives, and that any check or draft so taken may be handled in accordance with the practice of any collecting bank.[5]

It may be that some people fear that if they express themselves in simple language they will be looked at as simpletons. Perhaps that is why some educators use jargon and gobbledygook. They talk about training students to "successfully relate to others" or "interface with others" instead of saying that they want to teach their students to get along or cooperate. Maybe that is why some people have to *prioritize* instead of *decide what's most important*, or they have to examine *delivery systems* instead of evaluating teaching methods. People cannot just do their best anymore; they have to *maximize their potential*. Meetings to discuss important matters and decide what to do about them have been replaced with *quality conferences* or *intersegmental committees* that *essentialize priorities* and *take effective proactive stances*.

Finally, obscure language gives one an aura of complexity and profundity. Thus, jargon and gobbledygook are often encouraged, even though they are likely to lead to confusion and misunderstanding. We mistakenly think that obscure language is a sign of intelligence.

```
Exercise 2-4

    Find an example of gobbledygook in one of your textbooks.
```

2.4 False Implications

The final type of doublespeak we will consider is the *false implication*: language that is clear and accurate but misleading because it suggests something false. For example, a package of Carnation Breakfast Bars asserts that the product inside provides 25% of the daily-recommended amount of protein, if taken with a glass of milk.

```
Californians for Telecommunications Choice was the swell
name taken by a consortium of competitors to Pacific Bell in a
propaganda campaign led by AT & T.
```

What the package does not tell you is that almost all of the protein is provided by the milk. A package of *Healthy Choice* lunchmeat says that it is 97% fat-free, which is true if measured by weight, but when 25% of its calories come from fat, isn't the claim deceptive? Cow's milk and other dairy products are high in fat and cholesterol, but the dairy industry cleverly expresses fat content as a percentage of weight. Using this system, milk said to have 2% fat is actually 31% fat when fat is measured as a percentage of calories. Whole milk and yogurt are 49% fat, cheese is 60-70% fat. (There is no low fat butter; butter is 100% fat.)

```
We Just Want to Help

    The American Heart Association's "Heartguide' program awards a seal
of approval to products that meet certain guidelines for total fat, saturated
fat, cholesterol and sodium. Companies pay a fee of $15,000 to $640,000,
depending on product sales, for the right to put a red heart with a checkmark
on their products. The Heart Association won't reveal the criteria they use.
    One product already approved is Promise margarine. Dr. Jeffrey Blum-
berg, professor of nutrition at Tufts University, claims "this can give a mis-
leading impression that margarine is a heart-healthy food, and clearly it is
not."
    Dr. Dennis L. De Silvey, a cardiologist and a national board member of
the Heart Association, replies: "It is totally incorrect that margarine is a bad
food. People are going to eat margarine, and this makes it easier for them to
understand what is the appropriate amount."
    James S. Benson, acting commissioner of food and drugs for the Food
and Drug Administration, said that the Heartguide program "could very eas-
ily result in the endorsement of products--such as some varieties of marga-
rine, spreads and salad dressings--that quite simply do not represent the
kinds of foods that ought to be promoted to achieve healthy hearts."
    Bonnie Liebman, director of nutrition for the Center for Science in Pub-
lic Interest, said: "The American Heart Association is filling the gap left by
government. There are millions of people who want a simple thumbs up or
thumbs down."
```

The grocery store is one of the places where deceptive use of language is commonplace, especially the use of false implications. Deceptive food labeling is so extensive that the first Bush Administration announced plans for mandatory nutritional labeling on virtually all packaged foods.[6] The Secretary of Health and Human Services, Dr. Louis W. Sullivan, claimed that the "grocery store has become a Tower of Babel, and consumers need to be linguists, scientists and mind readers to understand the many labels they see." Not wanting to sound too alarmed, Sullivan added, "frankly, some unfounded health claims are being made." Sullivan didn't specify any particular claims that were unfounded but he did say that the government is concerned about claims such as "low fat," "high fiber," and "no cholesterol." That was a good start. In 1993, the Food and Drug Administration (FDA) and the U.S. Department of Agriculture's (USDA) Food Safety and Inspection Service set forth regulations regarding the use of terms such as "low," "high," and "light." A relative claim must identify a reference food and include the percent difference. For example, a beer can't just be "light." It must be light compared to something (e.g., "contains 20% fewer calories than our regular beer").

The FDA took 4,600 words to explain the difference between "natural" and "artificial" in its regulations on food labeling. Here are a couple of examples:

The term artificial flavor or artificial flavoring means any substance, the function of which is to impart flavor, which is not derived from a spice, fruit or fruit juice, vegetable or vegetable juice, edible yeast, herb, bark, bud, root, leaf or similar plant material, meat, fish, poultry, eggs, dairy products, or fermentation products thereof. Artificial flavor includes the substances listed in Secs. 172.515(b) and 182.60 of this chapter except where these are derived from natural sources.

The term natural flavor or natural flavoring means the essential oil, oleoresin, essence or extractive, protein hydrolysate, distillate, or any product of roasting, heating or enzymolysis, which contains the flavoring constituents derived from a spice, fruit or fruit juice, vegetable or vegetable juice, edible yeast, herb, bark, bud, root, leaf or similar plant material, meat, seafood, poultry, eggs, dairy products, or fermentation products thereof, whose significant function in food is flavoring rather than nutritional. Natural flavors include the natural essence or extractives obtained from plants listed in Secs. 182.10, 182.20, 182.40, and 182.50 and part 184 of this chapter, and the substances listed in Sec. 172.510 of this chapter. [Code of Federal Regulations, Title 21, Volume 2, Parts 100 to 169, Revised as of April 1, 1998.]

The USDA took nearly 3,000 words to define "organic" in the year 2000. Things may not be crystal clear yet, but at least we now have some standards for some of the terms used to hype products. However, there is still plenty of room for the clever marketing director. Ask yourself why do so many products have the following words in their names or labels: "health" or "healthy," "fresh" or "farm fresh," "nutritional" or "country?" Do these words imply something which is false?

You might think that a product called Country Time® Lemonade Flavor Drink might have some lemon in it. Not a chance. This Kraft Foods product has no lemon juice, no lemon pulp, not even any lemon peel in it. Here's a list of the ingredients: *Water, high fructose corn syrup and/or sugar, contains less than 2% of natural flavor, ascorbic acid (vitamin C), citric acid, sodium citrate, sodium benzoate and potassium sorbate (preserve freshness), ester of wood rosin, and yellow 5.* According to the distributor of this drink, "the name is reminiscent of a time when it was easier to get good old-fashioned lemonade."

When asked how Pillsbury could call a product that contains artificial flavorings and BHA (a preservative) "Natural Chocolate Flavored Chocolate Chip Cookies," a company representative replied that 'natural' modifies 'chocolate flavored' not 'cookie.' Says Lutz, "You'd better brush up on the syntactic structure of modification if you want to be able to read food labels these days" (Lutz 1989: 28).

Finally, what does it mean for the environment now that so many products are being touted as *recyclable, recycled, biodegradable,* or *ozone friendly*? What significance is there to Tetra Pak's and Combibloc's claim that their juice boxes are "easily recyclable" when there are few recycling programs that accept juice boxes? What was the point of Mobil Corp.'s claim that its Hefty trash bags are "degradable" when they degrade only if exposed to the ultraviolet light of the sun, but most such bags end up buried in landfills? Being made from recycled materials may not be significant if the *percentage* of recycled material in the product is negligible. Being compostable may be insignificant if there are not many facilities available to do the composting. Thus, what is the point of Proctor and Gamble, which has roughly half of the $3.8 billion U.S. market for disposable diapers, advertising that it is developing technology that converts disposable diapers into compost? "The fact that they're running these ads has led to a direct misleading effect," said John McCaull, general council for Californians Against Waste. "It's fostering a belief in the public that these facilities and programs actually exist when that's hardly the case."[7] It may be made of 75% recyclable material but it's still 100% garbage.

Exercise 2-5

Find three examples of false implications in product labeling or advertising.

3. Other abuses of language

Besides doublespeak, there are several other abuses of language the critical thinker should consider: *hedging, weasel words, vague comparisons, assuring expressions*, and *sneaking in opinions as if they were facts*....to name just a few.

3.1 Hedging

Hedging is using language that appears to commit one to a particular view, but because of its wording, allows one to retreat from that view. Hedging is a way to evade the risk of commitment. Former U.S. senator S.I. Hayakawa offers us one of the more effective examples of hedging. When asked, "Should the United States give back the Panama Canal to Panama?" he responded, "Hell no. We stole it fair and square." Hayakawa evaluated his response as being a "perfect political answer." (I always thought the perfect political answer was the one that said absolutely nothing, offended no one, and which everyone thought expressed their sentiments exactly!)

> *"I intend to open this country up to democracy and anyone who is against that I will jail, I will crush."*
> —*Joao Baptista Figueiredo, President of Brazil (1979)*

While serving as Lt. Governor of California, Mike Curb was consulted on all major decisions by his record company, Mike Curb Productions Inc. During his campaign, he had said "If I'm elected, I will reorganize my assets, whether it's a trust or whatever, so I am no longer involved." When Curb was accused of going back on the campaign promise, he responded by saying that he draws a distinction between "being involved" and "being consulted." "Being involved implies a day-to-day role," he said, "which I am obviously not doing."

President Ronald Reagan said in a televised speech "I will not stand by and see those of you who are dependent on Social Security deprived of the benefits you've worked so hard to earn. You will continue to receive your checks in the full amount due you." Had Reagan, who for years had publicly opposed increases in such federal programs, suddenly become the friend of those on Social Security? White House speaker David Gergen said that the President's words were "carefully chosen." Reagan was reserving the right to decide who was "dependent" on Social Security benefits, who had "earned" those benefits, and who was "due" what, and how much the "full amount due" to them amounted to (Lutz 1989: 15-16). In other words, Reagan had not changed his position. Although he had nothing to do with the increases, which were mandated by Congress, Reagan tried to give the impression that he was somehow responsible for making sure that the benefits were paid.

President Bill Clinton took hedging to new heights in his many depositions and testimonies regarding his relationship with White House intern Monica Lewinsky. She stated in a sworn affidavit that "I have never had a sexual relationship with the president." Clinton swore that what she said "is absolutely true." She later admitted to having oral sex with the president; he later admitted that he "did have a relationship with Miss Lewinsky that was not appropriate." Clinton tried to make a distinction between having a sexual relationship and engaging in sexual acts. Later, in his address to the people on August 17, 1998, he claimed that his previous "answers were legally accurate," and he admitted only that he had "misled people."

Secretary of Defense Donald Rumsfeld, in trying to explain why the Iraqi people were rebelling against the U.S. Military presence in their country, said: "We're trying to explain how things are going, and they are going as they are going. Some things are going well and some things obviously are not going well."

3.2 The language of advertising: weasel words, vague comparisons, and meaningless expressions

In order to hedge effectively, one must master a short list of **weasel words** that are often used to evade or retreat from direct, plainspoken statements. Weasel words give the impression of taking a firm position while avoiding commitment to any specific claim.

Advertisements tell us that products *help* or *may help* (prevent, stop, or fight) this or that. A toothpaste *helps fight* tooth decay. An aspirin *may help* relieve pain. Note that the ads do not say specifically what the product will or can do. The only weaker claim they could make would be that their products *may or may not help* this or that.[8]

Many ads note that "supplies are limited." That is true of just about anything in the sense that no consumer good exists in infinite quantities. But the claim suggests that you better hurry and purchase the product before they're all gone.

Then there is 'only,' a little word used to suggest a great deal. What is the difference between pork bellies that are $9.95 a lug and pork bellies that are *only* $9.95 a lug? The latter sounds like you are getting a great deal. The word 'only' suggests that the price is low. Those special offers for "a limited time only" imply that you better order *now* before it is too late.

'Only' can also suggest that a statistic is low. "*Only* half of all women who have been married one time say they would marry the same man if they had it to do over again, according to a new survey." If that were true then *only* half would *not* marry the same man again.

'Almost' is almost as slippery as *only*. Some products promise *almost* miraculous cures or *almost* superhuman healing secrets. Others promise to *almost* instantly get your dishes *virtually* spot-free. In other words, the product will not get your dishes spot-free instantly.

Another favorite expression of advertisers is 'up to,' as in "This pen lasts *up to* 20 per cent longer." The ad does not say that the pen *will* last twenty percent longer, but even if it did it still wouldn't mean much since it doesn't say longer than what. What does it mean when a package of almonds has the words "15% *more*" on it? Who knows? Or what is being promised by an ad which says "Come to our store and save *up to* 50 per cent." Even if you save nothing you still save below the promised limit. The ad only says that the most you can save is 50 percent; it says nothing about the least you can save. In fact, it does not even say that you will actually save anything—although that is clearly the inference the advertiser hopes the buyer will make.

It should be obvious that a critical thinker would not look to advertising as a source of reliable information, but as George Orwell pointed out, we need to keep asserting the obvious. Advertisements may be interesting, seductive, productive, sexy, humorous, enter-

> "One can like or dislike a television commercial....But one cannot refute it." -- Neil Postman, *Amusing Ourselves to Death*

taining, misleading, deceptive, false, or malicious, but they are rarely informative. It should go without saying that a critical thinker should not be seduced by the appeals of ads. True, many of our values and habits—even a few false needs—have originated in advertising (like our concern with bad breath or foot odor, or the color of our lips or hair). True, many of us feel like inferior human beings because we are not thin or muscular, or do not have good tans or thick hair, but we shouldn't be swayed by the constant bombardment of ads that try to persuade us of what is good and what will make us happy.

Ads often make *vague comparisons*:

"Colgate users have *fewer* cavities. . . ." [fewer than whom?]

"15 % *more* . . . ." (on a package of almonds) [more than what?]

"In a recent survey, *more* people preferred . . . ." [how large was the survey? How many more?]

Ads often use *absurd or meaningless expressions*: a detergent is said to get clothes "whiter than white," a beer is said to be the "King of Beers." General Electric thinks we will be impressed that it brings "good things to life." One ad tells us that "You can be sure if it's Westinghouse." Another declares: "Tandy. Clearly superior." We are invited to "Come to where the flavor is. Marlboro Country" or to become part of "The Pepsi generation."

In short, the language of advertising is like much of the language of politics: vague and deceptive. This should not be surprising, since most political speech is thinly disguised advertising. Press conferences and off-the-cuff remarks are often part of propaganda campaigns aimed at selling us on politicians and their ideas. It's no secret that political candidates and elected officials hire advertising agencies to sell the public on images: the candidate becomes another commodity to be sold to the masses.

Exercises 2-6

A. Find at least one example of a speaker, writer or advertisement that makes a *false implication* or which engages in *hedging*.

B. Find at least one example of a speaker, writer or advertisement that uses *weasel words*.

C. Find three examples of advertisements which make absurd or meaningless claims. (E.g., "Gets clothes whiter than white"; "King of beers"; "G.E. We bring good things to life"; "You can be sure if it's Westinghouse"; "Come to where the flavor is. Marlboro Country"; "Miller's: Made the American Way.")

D. Discuss each of the following expressions used in advertisements. Are the ads deceptive in any way? How?

 *1. Montsanto: "Without chemicals life itself would be impossible."
 2. Pacific Bell: "Reach out and touch someone."
 3. Marlboro Lights: "The spirit of Marlboro in a low tar cigarette."
 4. Colt 45 Malt Liquor: "If unique is what you seek."
 5. Beaulieu Vineyard (for a burgundy wine): "The anticipatory hush....The slow velvety pleasure."
 *6. Eve Light 120's cigarettes: "Tastes as good as it looks."
 7. L & M cigarettes: "The proud smoke."
 8. Virginia Slims : "You've come a long way, baby."
 9. Edge skin conditioner: "Switch to new Skin Conditioning Edge gel, for that closer, smoother feeling."
 10. Scholl exercise sandals: "Sometimes dreams are only a step away."
 *11. Pantene Pro-V: for hair so healthy it shines.
 12. There's no dog like your dog. And no heartworm protection like ours. Heartworm protection plus. Right from the heart.
 13. Just 5 calories per olive and tons of taste.
 14. (Ad for the Chrysler New Yorker) "Like Most New Yorkers, this one is sophisticated, refined and definitely has an attitude."
 15. Loro Piana's Tasmanian™ Fabric Performs Like No Other."

3.3 Assuring expressions and other no-brainers

One way to keep others from thinking about what you are saying is to assure them that what you have to say need not be questioned. This can be done very subtly by using *assuring expressions*. Many claims are preceded by expressions that assure us that they are warranted.

For example:

"As everyone knows...."
"As you already know...."
"The truth is...."
"Being reasonable, you will see...."
"Common sense tells us that...."

"It is certain that...."
"It has been shown that...."
"Experts agree that...."
"I assure you that...."
"That's a no-brainer...."

Why are such assurances made? If everyone knows something, then there is no need to say that everyone knows it. The truth is that such assurances do not inform us of what they literally assert. Rather, they inform us that the speaker does not consider what follows to be up for question. So, we should not expect to be given any reasons for what follows. If the speaker did not use the assuring phrase or word, then perhaps someone might ask her to back up her claim. But who would dare question what he already knows? Who would contradict common sense or what everyone knows? The fact is that each of the above assurances implies trust. In a context of honest discourse among people who trust each other, assuring phrases save time and simplify communication. But even in situations of trust, people can—and sometimes will—abuse their position. So, we should be aware of and beware assuring expressions. Of course, everyone knows this already, since it is just a matter of common sense!

3.4 Sneaking in judgmental words: opinions put forth as facts

Another way to keep others from thinking is to use *judgmental words* that evaluate the situation so they can be spared the agony of thinking for themselves. There is nothing wrong with making judgments and using the appropriate words to express those judgments. However, some writers may give you their *evaluation* of the situation under the guise of a factual report. For example, a writer says that "an *accurate* assessment of the situation was made by the Pentagon" or "the President took *justifiable* pride in signing the Trade Agreement with China." The writer is making judgments for you, telling you that an assessment is accurate or suggesting that a trade agreement was a good one. There are always those who are ready to give us the *right* view, the *correct* opinion, *trustworthy* advice, *reliable* information, or the *true* story about some *scoundrel, dishonest barracuda, interested party, pervert,* or *liberal dupe*! Beware of such language. It indicates people less interested in having you *think* than in having you *think as they do.*

Nowhere is this better exemplified than in the successful 1992 campaign in Colorado to pass a constitutional amendment barring laws that specifically protect homosexuals from discrimination. The leader of the campaign, Will Perkins, stated that "Language doesn't shape the campaign—it *is* the campaign." The hope was to influence and shape public opinion by characterizing homosexuals as people with a *sexual preference* rather than a *sexual orientation,* who have an *agenda* rather than *goals* to secure *special rights* rather than *civil rights*. On the other side, gay activists were trying to get the term "sexual preference" eliminated from public discourse because it implies that homosexuality is chosen rather than given to a person by nature or nurture.[9] Each side recognized that the words used to frame the issues would affect how people would think about those issues without actually thinking about the issues.

4. Clarity and language: ambiguity and vagueness

In chapter one, we described the Forer effect—the tendency of people to accept vague and general personality descriptions as applying uniquely to themselves. For example,

While you have some personality weaknesses you are generally able to compensate for them. You have considerable unused capacity that you have not turned to your advantage. You also pride yourself as an independent thinker, but you have found it unwise to be too frank in revealing yourself to others. Some of your aspirations tend to be rather unrealistic.

You're not told exactly what personality weaknesses you have. In fact, you're not given any guidance as to what might count as a personality weakness. It is left up to you to find something about yourself that you or others might consider a weakness. Most of us can find at least one or two things that we or others would consider a weakness. It is also unclear as to what is meant by being "generally able to compensate for them." The nature of our unused capacity isn't specified, nor is it clear how we have turned this to our advantage. Again, it is left up to you to provide the specific content of the personality profile. Words such as 'independent,' 'unwise,' and 'unrealistic,' and expressions such as 'too frank' are vague. No specific aspiration is mentioned. You must fill in the blank to give this profile any concrete meaning.

> **The following claims are taken from a list of written claims made by motorists who had been in accidents.**
>
> --I was taking my canary to the vet. It got loose in the car and flew out the window. The next thing I saw was his rear end and there was a crash.
> --The guy was all over the road. I had to swerve several times before I hit him.
> --I turned the wheel and found myself in a different direction going the opposite way.
> --A stop sign suddenly appeared where no stop sign had ever appeared before.
> --An invisible car came out of nowhere, struck my vehicle and vanished.

Vague or ambiguous language can be a hindrance to communication and to critical thinking, whether it is intentional or not. The vague language in personality profiles, horoscopes, and psychic readings is deceiving. It can make you think somebody has given you precise information, when *you* are the one who has provided the precision.

There are many other ways that unclear language can hinder critical thinking. Let's examine some of them and then let's look at some things we can do to improve the clarity of our communication.

4.1 Ambiguity

When a word or expression can be reasonably understood in more than one way, it is said to be *ambiguous*. For example, a group of parents opposing sex education classes at Catholic schools in the Sacramento diocese got together and called themselves *Irresponsible Sex Education Opponents*. Had they reflected a bit, they might have seen that their group's name would be found highly amusing by the supporters of the classes. The opponents of the classes seem to be saying that they themselves are the ones who are irresponsible. Or maybe they're saying that they are against education on irresponsible sex. Or maybe they're saying they're against sex education that is irresponsible, in which case they are suggesting that they believe there is a responsible form of sex education. In any case, it was a bad choice of words.

Ambiguity is often unintentional, due to carelessness. A writer or speaker intends to say one thing, but either says another or says it in such a way that it might be understood differently than intended. A headline states **LYING EXPERT TESTIFIES AT TRIAL.** Is the expert a liar? Is the one testifying an expert at telling when someone is lying? A highway billboard declares **PSA AIRLINES ONLY FLIES DIRECT TO BURBANK.** Is PSA the only airline that flies directly to Burbank? When PSA flies to Burbank does it only fly direct?[10] Or, is Burbank the only city to which PSA flies?

A headline says **CHILD MURDERER HAUNTS TOWN.** Is a child murdering people or is someone murdering children? **NUDE PATROL COMBS BEACH** states another headline. Are those on patrol patrolling in the nude or are they patrolling for nudists?

In 1978 the City Council of Florence, Oregon, passed an ordinance that made it illegal "to have sex while in or in view of a public or private place." They were trying to ban scandalous sexual behavior, not all sexual acts.

In 1987 California Governor George Deukmajian appointed Dan Lungren as state treasurer following the death of Jesse Unruh. The state Senate approved the nomination but the state Assembly rejected it. The governor knew that the State Constitution asserts that for an appointment to be valid a majority is required in both houses. He cited a 1976 amendment to the State Constitution, however, as justifying his contention that Lungren should become state treasurer although rejected by the Assembly. The amendment said that "if neither confirmed nor denied by both the Senate and Assembly within 90 days, nominees may take office." Lungren had been neither confirmed nor denied by both houses! The California Supreme Court ruled that the state Constitution's requirement of a majority in both houses was the law. Clearly, somebody goofed in writing the amendment and many legislators did not catch the goof, as they voted in favor of it. It seems that the intent was to insure a speedy process, to make sure that a vote was not delayed indefinitely but was taken within 90 days of nomination. But the governor was right; that's not all the amendment says.

While ambiguity is sometimes intentional, as in the earlier examples of hedging by Ronald Reagan, Mike Curb, and Bill Clinton, ambiguity is often the result of carelessness. In either case,

FOR SALE: Big dog. Beautiful animal, good watchdog. Will eat anything. Especially fond of children.

however, ambiguity is a hindrance to critical thinking. We cannot make reasonable judgments as to what to think and do if the information we receive is ambiguous. Often, even an astute critical thinker does not realize that an expression could be understood in another way, until it is too late.

4.2 Vagueness

Vagueness is often a considerable hindrance to critical thinking. Most communication, however, is vague to some degree. Vagueness only becomes a problem when language is less precise, specific, or definite than the context requires.

One kind of vagueness is due to not being precise or specific enough with numbers, directions, times, locations, etc. This kind of vagueness or *imprecision* can usually be cleared up by replacing the imprecise expression with a synonymous expression that is more precise. For example, "two hundred" is more precise than "many." "March 15, 1986" is more precise than "sometime." "San Francisco" is more precise than "somewhere north of Santa Barbara." There are many expressions that could be replaced by precise numbers, times, dates, etc. How precise one should be depends on the situation. If the situation does not require more precision, there is no need to replace a vague expression. "I'll pay you back soon" may be specific enough in most circumstances. But if one needs the money tomorrow, "soon" may be too vague. "The movie lasts two hours, four minutes, and seven sec-

onds" is probably too precise for most circumstances, but anything less precise would be too vague for someone writing the musical score for the film. If your partner asks you how much you have in your joint checking account, your answer may not need to be as precise as what you would expect from your bank's computerized records.

Another kind of problematic vagueness occurs frequently with qualitative terms and is due to lack of a definite boundary between two mutually exclusive **classes**. We might call this kind of vagueness *qualitative vagueness*. Two people may agree, for example, that only *justified killing* should be allowed, yet they may disagree as to the criteria for distinguishing *justified* from *unjustified* killings. That is, they may disagree as to the *definition* of the expression 'justified killing.' Or, they may agree on

A **class** is a set of items grouped together because of some shared characteristic or set of characteristics. For example, there is the class of doctors, which might be divided into the classes of *incompetent* doctors and *competent* doctors. Those classes would be mutually exclusive, i.e., a doctor can't be both competent and incompetent as a doctor.

The class of doctors might be divided up into doctors who are tall and doctors who have red hair. Those classes would not be mutually exclusive because the same doctor could be both tall and have red hair.

44

the defining criteria of the term 'justified killing,' but disagree in specific cases on the application of the criteria. For example, two people may agree that a killing is justified if it is necessary to save your own or another's life, or if it is done under orders in a time of war, or if it is done by the state as a punishment for murder. But they may disagree over whether a specific killing was really necessary, or whether a military order was correctly understood, or whether a person convicted of murder was really guilty.

Many qualitative terms will be vague in many of their uses, yet this fact need not be taken as a warning that the use of such words will always be *too* vague. Most of us would have little difficulty identifying certain teachers as *incompetent*, certain behavior as *cruel,* or a certain person as *rehabilitated.* The blatant cases are obvious and clear enough. It is the borderline cases that cause the trouble, as we shall see in the next section.

Exercise 2-7

Indicate whether the vagueness of the underlined words in the following passages is simply a matter of imprecision (which could be remedied by replacing the imprecise expression with a synonymous one that is more precise) or is a matter of qualitative vagueness (which could be made clearer only by giving defining criteria).

*1. We cannot allow police <u>brutality</u>. Any police officer guilty of <u>brutality</u> will be suspended or fired."
2. "I didn't take <u>much</u>, just <u>a little</u>--only <u>enough</u> <u>to get by</u>. What's a <u>few</u> dollars between friends?"
3. "We must get rid of the <u>fat</u> in government. The state and federal budgets should reflect <u>appropriate</u> cuts in the fat from the total budgets."
*4. "Inflation, I guarantee you my friends, will be curbed in the <u>near</u> <u>future</u>."
5. "We are calling for an end to the <u>exploitation</u> of the American worker!"
6. "It is high time we elect a <u>decent</u> President!"
7. "The foster child program is failing because we do not have enough <u>caring</u> people to take in a foster child."
8. "Our cuts in social welfare programs will not affect the <u>truly</u> <u>needy</u>.
9. "<u>Real</u> <u>Americans</u> <u>and</u> <u>true</u> <u>patriots</u> will stand behind the President's proposal."
10. "You will be hired as a permanent employee after six months, if your work has been <u>satisfactory</u>.

---

5. Definitions

Providing good definitions of key terms is essential to critical thinking. A good definition can prevent misunderstanding. A poor definition, on the other hand, can confuse or be used to sneak in questionable assumptions.

In our discussion of qualitative vagueness above, we mentioned borderline cases—those cases that were neither clearly in nor clearly out of a class. Some types of words are frequently used in ways that borderline cases cannot be resolved. Evaluative terms such as 'good' and 'bad' are notoriously vague. Relative terms cannot be used to express absolute or fixed quantities or qualities, e.g., 'tall,' 'not much,' 'shortly.' A relative term must have a fixed point of reference to relate it to, e.g., an elephant is big relative to a human being, but small relative to an ocean; a flea is small relative to a horse, but large relative to a proton. Clarification of qualitatively vague terms may be achieved by giving specific criteria for their application. To do so is to provide what is called a *precising* or *restrictive* definition. However, the criteria—even if not vague themselves—may still be open to criticism. For one thing, a precising definition of a term should bear a strong resemblance to its ordinary meaning. After all, the purpose of a precising definition is to *clarify* the meaning of a term or expression. Thus, for example, to define a machine as "that which is technologically developed for the facile breeding of pigs" would be a bad precising definition because it bears no resemblance to the ordinary usage of the term. On the other hand, to define an automotive vehicle as "a self-propelled machine meant to be driven by human adults but not used for recreational purposes" might be an acceptable precising definition for an insurance contract. A freeway sign which declares that a *car pool* is "2 or more persons" bears some resemblance to our ordinary usage of the term.

Even though most of us would require that the non-driving persons in the car fulfil some other requirements before we would say there is a *car pool*, the posted definition is adequate because it eliminates most vagueness.

Before accepting any criteria given to clarify the meaning of a vague term, one should first be clear as to why the clarification is needed. Also, one should be clear as to the likely consequences of accepting the criteria. If you want automobile insurance, you will have to accept the precising definition of 'motor vehicle' used in the insurance contract. If that definition excludes recreational vehicles, farm implements and boats, then if you want insurance for any of those items you had better get the contract rewritten or find another insurance company.

> In California there is a story—perhaps an urban legend—about a woman driving alone who was stopped by a Highway Patrol officer for violating the car pool lane law. She argued that since she was pregnant, she and her "child" counted as two persons. The officer was undaunted and asked if she would rather be cited for not having the "child" in a proper car seat.

If the school board must identify all the unqualified teachers in its district because the State has said it will cut off funds to any school district that employs unqualified teachers, then the school board must find out what criteria the State uses to determine which teachers are unqualified. The board would not only have to become aware of the likely consequences of accepting the criteria; they would have to become aware of the likely consequences of *not* accepting them. In such a case, the school board may have the power to object to the State's criteria, but no power to refuse to accept them.

Defining a vague expression may clarify its meaning, but one is under no obligation to accept the definition just because it is intelligible. Many arguments are grounded in definitions from which conclusions may be inferred.[11] Being a definition does not shield a claim from criticism. For example, *natural science* may be defined as "the attempt to understand and explain various aspects of physical, chemical, or biological entities through appeals either to supernatural or naturalistic mechanisms." However, such a definition implies that one must believe in the supernatural in order to do science. Since some scientists are atheists, this definition seems absurd. Are there two parallel sciences, then? One for those who believe in the supernatural and one for those who don't? Ken Ham, the executive director of the website Answers in Genesis, claims: "I don't use science to prove my 'religion' - I use the Bible to build my science." What he means by science can't be what most scientists mean by science, however. He is free to call his beliefs scientific if he so desires, but he should not expect the rest of the scientific world to pay much attention to him. In other words, one may stipulate that natural science includes supernatural explanations that are accepted on faith, but others will be quick to criticize the definition because it does not bear much of a resemblance to the ordinary meaning of the word 'science.'

The define science so that it includes theology and philosophy demonstrates that definitions can be packed with *theoretical implications*. If science is so defined then it makes sense to teach creation stories in science classrooms. Theories such as those of Zecharia Sitchin, L. Ron Hubbard, and Raël that humans originated from breeding experiments by aliens from other planets thousands or millions of years ago should also be taught in our science classes. Of course, if such topics were introduced into our science classrooms, there wouldn't be much time left for *science*, at least not as most of the scientific community understand that word.

5.1 Evaluating definitions

One cannot always resolve a disagreement over a precising definition by simply pointing out empirical facts. There may be no observations or experiences one can bring forth that would resolve the issue to everyone's satisfaction. For example, one person believes that science includes theological explanations. Another thinks this is false. Presumably, both are aware of the ordinary usage of the term 'science' and believe that the issue cannot be resolved simply by referring to the dictionary and what is called the *lexical* definition of the word. That is not to say that it would be irrelevant to bring up the ordinary or authoritative usage of the term as a reason for accepting one definition and rejecting another. Such a move would be appropriate. But it may not resolve the issue, for there may also exist a fundamental disagreement about many related issues. No resolution of the disagreement may be possible without one side abandoning many related beliefs and attitudes.

If a word may be used to *refer* to things or acts, etc., then the word is said to have a *denotation*. The denotation of the word *science*, for example, would be whatever may be correctly referred to by that word. If 'science' is defined in such a way that it denotes something that one believes is not science, then one would criticize the definition for being *too broad*, for including too much, for referring to things beyond the boundary, so to speak, of the class of things that one believes may properly be called science. On the other hand, if 'science' does not denote things that one believes are science, then one would criticize the definition for being *too narrow*, for not including what it should include, for not referring to what it should refer to. If a definition implies that a word denotes what it should not denote but fails to denote what it should denote, then that definition is said to be both too broad and too narrow. (It may seem contradictory to say that a definition is both too broad and too narrow, but being too broad only means that the definition denotes items beyond its proper boundary, while being too narrow means that the definition does not denote items within its proper boundary.) A definition that is both too broad and too narrow is like a misplaced boundary fence that both encloses land it should not and only encloses part of the land it should.

Since there is no agreed upon way to settle many of the disagreements over the definitions of terms, it is often the case that the best one can do is to compare the definitions to common usage. If a definition bears little or no resemblance to how a word is ordinarily used, then an explanation of the uncommon usage should be forthcoming. In any case, it is up to the listener or reader to decide whether to accept or reject the definition. In many cases, the best one can do is to try to understand how the definition fits in with other beliefs a person holds. For example, opponents on the abortion issue may begin with different definitions of the key term 'person.' The opponent of abortion may define 'person' so that it denotes fetuses. The proponent of abortion-on-demand may define 'person' in such a way that some or all fetuses are not denoted by the term. The issue is not an empirical one and cannot be resolved by appeals to observations or facts. Each may be using 'person' in a way that is consistent with common usage. Neither is able to accept the other's definition because to do so would not serve the theoretical purpose for which the definition was given. To accept the other side's definition would be to accept the other side's argument.

It should be noted that not all definitions that restrict the correct application of a word or expression occur in arguments over controversial issues. The meanings of key terms are often stipulated in contracts and in the social sciences. For example, most automobile insurance contracts give a precising definition of the expression 'motor vehicle' so that it is stipulated that the term does not denote recreational vehicles, farm implements, electric golf carts, or drivable lawn mowers. The purpose for such stipulations about the denotation of the term 'motor vehicle' is clear: The insurance company does not want to pay out for items it did not intend to cover and the insured person should know exactly what is covered under the conditions of the policy.

Finally, behavioral scientists often define terms by giving *operational definitions*, by describing the operations that are used to determine the correct application of an expression. For example, *quick reflexes* might be defined as "a reaction time to a tone under one-fifth of a second measured by a latency clock." Note how such a definition would eliminate the vagueness that would accompany most uses of the expression *quick reflexes*. Such a definition, however, may be packed with theoretical implications about behavior. It may imply that only behavior that is quantitatively measurable should be studied by behavioral scientists.

Exercise 2-8

Discuss each of the following definitions in terms of clarity (too vague, ambiguous or obscure) and extension of denotation (too broad, too narrow). [Exercises with an * are answered in Answers to Selected Exercises.]

*1. A biology text book defines *cetacean* as "of or pertaining to an order (Cetacea) of aquatic, mostly marine, mammals, consisting of the whales, dolphins, porpoises, narwhals, grampuses, etc., having a large head, fishlike hairless bodies, and paddlelike forelimbs."

*2. A student in a political science class is asked to define *demagogue* and answers that "a demagogue is someone with charisma."

*3. A character in a novel defines *freedom of speech* as meaning "the freedom to say whatever the government will allow you to say."

*4. A pamphlet from a local church defines an alcoholic as "someone who drinks two or more beers a day."

*5. A student delivers a speech in which she asserts that she means by the word *person* "a human being capable of social and political involvement with other human beings."

*6. A philosophy text gives as a definition of *spirit* the following: "non-material substance."

7. In an essay, an economist defines *recession* as follows: "a depression without the foreboding connotation of economic stagnation."

8. A humanities text defines *campanile* as "a freestanding bell tower."

*9. A book by an anthropologist defines *aggression* as "unprovoked physical attack aimed at elevating the aggressor to a position of higher status than his victim."

10. A lawyer is asked to define just law and she replies by saying that "a just law is one which has been passed by a duly elected legislature."

11. "Art is a selective re-creation of reality according to an artist's metaphysical value-judgments." --Ayn Rand, *The Romantic Manifesto* (New York: Signet Books, 1971, p. 64.

12. "Power may be defined as the production of intended effects." --Bertrand Russell, *Power* (New York: W.W. Norton & Co., 1969), p. 35.

13. "A vested interest...in ordinary intercourse is an improper advantage enjoyed by a political minority to which the speaker does not himself belong." --John Kenneth Galbraith, *The Affluent Society* (New York: Mentor Books, 1958) p. 146.

14. Inflation is "persistently rising prices." --John Kenneth Galbraith, *The Affluent Society* (New York: Mentor Books, 1958) p. 169.

15. "Thus we may define the real as that whose characters are independent of what anybody may think them to be." --Charles S. Peirce, "How to Make Our Ideas Clear."

16. *Joy* is man's passage from a less to a greater perfection....*Sorrow* is man's passage from a greater to a less perfection." --Baruch de Spinoza

17. "An instinct is defined as an inborn condition which imparts direction to psychological processes." --Calvin S. Hall, *A Primer of Freudian Psychology* (New York: Mentor Books, 1954), p. 37.

*18. "At any rate, hereafter the word *superstition* will be used in the sense of the kind of belief and action a reasonable man in present-day Western society would regard as being "superstitious.'" --Gustav Jahoda, *The Psychology of Superstition* (Great Britain: Pelican Books, 1970), p. 10.

19. "Artificial intelligence: Behavior by a machine that, if exhibited by a human, would be called intelligent."

20. "Immorality then, for the purpose of the law, is what every right-minded person is presumed to consider to be immoral." --Patrick Devlin, *The Enforcement of Morals*.

• • •

6. Statements of fact and statements of opinion

In the first chapter we noted that facts are what we take to be certain or true, and which we consider unreasonable to doubt. Opinions, on the other hand, are often contrasted with facts as being uncertain and reasonable to doubt. For example, someone claims (1) she perceived a dark object of human proportions moving across a field at night and (2) she believed that the object was her neighbor. Her first claim might be taken as a fact but the second claim would be taken as an opinion. The difference seems to be due simply to the amount of interpretation the perceiver does. If the perception requires simple and ordinary sense perception (of shapes, colors, and movement) and a minimal amount of interpretation, the event perceived is considered a fact. If the perception requires making judgments that go beyond simple sense perception (interpreting the moving shape as one's neighbor) the event related is considered an opinion. The opinion may turn out to be true, however. So, it is not accurate to say that facts are certain and true, while opinions are not. Some opinions are based on mounds of evidence and have a high degree of probability.

Another reason for not distinguishing facts and opinions as certain versus uncertain is that 'fact' is also used to mean 'event,' 'actuality,' or 'reality.' Many things which are claimed to be actualities or realities turn out not to be so after all. What was claimed to be a fact turns out to be false.

48

Rather than think of opinions as uncertain claims, it might be better to think of them as *beliefs that reflect judgments*. Judgments are based on interpretations or evaluations. It may be a fact that the local river is filled with dead fish, but it is a judgment (opinion) that the fish died because of lack of food. That judgment might come to be taken as a fact, however, if the evidence supports it beyond a reasonable doubt. There is, in other words, no clear line that separates facts from opinions in terms of certainty. Perhaps it would be less confusing if the distinction were made between *statements of fact* and *statements of opinion*, rather than between facts and opinions.

> "Experience is the name everyone gives to their mistakes."
> --Oscar Wilde

Determining whether something is a fact requires knowing whether or not it is true. Determining whether something is a statement of fact requires knowing only whether or not it is stated as if it were true. Determining whether it is a fact that the fish died because of lack of food requires more specific and detailed knowledge than would be required to determine whether the statement "The fish died because of lack of food" is stated as a fact or as an opinion. It is obvious that it is stated as a fact. If it were stated as an opinion, the speaker would indicate this by using expressions such as 'it is my opinion that,' or he would have used expressions such as 'might have' or 'probably,' e.g., "The fish *might have* died because of lack of food" or "The fish *probably* died because of lack of food."

In sum, facts and opinions both run the gamut from uncertain to very certain. A statement of fact, however, is asserted to be certain. A statement of opinion is asserted to be a judgment, but it is not necessarily asserted to be uncertain.

Exercise 2-9

For each of the following claims, identify whether it is stated as a fact or as stated as an opinion.

*1. Most welfare recipients are able-bodied persons who are too lazy to work and who would rather cheat the government than take an honest job.

*2. Homosexuals are more immoral than heterosexuals.

3. The major cause of violent crime is leniency in our courts.

*4. Anyone who supports legislation which would allow abortions condones the murder of innocent children.

*5. Prison guards are well-trained professionals capable of handling any disturbance prisoners might make.

*6. God probably exists.

*7. Ripe Macintosh apples are red.

8. The best counselors for juvenile delinquents are ex-convicts who were juvenile delinquents themselves.

*9. Cigarette smoking is hazardous to one's health.

10. Pornography is harmful to society.

*11. Nuclear reactors are unlikely to be unsafe.

12. Only physical things are real; there are no spirits.

13. It is immoral to use drugs for pleasure.

14. Drug dealers should be given capital punishment.

*15. Aliens from other planets may have visited earth in ancient times.

*16. My economic policies will reduce inflation by as much as 10 percent and increase employment by as much as 5 percent.

*17. The deaths of thousands of fish each year above Sacramento may be caused by a combination of problems, including a chemical in agricultural canals.

18. If gold is dipped in hydrochloric acid, the gold will not dissolve.

19. The essence of mind is thinking.

20. There might have been three stabbings of inmates by other inmates at the state prison last week.

*21. All persons have a natural right to life, liberty and the pursuit of happiness.

22. This person no longer has violent tendencies and is unlikely ever to rape and murder again.

23. The essence of physical reality is extension in space.

24. Cave paintings of animals done more than 25,000 years ago were probably done in order to assist the initiation of young men into the adult world of hunting.

*25. Interest rates may drop by as much as ten percent within the next six months.

26. It is necessarily the case that the soul has a beginning but is immortal.

27. People who love one another are happier and more productive than those who do not love one another.

28. Human beings are not naturally aggressive.

29. Anyone can have an out-of-body experience if they follow my easy ten-step plan.

*30. Only empirical statements are meaningful.

• • •

Chapter two self-test: true or false? (Check you answers in Answers to Selected Exercises.)

1. A euphemism is an offensive word used in place of an inoffensive one.

2. Emotive language is always inappropriate for a critical thinker.

3. When a word or expression can be reasonably understood in more than one way, it is said to be ambiguous.

4. An expression which precedes a claim and which indicates that the claim is not up for questioning is called an assuring expression.

5. A definition is too broad if its denotation does not include items it should include.

6. Definitions are rarely packed with theoretical implications.

7. Clarification of a term by giving specific criteria for the correct application of the term is to provide what is called a precising definition.

8. In contracts and in the social sciences the meanings of key terms are often stipulated.

9. Highly emotive language may be more effective than logical reasons in persuading others.

10. Social scientists often define terms by giving operational definitions, by describing the operations which are used to determine the correct application of an expression.

11. Language can be clear and accurate but misleading.

12. We cannot make reasonable judgments as to what to think and do if the information we receive is ambiguous.

13. A precising definition is one which gives specific criteria for the correct application of a word or expression.

14. A word's denotation is what the word refers to.

15. Expressions such as "cooking the books" or "creative bookkeeping" when used to refer to falsifying a corporation's accounting records are known as doublespeak euphemisms.

16. The language of advertising is usually misleading, deceptive, vague, or absurd.

17. How precise one should be depends on the situation.

18. Vagueness which is due to lack of a definite boundary between two mutually exclusive classes is called qualitative vagueness.

19. The primary meaning of euphemism is the "technical language of a science, trade, art or profession."

20. Gobbledygook is confusing or convoluted use of words which obscures thought.

21. The descriptive content of a word or expression is called its emotive content.

22. Emotive language used to bypass reasoning, to persuade without offering any logical reasons, or to stimulate people to action by preying upon their fears, prejudices, or hopes is called loaded language.

23. A definition is too broad if it excludes in its denotation items which should be included.

24. "Doublespeak" refers to language which is used to attempt to deceive or mislead.

25. Judgmental words are often used to sneak in evaluations, thereby sparing you the agony of thinking for yourself.

26. To call something a *fact* is to say that we take it to be certain and would consider it unreasonable to doubt it.

27. All opinions are uncertain and all facts are certain.

28. Opinions are beliefs which reflect judgments.

29. *Hedging* is to use language which appears to be clear and precise but which is vague or ambiguous enough to allow the user to back off from the apparent meaning.

30. True and clear claims can make *false implications*.

31. A critical thinker must be aware of people who state their opinions as if they were facts.

32. Expressions such as *save up to 50%* and *may help fight tooth decay* are called *weasel words*.

33. The cognitive meaning of a word is the attitude expressed by the word.

34. Jargon is the technical language of a trade or profession.

35. Some opinions are probably true.

50

Further Reading - Chapter Two

Kahane, Howard. (2001) *Logic and Contemporary Rhetoric, The Uses of Reason in Everyday Life*, 9th ed. Wadsworth Publishing Co.

Lutz, William. (1989) *Doublespeak*. Harper & Row.

Lutz, William. (1997) *The New Doublespeak: Why No One Knows What Anyone's Saying Anymore*. Harper Collins.

Newman, Edwin. (1975) *A Civil Tongue*. Bobbs-Merrill Company, Inc.

Notes - Chapter Two

[1]George Orwell's novel, *1984*, depicts a totalitarian state where language was one of the most important weapons used to control thought and action. "Newspeak" was Orwell's term for the official state language. And "doublethink" was his term for holding two opposing ideas at the same time, e.g., "War is Peace."

[2]Lutz distinguishes the use of *jargon* and *gobbledygook*, to be discussed below in separate sections. He also discusses the use of inflated language to make the ordinary seem special (e.g., calling a used car a "pre-owned vehicle'). We will discuss inflated language with jargon and gobbledygook, rather than in a separate section.

[3]"PBS 'commercials' draw more criticism than new revenue," Sally Bedell Smith, *The Sacramento Bee*, April 6, 1985, p. A15.

[4]These words are taken from a California State senator (Campbell) who proposed them as part of a Senate Bill (#1215).

[5]"Words CAN Really Hurt Me," by Sylvia Rubin, *San Francisco Chronicle*, July 20, 1979, p. 29.

[6]*New York Times*, March 7, 1990, p. 1.

[7]"State insists "green' labels be true-blue," Philip J. Garcia, *The Sacramento Bee*, Sept. 1, 1991.

[8] "Weasel words are words that suck all of the life out of the words next to them just as a weasel sucks an egg and leaves the shell." From the June 1900 issue of *Century Magazine*. Weasel words were first associated with politicians, who seem to have a penchant for saying things like "The public must be *duly* protected," instead of "The public must be protected." See *The Facts on File Encyclopedia of Word and Phrase Origins* by Robert Hendrickson (New York: Facts on File Publications, 1987).

[9]"Gay, Lesbian Groups Seek to Expunge Bias They See in Language," *Wall Street Journal*, May 23, 1993, p. A8.

[10]In airline doublespeak, a direct flight is not necessarily a nonstop flight. A direct flight is one which does not require a transfer of airplanes. So, all nonstop flights are direct but not all direct flights are nonstop. (Lutz, p. 22).

[11]We are using *argument* in a technical sense here. An *argument* is the presentation of reasons in support of some position. A *conclusion* is the position the argument tries to support. The nature of argument is the topic of chapter four.

Chapter Three - Sources

"...most newspapers do not deserve much public confidence."
—*Edwin Leavitt Clarke*

"Partisans of all stripes...value reliability over critical thinking." —*David Brock*

"If you give your point of view often enough and loudly enough, it becomes true."
—*Steve Hopcraft, Democratic political consultant*

At the end of World War II, 80 percent of American newspapers were independently owned. When Ben H. Bagdikian published *Media Monopoly* (Beacon Press) in 1982, 50 corporations owned almost of all of the major media outlets in the United States. Fifty corporations owned 1,787 daily newspapers, 11,000 magazines, 9,000 radio stations, 1,000 television stations, 2,500 book publishers and seven major movie studios. By the time Bagdikian put out the revised edition in 1987, ownership had shrunk to 29 corporations. By 1999, nine corporations owned it all. (Molly Ivans -- from Robert W. McChesney's *Rich Media, Poor Democracy: Communications Politics in Dubious Times* (University of Illinois Press).

1. Introduction

If our era is remembered for nothing else, it will be remembered as the age of entertainment. We live in an age of glitz and hype. It is called the information age and there is great talk about the information highway, but sifting out reliable and useful information from all the sexy garbage thrown our way is becoming nearly impossible for the average person. There is nothing wrong with being entertained and amused, but our society seems to have made amusement the goal of life (Postman: 1986). Even murder trials are televised and are not without their amusing moments as prosecutors, defense attorneys, and judges play to the camera and an audience of millions. Formerly reliable and dependable newspapers and television networks now feel obligated to report on tabloid gossip as part of their daily "news" coverage. At times it seems as if the news media pay more attention to the private lives of public figures than to their policies and decisions, although the latter are much more likely to affect us.

> "Again and again, facts--arson, plane crash, bomb [sex scandal]--are supplanted by controversies over how the stories were reported and who believes which version of reality." --Kurt Andersen, "The Age of Unreason," *The New Yorker*, Feb. 3, 1997.

Several highly publicized cases of journalists plagiarizing and faking sources have marred the reputation of institutions like *USA TODAY* (Jack Kelly) and *The New York* Times (Jayson Blair). A panel investigating the Jack Kelly case reported:

> Lax editing and newsroom leadership, lack of staff communication, a star system, a workplace climate of fear and inconsistent rules on using anonymous sources helped former *USA TODAY* reporter Jack Kelley to fabricate and plagiarize stories for more than a decade, an independent panel of editors has concluded. (Kevin McCoy, *USA TODAY*, April 22, 2004).

There must be something complex going on, because the consequences for a journalist of getting caught in a lie are terminal. Bill Vann, writing for the World Socialist Web Site, claims that Jayson Blair's flair for publishing interviews with people he never met and posting stories from places he'd never been, is not unusual among journalists. Vann blames "an unfortunate atmosphere of sensationalism combined with a competitive environment." Vann considers Blair's sins to be minor, however, compared to Judith Miller's. Her stories, seeming to substantiate the possession of weapons of mass destruction by Iraq, were published in the *Times* even

52

though her only source was the U.S. Military. Well, whether one considers plagiarism and faking news stories to be a greater or lesser evil than being manipulated, both kinds of grievances highlight the fact that there is a major credibility problem with today's mass media. Unfortunately, the media has a lot of company.

Police officers perjure themselves on national television (Mark Fuhrman); scientific researchers are caught plagiarizing or inventing data (Cyril Burt, Jan Hendrik Schön) to get grant money or to support personal agendas. Others pose as scientists and pass off worthless statistical data as if it were truth. Talk show hosts stand in line to present pseudo-scientists to their audiences because they often promote sexy themes, such as the kidnapping of hundreds of thousands of children (remember the photos on the milk cartons?), the sexual abuse of women and children, satanic ritual abuse of children, or the abduction of thousands of people by aliens from other solar systems. Reputable publishing houses seem to have little interest in the truth of what they publish, as long as it will sell. Many corporate executives seem to have little concern for their stockholders, the people who work for them, the law, or morals…until they get caught lying, evading taxes, paying bribes, or wasting corporate funds on personal pleasures.

How do we cut through the propaganda, the advertising, the hype and speculation of the mass media, the information and misinformation overloads? We are constantly blitzed with messages, images, phrases, notions, and ideas from myriad sources, some reliable and some not. Experts on every subject under the sun seem endless. With so many claims made by so many people, the critical thinker has a problem: Who do you trust? Who can you believe? Where is this unnamed 'reliable source' we keep hearing about but never seem to meet face to face?

As difficult as it is to know which sources to trust, there are some general guidelines we can follow. The guidelines will vary depending on whether we are evaluating an individual, a mass media corporation, or something as complex as the Internet. However, the rules will be basically the same whether we are evaluating a claim by a scientist, a newspaper reporter, a television or radio talk show host, a corporation CEO, or an author of a World Wide Web site.

The likelihood that a source is credible, unbiased, and accurate will depend on such things as the source's qualifications, integrity, and reputation. Does the source have the necessary qualifications for understanding and evaluating the kinds of claims he or she is making? Is there any reason to question the honesty or integrity of the source? Does the source have a reputation for accuracy? Does the source have a motive for being inaccurate or dishonest that is likely to outweigh the need to be accurate and honest?

Although the guidelines are the same for evaluating different types of sources, the *application* of the rules will vary for different sources.

2. Evaluating eyewitness testimony[1]

When evaluating the integrity and qualifications of an eyewitness, you should consider not only the reputation and motivation of the source, but also any environmental, physical, emotional, and intellectual factors that might significantly affect observation. Is the source physically and intellectually capable of making the observations he or she claims to have made? How reliable is the witness's eyesight or hearing? If the claim involves vision, consider whether the eyewitness wears corrective lenses or not. If the claim involves overhearing a conversation, consider whether the witness wears or needs a hearing aid. Consider the distance from the witness to what was observed. Consider the time of day or night, and factors such as the lighting. Consider whether the witness was under stress or in a state of excitement while making the observations. Consider whether any special experience or background knowledge is needed to make the observations in question. Does the witness have that experience or knowledge? If he says the gun he observed was a .22 caliber, for example, what qualifies him to describe the weapon that precisely? Consider the fact that eyewitness testimony involves interpretation of sense data and memory, both of which are fallible. Consider how long it has been since the observations were made.

Consider conflicting testimonies. The fact that a witness is confident and unhesitating in identifying someone or in describing something from memory does not mean the testimony is more accurate than that of a witness who hesitates or is cautious in giving testimony. Remember, too, that in choosing to believe one of two conflicting testimonies, you are not implying that one of the witnesses is lying. He or she could be mistaken.[2] Two people may observe "the same thing" and give inconsistent accounts of what they observed, and yet neither be lying. Their interpretations of what they perceive will depend in part on their past experience and their background knowledge. In part, it will depend on their prejudices and assumptions, and in part on their anticipations in the present situation. If you are not looking for something or expecting something, your observations will differ from someone who *is* looking for or expecting something specific. Probably most important, though, is the fact that some people are simply more attentive in their observations than others are. They see differently because they observe more, and they observe more carefully.

Consider also whether or not the eyewitness is being paid for his or her testimony. Greed or revenge will sometimes motivate a person to say things that are not true. Such motives are almost certainly at work in some of the testimony yielded by checkbook journalism: the practice of paying people for interviews. How reliable is the testimony of a Henry Kissinger or a Richard Nixon when they are doing interviews for hundreds of thousands of dollars? How reliable is the testimony of Michael Jackson's maid, Imelda Marcos's servants, Elvis's bodyguards, Elizabeth Taylor's cleaning lady, a cutlery salesman who claims he sold O.J. Simpson a long knife, etc., when these people are paid for their testimony? Are such people likely to feel obligated to exaggerate and invent, to give their benefactors their money's worth?

Be careful here. A person may have something to gain by lying, but it would hardly be worth it if discovery in a lie would mean the ruin of one's reputation or career. A paid expert, such as a lawyer, doctor or repairperson, may have a lot more to lose by being caught at being dishonest than he or she could gain if not caught. A tipster who is paid for information may have a lot more to gain by telling the truth than by feeding false information to the goose laying golden eggs. Also, although someone accused of wrongdoing would have a motive for inaccuracy or dishonesty if guilty, he or she would usually have an equally compelling motive for accuracy and honesty if innocent. Hence, it would not be reasonable to assume that anyone accused of wrongdoing is probably untrustworthy in giving testimony about the alleged wrongdoing. And it would not be reasonable to assume that anyone with something to gain by fraudulence or lying can't be trusted.

We should be most skeptical, however, of the testimony of those who not only have a lot to gain by false testimony, but also have nothing to lose if caught in a lie. We should be especially skeptical of the testimony of anyone who has much to gain by false testimony and who is the *sole source* of information. Such people know that they cannot be caught in a lie. There is no greater motivator to tell the truth than the certainty or high probability that a lie will be detected. The temptation to lie or embellish will be greater when one thinks that there is no chance of getting caught, e.g., when reporting "deathbed confessions" to which one is the only witness.

3. Experts

Remember how most of us had to deal with observation, memory, and authority as we developed from nearly totally dependent infants to independent adults. As infants we could not be critical thinkers. Our initial experiences were the basis for our earliest beliefs and those experiences were out of our control. We had to depend upon instinct and the guidance of others for our earliest beliefs. By the time we entered grammar school, we believed many things on the basis of untutored observation, untrained memory, and blind faith.

> "An expert is one who knows more and more about less and less." --Nicholas Murray Butler

As we passed through grammar school and high school, we may not have learned much about how to use authorities reasonably or how to become skilled observers. These matters may have been left to chance or—what is worse—were discouraged. Children are not often encouraged to question authority and those who do are not usually praised by parents or teachers, or by political or religious leaders. We come to resent many of those who do question authority.[3] Thus, forming a critical attitude toward the claims of experts and authorities may require much effort and many years of practice. It is not something that comes naturally to most people. But sometimes we must question authorities and experts. Just because we must depend on experts at times, does not mean that we should take everything they say on blind faith.

3.1 Qualifications, reputation, and motives

Consider the qualifications of the one making the claim. Does the claim imply special knowledge or expertise and does the claimant have that knowledge or expertise? Before one should accept a claim solely on the basis of expert testimony, one should determine that the expert is qualified in the subject matter that he or she is testifying about. What is the expert's educational background? What degree or degrees does he or she have? What professional work is he or she known for? Has the expert had books or articles published in his or her field of expertise? What professional awards or prizes has the expert earned?

What is the expert's reputation in the field? Is he or she generally respected by others in the field? Is the expert considered a maverick or oddball by other experts? If so, is the expert really an expert or an outsider claiming expertise? If the maverick really is an expert in the field, then the fact that his or her material is controversial means that it is the *evidence*, not the source, which must be given your full attention.

Does the expert have a hidden agenda? Just because one is an expert, even a scientific expert, does not mean that one is necessarily above using one's position to further a racist, sexist, religious, political, or personal agenda.

Is the expert paid for his or her testimony? In itself, getting paid does not taint testimony, but experts who make a career out of getting paid for testimony should be looked at with a very careful eye.

Some experts acquire their expertise not from academies but from experience. Many arts, crafts, and techniques have been learned by doing, without any formal training. For some fields, there are no higher degrees.

Most of the time, we are at the mercy of experts because we are totally ignorant of their field and their reputation. Consider, for example, the automobile mechanic. Imagine a situation with automobile mechanics that parallels that of psychiatric testimony in the courtroom. If whenever you had car trouble it were possible to line up mechanics on one side to say the car needs new spark plugs and another group of mechanics to say the car didn't need new plugs, would you ever take your car to a mechanic? Would it make you feel more comfortable if the mechanics who always diagnosed "needs new spark plugs" were paid by The Spark Club Lobby for their opinion and those who always rejected that diagnosis were paid by The Tow Truck Society?

Usually, the best guide for deciding whether to accept the claims of an expert who gained his or her expertise from experience is the *reputation* of the person. Usually we should seek out the testimony of satisfied customers. That's why many advertisers hire actors to pretend they are satisfied customers. That's why one of the most common forms of deception used by infomercial makers is to hire actors or *real people* to testify to the wonders of some product. However, you want to talk directly to someone who used the product or the services of the expert. You want someone who is unbiased, who isn't being paid or rewarded in some way for their testimony, and who has no interest in whether you do or don't follow their recommendation.

If we are uncertain of an expert's reputation, we can always seek a second opinion. Of course, experts can easily deceive us, since usually we lack the knowledge and experience necessary to judge their opinions. However, unless deceit is common in a profession or in a particular business, the fear of acquiring a reputation for dishonesty would be a major disincentive to deceive. If, on the other hand, there is little chance of getting caught and a good chance of making money by being dishonest, then the major disincentive to cheating is gone and the buyer should beware. Let's not forget the Sears Auto Shop scandal in California in 1992. A whole area of auto repair in Sears' Shops—brake and shock absorber repair and replacement—was discovered to be fraudulent. Sears' auto shop personnel systematically lied to customers about needing brakes and shocks. They took advantage of the customer's vulnerability and the fact that there was little chance they would be found out. Unfortunately for Sears, agents of the State of California brought in vehicles with known good brakes and shocks but they were told repeatedly in stores across the state that the brakes and shocks needed to be replaced. Sears took out full-page ads across the state and said something like "mistakes were made" and they will not happen again. They sincerely regretted the loss of business.

Because some fields of expertise are so controversial, however, finding satisfied customers can sometimes be misleading. For example, it is easy to find many people willing to vouch for any number of phony healers. In evaluating an expert source, we must consider not just the reputation of the expert and the testimonials of the expert's following; we must consider the field of expertise itself.

3.2 Fields of expertise

Some fields are so controversial that there is scarcely a claim in the field that is not defended by one expert and rejected by another. On the other hand, some fields are relatively free of controversy about facts and fundamental issues. For example, chemistry and physics are fields that use impersonal methods of inquiry and whose results can be tested by anybody with the proper training. The science texts you are likely to read will most likely be read mainly to learn factual information and established techniques and procedures. Yes, there are controversial areas in the sciences. But you can expect to find much more agreement about fundamental matters (facts, definitions of basic terms, and techniques of inquiry) in the sciences than in either the social sciences (such as history, psychology and sociology) or the humanities (such as philosophy, literature and art).

The humanities and social sciences are more personal than the physical sciences; they are more likely to be affected by individual interests, purposes, and beliefs. The great diversity of opinion in these fields is not considered a drawback, but reflects the richness of human interest and design. Usually experts in the humanities and the social sciences should be read not just to gather facts. Such experts are likely to express personal opinions in their professional publications more often than science writers. It is those *opinions* that should interest us. But all experts, regardless of subject matter, ought to be used with caution. Facts ought to be separated from opinions, and opinions ought to be appealed to more as stimuli to thinking than as oracles of truth.

Yet, sometimes it is difficult to separate fact from opinion, especially when self-proclaimed (or media-proclaimed) experts reinforce each other's opinions to the point where they treat total fabrication as scientific fact. In chapter one we mentioned a group of authors who have written books on child abuse.[4] Through the communal reinforcement of many empirically unsupported notions, including the claim that about half of all women have been sexually abused, they have managed to get many people to treat this and other unproven claims as a facts. Psychologist Carol Tavris writes

> In what can only be called an incestuous arrangement, the authors of these books all rely on one another's work as supporting evidence for their own; they all endorse and recommend one another's books to their readers. If one of them comes up with a concocted statistic--such as "more than half of all women are survivors of childhood sexual trauma"-- the numbers are traded like baseball cards, reprinted in every book and eventually enshrined as fact. Thus the cycle of misinformation, faulty statistics and invalidated assertions maintains itself.[5]

The main difference between this group of experts and, say, a group of physicists is that the child abuse experts have achieved their status as authorities not by scientific training but either (a) by experience [they were victims of child abuse or they treat victims of child abuse in their capacity as social workers] or (b) by writing a book on child abuse. The child abuse experts aren't trained in scientific research, which, notes Tavris, "is not a comment on their ability to write or to do therapy, but which does seem to be one reason for their scientific illiteracy."

Whole industries have been built up out of the hysteria that inevitably accompanies charges of the sexual abuse of children. Therapists who are supposed to help children recover from the trauma of child abuse are hired to interrogate children to find out if they have been abused. But too often the therapist suggests the abuse to the child and the child develops false memories of being abused. The therapist is then ready to testify to the abuse, but no reasonable person should find a parent or caretaker guilty *solely* on the basis of such tainted "expert" testimony.[6]

There are qualified experts in the field of child abuse, of course. They are trained in scientific methodologies, are *not* driven by extra-scientific motives, and do not use their science to promote personal agendas. For the critical thinker, however, it is often not an easy task to determine which experts to trust. Remember that some fields are controversial by nature, i.e., the experts in the field do not agree on fundamental issues. The opinions of experts in such fields should never be accepted solely on the basis of expert testimony; otherwise, it would be reasonable to accept contradictory opinions. The humanities and many areas of the social sciences are such fields. So are all those fields introduced by the term "alternative": *alternative medicine, alternative science, alternative history*, and the like. On the other hand, fields such as mathematics, physics, and chemistry are fields where the experts agree on fundamental matters and definitions of basic terms.

> "In this age, the mere example of nonconformity, the mere refusal to bend the knee to custom, is itself a service." --John Stuart Mill (1806-1873)
>
> "All men are partially buried in the grave of custom. . . ." --Henry David Thoreau (1817-1862)

Also, simply because one is an expert in one field does not give one license to make proclamations in fields beyond one's area of expertise. Of course, experts in one field are as free as anyone else to state their opinions in fields outside their sphere of expertise. But they should not expect us to treat their opinions in such matters any differently than we would treat any non-expert's.

4. Custom and tradition

Many of our beliefs are customary beliefs. They have come to us more or less unconsciously through our cultural traditions and social institutions. As such, custom and tradition can be seen as a powerful source of beliefs.

How much trust should we put in customary and cultural beliefs, in the traditional wisdom of our predecessors, in the advice and instructions of our parents, and in the claims of our religious, educational, and political leaders? Our first guiding rule might be: *Rely on customary and traditional beliefs only if you must.* If the matter is something that you can easily discover for yourself, do so. Use your own knowledge and experience as a check against traditional, as well as against new claims.

> "It is obvious that the mere fact that a belief is 'old' is no evidence in its favor. On the contrary: that merely means that the belief must have originated at a time when much less was known than is known today; and when people generally were more credulous about alleged 'facts'; less critical of ideas; without the desire (or technique) to examine, test, and verify acceptance." --A.E. Mander, *Logic for the Millions*, pp. 177-178.

Sometimes our specific knowledge in a field will be the standard against which we will measure a claim. But what if we have no specific knowledge about what is being claimed? And what if the claim is made in a field that requires special training and education? In that case, we will have to base our decision on the amount of trust we have in the one making the claim. When is such trust reasonable? And how far should it extend? These are questions every critical thinker must consider.

Exercise 3-1

The following passages each contain claims made by different sources. In each case, identify whether the source is either (a) an expert or authority or (b) a non-expert. If the source is an expert or authority, state whether the expert's

field is controversial or not (do experts tend to disagree about fundamental matters in the field?). For each source, what would you need to consider to determine the source's credibility. [Exercises with an * are answered in Answers to Selected Exercises.]

*1. The President of the United States claims that his policies may reduce inflation by as much as 10 percent and increase employment by as much as 5 percent.

2. A police officer commenting on the behavior of a man who began shooting at investigators from the district attorney's office who had come to serve a warrant of arrest: "It was just happenstance. The same thing would have happened had he been pulled over for a traffic violation."

*3. "A state biologist said Tuesday that the deaths of thousands of fish each year above Sacramento [California] may be caused by a combination of problems, including a chemical in agricultural canals."

4. A chemist claims in a lecture that if gold is dipped in hydrochloric acid, the gold will not dissolve.

5. A philosopher declares that the essence of mind is thinking.

*6. A newspaper reports that there were three stabbings of inmates by other inmates at a state prison.

7. You are handed a flyer by a stranger. It says it's printed by the California Agrarian Action Project, and it claims that the department of Food and Agriculture has not released information regarding the health effects of pesticides.

*8. Fidel Castro accuses America of using germ warfare against his regime.

9. A speaker at a political rally claims that all persons have a natural right to life, liberty and the pursuit of happiness.

10. A psychiatrist declares of a person who has been serving time in a state mental hospital for the criminally insane that this person no longer has violent tendencies and is unlikely ever to rape and murder again.

*11. A philosopher declares that the essence of physical reality is extension in space.

12. A spokesperson for a Detroit automobile manufacturing firm asserts that Japanese automobile import quotas are too large.

* 13. Loren Coleman, director of a suicide-prevention project at the University of Southern Maine (in Portland, Maine), says "the reappearance of Halley's comet brings forth the realization of larger cycles that interplay with the phenomenon of suicide." Coleman noted that a wave of teenage suicides and airline crashes coincided with the appearance of Halley's comet. He said that the word 'disaster' evolved from 'evil star' and that an analysis of suicides or epidemics and the appearance of comets "demonstrates some interesting correlations." "Halley's comet appeared like a 'sword' over Jerusalem in 66 A.D.," said Coleman, "foreshadowing its destruction at the hands of the Romans."

14. An art historian claims that cave paintings of animals done more than 25,000 years ago were done in order to assist the initiation of young men into the adult world of hunting.

* 15. An expert from the New York Stock Exchange claims that interest rates will drop by as much as ten percent within the next six months.

16. A music reviewer writes: "A lively, lifelike, brilliant performance, extremely well-recorded, of one of Bach's greatest masterpieces."

17. A preacher says from the pulpit that faith alone will save your soul.

18. An actress on a soap opera which specializes in infidelity, adultery, lechery in personal affairs and dishonesty in business affairs, says that "the program saves marriages by providing a harmless outlet for fantasies of unfaithfulness."

* 19. A newspaper article reports: "Lifesaving antibiotics are increasingly losing their disease-fighting power because of flagrant world-wide overuse, 150 doctors and medical scientists in 25 nations charged Tuesday. In news conferences in Boston, Mexico City, Santo Domingo in the Dominican Republic, and Sao Paulo Brazil, the group issued a joint statement urging international action to curb 'global drug abuse'."

20. Dean F. Martin, a professor of chemistry at the University of Southern Florida in Tampa said that he had discovered a marine organism which can destroy 'red tide' (a marine algae which can kill fish and irritate the eyes and throats of bathers). William Taft of the Mote Marine Laboratory in Sarasota said that he put a teaspoonful of Martin's marine organism in a 20-gallon aquarium with 20 million per liter of the red-tide organism. Said Taft, "It killed them all."

21. A theologian asserts that the soul has a beginning but is immortal.

22. An author of numerous books and articles on human relationships claims that people who love one another are happier and more productive than those who do not love one another.

* 23. An eminent anthropologist claims that she has discovered conclusive evidence that human beings are not naturally aggressive.

24. You read an article in the newspaper which indicates it originated in WASHINGTON(AP). The article states that according to the Census Bureau one in nine American manufacturing workers owes his or her job to buyers in foreign countries.

* 25. James Woodford, an Atlanta chemist who frequently testifies in court cases concerning drug abuse, claims that pigments (viz., melanin) in dark-skinned people are chemically similar to marijuana (viz., THC, tetrahydrocannabinol) and may lead to wrongful accusations of marijuana use based on inaccurate urine tests.

26. An author of numerous books on astral projection [soul travel] says that anyone can have an out-of-body experience if they follow her easy ten-step plan.

27. Arthur McBay, a drug-testing expert with the state medical examiner's office in North Carolina, said that equipment used to test urine for evidence of marijuana usage will frequently produce positive results even with empty samples.

28. A famous talk show host announces that the guests on his program are just the tip of the iceberg in a nationwide network of Devil Worshipping Child Eaters.

29. Dr. Lenore Terr, psychiatrist and author of *Unchained Memories*, testified as an expert witness regarding repressed memory in the trial of George Franklin. Franklin's daughter, Eileen Franklin Lipsker, said she suddenly remembered, 20 years after the crime, that her father raped and then killed her best friend, 8-year-old Susan Nason. Lipsker had told Terr that as a child she had torn out her hair, creating a bloody bald spot on her head. In her book, Terr writes: "Most likely, young Eileen unconsciously set out to duplicate the horrible wound she had seen on Susan Nason's head." [By the way, Eileen's mother, Leah Franklin, says she does not remember seeing a bald spot on her daughter's hair during her childhood years when she combed, braided and cut her child's hair. Leah Franklin also says she gave prosecutors more than forty photographs of Eileen as a child and that none of them showed any hair problems.]

30. You are surfing the Internet and you come upon something called THE DRUDGE REPORT which has very impressive graphics. You read there that the President of the United States has been seen having sex with White House visitors by Secret Service Agents.

5. Popular mass media

Television, radio, newspapers, magazines, and the Internet are some of our main sources of information about the world. Special attention to evaluating claims made in the popular mass media is required by anyone desiring to become a critical thinker today.

One would think that journalists would be trained to be critical thinkers and observers, and that their training would reveal itself in their work, thus easing our task as critical readers and viewers. Even granting that journalists are trained critical thinkers, they are still human beings with worldviews, political affiliations, loyalties, ambitions, hopes, religious beliefs, biases, and prejudices. Like the rest of us, their patriotism, sexism, ethnocentrism, laziness, wishful thinking, greed, ambition, and the like will sometimes affect the way they go after or report a story. For example, in 1983 a Korean Air Lines plane [KAL 007] with 269 people aboard was shot down over the Soviet Union by

> In December 1996, NBC reportedly paid more than $500,000 to Richard Jewell, a security guard at the Atlanta Olympic games wrongly accused in the Olympic Park bombing. Why? Because Tom Brokaw announced on the evening news that the cops "probably have enough to arrest [Jewel] right now [and] probably enough to prosecute him."

the Soviet Air Force. Most of the headlines and stories in the American mass media regarding the event clearly asserted that the Soviets knew the passenger airliner had accidentally drifted over Soviet territory. It is to the credit of the American free press that these assertions were later admitted to be wrong. We were eventually informed that the story was much more complicated than we had been led to believe by the initial reports coming from United States government sources. The Soviets, we were later told, were justified in believing that the plane was on a spy mission and their action could be seen not as a malicious act of mass murder but as a reasonable act of self-defense. Nevertheless, the initial reports and allegations are the ones that remain in the minds and hearts of many Americans.

> "TV news is just a tail on the dog of entertainment." — Walter Cronkite

Some fifteen years after the KAL incident, Alvin A. Snyder, who was director of worldwide television for the U.S. Information Agency in 1983, revealed that he was pressured to lie about KAL 007 by the U.S. State Department. Snyder claims he was given an audio tape and instructed to produce a video, based on the tape, to be shown to the United Nations Security Council two days later. The video, he says, was beamed around the world by satellite. "It was powerful, effective and wrong," says Snyder. Secretary of State George Shultz knew of the video and wrote in a memo to President Reagan that there would be a massive public disinformation effort "to exploit the incident." Reagan was made fully aware by the State Department that the Soviet pilots were confused as to the identity of the plane they had intercepted and shot down. Jeanne Kirkpatrick, U.S. ambassador to the UN, introduced the tape, and the mass media passed on the propaganda piece.[7]

When the USS Vincennes shot down an Iranian passenger jet over the Persian Gulf, killing 290 people, on July 3, 1988, the Iranian media treated the incident much as the U.S. media had treated KAL 007. The position of the U.S. government and of our mass media, however, was that the plane was shot down by mistake

The way the press handled the shooting down of KAL 007 by the Soviets and the shooting down of the Iranian passenger plane by the Americans is typical of American journalism. First, an *interested party*--in this case, the U.S. government--is the original source of the information. Then, the material is interpreted and edited by journalists before being passed on to you and me. Much of the information presented in the mass media is not the result of investigative or eyewitness reporting. It is handed to the media in the form of press releases by people representing those who have a stake in the public's response to the information. The worst part of this is not that opinions are sometimes presented as facts or that outright lies are sometimes leaked to the press to misinform the public about some political enemy. The worst part is that only part of the story gets reported—at least initially—the part that favors the way of looking at things held by the source of the information.

Not only do mass media reports often serve the interests of those in power, they exaggerate the significance of much of what they report. We have become accustomed to being informed on anything the President of the United States says or does, no

> "…self-criticism and introspection are not the order of the day for people clinging to power." --David Brock

matter how trivial, personal, or political. If the President wants to help out a political ally, all he has to do is speak; the press will report whatever he says. For example, when conservative Republicans led the charge to oust California Supreme Court Chief Justice Rose Bird, President Reagan joined in the attack when he singled out Chief Justice Bird for special criticism as he "assailed judges who approve 'outrageous' awards in injury cases and drive up liability insurance rates," according to an article in the *Sacramento Bee*.[8] The President's assertions were headlined and reported. Although President Reagan's remarks were criticized and challenged throughout the article as being misleading, incomplete, and erroneous, they were treated with the dignity and respect worthy of a Nobel laureate speaking in his or her field of expertise. Even the fact that on the same day in the same newspaper another article appeared that was headlined, "Report: Liability 'crisis' is a myth," could not mitigate the impact of the President's misinformed and misleading comments. The other article begins: "Sharp increases in liability insurance premiums for doctors, governments, businesses and other groups are caused by the insurance industry's own decisions and not excessive lawsuits, according to a new study prepared for the nation's attorney general." The inconsistency of this information with President Reagan's claims should alert the critical reader that something is awry. The newspaper did try to make the reader's task easy, as it put the article claiming that the liability crisis is a myth on page 3 with a note about the Reagan claim and a reference to its location on page 22 of the paper. Yet, it is clear that the only reason Reagan's assertions were published was that at the time he made them he was President of the United States.

60

Another way that the mass media exaggerate the significance of what they publish is the hype they use to sell what is called "news." In 2004, as the latest edition of this book is being prepared, terrorism and America's war against Iraq dominate the news. In 1999, when the previous edition of this book was being prepared, there was an extraordinary amount of attention being paid to Kosovo. The year before that, the hot topic was President Clinton's sex life, as it was in 1994. Before that it was illegal aliens. Before that it was O.J. Simpson and battered women. In 1994, the focus was not only on Clinton's sex life, but on child abuse and national health care reform. Before that the hot topics were the homeless, cocaine and 'crack' usage, and AIDS. Before that there was a great deal of attention paid to each of the following: drunken driving, teenage pregnancy, Eastern European nations and their struggle for democracy and freedom, the federal deficit, taxes, the Gulf War, droughts and floods, and the alleged kidnapping of thousands of children. One wonders how the nation continues to exist, given all the crises we're undergoing. Topics seem to take on a life of their own; they have a kind of 'cash-value' as a bizarre form of entertainment. Each topic is like a fireworks display. It appears in a blaze of glory and disappears as it is replaced by another.

"...raw news...is to the newspaper readers for the most part inedible and indigestible. The raw news has, therefore, to be processed in order to make it intelligible, for if it is not intelligible, it will not be interesting. And if it is not interesting, it will not be read....If we tried to print only the facts of what had happened...the news items would be like the pieces of a jigsaw puzzle thrown in a heap upon the table."-- Walter Lippmann, Washington Post, September 24, 1949, p. 16. [From *Argument and Advocacy*, Russel R. Windes and Arthur Hastings (New York: Random House, 1965), pp. 139-140.]

If an alien were to fall to earth and read several daily newspapers, she might come to the conclusion that earthlings are devoted to war, violent crimes, natural and human disasters, drugs, sex, and sports. Despite the fact that most persons on earth are law abiding and non-violent, our mass media publications focus so much attention on violent criminals that it is not uncommon for children to grow up fearing most of the human race. Our worldviews are molded by what we deem significant, and the mass media, by their emphasis on certain kinds of events, greatly affect, in a perverse way, our overall outlook on life. Educational, judicial, and penal institutions are reported on primarily when the *unusual* occurs. We read about the student who graduates from high school although he or she is illiterate; we do not read about the hundreds of thousands of students who graduate and can read quite well. We read about the murderer who serves ten years in prison and commits a murder within a month of being released. Or we read of the innocent man who spent ten years on death row before being exonerated. We do not read about the thousands of criminals who are processed by our courts every day in an orderly and just fashion and who are punished appropriately. We read of the mentally ill person who shoots people in a shopping mall after warnings by her mother to the police. But we do not read about the thousands of police officers who in the course of an average day filled out thousands of reports, resolved thousands of disputes, and saved a few hundred lives. We rarely hear about any of our institutions until something goes wrong. The usual, the everyday efficient and appropriate functioning of our institutions, is ignored. It is the unusual which makes the headlines and, too often, affects our beliefs and attitudes.

"I fear it is just a matter of time before newspapers will be considered the same as any business, a fit prize for investment by interests that do not care about the principles of good journalism." --C.K. McClatchy, editor and Chairman of the Board of McClatchy Newspapers

Of course, it is not only the unusual that grabs the attention of the mass media. There has been a noticeable decline in journalistic standards with respect to the privacy of public figures. Compounding this decline is a growing disregard for accuracy. Much of this decline is reflective of changes in American society. There is a growing acceptance of rudeness, invasion of privacy, and vulgarity. We have become a tabloid society. Our news and entertainment are a reflection of our growing indecency. We not only tolerate false and misleading stories if they are sexy enough, we encourage them by our support. As a nation, we seem less interested in truth than in our own personal titillation. Give us a story about President Clinton's or Princess Diana's alleged sex life. We not only don't seem to care whether these stories are true, we don't even ask whether this is the kind of story we should be demanding. Innuendo and rumor suffice. We do not demand good evidence. We certainly do not require that several sources be able to back up a claim which, if true, could ruin someone's reputation. We do not seem to care that false claims can ruin lives. We do not seem to realize that anyone with enough money can buy journalists to dig up dirt on anyone. Just give us the dirt. We do not care whether it is real dirt or where it came from or who paid for it.

Our own standards have declined in other ways as well. We seem to accept the notion that even if one story has about zero credibility, when we add up a half dozen such stories we now have credibility. Yet, no matter how many zeros are added together the result is still zero.

I do not advocate different goals for the mass media. What I am advocating is that as critical thinkers we put the reports of the mass media into proper perspective. Recognize them for what they are: almost always one-dimensional and relatively superficial accounts, often biased or slanted, one-sided or even false. While the purpose of the mass media includes providing information, it often seems that the main purpose of most media work is entertainment. The news media provide us with accounts of generally unusual or entertaining events whose significance is often to be found in their tragic or comic entertainment value. This function of the mass media is most obviously witnessed every evening on television where not only are accounts of mass murders and military invasions sandwiched around commercials for laxatives, but stories about the sex lives of celebrities are juxtaposed to stories about sexual harassment and rape, and accompanied by commercials featuring sexy men and women using sex to sell everything from automobiles to refrigerators.

The mass media must cater to their audience, of course. The things the media emphasize seem to be the things the masses desire to see or read and hear about. The way the mass media present material reflects their audience. We complain loudly about negative ads during political campaigns, where candidates are advertised as if they were a better deodorant or a can of soup while their opponents are accused of stinking up the world with their presence. However, how many of us would tune in to a rational debate (assuming it were even possible) that focused on specific issues of concern to the nation? How many of us would be willing to try to follow a complex political issue for more than five or ten minutes, were the media willing to present it? Such programs are presented occasionally, either on television or in print or in public halls, and they are attended by goodly numbers of people at times. Nevertheless, nobody ever got rich catering to the good citizenship of our fellow Americans.

Besides being oversimplified, the information in the mass media is likely to be incomplete and one-sided. On the one hand, journalists report what they take to be news; they do not necessarily evaluate or judge what they report on. If a district attorney charges several day care operators with sexual abuse of children, the reporter will report it.

> Brit Hume and T.R. Reid, in their syndicated column *Computing,* claim that "Most of the computer trade press is not a skeptical outside observer of the industry it covers; it is, instead, very much a part of that industry." They cite *PC Magazine* in particular as one which calls itself "The Independent Guide to IBM-Standard Computing", but which in fact steers and advises companies on programs it then reviews and recommends.
> *PC* defends this practice on the grounds that it leads to better products for computer users. Maybe. All we can be sure of is that it leads to products favored by the editors of *PC*. How much computer users benefit from this intimate relationship is questionable, according to Hume and Reid. See their column "Computer mag's no Consumer Reports," *Sacramento Bee*, July 16, 1990, p. C3.
> In the same issue of the *Bee* (page C2), there was another article titled "Magazine radiation piece irks advertisers." It seems that *MacWorld*, a magazine for Apple MacIntosh users, is not one of those in the trade that is in cahoots with the industry. They printed an article in their July 1990 issue on the possible health hazards caused by the electromagnetic emissions of computer terminals. The article angered some important advertisers. James Martin, president of MacWorld Communications, said that other articles critical of computer hardware and software products had cost the magazine as much as $500,000 annually in lost ad revenue. "We're walking a thin line between helping our readers and hurting our advertisers," said *MacWorld* staffer Jerry Borrell. The article noted that relations between Apple and Macworld have become strained over the past two years because of articles criticizing Apple.

It is not the reporter's job to investigate the district attorney to make sure that the charge is justified before anything is printed in the paper. If it turns out that the district attorney drops all the charges at a later date, the news media sees its job as being done if it simply reports that the charges have been dropped, and perhaps states why. No matter that lives may have been irreparably harmed by the initial charges and reports. That is how we run things in this country. The news media may report anything about a current court case, unless specifically

62

ordered not to by a judge.

The critical reader must be careful to separate what is reported from what may really be the case. Charges do not imply guilt. Accusations do not imply facts. Yet, it is easy to draw conclusions when a reporter, while not specifically asserting his or her own opinion about a matter, quotes from this or that source. It is a perfectly legitimate reporting practice to quote anyone, no matter how idiotic, misleading, or reprehensible. Thus, one can easily slant or slip in judgments on events by quoting people who express one's own sentiments or who express, in a foolish way, ideas one opposes. Also, it ought to be remembered that "news" must go through several screenings before it is presented to readers or viewers. Events must occur and be witnessed. Decisions must be made as to which events are worth reporting on. Reports of those events must be made; to do so, the reporter must select what to report and, necessarily, what *not* to report. Or, press releases and so-called 'public information' releases are received by an editor. Decisions must be made as to which reports and releases will be published. Before they are published, they may have to be edited. Then, when what is to be reported has been selected, decisions have to made as to how to present it. Judgments will be made as to where to place a story, how big a headline to give it, what kind of language to use in presenting the story, etc. For television, decisions will have to be made as to what order to present material, what film footage to show, etc. In other words, what and how the mass media present material depend on many judgments made by many people.

> **"Since 1993, the homicide rate nationwide has dropped by 20 percent. Yet in the same period, the coverage of murders on the ABC, CBS and NBC evening news has increased by 721 percent."** -- **Vincent Schiraldi, director of the Justice Policy Institute, 1998.**
>
> **The homicide rate went down 13% between 1990 and 1995. During the same period, network news coverage of homicide increased 336%.** --**"Living in Fear," Los Angeles Times, August 23, 1998.**

Some of those judgments may be affected by the very nature of the mass media. Newspapers and television networks are businesses that depend on advertising for their survival. They are also legislated and government regulated businesses. What is the likelihood that a local newspaper is going to initiate an investigation of local supermarkets (say with regard to the accuracy of their scales) or of local department stores or automobile dealerships? What is the likelihood that a magazine that depends heavily on cigarette advertising revenue to pay its employees their monthly checks is going to launch an all out media blitz on the hazards and social harms caused by smoking? Is a psychology magazine that has an advertisement for hard liquor on every fourth or fifth page likely to present its readers with a fair and honest portrayal of the social and psychological effects of alcohol?

Personal interest may affect not only what does get reported but also what does *not* get reported. "During the enormous business enthusiasm for mergers, acquisitions, junk bonds, deregulation, 'getting government off the backs of business,' the news was full of the glories of these policies."[9] Little was offered from economists with opposing views. A critical reader and viewer of the mass media must pay attention not only to what is presented but also to what is being omitted.

One wonders where the mass media was while billions of dollars were being ripped off by wealthy bankers and investors following President Reagan's decision to deregulate the banking industry? The most expensive public finance scandal in our history was not treated with much significance by the mass media until most of the damage had been done. Why? Ellen Hume, executive director of Harvard's Shorenstein Barone Center on the Press, Politics and Public Policy, offers these reasons:

1. The Savings and Loan scandal was a *numbers* story, not a *people* story. It was complicated and boring to many mainstream journalists. There were articles written on the subject in the early 1980's but they appeared in local papers or in the trade press, e.g., the *National Thrift News* (now called the *National Mortgage News*). Local reporting "generally isn't read by journalists from the national news organizations." "Financial stories are particularly hard for television." NBC president Michael Gartner commented that the S & L story didn't lend itself to images. Without images, he said, "television can't do facts."

2. Many relevant documents were kept secret by law. Reporters didn't have access to credit reports and crucial loan documents. So, even if they had wanted to, they couldn't have examined documents protected by law because lawmakers

fear such information might cause bank panics.

3. The victims didn't complain. After all, the federal government was covering the losses. "There weren't any pictures of anguished citizens lining up outside closed savings and loans" in the early days of the scandal. There were in the final days and those pictures began to make the nation realize just how bad things were.[10]

Hume also claims that the mass media did not pick up on the Savings and Loan scandal until very late in the game because the villains were a politically powerful bipartisan group. But three reasons she lists especially interest us:

1. "The press simply isn't equipped to do everything the public expects it to do....

2. Journalists have gotten used to having their information predigested" and

3. "Serious investigative journalism is considered too wasteful for today's bottom-line oriented journalism corporation managers.[11]

In other words, had some of these bank-robbing executives been caught having sex with children or murdering one another, some journalist might have investigated them and uncovered, purely by accident, the S & L scandal.

Finally, the critical thinker ought to consider the conditions under which the news is gathered and reported. For example, what is the likelihood that correspondents in foreign countries where there are civil wars and revolutions going on are going to be able to have free access to all the information they desire? What government is going to allow journalists to freely roam amongst the enemy? How complete is information likely to be issuing from a country where journalists are licensed by the government, as is the case in many countries?

5.1 Accuracy of the mass media

Just how accurate is your daily newspaper or the national evening news? Milton Mayer analyzed a page-one story in the *Chicago Tribune* of about 2,500 words and found at least 122 inaccuracies and distortions in it.[12] Accounts of reporters writing of events they didn't attend or making inaccurate quotes (many times invented by the reporter), are well-documented.[13] A study done by Walter Lippmann and Charles Merz examined news articles on the Russian Revolution in the *New York Times* from March, 1917, until March, 1920.[14] What they found was paralleled during the Vietnam War, and, more recently, during the revolutions in Eastern Europe which in no way

> "We have thousands of highly trained, experienced American correspondents in Washington, but despite many early warnings available to all, they never caught or ran with the depth of the Iran Contra scandal, corruption and waste in the Department of Housing and Urban Development, the savings and loan industry, large-scale nuclear poisoning of community water supplies, misman-agement of our nuclear weapons plans, and so on."
> -- Ben H. Bagdikian

were anticipated by our general press. The optimism about a U.S. victory during Vietnam was as unjustified as was the optimism that the Russian Revolution would be crushed eighty years ago. Lippmann and Merz concluded that "a great people in a supreme crisis could not secure the minimum of necessary information on a supremely important event." Why? "Because," they said, "Reports on extremely important events are likely to be written to harmonize with generally accepted beliefs and prejudices." Official sources of information are likely to be partisan and less than honest in their reports to the reporters. "Most men...tend to accept or to reject in the light of their prejudices" (Clarke 1929: 276).

In 1922 the Chicago Commission on Race Relations published a report entitled *The Negro in Chicago*. The Commission had studied articles dealing with the Negro that had appeared in 1916 and 1917 in the three Chicago

64

daily papers with the largest circulations.[15] The Commission wrote:

> Generally these articles indicated hastily acquired and partial information, giving highlights and picturing hysteria. Frequently they showed gross exaggeration....The subjects receiving most frequent and extended treatment in these three papers were: crime, housing, politics, riots, and soldiers....For a public which depends upon newspapers for its information an inordinately one-sided picture is presented. This emphasis on individual crimes specifying Negroes in each offense tends to stamp the entire Negro group as criminal.

We hear African-American leaders making the same charges today. The only difference is the word "Negro."

On October 23, 1989, it was reported by the Boston mass media (and then around the nation) that a black

> **"...damn it, we make too many mistakes of fact and context. Then too few of us hurt enough inside when we do make mistakes. Too few of us correct those mistakes forthrightfully."** --David Lawrence Jr., Executive Editor of the *Detroit Free Press*, "Is the Press Fair?" *Parade Magazine*, August 19, 1984, p. 8.

man in a jogging suit had shot Charles and Carol Stuart as they got in their car at a busy intersection in Boston. They had just attended a childbirth class; Carol was 6 months pregnant. The next day doctors performed a Caesarean section on Carol. She died, but delivered an 8-week premature child who also eventually died (on November 9). Charles Stuart, who was shot in the abdomen, described the killer as a black man in a jogging suit with a raspy voice.

Boston mayor Ray Flynn ordered every available cop to hunt for the black killer. *Newsweek* reported that residents of the racially mixed area where the Stuarts had been attending the birthing class "complained that as many as 150 black men were illegally stopped and frisked every day."[16] The police arrested William Bennet, "a two-time loser with a long rap sheet." On Nov. 21st Charles Stuart reportedly had shown "a strong physical reaction" when shown a mug shot of Bennet. On December 28, Stuart identified Bennet from a lineup saying he looked "most like" the killer. *Newsweek* also reports that "A court document submitted by the prosecutor cited five witnesses as a reason to suspect Bennet....Only a day after the murder, the document said, three teenagers told police that Bennet's nephew had 'said his uncle shot the Stuarts.' A woman also said she saw Bennet on the night of the shooting with jewelry and a gun similar to the one Charles Stuart had described. Another woman reported that Bennet told her Stuart owed him money for drugs; she said Bennet added that the bullet 'wasn't meant for the woman, it was meant for the man'."

On January 4, 1990, Charles Stuart committed suicide. The day before, his brother Matthew had gone to the police and gave them Carol Stuart's wedding ring (which had allegedly been stolen by the killer) and told them that Charles had murdered Carol Stuart and had shot himself in an effort to make it look like someone else had done it. Not long afterwards the gun and Carol's handbag were found in a river where they had been thrown by Jack McMahon, Matthew's friend who had helped him dispose of the incriminating evidence.

Why did Charles Stuart do it? Who knows, but the evidence seems to indicate that he did not want a child and he did not want a wife who did not work. A friend of Charles Stuart, David MacLean, testified before a grand jury that Charles and he were out drinking in September when Stuart had asked him if he knew anyone who would kill his wife. MacLean said that Stuart had told him that Carol had refused to have an abortion and that he was afraid she wouldn't return to her job as a tax attorney after the baby was born. Carol made $41,000 a year; Charles made about $100,000 a year as a manager of a fur store. MacLean said that Charles told him he wanted the insurance money to open a restaurant, that he "didn't want to spend the rest of his life busting his ass for somebody else."[17]

The press just reported what the police and Charles Stuart asserted. When Charles made a tearful wheelchair visit to his dying newborn son, the TV cameras were there. When a friend of Charles read a letter at Carol's funeral, it was reported by the press. ("Good night, sweet wife, my love," wrote Charles, "Now you sleep away from me. I will never again know the feeling of your hand in mine, but I will always feel you...")

Newsweek wrote: "If it does nothing else, [Stuart's] suicide may help clarify the double standards and prejudices that allowed Stuart to succeed with his plot in the first place." After describing the "media circus," the "rationalized racism," and other inadequacies and failures of the press and police to be fair, skeptical, non-judgmental, and honest, *Newsweek* wrote: "When the police, under pressure from frenzied press coverage, are desperate to make an arrest--that's the time when the standards of evidence should be at their strongest, not weakest."[18]

A final note on the affair: minutes after she heard about Stuart's suicide, literary agent Jane Dystel phoned writer Joe Sharkey. That afternoon Sharkey was in Boston interviewing figures in the Stuart case. A few days later, Dystel and Sharkey had a 26-page book proposal on an editor's desk. As news stories get turned into books and movies almost as soon as they are reported, the line between news and entertainment gets blurrier and blurrier. Before the year was out, "Good Night Sweet Wife: A Murder in Boston" showed on TV and was billed as a "fact-based story." Authorship was credited to Daniel Freudenberger.

As further evidence of how entertainment drives the news—even news regarding brutal murders—witness the number of books written by the attorneys involved in the O.J. Simpson trial. Prosecution lawyers have two books out; and at least two defense team members have published books on the trial. Marcia Clark of the prosecution and Johnny Cochran of the defense have each found work on television doing talk shows on law and crime. Even O.J. Simpson was hired to do commercials for a legal firm.

5.2 Managing the news

After the Geneva Conference in 1955, the term "managing the news" was coined by James Reston of the *New York Times* to describe "any governmental policy of issuing false evidence, suppressing evidence, distorting evidence, or harassing unfriendly critics." About the Geneva conference, Reston wrote:

> I think there was a conscious effort to give the news. . .an optimistic flavor. I think there was a conscious effort there, decided upon even perhaps ahead of time, for spokesmen to emphasize all the optimistic facts coming out of that conference and to minimize all of the quarrels at that conference. . . .

> After the Geneva conference a decision was taken in the government that perhaps this was having a bad effect, that the people in the Western countries were letting down their guard, and therefore a decision was made . . . that the government should strike another note. So that after the Geneva smiling, the new word went out that it might be a good idea now to frown a little bit, so the President made a speech at Philadelphia, taking quite a different light about the Geneva Conference. That is what I mean by managing the news (Clarke: 148).

The actions of modern politicians to manage the news are not completely without precedent. Abraham Lincoln suppressed the Emancipation Proclamation for three months because his advisers feared its release might cost the Republican Party an election. Today's presidents manage the news in ways Lincoln could not have imagined. We will give two examples. The first concerns President Bush and how he allowed himself to be manipulated for political reasons by a public relations firm representing the emir of Kuwait. The other concerns the way Presidents Clinton and Bush used the press.

5.2.1 Hill & Knowlton manipulate a nation

One of the more egregious examples of TV news manipulation is the work done by the public relations firm of Hill and Knowlton after the invasion of Kuwait by Iraq. Hill and Knowlton worked for *Citizens for a Free Kuwait*, funded by the emir of Kuwait. Hill and Knowlton ignited public opinion to go to war in Iraq by coaching the daughter of Kuwait's ambassador to the U.S. to lie about herself to a Congressional committee (she said she was Nayirah, a Kuwaiti refugee) and claim that she had witnessed atrocities against babies by Iraqi soldiers. She claimed the soldiers stormed a hospital in Kuwait and pulled premature babies from their incubators, leaving them to die. President Bush cited the infants' deaths as an example of the kind of brutal aggression these modern day Nazis would continue to engage in if they were not stopped.[19] Hill and Knowlton also made available to news agencies videotapes of Kuwaiti refugees whose stories served their client's interests. At the time, Craig Fuller, President Bush's former chief of staff, headed Hill and Knowlton. The public relations firm had unrestricted travel privileges in Saudi Arabia, while journalists were severely limited in where they could travel to. The PR firm also was the source for many amateur videos shot inside Kuwait and smuggled out to be edited and distributed by Hill and Knowlton on behalf of their client. These videotapes were widely used by TV news networks. The PR firm also coached Fatima Fahed for her lying testimony before the United Nations Security Council about atrocities she alleged she had witnessed in Kuwait. Morgan Strong interviewed Fahed, a close relative of a senior Kuwaiti official and the wife of Kuwait's minister of planning, in Jedda, Saudi Arabia, *before* her UN testimony and she told him she had no firsthand knowledge of atrocities.[20] Says Strong, "It is an inescapable fact that much of what Americans saw on their news broadcasts, especially leading up to the Allied offensive against Iraqi-occupied Kuwait, was in large measure the contrivance of a public-relations firm."[21]

5.2.2 Clinton & Bush manipulate the press

Another example of managing the news is the way President Clinton used local television stations to bring his agenda to the American people on issues such as health care, the U.S. role in Somalia, tax reform, etc. For example, Mr. Clinton appeared on a television program in Sacramento, California, in October 1993, called "California Town Hall." It was moderated by KCRA Channel 3 anchor Stan Atkinson. The ninety minute program was broadcast statewide to NBC affiliates. After Sacramento, Clinton would take his "town hall" show to some other town in some other state. Why not just have a press conference in Washington, D.C., with the national and international press asking the questions? Because you cannot manage the Washington press corps the way you can local anchors or "town hall" sessions. The town hall audience and the questions they would ask the president were screened and selected by KCRA. We wanted "real people, not political types" in the audience, said KCRA new director Bill Bauman. "We tried to pick questions that deal with a wide variety of issues."[22] *Real people* asking a *variety of questions*: what more could a president ask for? No seasoned veteran of Washington manipulation asking follow-up questions to pointed inquiries. No relentless pressure to address rather than evade issues. Just soft questions, maybe a few tears and heartfelt expressions of sympathy to someone in the audience. Clinton could get out his message in a no-risk, easy-to-control, non-threatening setting.

A similar technique was used by both Bush and Clinton during their presidential campaigns. They would rent a small TV studio and satellite time. They would beam to local stations so that they could be interviewed by local anchors. These were paid interviews. That is, the candidates paid for the studios and the use of the satellite transponder. The candidates could get their messages out to a large television audience while appearing to be interviewed by the local anchor of every city in America. From a studio in Arkansas, Clinton conducted 40 interviews with stations in 25 states. His campaign paid for the interviews. He was doing

> Paramount studios stopped all company advertising in *Daily Variety* because of a scathing review by Joseph McBride of Paramount's "Patriot Games." McBride has been a staff critic and reporter for *Daily Variety* for over 20 years. He described the movie based on the novel by Tom Clancy a "right-wing cartoon of the British-Irish political situation." How did the editor of *Daily Variety*, Peter Bart, respond to McBride's politically influenced review of a politically influential movie? He apologized to Paramount and said not only would McBride not review any more Paramount films but his "situation as critic is being reviewed." Bart said he was especially disturbed by "the political nature of the review." Would Bart have been disturbed if McBride's review had expressed political sympathy with Clancy's?

commercials, in fact, but it is much cheaper this way.[23]

5.2.3 Special interest groups

Presidents and powerful PR firms are not the only ones who manage the news. Special interest groups also actively attempt to manage the news and manipulate public opinion. For example, on June 13, 1991, the *CBS Evening News* did a story on the hazards of automobile safety belts. A videotape was shown of a car tipping on its side, the car door opening, and the shoulder strap failing to hold a dummy, which fell out of the car and was crushed. CBS news correspondent Mark Phillips stated that shoulder straps are "a labor-saving device that may be costing lives instead of saving them." CBS's "eye" logo ran throughout the video segment of the story. The video, however, was not done by CBS. It was a video news release (VNR) sent to CBS by the Institute for Injury Reduction (IIR) which, says David Lieberman, is "a swell-sounding name for a lobby group largely supported by lawyers whose clients often sue auto companies for crash-related injuries." [24] Lawyers for IIR often show reports like the CBS segment in court, hoping it will help them win cases and increase their settlements and thus increase their fees. Juries find reports aired by CBS and other major news agencies to be more credible than some taped test by a lobbying group with an obvious axe to grind.

According to Lieberman, some 4,000 VNRs were made available to newscasters in 1991. A Video News Release is the video equivalent of printed propaganda provided by interested parties to newspapers and magazines. One firm, Medialink of New York, distributed about half of these VNRs. About 80 percent of the country's news directors say they use VNR material at least several times a month. The opportunity for manipulation of the TV news media is perhaps better than that for print media being influenced by press releases simply because the value of video footage can be completely independent of its news value. The image, not the information, will capture the audience.

TV Guide recommends that the label **VIDEO SUPPLIED BY [COMPANY OR GROUP NAME]** be visible for as long as VNR material is on-screen. [25] Something similar should be required of all infomercials, those half-hour or hour-long commercials that are presented as if they were news or entertainment programs. David Bartless, president of the Radio-Television News Directors Association, believes that stations should tell their viewers when they are watching a campaign-supplied interview. Such interviews, he believes, should be treated as if they were VNRs. [26]

In March, 2004, nineteen journalist groups asked "that public agencies stop producing videos that imitate television news stories or use announcers that identify themselves as reporters. Viewers expect a reporter to be a journalist employed by a news organization." In VNRs, so-called reporters are often working for a public relations firm hired by a government agency. "We find that misidentification unacceptable," they said. About the same time the journalist groups were complaining about the misuse of VNRs, Congress was investigating a claim that VNRs were produced by the Bush administration in which actors posed as journalists praising the benefits of the new Medicare law.

In considering the issue of managing the news, we must remember that many news organizations are part of huge conglomerates that have many special interests. For example, General Electric owns NBC, the PAX Television Network, Telemundo Communications Group, CNBC, MSNBC, and Bravo, in addition to numerous local television and radio stations. When the *Today* show (NBC) did a program on shoddy products and their manufacturers that originally mentioned General Electric as one of the manufacturers, the GE name was deleted. [27] GE invests heavily in defense and nuclear power. When do you think we will see a major documentary on NBC on either of those subjects? Also, soon after GE bought NBC in 1986, a corporate executive sent out a memo advising NBC employees to start a political action committee with the aim of influencing congressional legislation on favored company projects. Failure to do so would raise questions about an employee's "dedication to the company." When GE sold its home appliance division (which is what most Americans identify GE with,

> "No people can be really free if its press is spoon-fed with government pap or if the news which provides a democracy with the rationale for its actions is so controlled, restricted, managed, or censored that it cannot be published."--Hanson W. Baldwin, "Managed News: Our Peacetime Censorship," *Atlantic Monthly* (April, 1963), pp. 53-59.

68

thanks to decades of advertising) to a foreign firm, the news was not reported by NBC. It was reported by ABC and CBS.

On the other hand, Disney owns ABC, which was one of the first to report that Kathy Lee Gifford's Wal-Mart clothing line is made by child laborers making pennies a day. Gifford's TV talk show was on rival CBS. However, no ABC newscaster mentioned that much of Disney's clothing is also made by children in foreign countries. Disney also owns A&E, the History Channel, ESPN, and Lifetime, as well as many local television and radio stations.

> "In a universe that values entertainers more than it values journalists, the journalists are becoming entertainers....partly paid for by profits from entertainment shows...."The greatest risk in this news-as-entertainment urge is the most obvious--the trivialization of important issues once deemed worthy of serious treatment even at the cost of lower ratings.... -- Peter J. Boyer, *Who Killed CBS?- the undoing of America's number one news network* (New York: St. Martin's Press, 1989).

The other major network, CBS, is owned by Viacom, which also owns Simon and Schuster, Blockbuster, Paramount Pictures, and numerous radio stations. Rupert Murdochs' News Corporation owns Fox Broadcasting, 20th Century Fox film productions, numerous television stations and newspapers (mostly in Australia and the United Kingdom), HarperCollins publishing house, and TV guide, among other things. Time-Warner is the largest media company in the world. It owns CNN, Court TV and Turner Broadcasting. It owns AOL and MapQuest.com, in addition to TimeLife Books, numerous magazines, and many film, TV, and music production companies.

So what is new? What is new is the kind of ownership of today's TV and radio stations and newspapers. Most are not family or locally owned. Today, multinational corporations own many of the mass media broadcasting or newsprint businesses. They are in competition with each other for more than just news stories. They have many economic interests, and their reports can affect those interests. Is this situation ideal for assuring that the public gets fair and accurate information from the sources of that information?

Finally, individual rich persons can manage the news because they can either buy newspapers and television stations or they can hire journalists to produce stories for them: e.g., Rupert Murdoch (Fox network and various publications), the Rev. Sun Myung Moon (*Washington Times*), Bill Gates (richest man in the world and owner of Microsoft) or Richard Mellon Scaife. In the case of Microsoft's Gates, they can wage fake "grassroots" support for their company by soliciting opinion pieces from free-lance writers and letters to the editor from business leaders expressing their support of Microsoft in one of its many anti-trust battles with the government. Scaife has spent millions of his inheritance from the Mellon banking family to hire "journalists" to destroy President Clinton's reputation by proving that deputy White House Counsel Vince Foster did not kill himself. Scaife also owns the *Pittsburgh Tribune-Review* whose Clinton-bashing reporter Christopher Ruddy has financial ties to Jerry Falwell and others on the Christian right who would like to replace Clinton with one of their own. Falwell's associates produced *The Clinton Chronicles* (1994), a videotape accusing Clinton of everything from Foster's murder to cocaine smuggling. The video was narrated by Larry Nichols, who was fired from a state agency for malfeasance in 1987 by Arkansas Governor Clinton. Nichols received more than $89,000 from *Citizens for Honest Government*, the front name for the group that produced the video. Falwell's buddies have set up the Rutherford Institute which, among other things, funded the Paula Jones' sexual harassment suit against President Clinton. The Rutherford Institute pretends to be a "civil liberties" group, but its main aim seems to promote hatred of Clinton and saving the world through prayer in the schools and opposing abortion. Its founder, attorney John W. Whitehead, worked for Falwell's Moral Majority Legal Defense Fund. Add to this mix R. Emmet Tyrell's *American Spectator*, and you have what Hillary Rodham Clinton referred to as a "vast right wing conspiracy" to smear and ruin her husband. David Brock, who used to be one of the darlings reporting for *American Spectator*, fell out of favor with the entire conservative community when he wrote a book on Mrs. Clinton that did not demonize her. Brock was the one who started the Paula Jones debacle by writing an article based on the claims of Arkansas state troopers Larry Patterson and Roger Perry who claimed they witnessed Clinton in various sexual escapades when he was governor of Arkansas. Brock now doubts the veracity of the troopers' story and admits that his purpose in writing the story was "ideological." He now claims that "in 1994, Nichols and state trooper Patterson opened a joint bank account and began making payments to at least six other people from Arkansas who made allegations about Clinton's personal life." Patrick Matrisciana, the president of *Citizens for Honest Government*, held a joint bank account with Christopher Ruddy with total assets of $3.069 million which was used to make "payments to critics of the president."[28] Many of the claims originating with these conservative groups were reported without further investigation by mainstream newspapers such as the *Wall Street Journal* and the *Dallas Morning News*. Each of those newspapers reported and then retracted false stories about an eyewitness to sex between the President and Monica Lewinsky. The irony is that Clinton's behavior was so reckless that very little effort would have been needed to discredit him.

These efforts to inform, misinform, and disinform (purposely provide false and misleading claims as if they were accurate information) cross the line between managing the news and *faking* the news, the topic to which we now turn.

5.3 Fake news

In 1985 the syndicated columnist Richard Reeves claimed that "The people taking over television are blithely going about the business—the very profitable business—of screwing up America's heads so bad that by the time they're finished we won't know up from down, truth from fiction."[29] Reeves feared that a new generation of television journalists "trained in sales conferences and dressing rooms" would significantly affect our perception of reality with its penchant for "fiction news." Today it is not called "fiction news" but *docudrama* or *news re-enactment*. Reeves was concerned that programs such as NBC's mini-series *Fatal Vision* would be just the beginning of presenting fictionalized accounts as if they were documentaries. *Fatal Vision* was about the murders of the wife and children of Dr. Jeffrey MacDonald, who was found guilty of the crimes. A poll done in MacDonald's hometown by *Newsday* found that before the film was shown 20 percent thought MacDonald was guilty; after the film was shown 50 percent thought he was guilty. Many people, said Reeves, "believe that the camera doesn't lie."

Reeves was ahead of his time. Re-enactments present fiction as fact, and they do so in a medium that uses images to give the illusion of reality. Re-creations of events can be misleading and deceptive, making the viewer think an alleged event actually occurred. The opportunity for abuse of journalistic power has rarely been as great. For example, ABC's *World News Tonight* aired a dramatization of alleged spy Felix Bloch passing a briefcase to a Soviet agent. The scene looked like the real thing and it was not labeled a simulation. It made an alleged event look like it was a recorded fact.[30]

5.3.1 Faking crimes: the American posse

Presenting re-enactments of crimes, as in the programs *America's Most Wanted* and *Unsolved Mysteries*, has become very popular. These programs worry some people other than

> *Anyone who thinks the camera doesn't lie, doesn't think.*

wanted criminals. Civil-liberties lawyers and media-ethics experts "have become increasingly uneasy" about such programs, according to Edward Felsenthal of the *Wall Street Journal*. "They argue that the shows present a one-sided version of how a crime took place, often pinning blame on suspects before they've even been indicted. And they worry that suspects won't get a fair trial if potential jurors form opinions on the basis of the television show, even though judges often disqualify jurors who have been exposed to pretrial publicity."[31] Not only are the crimes presented from the point of view of the police, but also the concern for ratings may have the shows turning petty crimes into major ones and minor offenders into major criminals.

More important, though, than the potential for distortion and prejudicing a criminal case, is the fact that such shows require an intimate rapport between the police and journalists. According to Felsenthal, law-enforcement officials praise programs that turn millions of viewers into "the largest posse in the history of police work." At least one viewer, Tom Goldstein, is concerned. "One of the roles of the media is to be a watchdog on law enforcement," says Goldstein, dean of U.C. Berkeley School of Journalism. "When the two become partners, it leads to mischief."[32]

It should be added that it is not just *fiction* news that concerns lawyers and media-ethics experts. The way the news media covers ongoing criminal investigations, preliminary hearings, and trials in high profile cases can be just as one-sided and manipulative as faked news.

5.3.2 *Dateline*: the faked truck explosion

Advertising executive Jim Morrissey said: "The facts are never enough....Imagery lives on." Unfortunately, sometimes the desire for vivid imagery compromises the presentation of the facts not only in advertising but also in news reporting, leading some television news programs to commit serious violations of even the most lenient media-ethics. I am referring to the practice of not just re-creating the news but of *faking the news entirely*.

One of the most publicized example of fake news in recent times is the case of NBC's faking a crash test in a story about trucks made by General Motors. The story, labeled "Waiting to Explode?", first appeared on *Dateline*, which was then cited as the source for the "news" story on NBC and other networks. In explicit video, NBC "proved" that GM trucks with gasoline tanks mounted outside the trucks' underframe are prone to explosion when hit from the side. In the NBC demonstration video, a GM truck burst into flames after being hit from the side. A man identified as Byron Bloch, safety consultant, went on the air and described the fire as a "holocaust." NBC reporter Michele Gillen claimed that the crash had punctured a hole in the gasoline tank. No mention was made of the fact that the producers of the show had attached toy rockets to the truck's fuel tank and then detonated the rockets by remote control at the moment of impact. Nevertheless, even when this fact became known, Michael Gartner, president of NBC at the time, said: "The segment that was broadcast on *Dateline NBC* was fair and accurate."[33] Harold Pearce, GM's executive vice-president and general counsel, did not think so. He called the NBC program "outrageous misrepresentation and conscious deception."

The truth about the fake news came about due to the investigative journalism of Pete W. Pesterre, editor of *Popular Hot Rodding* magazine, and GM itself. For reasons unrelated to the faking of the story, Pesterre had criticized the *Dateline* show in an editorial. A reader called him and told him of Fire Chief Glen R. Bailey Jr., who was at the scene and thought the test was rigged. GM hired its own investigators who asked NBC to let them look at the trucks used in the tests. NBC refused. The investigators checked 22 junkyards before they found the trucks, but the fuel tanks were missing. Bruce Enz, who calls himself a "news gatherer," was president of the consulting firm hired by NBC to do the crash tests. He had given the tanks to a neighbor. GM got the tanks but Mr. Enz would not answer any questions about the faked test, claiming he had First Amendment protection from interrogation.[34]

So, with little or no help from NBC, GM discovered that the fire that was described as a "holocaust" was a small, 15-second flame; that a non-standard gas cap was used and it blew off at impact, releasing gasoline that caught fire; and that X-rays showed no puncture in the gas tank. It cost General Motors nearly $2 million to investigate a piece of faked news. Who knows what it cost NBC to fake the story.

The question that must be asked is: Was this just a lapse of judgment of one TV news network or was it symptomatic of more widespread dishonesty, or at least incompetence, in the media?

Expert opinions are divided on this issue.

5.4 Experts on the news

My father-in-law's favorite television program was the McNeil/Lehrer Report (now the "NewsHour with Jim Lehrer"), a public television program that focuses on one or two issues in more depth than the evening news. The common format is to interview experts and major players. One thing my father-in-law did not like about the program, though, was that he thought they kept interviewing the same people. He was right. This is a problem with all major news organizations. They keep interviewing the same experts.

Stephen Hess is one of those experts the media keep interviewing. He is a senior fellow at the Brookings Institution, a Washington, D.C., "think tank" that specializes in research into economic, governmental, and international problems. In an article he wrote for the Washington Post, Hess claimed he got 301 calls the previous year from TV journalists. "Basically, this is what happens," writes Hess. "A producer calls to check me out asking enough questions to know whether I am likely to say what they are after. If I do not respond appropriately, they say they will get back to me. Which means they won't. This is a big city and someone else is sure to have the magic words they are looking for." Hess admits that the producers never tell him what to say. "If they choose to interview me on camera, someone shows up and asks a question in as many permutations as it takes to get the answer that is the chip that I'm supposed to represent in the mosaic that is their 'package'." In short, Hess believes experts like him are used not to test hypotheses or get information, but to find facts or quotes that fit a preconceived hypothesis. This, Hess notes, is dishonest. "TV news is increasingly dishonest in that increasingly its stories are [a] gathering of quotes or other material to fit a hypothesis....Reporters tend to interview only those who fit a preconceived notion of what the story will be, and a story's hypothesis becomes self-fulfilling." It is interesting to note that Hess does not feel that print journalists shop for quotes the way TV journalists do. Hess bases his opinion on the 789 calls from print reporters that he received in the previous year.

Thus, when evaluating the claims of experts used in TV sound bites, we have to consider the possibility that the expert is being used to bolster the viewpoint of the TV journalist or news producer. What the expert says may well be true or reasonable, but what other equally qualified and reasonable experts would say, if they were given the opportunity, might contradict the "news" we have been given.

6. Liberal bias in the media

One common complaint about the media is that they have a liberal bias. This complaint frequently comes from anti-liberal members of the media. Popular media figures like Rush Limbaugh, Bill O'Reilly, Ann Coulter, George Will, or Sean Hannity try to promote themselves as antidotes to this liberal bias. Former TV journalist Bernard Goldberg wrote a book of anecdotes about the liberal bias of the media (2003: Perrenial), but it was countered by another journalist, Eric Alternam, who claims that conservative journalists, politicians and talk show hosts are wrong about liberal bias. Alternam argues that the perception of bias has intimidated many media outlets into presenting more conservative opinions to counterbalance a bias that does not exist (2003: Basic Books).

Is there a liberal or conservative bias in the media? It depends on your viewpoint. If you are liberal, you probably think the media slant news and information toward the conservative side. If you are conservative, you probably agree with Goldberg. My view is that most criticism of the media for being either too liberal or too conservative is misguided. Most of us would like the media to be an advocate for our own viewpoint. Unmasked, most complaints about media bias are really laments over the lack of power to control what the media present and how they present it. For example, conservative Christians would like the media to portray gay marriage and abortion as sinful. Some critics would like the media to play down reports of U.S. soldiers torturing prisoners in Iraq. The President would like only the good news about the economy to be publicized. Atheists would like to see newspapers drop their sections on religious issues.

The fact is that if anyone controls the bias of the media it is the *owners* and their CEOs, not the managers, reporters, and editors. Owners and CEOs tend to be more conservative than liberal.

It may be true that the majority of journalists are more liberal than conservative. However, it does not follow from that fact, if it is a fact, that journalism has a liberal bias. It is not justifiable to assume that a liberal (or conservative) journalist can't be fair when doing a story on an issue unless it fits with his or her own biases.

Some critics think the concern over liberal bias is a diversion from other serious problems with the media. They think the media promote superstition and pseudoscience when they produce positive stories about such things as graphology, alleged psychics, the polygraph, or astrology. Rather than encourage people to think more critically, the media too often encourage lazy thinking—locking onto paranormal or supernatural explanations for events rather than stimulating viewers, listeners, or readers to investigate natural and scientific explanations. Some take the media to task for their use of fear to attract audiences (Glassner: 2000) and their devotion to superficial issues like the private lives of politicians and other famous people. Real news—the stories about the kinds of things that have real impact on many people's lives—are neglected for scare stories and celebrity anecdotes (Radford: 2003). Scare stories are especially popular on local TV news programs: *How household items like toothpicks and staples are shaving off years of your life! Tune in tonight to find out what you can do about it and lose weight in the bargain!*

In the fall of 1995, Rocky Mountain Media Watch analyzed tapes of local evening news programs of 100 television stations in 35 states that aired the same day. Thirty percent of the news was devoted to crime. Coverage of government came in a distant second at 11 percent and environmental stories accounted for 2 percent of the stories covered that day. Poverty received 1.8 percent of air time. Unions and labor got 1.6 percent and civil rights got 0.9 percent. Other news of the day included a Miss Bald USA contest, a beauty contest for cows, a bourbon-tasting contest, and a story about a kangaroo who fell into a swimming pool in Australia. The motto of local TV news seems to be *if it bleeds, it leads*. "Stories about crime, disaster and war averaged 42 percent of the news on all 100 stations."

There does seem to be a bias here, but it does not seem to be either liberal or conservative. In 1990, the *Columbia Journalism Review* published an article by John McManus, who spent 50 days inside TV newsrooms in several metropolitan areas. According to McManus, "Overall, 18 of the 32 stories analyzed—56 percent—were inaccurate or misleading." There was a pattern, too. "There is an economic logic to these distortions and inaccuracies. All but one...were likely to increase the story's appeal, help cut down the cost of reporting or oversimplify a story so it could be told in two minutes." The bias is toward cutting costs while increasing ratings.

7. The Internet and the World Wide Web (WWW)

The Internet is more a *conduit* of sources than a source itself. Millions of people use the Internet to post facts and opinions. One site links you to many other sites. The accuracy and reliability of the data vary from site to site, just as they do with information in newspapers, magazines, and books. The same critical thinking skills needed to evaluate information from traditional print, audio, and video sources are needed when researching on the Internet. However, a few unique qualities of the Internet require special consideration. (While there are other parts of the Internet, the comments below are intended to apply only to that part of the Internet known as the World Wide Web. Claims made in chat groups or on Usenet sites should usually be considered anonymous hearsay.)

It is often difficult to know the purpose of a World Wide Web site. This often makes it difficult to evaluate the claims found there. Whether a site is an attempt at news, parody, satire, or fiction is not always immediately apparent. Before you can evaluate the claims on a site, you must first determine what the purpose of the site is. This is not typically a problem with printed materials. There is a similar problem at times with television programs, however. When you first tune into a program, it is often not immediately apparent whether the show is aimed at entertaining, educating, or selling a product. However, one can usually figure out the purpose of a television program by watching it for a few minutes or looking up a description in a television program guide. To determine the purpose of a website, you may have to go to a Main Page or Home Page from the site and use data provided there to determine its purpose. If you cannot determine the purpose of the site, then you should not rely on the claims made there.

The author of a website is not always identified. This makes it impossible to evaluate the author's credentials, background, track record, etc. If the author is anonymous to you, you cannot assume he or she is credible.

There is often no screening process for a website. Literally anyone can now be an internationally published author simply by having a website. There is no screening process, no credentials or degrees required, no training necessary. With many other forms of publication, one can depend somewhat on others to do a fair amount of screening, not for the *truth* of claims, but for competency and general reliability. Incompetent and unreliable authors do not usually succeed in getting published in the real world. Some do, of course, but editors and referees at journals, newspapers, magazines, and publishing houses do a great deal of screening. Nevertheless, one cannot assume that just because something is printed in a reputable newspaper or in a book by a reputable publishing house that it is true. One still has to use one's critical reading and thinking skills to ferret out what is reasonable to believe from what is likely to be speculation or false. One still has to be able to tell the difference between statements of fact and statements of opinion. One still has to learn as much as possible about a source and rely on what is known about a source to determine who is reliable and who is not.

There is no policing on the Internet, either. Thus, anyone can say he or she is a Ph.D. or a rocket scientist or works for a secret government organization. It is often impossible to verify such credentials. If a person claims he or she is affiliated with an educational institution, one can usually verify that since most such institutions have their own websites (which will have *.edu* in their URLs, i.e., uniform resource locators, or addresses) and they often publish lists of their faculties. If not, one can usually contact the universities to verify the claims made. A URL ending in *.gov* is a government site and is probably well monitored.

The currency of data is often difficult to establish for a website. Many websites do not provide a date when the data was posted nor do they have copyright notices. With newspapers, magazines, and books, one usually can figure out quickly whether information is outdated. This is not always possible with a website.

Disinformation is often difficult to correct because of the high transmission speed of information on the Internet and because of the number of people who will repeat false or questionable claims as if they were authoritative. One problem the Internet poses is that the same story can get repeated by a thousand different people in a dozen countries and yet the basic claims of all these documents might issue from a single source deliberately planting false information or speculating about a favorite paranoid fear. Rumors spread in any medium, but on the Internet they can spread around the world almost instantly. When newspapers and television people are used as conduits of disinformation, they can try to make amends by retracting or correcting false stories. There is no such thing as retraction or correction by the Internet.

Publication on the Internet is ephemeral. It is common to find that an Internet site you once visited no longer exists. This makes it difficult or impossible to reference websites the way one can reference a book, magazine, or television program. The book may go out of print, but it will always have a publication or copyright date. With the Internet, material you cite today may be gone tomorrow, or it may have "moved" (i.e., have a new "address" or URL).

Despite the above caveats, the Internet can be an excellent source of reliable information provided by credible sources. Many sources do identify their authors and provide enough information for one to determine their credibility. Many sources are recognizable as generally reliable; for, they are the same sources one finds off the Internet: *The New York Times, CNN, The Smithsonian, Nova, Scientific American, Encyclopedia Britannica,* etc., as well as authors who are known to you from their print publications.

Note: any messages in unsolicited e-mail should be regarded as suspect. If in doubt, consult *snopes.com*, the Urban Legends Reference Pages of Barbara and David Mikkelson, who make a living tracking down rumors and questionable claims.

Exercise 3-2

Compare the treatment of the same news story by two or three daily metropolitan newspapers. Examine the articles for similarities and differences in sources, language, slant or bias, positioning (where is the article located?), headlines, etc. Do the same for two or three newsmagazines (e.g., *Newsweek*, *The Nation*, and *National Review*).

Chapter Three Self-test: true or false? (Check your answers in Answers to Selected Exercises.)

1. Whenever possible one should use one's own knowledge, general and specific, to determine whether to believe a claim.
2. Greed or revenge will sometimes motivate a person to say things that are not true.
3. When evaluating the credibility of a source it is not important to consider the source's motives.
4. Checkbook journalism is the practice of paying people for interviews.
5. We should be especially skeptical of the testimony of anyone who has much to gain by lying and who is the sole source of information.
6. If a claim is made by an eyewitness, you should consider not only the integrity of the source but also the environmental, physical, emotional, and intellectual factors that might affect observation.
7. The fact that a witness is confident and unhesitating in identifying someone or in describing something from memory indicates that the testimony is probably accurate.
8. In choosing to believe one of two conflicting testimonies, you are not implying that one of the witnesses is lying.
9. Some people are more attentive in their observations than others are.
10. Before one should accept a claim solely on the basis of expert testimony, one should determine that the expert is really qualified in the subject matter that he or she is testifying about.
11. If one is an expert in one field, one's testimony in other fields becomes more reliable than other non-experts in those other fields.
12. Some fields are so controversial that there is scarcely a claim in the field that isn't defended by one expert and rejected by another.
13. You should not expect to find more agreement among experts about fundamental matters in the sciences than among experts in either the social sciences or the humanities.
14. The great diversity of opinion in the humanities and social sciences reflects the lack of useful information and opinion to be found in those disciplines.
15. False or unsubstantiated claims can come to be accepted as true among experts in a field through *communal reinforcement* (the process of self-proclaimed or media-proclaimed experts reinforcing each other's opinions).
16. Those who have the authority of power also have the authority of knowledge or experience.
17. Journalists have worldviews, political affiliations, loyalties, ambitions, hopes, religious beliefs, biases, and prejudices, and are subject to the same hindrances to critical thinking as the rest of us.
18. The worst part about journalism based upon information provided by interested parties is that only part of the story gets reported—at least initially—the part that favors the way of looking at things held by the source of the information.
19. Not only do mass media reports often serve the interests of those in power, they exaggerate the significance of much of what they report.
20. Our worldviews are molded by what we deem significant.
21. In general, the fact that experts are paid for their expertise is a good reason in itself to distrust them.
22. The *reputation* of a person is the best guide for deciding whether to trust an expert who gained his or her expertise from experience.
23. Experts can easily deceive us, since we usually lack the knowledge and experience necessary to judge their opinions.
24. According to Walter Lippmann and Charles Merz, the stories of journalists on important events are likely to be written to harmonize with generally accepted beliefs and prejudices.
25. According to Walter Lippmann and Charles Merz, most of us tend to accept or to reject news stories according to our prejudices.
26. Police officers, district attorneys, and newspersons do not mirror the society in which they live; they are not subject to the same prejudices and failures as the rest of us, and they are rarely led by their emotions instead of their brains.
27. "Managing the news" was coined by James Reston of the *New York Times* to describe the government's policy of issuing false evidence, suppressing evidence, distorting evidence, or harassing unfriendly critics.

28. According to Morgan Strong, much of what Americans saw on news broadcasts leading up to the offensive against Iraqi-occupied Kuwait was in large measure an example of managing the news by the public-relations firm of Hill and Knowlton.

29. According to David Lieberman, about 80 percent of the country's news directors say they use Video News Releases at least several times a month.

30. A Video News Release (VNR) is the video equivalent of printed propaganda provided by interested parties to newspapers and magazines.

31. There is careful screening by the International Truth Organization of all claims posted on the Internet.

32. An example of managing the news is the way President Clinton used local television stations to bring his agenda to the American people on issues such as health care, the U.S. role in Somalia, and tax reform.

33. Special interest groups rarely attempt to manage the news but when they try, they are never successful.

34. The ability to manipulate TV news with VNRs is enhanced because the value of video footage can be completely independent of its news value.

35. Experts are often used by the mass media not to test hypotheses or get information, but to find facts or quotes that fit a preconceived hypothesis.

36. Besides being oversimplified, the information in the mass media is likely to be incomplete and one-sided.

37. A journalist can easily slant or slip in judgments on events by quoting people who express the opinion the journalist wishes to express.

38. The Internet can often be a source of reliable and credible information.

39. The news media are highly reliable sources of information about government and special interest blocs although the government and special interest groups themselves are managing information that might affect our opinion of them.

40. The way the news media cover ongoing criminal investigations, preliminary hearings and trials in high profile cases can be just as one-sided and manipulative as faked news.

41. Re-creations of events for television docudramas can be misleading and deceptive, making the viewer think an alleged event actually occurred.

42. Many civil-liberties lawyers and media-ethics experts believe that a docudrama of an alleged crime presents a one-sided version of how a crime took place, often pinning blame on suspects before they've even been indicted.

43. Mass media do not depend on advertising for any significant income.

44. The potential for distortion and prejudicing a criminal case exists when an intimate rapport exists between the police and journalists.

45. The members of the mass media can be diligent watchdogs on law enforcement when they become partners with law enforcement.

Further Reading - Chapter Three

Alterman, Eric. (2003) *What Liberal Media? The Truth About Bias and the News*. Basic Books.

Clarke, Edwin Leavitt. (1929) *The Art of Straight Thinking*. D. Appleton-Century Company.

Glassner, Barry. (2000) *The Culture of Fear: Why Americans Are Afraid of the Wrong Things*. Basic Books.

Goldberg, Bernard. (2003) *Bias: A CBS Insider Exposes How the Media Distort the News*. Perrenial.

Postman, Neil. (1986) *Amusing Ourselves to Death: Public Discourse in the Age of Show Business*. Viking Press.

Postman, Neil and Steve Powers. (1965) *How to Watch TV News*. Penguin Books.

Radford, Benjamin. (2003) *Media Mythmakers: How Journalists, Activists, and Advertisers Mislead Us*. Prometheus Books.

Windes, Russel R. and Arthur Hastings. (1965) *Argument and Advocacy*. Random House.

Notes - Chapter Three

[1]Testimony here refers not only to testimony under oath in a court of law, but also to testimony given to reporters or others where no such oath is involved.

[2]Adolph Beck served seven years in prison after being mistakenly identified by twenty-two eyewitnesses. Seven eyewitnesses identified Bernard Pagano, a Catholic Priest, as having robbed them at gunpoint. Robert Clouser confessed to the crimes when it became apparent to him that the priest was going to be convicted. More recently, Randall Lynn Ayers spent eight years in prison for the rape, robbery and shooting of a 15-year-old girl. Randall was 17 when he was convicted in 1982. Eight years later Robert Minton, charged with slaying two Cincinnati women, confessed to the earlier crime. Minton offered details of the crime that convinced investigators he was telling the truth. When the victim of the 1981 attack looked at Ayers and Minton, who strongly resembles Ayers, she could not identify which was her assailant. *Sacramento Bee*, July 22, 1990. See *Witness for the Defense: The Accused, the Eyewitness and the Expert Who Puts Memory on Trial* by Elizabeth Loftus and Katherine Ketchum (St. Martin's Press 1992).

[3] We do admire some people who question authority. For example, if the challenger is attacking someone we disagree with. Criticism of one's own democratic government is often attacked as treasonous, but the same people admire critics in non-democratic countries who attack their government's policies.

[4]Ellen Bass, Laura Davis, Wendy Maltz, Beverly Holman, Beverly Engel, Mary Jane Williams and E. Sue Blume. See above, page 10.

[5]Carol Tavris, "Hysteria and the incest-survivor machine," *Sacramento Bee*, Forum section, January 17, 1993, p. 1. Tavris is the author of several works in psychology, including *The Mismeasure of Woman* (New York: Simon & Shuster, 1992). She is also the editor of *Every Woman's Emotional Well-being* (Garden city, N.Y.: Doubleday, 1986).
Here are a few of the unproved, unscientifically researched notions that are being bandied about by these child abuse experts: (1) If you doubt that you were abused as a child or think that it might be your imagination, this is a sign of "post-incest syndrome" [Blume]. (2) If you can't remember any specific instances of being abused, but still have a feeling that something abusive happened to you, "it probably did" [Bass and Davis]. (3) When a person can't remember his or her childhood or has very fuzzy memories "incest must always be considered a possibility" [Maltz and Holman]. And, (4) "If you have any suspicion at all, if you have any memory, no matter how vague, it probably really happened. It is far more likely that you are blocking the memories, denying it happened" [Engel].

[6]Yet, it has happened. In a modern version of the Salem witch hunts, the McMartin pre-school case exemplifies the very worst in institutionalized justice in the hunt for child molesters. See Mary Ann Mason, "The McMartin case revisited: the conflict between social work and criminal justice," [on evaluating the credibility of children as witnesses in sexual abuse cases] *Social Work, v.* 36, no. 5 (Sept, 1991), pp. 391-396, and Marion Zenn Goldberg, "Child witnesses: lessons learned from the McMartin trials," *Trial*, v. 26, no. 10 (Oct, 1990), pp. 86-88. See also Richard Lacayo, "The longest mistrial; the McMartin Pre-School case ends at last," *Time* (August 6, 1990), p. 28; Frank McConnell, "The trials of television: the McMartin case," *Commonweal* (March 23, 1990), pp. 189-190; Douglas J. Besharov, "Protecting the innocent," *National Review* (Feb 19, 1990), pp. 44-46; Margaret Carlson, "Six years of trial by torture: children, defendants, jurors and judge were all abused in the wasteful McMartin case," *Time* (Jan 29, 1990), pp. 26-28; and "The child-abuse trial that left a national legacy," *U.S. News & World Report* (Jan 29, 1990), p. 8.

[7] Alvin A. Snyder, "Lies the government made me tell about KAL 007," *Sacramento Bee*, Forum 2, September 8, 1996.

[8] "Reagan ties Bird to insurance bind," by Leo Rennert, *Sacramento Bee*, May 31, 1986, p. A22.

[9] Ben H. Bagdikian, "Journalism's sins of omission," *Sacramento Bee*, Jan 24, 1990 p. B5.

[10]*ibid.* Hume also notes that the media's handling of the S&L scandal was not much different from "our inability to unravel and explain the importance of the Iran-Contra abuses, [and] the Housing and Urban Development influence-buying schemes.

[11] *ibid.*

[12] "How to Read the Chicago Tribune," *Harpers Magazine* (April, 1949). pp. 24-35.

[13] Here is just one example. Reporter Don Stanley once wrote an article for the *Sacramento Bee* that gave every appearance of being an eyewitness account of a talk given by Gloria Steinem at U.C. Davis. In fact, Stanley left the lecture hall before the talk began. He had an 11 p.m. deadline to meet and the talk was delayed until after 9 p.m. due to a bomb threat. Stanley didn't even know there was a bomb threat, though it was announced over the public address system. He claims he "asked the guy alongside me" what was announced on the P.A. and "he simply told me that the hall was going to be cleared and the talk started at 9 p.m." Steinem gave Stanley a personal interview and summarized for him what she was going to talk about. Unfortunately for him she changed her mind. Those who read his article and had been at the talk were very confused as he (1) made no mention of the bomb threat and (2) reported on a speech nobody heard. See the *Sacramento Bee*, Nov. 27, 1983, p. B1. Some high profile journalists caught faking it (besides those already mentioned in this chapter) should be noted: Janet Cooke (*Washington Post*), Steven Glass (*New Republic*), and Patricia Smith and Mike Barnicle (*Boston Globe*).

[14] "A Test of the News, *New Republic*, Supplement. Aug. 4, 1920 (Windes and Hastings, 276 ff.).

[15] *The University of Chicago Press*, 1922. See Clarke, *op. cit.,* p. 284.

[16] "A Murderous Hoax," January 22, 1990, pp. 16 ff.

[17] "Race and Hype in a Divided City: the double standards of police and press," by Jonathan Alter and Mark Starr, *Newsweek*, January 21, 1990, p. 22.

[18] *ibid.*

[19] After the war ended, ABC television reported (March 15, 1991) that it was true that 312 babies had died in a maternity hospital but they had not died because Iraqi soldiers killed them or stole their incubators. The babies died because the doctors and nurses abandoned the hospital. Dr. Mohammed Matar and his wife, Dr. Fayeza Youssef, who ran the hospital, said that the babies died because "no one stayed to care for them" after the invasion. Matar admitted that the reports on Iraqi atrocities about the babies were "for propaganda." See *Sacramento Bee*, "Iraqis didn't kill babies, ABC says," March 16, 1991, p. A-19.

[20] "Portions of the GULF WAR were brought to you by...the folks at Hill and Knowlton," Morgan Strong, *TV Guide*, February 22, 1992, p. 11.

[21] *ibid.*, p. 13.

[22] "Spontaneity scripted at town hall/ KCRA's staff doesn't want any surprises during Clinton Forum," by Jennifer Bojorquez, *Sacramento Bee*, September 29, 1993.

[23] David Lieberman, "Fake News," *TV Guide*, Feb. 22, 1992, p.16. According to Frank Geer, a Clinton media advisor, it costs about $600 an hour to rent a satellite transponder.

[24] "Fake News," *TV Guide*, Feb. 22, 1992, p. 11.

[25] *ibid.* p. 26.

[26] *ibid.*, p. 16.

[27] "Journalism's sins of omission" by Ben H. Bagdikian, former reporter and editor who now teaches at UC Berkeley in the Graduate School of Journalism. The original article was in *Newsday*; it was reprinted in the *Sacramento Bee*, Jan 24, 1990, p. B5. The information on General Electric and NBC is taken from Bagdikian's article.

[28] The information regarding the right-wing conspiracy outlined in this section came from two Internet sources: *Conspire.com Weekly* (conpire.com) and *Salon* (salonmagazine.com). Evaluating Internet sources is discussed below in section 6 of this chapter.

[29] "Re-Creating News for Television," *Sacramento Bee*, January 13, 1985, FORUM, p. 5.

[30] "TV News Goes Hollywood," by Richard Zoglin, *Time*, October 9, 1989, p. 98. In an accompanying article, "Truth and

Consequences," *Time* reports that CBS anchorman Dan Rather was charged with using faked footage of events in Afghanistan. The images were of troops in battle and suffering civilians. They won CBS an award for news coverage. An Afghan rebel claimed that the photographer of the events arrived twelve days after they had happened and persuaded the rebels to restage their blowing up of electric-power pylons. The action was supposed to have been the "largest sabotage operation of the war." Other events were allegedly staged as well, or misrepresented. *ibid.* p. 98.

[31] "TV Cops May Right Wrongs, Wrong Rights," *Wall Street Journal*, March 10, 1993, p. B1.

[32] *ibid.*

[33] "GM Accuses NBC of Rigging Test Crash of Pickup Truck on 'Dateline' Program," *Wall Street Journal*, Feb. 9, 1993, p. A6.

[34] "How GM One-Upped an Embarrassed NBC on Staged News Event," *Wall Street Journal*, Vol. cxxviii No. 29; "Exposing the 'Experts' Behind the Sexy Exposés: How Networks Get Duped by Dubious Advocates," Walter Olson, *The Washington Post* (Sunday "Outlook"), February 28, 1993.

Chapter Four - Arguments

Arguments are to be avoided:
They are always vulgar and often convincing.
--Oscar Wilde

Truth springs from argument amongst friends.
--David Hume

1. Introduction

At the heart of critical thinking is the ability to recognize, construct, and evaluate **arguments**. By **argument** we mean *the presentation of a reason or reasons in support of some claim or action*. A single statement of a belief or position is not an argument. There must be at least two statements in an argument. One of those statements must represent a claim or action being defended, and one of the statements must represent a reason given in support of that claim or action. The reasons given in an argument are called the **premises** of the argument. The claim they try to support is called the **conclusion** of the argument.

Arguments can be on any topic. One can argue for legalized abortion; one can argue against legalized abortion. Some argued for intervention in Iraq; others argued against intervention. Some argue that dogs and cats and other non-human animals have moral rights; others argue that non-human animals have no moral rights. Some argue that pornography should be banned; others argue that it should not be banned. Some argue that there is life on other planets. Some argue that vitamin C can prevent colds. Some argue for three-strikes laws that send people to prison for life for a third felony; others argue that sometimes such punishment is cruel and unusual and therefore violates the eighth amendment to the Constitution.

What makes an argument a good one will be discussed in the next chapter. Here our concern is with learning how to identify arguments and their components. The first thing to consider is the **language of argument**.

2. The Language of Argument

Above we defined an argument as *the presentation of a reason or reasons in support of some claim or action*. We said that the claim for which support is given is called the **conclusion** and the reasons given in support of the claim are called the **premises**. These are the technical terms of logic: 'premise', 'conclusion', and 'argument'. However, there are many non-technical terms that describe premises or conclusions. In a court of law, *evidence* (premises) is presented to support a *verdict* (conclusion). In a scientific paper, results of experiments or *data* (premises) are used to support conclusions. In the legislature, *reasons* (premises) are given to support voting for or against a bill (conclusion). On the automobile sales lot, the salesperson presents *facts* and *opinions* (premises) to convince a customer to buy a car (conclusion). In a scholarly mathematical paper, *proofs* (premises) are given to justify certain propositions (conclusions) and certain propositions (conclusions) are said to follow from other propositions (premises). In formal logic, a set of statements (premises) is said *to imply or to entail* another statement (conclusion). A security guard asks for *verification* (premise) that a person is who she says she is (conclusion). An English teacher demands that students give *support* (premises) for claims (conclusions).

In the courtroom, a defense lawyer is not likely to say that "the premises do not prove that the conclusion that should be drawn is *guilty*." A lawyer is more likely to say "the *evidence* does not warrant finding the defendant *guilty*. A scientist is not likely to write that her *premises* prove her conclusion. She is more likely to say that her *data* support her conclusion. The facts and opinions heaped on the poor car buyer are the premises of the salesperson's argument. The conclusion is that you ought to buy the car.

In ordinary English, many different words are used for the technical terms 'premise' and 'conclusion'. Depending on the situation, *evidence, support, data, fact,* and *opinion* mean the same as *premise*. A *verdict* or an *inference* is a *conclusion*. *Proofs* or *verification* are *arguments*. Conclusions are not only said to be *supported by* premises; conclusions are said to *follow from* premises, to *be implied by* or to *be entailed by* premises. Finally, premises are said to *support* or *imply* conclusions.

Thus, even though in most ordinary-language arguments we do not use the technical language of argument (i.e., the terms 'premise' and 'conclusion') we may still be arguing in the logical sense of that word: *presenting reasons in support of some claim or action.*

Clearly, before one can begin to evaluate an argument, one must be able to recognize when an argument is being made. One must be able to separate premises and conclusions from other material. Only then can one begin to evaluate the *reasons* and the *reasoning* of the argument. Knowing the language of argument can help in the process of identifying premises and conclusions.

2.1 Sentences and statements

Premises and conclusions are expressed in sentences. Sentences that are used as premises or conclusions must be *complete* sentences, not fragments of sentences. For example, the sentence 'No drug should be illegal' could be a premise or a conclusion. The expression 'illegal drugs' could not be a premise or a conclusion, since it is not a complete sentence.

In addition to being complete, the sentences used as premises or conclusions must assert something about which it makes sense to say such things as 'Yes, that's true' or 'No, that's false' or 'That's reasonable to believe' or 'That doesn't seem reasonable to accept.' A command, such as 'Shut the door', could not be a premise. The imperative sentence is used to issue a command, not to make a claim. Hence, imperatives are not statements. Neither are exclamations. Nor could a question such as 'What time is it?' be a premise or a conclusion. Interrogative sentences generally ask questions. Hence, they do not make statements. The exception is the *rhetorical question.* "Is he greedy or what?" is not asked to get an answer but to make a statement. It may have the grammar of a question but its function is to make a statement. It is the *function* of the sentence, not its grammatical form, that determines whether it is a statement. Any sentence used to state or assert that something is the case *could* be used as a premise or a conclusion. It is generally the declarative sentence, however, that is used to make a statement.

A sentence makes a statement or an assertion when it is used to state some fact (*There were three hundred and twenty robberies in Chicago last week*), assert some opinion (*Capital punishment is immoral*), or make some claim (*There could be life on other planets in other solar systems in other galaxies*). Statements can be simple (*The crime rate is declining*) or complex (*The crime rate is declining but press coverage of crime is increasing*; or *Either the crime rate is rising or the drug rate is increasing*; or *If the drug rate is increasing, then the crime rate is rising*).

Statements become premises or conclusions when they are related to one another as **reason** *to* **claim** *or* **action supported**. Not every group of statements makes an argument, because not every group of statements consists of premises or conclusions. For example, some groups of statements are purely descriptive, such as a listing of what fines a city will levy for various kinds of parking violations. What makes a group of statements an argument is that at least one of the statements is put forth as a reason for accepting at least one other statement. In other words, no statement is a premise or conclusion in and of itself. A statement becomes a premise only if it is used to support another statement. A statement becomes a conclusion only if another statement or set of statements is offered in support of it. For example, the assertions 'Jack is a politician' and 'Don't vote for Jack' might be used in an argument by using the first statement to support the second:

Don't vote for Jack because he's a politician.

'Don't vote for Jack' is the action supported (**the conclusion**). 'He's a politician' is the reason given (**the premise**) in support of that action. The word 'because' relates the two assertions as premise to conclusion.

Here is another example of an argument.

Jack's conservative; so, he's probably a Republican.

'Jack's conservative' is the reason (premise). 'He's probably a Republican' is the claim supported (the conclusion). The word *so* relates the two assertions as premise to conclusion.

Finally, notice that in the two examples of arguments just given, each *sentence* contains more than one *statement*. Though an argument must have at least two *statements*, a single sentence may contain one or more statements.

2.2 Argument indicators

In the examples of arguments given at the end of the previous section, the words 'because' and 'so' were used to relate two claims as premise to conclusion. Such words are called *argument indicators*. 'Because' is called a *premise indicator* and 'so' is called a *conclusion indicator*. Many words and expressions may be used to indicate that a premise or a conclusion follows.

SOME PREMISE INDICATORS	SOME CONCLUSION INDICATORS
since; because; for; for the reason that; as indicated by	*therefore; thus; so;, hence; it follows that; consequently*

Note that conclusions *never* immediately follow premise indicators and premises *never* immediately follow conclusion indicators. Remember, too, that many arguments have no indicators. The *context* alone must be used to distinguish the argument. How can one tell when a word is being used as an argument indicator or not? The only way to tell is to *examine how the word is used in context*. Although it is useful to look for premise and conclusion indicators, it would be a mistake to think that the words in the above lists are *always* used to indicate premises and conclusions. Most words have several possible uses or functions. Premise and conclusion indicators are no exceptions. 'Since' can be used as an adverb; e.g., "I've known her *since* she was a baby." 'For' is often a preposition; e.g., "She was here *for* an hour." 'Thus' can be used as an adverb; e.g., "*Thus* goes the wheel of fortune."

Even though these words aren't *always* used to indicate premises or conclusions, they are used in this way frequently enough to make it worth your while to become familiar with them.

Exercise 4-1

Indicate whether or not each of the following *could* be used as a premise or a conclusion. [Exercises with an * are answered in Answers to Selected Exercises.]

*1. No one was at the scene of the crime.
2. An ugly incident.
3. Only a tall person could have gotten through that window.
4. Since.
*5. Nevertheless, if that is what.
6. Why drugs shouldn't be legal.
7. Drugs should be legalized.
*8. Opium should be cheap and it should be legal.
9. Either drunk drivers should be imprisoned or they should have their licenses taken away.
10. If drugs were legalized there would be fewer crimes.
11. If the test results are positive.
*12. Either the wind was blowing.
13. Wow!
14. The zombie only wakes at night.
*15. No person is an island.

Exercise 4-2

For the following arguments, underline the premises, circle the conclusions and box any premise or conclusion indicators.

*1. Justice can't exist for the poor because justice is nothing but the way the rich protect their interests.
2. God exists; for, the world needs a Creator.
3. A politician can't get elected unless she lies. Therefore, all elected officials are liars.
4. Since women are smaller than men, it follows that men are stronger than women.
*5. Because size is irrelevant to intelligence, it is necessarily the case that you are wrong in stating that women must be less intelligent than men.
6. We're out of gasoline. Therefore, you had better start walking to the nearest gas station.
7. Children should not enter child beauty contests because photographers will make them pose for sleazy pictures and judges will give them drugs.
8. You don't have a suntan. So, you're not from California.
9. Since that noise you listen to has no rhythm, harmony or melody, it is not music.
*10. King Tutankhamen was not a great king because he died before his twentieth birthday.
11. All women are mortal. Xanthippe is a woman. So, Xanthippe is mortal.
12. Everybody does it. So, I ought to be allowed to do it, too.
13. The President's action was a mistake because he has put his own children in extreme danger. And, it will not reduce, but escalate terrorism. It will lead to further retaliation on our part. It will strengthen the resolve of our Arab enemies. Finally, it will push friendly Arab states into the arms of the Soviet Union.
*14. "Astronomy was born of superstition; eloquence of ambition, hatred, falsehood and flattery; geometry of avarice; physics of an idle curiosity and even moral philosophy of human pride. Thus, the arts and sciences owe their birth to our vices."
--Jean Jacques Rousseau, *Discourse on the Arts and Sciences.*

Exercise 4-3

Create your own arguments for each of the following groups of statements. Use either a premise or a conclusion indicator in each argument you make.

*1. a. Nude bathing should not be allowed.
   b. Immorality has to stop somewhere.
   c. Decent people have to start standing up for their rights.

2. a. The speaker's defense of Mill is not worth considering.

    b. The speaker is a friend of Mill's.
    c. The speaker is a notorious drunk.

3.   a. A free press is necessary to a free society.
    b. Without a free press, the people won't know who to vote for.
    c. Communist countries don't have a free press.

4.   a. The Greeks had a low opinion of life.
    b. They killed each other with reckless abandon.
    c. They went to war for ten years over a woman.

5.   a. I am not guilty.
    b. I never went near the scene of the crime at any time.
    c. I was in another city at the time of the crime.

*6.   a. Slavery was ordained by God.
    b. The Bible is the word of God.
    c. There is nothing in the Bible which forbids slavery.

2.3 Arguments without indicators

Not all arguments have premise or conclusion indicators. Often, one must tell from the context alone whether an assertion is intended as a premise, a conclusion, or neither. Since the function of statements is not always made clear by the context, there may be times when it is not possible to tell whether an argument is being made. Don't let this worry you. Most of the time it will be clear enough whether someone is arguing.

    The most important contextual indicator is *background knowledge*. For example, if you are going into a meeting to discuss whether you should fire Jones, statements without argument indicators (such as 'since' and 'therefore') will be made that you would undoubtedly recognize as being intended to support either firing or not firing Jones. For example, "Jones is always sick on Mondays" (premise); He took the company car without asking and used it for his vacation" (premise); "We should fire him" (conclusion).

    If an article is titled "Why Drugs Should Be Legal," statements without argument indicators will probably be used, but the context will indicate that certain statements are put forth as reasons in support of the view that drugs should be legal. For example: "It would cut down on street crime" or "We'd save a lot of money."

    Other contextual indicators are the *tenses* of sentences, and *cause/effect* relationships asserted by the claims. Statements in the present tense are often used to support statements in the future tense. A statement that claims something is a cause of something else is often used as a premise in support of the claim asserting the effect.

Exercises 4-4

For each of the following arguments, underline the premises and circle the conclusions.

*1. "There should be no law which regulates when and where an individual may smoke. Such a law would allow government to substitute its laws for our freedom to make individual decisions. It didn't work with liquor prohibition; it won't work with smoking prohibitions."
2. "You're eating too fast. You're going to get sick."
3. "You can't prove that I cheated on the test. I must be innocent."
4. "Free speech will be abused. Every liberty is abused."
5. "You should vote 'yes' on proposition 45; it could save your job."
*6. "Men are all insecure babies. My first four husbands were."

7. "Ann Landers is divorced; any advice she gives on marriage is worthless."

8. "Our diet plan is healthy; no one has been able to prove it isn't."

*9. "As Superintendent of Schools, you have a vested interest in the funding bill before this legislative committee. Your arguments for increased funding of the public school system may be justifiably ignored."

10. "Philosophy requires a lot of hard thinking. If you take a philosophy class, you will have to exercise your brain extensively."

11. We never should have listened to Wilberforce. The man's a moron and he lies like a rug.

*12. No one ever did anything he or she did not want to do. If Smith robbed that bank, then he wanted to do it.

13. Either Gordonski is lying or she's telling the truth. She isn't lying. She must be telling the truth.

14. It's a good idea to believe in free will. If there is no free will, then no one is responsible for their actions. If no one is responsible for their actions, then no one can justifiably be held accountable for their actions. If no one is held accountable for their actions, there would be chaos. No one wants chaos.

*15. If fatalism is true, then everything that happens has to happen. If no one can change what must happen, then there is no sense in worrying about what happens, whether it is good or bad. Fatalism should take away our worries.

16. Alcoholic drinks should be avoided at meals. Liquor taken before or during meals encourages overeating.

17. "Milk is the only perfect, complete or standard food combination in Nature. This is evident from the fact that it contains all the elements of nutrition which the new born infant body needs, not only for its vital activities but also for the building of its rapidly multiplying cells and tissues." --Henry Lindlahr, M.D., *The Practice of Nature Cure*

18. All cows are bovine. Either Max is a cow and bovine or Max is not bovine.

19. If Nobody is on first, then Who is on second. Nobody is on first. Who must be on second.

20. You should give the man a raise. After all, he's worked for you for fifty years and he's never once taken a day off.

2.4 Simple and complex statements

A simple statement is one that cannot be broken down into simpler statements. For example: *There should be no letter grades given for college level courses.*

A complex statement is one that consists of two or more simple statements. For example: *Letter grades make the clever feel superior and they destroy the confidence of those who fail.*

Since premises and conclusions must be statements, and statements can be simple or complex; it follows that premises and conclusions must be either simple statements or complex statements.

Three of the more common types of complex statements are: **the conjunction, the disjunction,** and **the conditional statement.**

A *conjunction* joins statements together in a string or list, usually using the word 'and' or 'but' to join the statements. For example,

Sheila cheated but she failed the exam.

A *disjunction* also joins statements together, usually using the word 'or', or using the expression 'either...or'. For example,

Either Sheila cheated or she failed the exam.

or

Sheila cheated or she failed the exam

The conjunction asserts both that *Sheila cheated* and that *she failed the exam.* The disjunction, on the other hand, does not assert that Sheila cheated. Nor does it assert that she failed the exam. The disjunction asserts that one of those statements is true, but not both. Furthermore, it does not give any clue as to which of the statements is thought to be the true one.[1]

A **conditional statement** joins statements together with the connective 'if' or the connectives 'if...then'. The *if* statement is called the **antecedent**; the *then* statement is called the **consequent**.

If Sheila cheated, then she passed the exam.

or

If Sheila cheated, she passed the exam.

The conditional is like the disjunction in that it does not assert that its component statements are true. The disjunction asserts that one of the disjuncts is true. The conditional asserts that if the antecedent is true, the consequent is true.

Unless statements are also conditionals.

Unless Sheila cheated, she failed the exam.

or

Shelia failed the exam unless she cheated.

These statements mean the same as the *if...then* statement

If Sheila did not cheat, then she failed the exam.

My favorite kind of conditional statement is the **contrary-to-fact conditional**. For example, *I would have passed the exam if I had studied.* (We'll never know because I didn't study.) *I would have made the field goal to win the game if I hadn't had donuts for lunch.* (We'll never know because I did have donuts for lunch.) *I could have made this chapter less boring if I had tried harder.* (We'll never know because I didn't try harder!)

2.5 Distinguishing arguments from conditional statements

Conditional statements are sometimes mistakenly thought to be arguments. However, it is quite easy to recognize the essential differences between the two. An argument's function is to state a claim and to state reasons sufficient to support that claim. A conditional statement's function is to claim that one statement is a sufficient reason for accepting some other statement; that is, that the antecedent *implies* the consequent. There are some similarities between arguments and conditionals. In an argument one gives reasons. In a conditional statement, one says one claim is a reason for accepting another claim.

A conditional statement asserts a *single, complex* claim. Arguments make at least two claims. To be an argument, at least once claim must be *given* as a reason for accepting another claim.

The following is an example of a conditional statement. It is not an argument.

"*If* Sheila passed the exam, *then* she cheated."

86

This statement asserts a single, complex claim. It does not claim that Sheila passed the exam; it does not claim that she cheated. It claims that *if* Sheila passed the exam, *then* she cheated. That is, it claims that the statement 'she cheated' is *implied* by the statement 'she passed the exam.' (Put another way, it says that 'she cheated' may be *inferred from* 'she passed.')

In an argument, one makes a claim and asserts that that claim supports the truth or reasonableness of another claim. In a conditional statement, one statement (the **antecedent**) is put forth as being a condition which, if true, is sufficient to warrant accepting another statement (the **consequent**). The antecedent of a conditional is *not* a premise for the consequent, and the consequent is *not* a conclusion based on the antecedent.

It would be possible, of course, to make an argument out of the statements "Sheila cheated" and "Sheila passed the exam." All that needs to be done is to put one of these statements in relation to the other as premise to conclusion. One must *give* one of the claims as a reason for accepting the other claim. For example,

"Since *Sheila passed the exam*, one must conclude that *she cheated*."

Here there are two separate claims made: *Sheila passed the exam* and *she cheated*. One of the claims is given as a reason for accepting the other claim. Thus, here we have an argument.

In an argument, a premise is asserted *un*conditionally. In the conditional, the antecedent is asserted *conditionally*. That is, 'if' functions quite differently than 'since.' 'If' is a *connective*, not a premise indicator. 'If' connects an antecedent with its consequent. Putting 'if' in front of the statement "Sheila passed the exam" is a way of saying that you are not claiming that she passed the exam. By using the *conditional* you are only saying that *her passing the exam would be a sufficient reason for believing some other claim* (namely, that she cheated). Putting 'since' before "Sheila passed the exam" in the argument not only indicates that her passing the exam is a sufficient reason to believe that she cheated, but also asserts that she did pass the exam and she did cheat.

Conditional statements, then, are not arguments but *single, complex statements*. Of course, being statements, conditionals could be used as premises or conclusions in arguments just as any other kind of statement may. (If this is not clear, refer to section 2.4 above, which discusses using complex statements in arguments.)

Finally, there is another important difference between arguments and conditional statements. The antecedent and consequent of a conditional must always be in the same sentence. The premises and conclusions of arguments, however, may be either in the same or in separate sentences.

Exercise 4-5

Underline the premises, circle the conclusions, and box any premise or conclusion indicators in the following arguments. Note any cases where 'and', 'but' 'either' or 'or' are NOT used to join statements together.

*1. Holding in one's feelings is not healthy, since it might lead to psychosomatic illness or it might result in anti-social behavior.

2. Computers cannot think; for, if something is a machine, then it cannot think.

3. Since 7 is greater than 5, it follows that 12 is greater than either 7 or 5.

4. Civilization has caused more harm than good to mankind because it not only has given human beings the chance to be moral, but it has also made possible immorality. And, the pernicious and cruel effects of immorality seem to far outweigh the benefits of what little moral behavior there is.

5. If 'A' is greater than 'B' and 'B' is greater than 'C' then 'A' is greater than 'C'. 'A' is greater than 'B' and 'B' is greater than 'C'. So, 'A' is greater than 'C'.

6. If the Dodgers come in first, then the Reds will come in second. The Dodgers will come in first. Therefore, the Reds will come in second.

*7. Either it will rain or it will snow. It will not snow. Therefore, it will rain.

8. It has never snowed in June or July here, so it shouldn't snow this summer either.

9. Agriculture must be the least lucrative of all arts because its products are indispensable and their price must be proportionate to the abilities of the poorest. --J.J. Rousseau, *Discourse on the Origin of Inequality*

10. Since human history is the story of one war after another, either there will be more wars in the future or human nature will change.

*11. If the President is telling the truth then the Russians will not invade Poland. The Russians will invade Poland. So, the President is lying.

*12. Either the Germans will not quit the United Nations or the moon will turn to green cheese. Since the moon will not turn to green cheese, it follows that the Germans will not quit the United Nations.

13. "Remembering, which occurs now, cannot...possibly prove that what is remembered occurred at some other time, because the world might have sprung into being five minutes ago, exactly as it then was, full of acts of remembering which were entirely misleading." --Bertrand Russell, *An Outline of Philosophy*

14. All unhappiness is due to unsatisfied desires. All satisfaction is due to satisfied desires. And, no one can satisfy all his or her desires. Therefore, either one must give up desires and be happy or one must resign oneself to a life of unhappiness. (This is a paraphrase of one of the teachings of the Buddha, Siddhartha Gautama.)

Exercise 4-6

For each of the following, first determine if the passage contains an argument. If it does, underline premises, circle conclusions, and box off any premise or conclusion indicators. If the passage does not contain an argument, put a check in the margin and indicate whether or not it contains a conditional statement.

*1. There must be simple substances because there are composites; for a composite is nothing else than a collection or aggregate of simple substances. --Leibniz, *Monadology*

*2. "It is a test of true theories not only to account for but to predict phenomena." --William Whewell, *Philosophy of the Inductive Sciences*, aphorism 39.

*3. If the water is black, then the well is polluted.

*4. The water is black and the well is polluted.

5. "It is not enough to have a good mind. The main thing is to use it well." --René Descartes, *Discourse on Method*

6. Since the water is black, the well is probably polluted.

7. The water is black; therefore, the well is polluted.

* 8. Memory should not be trusted as the sole judge of the truth of any claim, since memory is fallible and memory sometimes is constituted by later acts.

9. Computers are extremely useful. I bought one last year and am glad I did.

10. A man's conscience and his judgment is the same thing. The judgment may be erroneous. So, the conscience may be erroneous, too. --Thomas Hobbes

11. You ought to buy a computer because they're extremely useful.

12. I bought a computer; so, I must be smarter than you are.

*13. She did well on the exam; so, she'll probably graduate.

14. "If women do not put forth, finally, that effort to become all that they have it in them to become they will forfeit their own humanity." Betty Friedan, *The Feminine Mystique*

15. Women should put forth their best effort. Actually, men should, too.

*16. If the world were to end today, could you say that your life had been worth living?

17. "There must have been a burglary at my house because the place was a shambles: drawers were open and papers were strewn all over the floor. And my silver collection was gone."

18. If you are a defense attorney for someone you know is guilty, you must nevertheless make the best defense possible for your client.

*19. "...[W]e ought mutually to tolerate one another, because we are all weak, irrational, and subject to change and error." --Voltaire, "Toleration"

20. "The first man who, having fenced in a piece of land, said, 'This is mine,' and found people naïve enough to believe him, that man was the true founder of civil society." --Jean Jacques Rousseau

*21. If cows could talk, their gods would be bovine.

22. "Religion is the opium of the people." Who said that?

23. Since dogs have no free will, they should not be held morally responsible for attacking or killing humans.

24. Dogs have no free will. They don't even know what 'moral' or 'immoral' means.

88

*25. The drug problem is out of control. I don't know who is in charge of solving this problem. If it gets much worse we'll be in too much trouble to do anything about it.

26. Electrons do not exist because they cannot be seen or tasted or touched. And, anything which cannot be seen, tasted or touched does not exist.

*27. There must be life on Mars since nobody has been able to prove there isn't life there.

28. If the key works, I'll open the door.

29. The key didn't work. The door was locked. We left at 5:00 p.m.

30. Around here 'free speech' means 'free to say whatever you want as long as you don't offend anyone.'

3. Complex arguments

The simplest argument has a single premise and a single conclusion. Complex arguments may have several premises and one or more conclusions. Some complex arguments are constructed by linking together several simpler arguments. The linkage may be made by having the conclusion of one argument serve as a premise in another argument. A very common form of complex argument is to present several sub-arguments in support of a single main conclusion. *A sub-argument is one whose conclusion is **not** the main conclusion of the argument.*

For example:

> **Drugs should be legalized because it would cut down on street crime. Criminals wouldn't have to commit crimes to get their drugs because their drugs would be cheap. And it would save the taxpayer a lot of money. We wouldn't have to build so many jails and we wouldn't have to hire so many cops to enforce drug laws.**

This argument has sub-arguments. A tree diagram might be helpful to illustrate this point. First, let's rewrite the argument, numbering each statement. Then, we'll diagram the argument using the numbers of the statements to represent the statements in the diagram. To give a visual representation of the role of premises as *supports* in an argument, we represent premises *below* their conclusions, as in diagram 1.

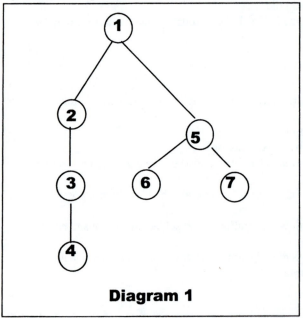

Diagram 1

[1] Drugs should be legalized because [2] it would cut down on street crime. [3] Criminals wouldn't have to commit crimes to get their drugs because [4] their drugs would be cheap. And [5] it would save the taxpayers a lot of money. [6] We wouldn't have to build so many jails and [7] we wouldn't have to hire so many cops to enforce drug laws.

"Drugs should be legalized" [statement 1] is the main conclusion of the argument, which is represented at the top in the diagram. "It would cut down on street crime and it would save the taxpayers a lot of money" [statements 2 and 5] are the main reasons given in support of the main conclusion. Those statements are put *below* the statement they support. But statements 2 and 5 are also conclusions of sub-arguments. "It would cut down on street crime [statement 2] is supported by the claim that "criminals wouldn't have to commit crimes to get their drugs"

[statement 3]. So, 3 is placed below 2 in the diagram. Furthermore, statement 3 is itself also a conclusion of a sub-argument with "their drugs would be cheap" [statement 4] given as a reason for accepting it. "It would save the taxpayers lots of money" [statement 5] is supported by the claims that "we wouldn't have to build so many jails" [statement 6] and "we wouldn't have to hire so many cops to enforce drug laws" [statement 7].

The diagram shows the sub-arguments. Statements 2, 3, and 4 make up a *chain argument*: Statement 4 supports statement 3 and statement 3 supports statement 2. Statements 5, 6, and 7 make up another sub-argument. (Each of these groups of statements has a conclusion that is not the main conclusion of the argument.) And each of the sub-arguments has a statement that serves as both a premise and a conclusion in the overall argument. (Remember: the terms 'premise' and 'conclusion' are *relational* terms. Just as the same man can be both a son and a father, the same statement can be both a premise and a conclusion in an argument.)

3.1 Diagramming complex arguments

Diagramming an argument may help you see the logical structure of the argument. To diagram an argument, first number each statement in the argument. Then use circled numbers to represent the statement in your diagram. Connect the circled numbers in such a way that premises are displayed beneath (as supports of) conclusions. Indicate that a statement is both a premise and a conclusion by putting the circled number of the statement beneath the statement it is a premise for and above the statement it is a conclusion of.

For example, the following argument would be numbered and diagramed as indicated in the box below.

[1] I don't know why people are always arguing about the existence of God.[2] You cannot disprove that God exists, for [3] it is impossible to prove the negative existence of anything. [4] If you can't disprove something, then it seems reasonable to believe whatever you feel like believing about it. So, [5] if you feel like believing in God, then you should.

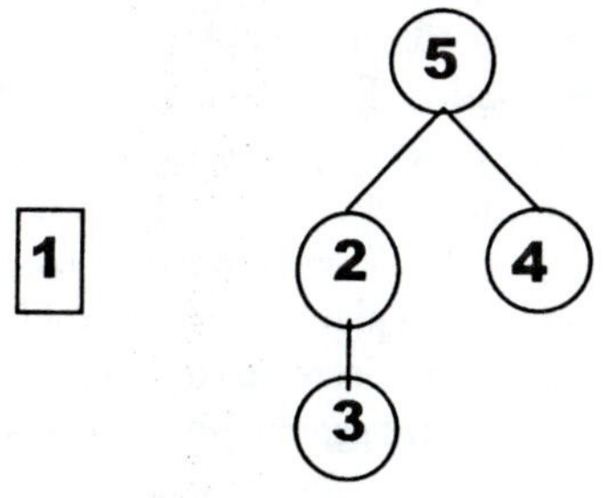

In **Diagram 2**, statement 5 is the *main conclusion*. Statement 1 is drawn off to the side because it simply introduces the topic and is not part of the argument; that is, it is neither a premise nor a conclusion. Statement 2 is diagramed as being both a premise (with respect to statement 5) and a conclusion (with respect to statement 3). Statements 2 and 3 together make up a *sub-argument*.

Diagram 2

In diagram 2, the premises that are not also conclusions (statements 3 and 4) are the *assumptions* the main conclusion is based on. **Assumptions** are those statements for which no reasons are given. *An assumption is something that is taken for granted.* Every argument is based on one or more assumptions. In the argument above, only statement 2 is a premise that is not an assumption. It is not an assumption because statement 3 is offered as a reason for statement 2.

A tautology is a statement composed of simpler statements in a fashion that makes it true whether the simpler statements are true or false; for example: *"Either you will live forever or you will not live forever."* Such statements are said to be empty or vacuous. On the bright side, a tautology can't possibly be false.

Another thing to remember before doing the next set of exercises is that certain kinds of statements are not likely to be anything but premises in most arguments. *Definitions*, for example, are likely to be used as a basis from which to reason, along with other premises, to a conclusion. *Self-evident claims* and *tautologies*—claims which cannot be false—are also likely to be used as premises, along with other premises, to argue to a conclusion. It would be rare to find an arguer trying to prove a self-evident claim!

Exercise 4-7

For each of the following, first determine if the passage contains an argument. If it does, underline premises, circle conclusions, and box off any premise or conclusion indicators; or number the statements and diagram the argument. If the passage does not contain an argument, put a check in the margin and indicate whether or not it contains a conditional statement.

*1. "Since [beauty] is no creature of our reason...[and] since it strikes us without reference to use...we must conclude that beauty is, for the greater part, some quality in bodies acting mechanically upon the human mind by the intervention of the senses."

2. Nothing can have value without being an object of utility. Therefore, only labor which is useful has any value.

3. "For over two thousand years mathematicians have been making correct inferences of a systematic and intricate sort, and logicians and philosophers have been analyzing the character of valid arguments."
--Patrick Suppes, *Introduction to Logic*

4. The unleashed power of the atom has changed everything except our modes of thinking. Therefore, we will drift toward unparalleled catastrophes. --Albert Einstein

5. "No testimony is sufficient to establish a miracle, unless the testimony be of such a kind that its falsehood would be more miraculous than the fact which it endeavors to establish." --David Hume, *An Enquiry Concerning Human Understanding*

*6. "We are an intelligent species and the use of our intelligence quite properly gives us pleasure. In this respect the brain is like a muscle. When it is in use we feel very good. Understanding is joyous." --Carl Sagan

*7. "Women are directly fitted for acting as the nurses and teachers of our early childhood by the fact that they are themselves childish, frivolous and short-sighted; in a word, they are big children all their life long...." --Arthur Schopenhauer, *Studies in Pessimism*, "Of Women"

8. "Surely human affairs would be far happier if the power in men to be silent were the same as that to speak. But experience more than sufficiently teaches that men govern nothing with more difficulty than their tongues." --Spinoza, *Ethics*, pt. III, proposition 2, note.

9. "If happiness is activity in accordance with excellence, it is reasonable that it should be in accordance with the highest excellence." --Aristotle, *Nicomachean Ethics*, bk. X, ch. 17.

10. "He whose honor depends on the opinion of the mob must day by day strive with the greatest anxiety, act and scheme in order to retain his reputation. For the mob is varied and inconstant." --Spinoza, *Ethics*, pt. IV, proposition 58, note.

11. "No violation of justice among citizens may be justified...by appeal to the ideal of equality, for that ideal is logically dependent upon the notion of justice. Reverse discrimination, then, which attempts no other justification than an appeal to equality, is wrong." --Lisa H. Newton, *Reverse Discrimination as Unjustified*

*12. "No educated man stating plainly the elementary notions that every educated man holds about the matters that principally concern government could be elected to office in a democratic state, save perhaps by a miracle. His frankness would arouse fear, and those fears would run against him; it is his business to arouse fears that will run in favor of him." --H.L. Mencken, *Notes on Democracy*

13. "The figure of the tyrant-monster is known to the mythologies, folk traditions, legends, and even nightmares, of the world; and his characteristics are everywhere essentially the same. He is the hoarder of the general benefit. He is the monster avid for the greedy rights of 'my and mine.'"--*The Hero with a Thousand Faces*, Joseph Campbell

14. "Affirmation of life is the spiritual act by which man ceases to live unreflectively and begins to devote himself to his life with reverence in order to raise it to its true value. To affirm life is to deepen, to make more inward, and to exalt the will to live." --Albert Schweitzer, *Out of My Life and Thought*

15. "If all mankind minus one were of one opinion, and only one person were of the contrary opinion, mankind would be no more justified in silencing that one person than he, if he had the power, would be justified in silencing mankind." --John Stuart Mill, *On Liberty*

16. Psychiatry is a fraud because it decides what is or is not a mental illness by democratic vote of its members: that's what it did with homosexuality. Before the vote was taken, homosexuality was a treatable mental illness; after the vote, homosexuality was no longer a mental illness.

17. "Two things fill the mind with ever-increasing wonder and awe, the more often and the more intensely the mind of thought is drawn to them: the starry heavens above me and the moral law within me." --Immanuel Kant, *Critique of Practical Reason*

18. "I refer those actions which work out the good of the agent to courage, and those which work out the good of others to nobility. Therefore temperance, sobriety, and presence of mind in danger, etc., are species of courage; but modesty, clemency, etc., are species of nobility." --Spinoza, *Ethics*, pt. III, proposition 59, note.

*19. I just don't see why multi-cultural education is so popular or why people think it is value-free. Multi-cultural education is not value-free, despite what its proponents say. It teaches children to respect and accept the evil values and practices of other cultures such as genital mutilation of young girls in Africa and handing out death sentences for blasphemy in Iran.

20. "The majority of men, I maintain, are dominated by a high opinion of their own skill and accomplishments, especially the perfection of their intellects for distinguishing true from false and sure guidance from misleading suggestion. It is therefore necessary, I maintain, to shut the gate so as to keep the general public from reading the books of the misguided as far as possible." --Algazali, *The Deliverance from Error*

21. "...[H]owever much health may contribute to that flow of good spirits which is so essential to our happiness, good spirits do not entirely depend upon health; for a man may be perfectly sound in his physique and still possess a melancholy temperament and be generally given up to sad thoughts." --Arthur Schopenhauer, *The Wisdom of Life*, "Personality, or What a Man Is"

22. "In our time, political speech and writing are largely the defense of the indefensible. Things like the continuance of British rule in India, the Russian purges and deportations, the dropping of the atom bombs on Japan, can indeed be defended, but only by arguments which are too brutal for most people to face, and which do not square with the professed aims of political parties. Thus political language has to consist largely of euphemism, question-begging, and sheer cloudy vagueness." --George Orwell, *Politics and the English Language*

*23. Restitution, rather than imprisonment should be required in those cases where property damage is the issue; for, sending a person to prison ought to be avoided whenever possible and the victim of a property crime is likely to be much more satisfied with our criminal justice system if he or she is repaid. If a criminal goes to prison, he is not going to be able to make restitution.

24. "Man can will nothing unless he has first understood that he must count on no one but himself; that he is alone, abandoned on earth in the midst of his infinite responsibilities, without help, with no other aim than the one he sets himself, with no other destiny than the one he forges for himself on this earth." --Jean Paul Sartre, *Being and Nothingness*

25. "A celebrated author and divine has written to me that 'he has gradually learnt to see that it is just as noble a conception of the Deity to believe that He created a few original forms capable of self-development into other and needful forms, as to believe that He required a fresh act of creation to supply the voids caused by the action of His laws.'" --*The Origin of Species*, Charles Darwin

26. "Homosexual pornography features an inordinate amount of sadomasochism....It is a striking fact that homosexuals seldom (to my knowledge, never) object to homosexual pornography on similar grounds; from which it would seem that the homosexual subculture makes no value distinctions among kinds of sexual relations but is, in principle, promiscuous." --Joseph Sobran, *Bogus Sex: Reflections on Homosexual Claims*

27. "Until philosophers are kings, or the kings and princes of this world have the spirit and power of philosophy, and political greatness and wisdom meet in one, and those commoner natures who pursue either to the exclusion of the other are compelled to stand aside, cities will never have rest from their evils--no, nor the human race, as I believe--and then only will this our State have a possibility of life and behold the light of day." -- Plato *The Republic*, V, 473-C.

*28. "To protect the workers in their inalienable rights to a higher and better life; to protect them, not only as equals before the law, but also in their health, their homes, their firesides, their liberties as men, as workers, and as citizens; to overcome and conquer prejudices and antagonism; to secure to them the right to life, and the opportunity to maintain that life; the right to be full sharers in the abundance which is the result of their brain and brawn, and the civilization of which they are the founders and the mainstay...The attainment of these is the glorious mission of the trade unions." -- Samuel Gompers

29. "Since I do not foresee that atomic energy is to be a great boon for a long time, I have to say that for the present it is a menace. Perhaps it is well that it should be. It may intimidate the human race into bringing order into its international affairs, which, without the pressure of fear, it would not do." --Albert Einstein, *Atlantic Monthly*, Nov. 1945.

30. "Philosophy is written in this grand book—I mean the universe—which stands continually open to our gaze, but it cannot be understood unless one first learns to comprehend the language and interpret the characters in which it is written. It is written in the language of mathematics, and its characters are triangles, circles, and other geometrical figures, without which it is humanly impossible to understand a single word of it; without these, one is wandering about in a dark labyrinth." --Galileo Galilei, *Il Saggiatore*

31. "Equal and exact justice to all men, of whatever state or persuasion, religious or political; peace, commerce, and honest friendship with all nations, entangling alliances with none...Freedom of religion; freedom of the press, and freedom of person under the protection of the habeas corpus, and trial by juries impartially selected. These principles form the bright

constellation which has gone before us, and guided our steps through an age of revolution and reformation. The wisdom of our sages and the blood of our heroes have been devoted to their attainment." --Thomas Jefferson, *First Inaugural Address*.

Exercise 4-8

The statements in each of the following passages are numbered. Diagram each argument and answer the questions that follow each passage. Do the asterisked problems first and check your answers in Answers to Selected Exercises.

*1. *[1] If Mary deliberately harmed Jane, then she ought to be punished. [2] Mary deliberately hurt Jane. Therefore, [3] Mary ought to be punished. And, since [4] Mary ought to be punished, [5] we should not invite her to dinner tonight.*

   1.1 Statement [1] is (a) a premise (b) a conclusion (c) both a premise and a conclusion (d) neither a premise nor a conclusion

   1.2 Statement [2] is (a) a premise (b) a conclusion (c) both a premise and a conclusion (d) neither a premise nor a conclusion

   1.3 Statement [3] is (a) a premise (b) a conclusion (c) both a premise and a conclusion (d) neither a premise nor a conclusion

   1.4 Statement [4] is (a) a premise (b) a conclusion (c) both a premise and a conclusion (d) neither a premise nor a conclusion

   1.5 Statement [5] is (a) a premise (b) a conclusion (c) both a premise and a conclusion (d) neither a premise nor a conclusion

   1.6 This argument has (a) a premise indicator (b)a conclusion indicator (c) both a premise and a conclusion indicator (d) neither a premise indicator nor a conclusion indicator

*2. *[1] You might think pornography is harmless, but let me tell you something. [2] If your mind is always in the gutter, you'll develop into a dirty old man. For, [3] the kinds of things you occupy your mind with will affect your character for the rest of your life.*

   2.1 Statement [1] is (a) a premise (b) a conclusion (c) both a premise and a conclusion (d) neither a premise nor a conclusion

   2.2 Statement [2] is (a) a premise (b) a conclusion (c) both a premise and a conclusion (d) neither a premise nor a conclusion

   2.3 Statement [3] is (a) a premise (b) a conclusion (c) both a premise and a conclusion (d) neither a premise nor a conclusion

   2.4 This argument has (a) a premise indicator (b) a conclusion indicator (c) both a premise and a conclusion indicator (d) neither a premise indicator nor a conclusion indicator

3. *[1] A miracle is a violation of the laws of nature. [2] Unalterable experience has established these laws. Therefore, [3] to believe in a miracle is to reject unalterable experience as a basis for belief in the laws of nature. Since [4] science is based upon a firm belief in the laws of nature, [5] to believe in miracles is to reject science.*

   3.1 Statement [1] is (a) a premise (b) a conclusion (c) both a premise and a conclusion (d) neither a premise nor a conclusion

   3.2 Statement [2] is (a) a premise (b) a conclusion (c) both a premise and a conclusion (d) neither a premise nor a conclusion

   3.3 Statement [3] is (a) a premise (b) a conclusion (c) both a premise and a conclusion (d) neither a premise nor a conclusion

   3.4 Statement [4] is (a) a premise (b) a conclusion (c) both a premise and a conclusion (d) neither a premise nor a conclusion

   3.5 Statement [5] is (a) a premise (b) a conclusion (c) both a premise and a conclusion (d) neither a premise nor a conclusion

   3.6 This argument has (a) a premise indicator (b)a conclusion indicator (c) both a premise and a conclusion indicator (d) neither a premise indicator nor a conclusion indicator

*4. [1] If God is All-Powerful, then nothing a human being does could affect Him. For, [2] if a human act could please or displease God, then human beings would have power over God. So, [3] either God is not All-Powerful or God doesn't give a hoot what you or I do. But, [4] if God isn't All-Powerful, then He isn't really God and He couldn't send us to Hell even if He wanted to. So, [5] sin at will; for, [6] either God doesn't care what we do or he cares but can't do anything about it.

4.1 Statement [1] is (a) a premise (b) a conclusion (c) both a premise and a conclusion (d) neither a premise nor a conclusion

4.2 Statement [2] is (a) a premise (b) a conclusion (c) both a premise and a conclusion (d) neither a premise nor a conclusion

4.3 Statement [3] is (a) a premise (b) a conclusion (c) both a premise and a conclusion (d) neither a premise nor a conclusion

4.4 Statement [4] is (a) a premise (b) a conclusion (c) both a premise and a conclusion (d) neither a premise nor a conclusion

4.5 Statement [5] is (a) a premise (b) a conclusion (c) both a premise and a conclusion (d) neither a premise nor a conclusion

4.6 Statement [6] is (a) a premise (b) a conclusion (c) both a premise and a conclusion (d) neither a premise nor a conclusion

4.7 This argument has (a) a premise indicator (b) a conclusion indicator (c) both a premise and a conclusion indicator (d) neither a premise indicator nor a conclusion indicator

*5. [1] To me the whole thing is simple. [2] If the white man's Holy book has the Truth, then there should be no disagreement about the Truth in the Holy Book. Therefore, [3] the white man's Holy Book does not have the Truth.

5.1 Statement [1] is (a) a premise (b) a conclusion (c) both a premise and a conclusion (d) neither a premise nor a conclusion

5.2 Statement [2] is (a) a premise (b) a conclusion (c) both a premise and a conclusion (d) neither a premise nor a conclusion

5.3 Statement [3] is (a) a premise (b) a conclusion (c) both a premise and a conclusion (d) neither a premise nor a conclusion

5.4 This argument has (a) a premise indicator (b) a conclusion indicator (c) both a premise and a conclusion indicator (d) neither a premise indicator nor a conclusion indicator

6. [1] Let me tell you my theory of crime and punishment. [2] If the behavior of criminals is determined by their heredity and environment, then they're not responsible for their crimes. [3] If they're not responsible for their crimes, then they shouldn't be punished. So, [4] if the behavior of criminals is determined by their heredity and environment, then they shouldn't be punished. For [5] a person should be punished only if he deserves it and a person can only deserve to be punished if they're responsible for their actions. [6] That's my opinion, anyway.

6.1 Statement [1] is (a) a premise (b) a conclusion (c) both a premise and a conclusion (d) neither a premise nor a conclusion

6.2 Statement [2] is (a) a premise (b) a conclusion (c) both a premise and a conclusion (d) neither a premise nor a conclusion

6.3 Statement [3] is (a) a premise (b) a conclusion (c) both a premise and a conclusion (d) neither a premise nor a conclusion

6.4 Statement [4] is (a) a premise (b) a conclusion (c) both a premise and a conclusion (d) neither a premise nor a conclusion

6.5 Statement [5] is (a) a premise (b) a conclusion (c) both a premise and a conclusion (d) neither a premise nor a conclusion

6.6 Statement [6] is (a) a premise (b) a conclusion (c) both a premise and a conclusion (d) neither a premise nor a conclusion

6.7 This argument has (a) a premise indicator (b) a conclusion indicator (c) both a premise and a conclusion indicator (d) neither a premise indicator nor a conclusion indicator

7. [1] A person should strive above all to achieve his or her own personal happiness. Therefore, [2] if an ethical system has the consequence of making people unhappy, it cannot be a good ethical system. So, [3] The ethics of self-sacrifice, of always

choosing what will make other people happy, without regard for your own well-being, cannot be a good ethical system.

7.1 Statement [1] is (a) a premise (b) a conclusion (c) both a premise and a conclusion (d) neither a premise nor a conclusion

7.2 Statement [2] is (a) a premise (b) a conclusion (c) both a premise and a conclusion (d) neither a premise nor a conclusion

7.3 Statement [3] is (a) a premise (b) a conclusion (c) both a premise and a conclusion (d) neither a premise nor a conclusion

7.4 This argument has (a) a premise indicator (b) a conclusion indicator (c) both a premise and a conclusion indicator (d) neither a premise indicator nor a conclusion indicator

8. *[1] To not hold a person responsible for their behavior is to treat them as if they were just a `thing', an object following laws of nature, not a human being with a moral sense and the freedom to choose to do or not do evil actions. Therefore, [2]to blame the environment or a person's heredity for their criminal behavior is to deny the criminal's humanity. [3] You might not agree, but that's how I feel.*

8.1 Statement [1] is (a) a premise (b) a conclusion (c) both a premise and a conclusion (d) neither a premise nor a conclusion

8.2 Statement [2] is (a) a premise (b) a conclusion (c) both a premise and a conclusion (d) neither a premise nor a conclusion

8.3 Statement [3] is (a) a premise (b) a conclusion (c) both a premise and a conclusion (d) neither a premise nor a conclusion

8.4 This argument has (a) a premise indicator (b) a conclusion indicator (c) both a premise and a conclusion indicator (d) neither a premise indicator nor a conclusion indicator

9. *"[1] If men and women try to create a society in which there is no fundamental agreement about good and evil they will fail; if, having based it on common agreement, the agreement goes, the society will disintegrate. For [2] society is not something that is kept together physically; it is held by the invisible bonds of common thought."* --Patrick Devlin, *The Enforcement of Morals*

9.1 Statement [1] is (a) a premise (b) a conclusion (c) both a premise and a conclusion (d) neither a premise nor a conclusion

9.2 Statement [2] is (a) a premise (b) a conclusion (c) both a premise and a conclusion (d) neither a premise nor a conclusion

9.3 This argument has (a) a premise indicator (b) a conclusion indicator (c) both a premise and a conclusion indicator (d) neither a premise indicator nor a conclusion indicator

10. *"[1]...[S]tereotyping involves not merely the attitudes of rigid people discriminating against racial and ethnic outgroups. [2] It is an inherent and inevitable aspect of every human appraisal of every person encountered. [3] It is therefore misleading to inquire about the presence or absence of stereotypes and prejudgments."* --G. McCall and J. Simmons, "Social Perception and Appraisal"

10.1 Statement [1] is (a) a premise (b) a conclusion (c) both a premise and a conclusion (d) neither a premise nor a conclusion

10.2 Statement [2] is (a) a premise (b) a conclusion (c) both a premise and a conclusion (d) neither a premise nor a conclusion

10.3 Statement [3] is (a) a premise (b) a conclusion (c) both a premise and a conclusion (d) neither a premise nor a conclusion

10.4 This argument has (a) a premise indicator (b) a conclusion indicator (c) both a premise and a conclusion indicator (d) neither a premise indicator nor a conclusion indicator

*11. *[1] If, throughout life, a person continues to define his or her life in terms of the concepts absorbed from his or her society as a child, then one will only be as rational and critical as one's society. [2] If a person is only as rational and critical as his or her own society, then in an irrational society, one will grow up to be irrational. Thus, [3] a person who does not reflect on the concepts absorbed as a child in an irrational society will grow up to be irrational. [4] Being unreflective, even in an irrational society, can be dangerous since [5] to be unreflective is to ignore life as one is actually* *finding it by experience to be. And [6] it is always more dangerous to live in a delusional world.*

11.1 Statement [1] is (a) a premise (b) a conclusion (c) both a premise and a conclusion (d) neither a premise nor a conclusion

11.2 Statement [2] is (a) a premise (b) a conclusion (c) both a premise and a conclusion (d) neither a premise nor a conclusion

11.3 Statement [3] is (a) a premise (b) a conclusion (c) both a premise and a conclusion (d) neither a premise nor a conclusion

11.4 Statement [4] is (a) a premise (b) a conclusion (c) both a premise and a conclusion (d) neither a premise nor a conclusion

11.5 Statement [5] is (a) a premise (b) a conclusion (c) both a premise and a conclusion (d) neither a premise nor a conclusion

11.6 Statement [6] is (a) a premise (b) a conclusion (c) both a premise and a conclusion (d) neither a premise nor a conclusion

11.7 This passage has (a) a premise indicator (b)a conclusion indicator (c) both a premise and a conclusion indicator (d) neither a premise indicator nor a conclusion indicator

*12. [1] There are only three alternatives possible for the origin of the world: it is self-existent, or self-caused, or caused by some external agency. And [2] each of these alternatives is really without meaning to our minds. [3]We cannot conceive that a thing exists in its own right without any source beyond itself; [4]we cannot conceive self-creation, for [5] that implies that the thing exists before it exists; and [6] to refer it to an external creator merely defers the question. For [7] we have to ask, Whence the creator?" --*William Ernest Hocking, *Types of Philosophy*

12.1 Statement [1] is (a) a premise (b) a conclusion (c) both a premise and a conclusion (d) neither a premise nor a conclusion

12.2 Statement [2] is (a) a premise (b) a conclusion (c) both a premise and a conclusion (d) neither a premise nor a conclusion

12.3 Statement [3] is (a) a premise (b) a conclusion (c) both a premise and a conclusion (d) neither a premise nor a conclusion

12.4 Statement [4] is (a) a premise (b) a conclusion (c) both a premise and a conclusion (d) neither a premise nor a conclusion

12.5 Statement [5] is (a) a premise (b) a conclusion (c) both a premise and a conclusion (d) neither a premise nor a conclusion

12.6 Statement [6] is (a) a premise (b) a conclusion (c) both a premise and a conclusion (d) neither a premise nor a conclusion

12.7 Statement [7] is (a) a premise (b) a conclusion (c) both a premise and a conclusion (d) neither a premise nor a conclusion

12.8 This argument has (a) a premise indicator (b)a conclusion indicator (c) both a premise and a conclusion indicator (d) neither a premise indicator nor a conclusion indicator

13. *[1] It is unreasonable to believe in punishment in the afterlife. For, [2] either there is no afterlife or there is one. [3] If there is none, then it is absurd to believe in punishment after death. [4] If there is an afterlife, then an all-just and all-merciful God would not punish a creature for being too weak to resist desires instilled by the Creator.*

13.1 Statement [1] is (a) a premise (b) a conclusion (c) both a premise and a conclusion (d) neither a premise nor a conclusion

13.2 Statement [2] is (a) a premise (b) a conclusion (c) both a premise and a conclusion (d) neither a premise nor a conclusion

13.3 Statement [3] is (a) a premise (b) a conclusion (c) both a premise and a conclusion (d) neither a premise nor a conclusion

13.4 Statement [4] is (a) a premise (b) a conclusion (c) both a premise and a conclusion (d) neither a premise nor a conclusion

13.5 This argument has (a) a premise indicator (b)a conclusion indicator (c) both a premise and a conclusion indicator (d) neither a premise indicator nor a conclusion indicator

14. *[1]The death penalty does not deter potential murderers. Therefore, [2] it ought to be abolished. And, [3] even if it does deter others, it still ought to be abolished; for, [4] the only reason which could justify intentionally killing anyone would be that the person deserved to be killed.*

    14.1 Statement [1] is (a) a premise (b) a conclusion (c) both a premise and a conclusion (d) neither a premise nor a conclusion
    14.2 Statement [2] is (a) a premise (b) a conclusion (c) both a premise and a conclusion (d) neither a premise nor a conclusion
    14.3 Statement [3] is (a) a premise (b) a conclusion (c) both a premise and a conclusion (d) neither a premise nor a conclusion
    14.4 Statement [4] is (a) a premise (b) a conclusion (c) both a premise and a conclusion (d) neither a premise nor a conclusion
    14.5 This argument has (a) a premise indicator (b)a conclusion indicator (c) both a premise and a conclusion indicator (d) neither a premise indicator nor a conclusion indicator

15. "[1] Belief must have an object. For, [2] he that believes must believe something; and [3] that which he believes is called the object of his belief. [4] Of this object of his belief, he must have some conception, clear or obscure; for [5] although there may be the most clear and distinct conception of an object without any belief of its existence, there can be no belief without conception." --Thomas Reid, Essays on the Intellectual Powers of Man

    15.1 Statement [1] is (a) a premise (b) a conclusion (c) both a premise and a conclusion (d) neither a premise nor a conclusion
    15.2 Statement [2] is (a) a premise (b) a conclusion (c) both a premise and a conclusion (d) neither a premise nor a conclusion
    15.3 Statement [3] is (a) a premise (b) a conclusion (c) both a premise and a conclusion (d) neither a premise nor a conclusion
    15.4 Statement [4] is (a) a premise (b) a conclusion (c) both a premise and a conclusion (d) neither a premise nor a conclusion
    15.5 Statement [5] is (a) a premise (b) a conclusion (c) both a premise and a conclusion (d) neither a premise nor a conclusion
    15.6 This passage has (a) a premise indicator (b)a conclusion indicator (c) both a premise and a conclusion indicator (d) neither a premise indicator nor a conclusion indicator

16. *Since [1] beauty "is no creature of our reason, since [2] it strikes us without any reference to use, and...since [3] the order and method of nature is generally very different from our measures and proportions, we must conclude that [4] beauty is, for the greater part, some quality in bodies acting mechanically upon the human mind by the intervention of the senses."* --Edmund Burke, *On the Sublime and Beautiful*, III.xii

    16.1 Statement [1] is (a) a premise (b) a conclusion (c) both a premise and a conclusion (d) neither a premise nor a conclusion
    16.2 Statement [2] is (a) a premise (b) a conclusion (c) both a premise and a conclusion (d) neither a premise nor a conclusion
    16.3 Statement [3] is (a) a premise (b) a conclusion (c) both a premise and a conclusion (d) neither a premise nor a conclusion
    16.4 Statement [4] is (a) a premise (b) a conclusion (c) both a premise and a conclusion (d) neither a premise nor a conclusion
    16.5 This argument has (a) a premise indicator (b)a conclusion indicator (c) both a premise and a conclusion indicator (d) neither a premise indicator nor a conclusion indicator

17. *[1] All is One. [2] If all is One, then individuals do not exist. Therefore, [3] individuals do not exist. And since [4] murder is the unjustified killing of one individual by another, it follows that [5] murder does not exist. [6] If murder does not exist, then my client cannot be guilty of murder. Therefore, [7] my client cannot be guilty of murder.*

    17.1 Statement [1] is (a) a premise (b) a conclusion (c) both a premise and a conclusion (d) neither a premise nor a conclusion

17.2 Statement [2] is (a) a premise (b) a conclusion (c) both a premise and a conclusion (d) neither a premise nor a conclusion

17.3 Statement [3] is (a) a premise (b) a conclusion (c) both a premise and a conclusion (d) neither a premise nor a conclusion

17.4 Statement [4] is (a) a premise (b) a conclusion (c) both a premise and a conclusion (d) neither a premise nor a conclusion

17.5 Statement [5] is (a) a premise (b) a conclusion (c) both a premise and a conclusion (d) neither a premise nor a conclusion

17.6 Statement [6] is (a) a premise (b) a conclusion (c) both a premise and a conclusion (d) neither a premise nor a conclusion

17.7 Statement [7] is (a) a premise (b) a conclusion (c) both a premise and a conclusion (d) neither a premise nor a conclusion

17.8 This argument has (a) a premise indicator (b)a conclusion indicator (c) both a premise and a conclusion indicator (d) neither a premise indicator nor a conclusion indicator

4. Inductive and deductive arguments

Traditional logic divides arguments into two types: *deductive* and *inductive*. We will conclude this chapter with a brief description of the nature of both types of argument, as well as of their major differences. The two types of arguments may be evaluated by quite different methods, as we will see in the following chapter.

4.1. Deduction

Aristotle (384-322 B.C.E.) is considered the father of Logic because he was the first philosopher to develop a systematic way of analyzing and evaluating reasoning. He developed techniques for distinguish good reasoning from bad reasoning. His Logic is based upon a theory of the relationship of reality to thought and of thought to language. His goal seems to have been to develop a systematic way to *demonstrate* the truth of every true statement. Aristotle knew, as every logician since has known, that *language* itself is the main stumbling block to developing a systematic way to prove the truth of all true statements. Everyday language is not clear and precise enough to do the job.[2] Even if the mind grasps the truth, stating that truth in clear, unambiguous terms proves to be a very difficult task. Worse, though, is the fact that using ordinary language with its sloppy and undisciplined ways of expression tends to make us sloppy and undisciplined thinkers. The solution: translate those thoughts that truly reflect reality into an artificial language in which every term is clear, precise, and unambiguous. Language can then be used not only to communicate the truth but to deduce further truths. The problem, however, is that something is lost in the translation. One thing that is lost is the truth about language itself. Language has many equally legitimate functions. Communicating the truth is just one of them.

Furthermore, not only language, but *reality* is more elusive and less fixed than Aristotle thought. The attempt to connect reality, thought, and language through a system of logic gets very complicated. Nevertheless, one very important element of Aristotle's Logic will always remain significant and essential. This element is perhaps best seen by examining his definition of a *syllogism*.

Aristotle defined a *syllogism* as "discourse in which, certain things being stated, something other than what is stated follows of necessity from their being so" (*Prior Analytics*, I.1). The concept of *following of necessity* is now considered the essential defining characteristic of *deduction*. The kind of reasoning Aristotle evaluated was a direct outcome of his beliefs about reality, truth, and language, especially his notion that language can reflect thought which in turn can reflect reality. Today, only one part of deductive logic is devoted to evaluating Aristotelian syllogisms. Still, the concern of modern deductive logic focuses, as does Aristotelian logic, on the concepts of *logical inferences* and *logical implications*. What matters in the analysis of reasoning according to the standards of modern deductive logic is whether one sentence or set of sentences *implies* the truth of another sentence. Modern logic is concerned with what Aristotle was concerned with: "discourse in which, certain things being stated, something other than what is stated follows of necessity from their being so."

What does it mean for one sentence to *follow of necessity* from another sentence or set of sentences? For example, what does it mean to say that from the statements "All men are mortal" and "Socrates is a man", *it follows of necessity* that "Socrates is mortal"? It means that if it is true that all men are mortal and that Socrates is a man, then *it must also be true* that Socrates is mortal. In Logic, when a statement (call it "q") is said to follow of necessity from another (call it "p"), we say that **p implies q**. Or, we say that **q may be logically inferred from p**. For example, the statement "All bachelors are unmarried and Sergio is a bachelor" *logically implies* "Sergio is unmarried." And the statement "Sergio is unmarried" may be *logically inferred* from the statement "All bachelors are unmarried and Sergio is a bachelor."

4.2 Induction

We have seen that the concept of *necessary connection* between statements is the defining characteristic of deductive arguments. A deductive argument claims that its premises provide sufficient proof of the truth of its conclusion. There are many arguments, however, that do not claim that their premises are sufficient to *prove with necessity* that a conclusion is true. Many, if not most, arguments one is likely to hear in daily life will make the claim that their premises provide *reasonable grounds* (rather than necessity) for their conclusions. Such arguments are called *inductive* arguments. The premises of inductive arguments, even if true, do not provide sufficient grounds for establishing the truth of their conclusions. No matter how strong the evidence is in an inductive argument, it will never prove its conclusion with necessity. At best, an inductive argument can provide proof to a high degree of *probability*.

Since the conclusions of inductive arguments do not follow with necessity from their premises, it is possible for a good inductive argument to have true premises but a false conclusion. How a *good* argument could have a *false* conclusion needs some explaining. It is attributable to the nature of induction. Our notion of *inductive* reasoning is based on our belief that *induction* is usually *empirical*. Empirical induction is based on observation or experience or the testimony of others. Nothing based on experience, observation, or testimony can be known with *infallible certainty*. The best that can be hoped for with regard to empirical truth is a *high degree of probability*. Empirical inferences are interpretations or explanations of sense experience; they are by nature fallible. Nevertheless, most human affairs can be conducted quite reasonably based on less-than-perfect evidence and reasoning. For example, no criminal court requires proof stronger than proof *beyond a reasonable doubt*. No conclusion of guilt will ever follow necessarily from evidence presented in a court of law, nor could the evidence itself ever be proved to be necessarily true. Even if a defendant confesses, guilt cannot be logically inferred from the confession. He could be lying to protect someone else. He could be deluded and think he did something he did not actually do. Even a dozen reliable witnesses could be wrong in identifying an individual as the perpetrator of a crime. No matter how incriminating the evidence might be, there is always some possible doubt that could be presented.

In a court of law, a prosecutor does not have to present evidence sufficient to prove that the defendant is *necessarily* guilty. Such proof would be unreasonable. On the other hand, the defense cannot refute the prosecutor's argument by introducing a *possible* doubt as to guilt. That, too, would be unreasonable. Before a jury decides that a defendant is guilty, the evidence should be strong. It should prove guilt beyond a *reasonable* doubt. It may be *possible* that twelve reliable witnesses are wrong about who they saw commit a crime, but is it *reasonable* to believe they are all in error? Those are two different questions. Only the latter one is relevant in a court of law.

A jury may conclude that an innocent person is guilty as charged beyond a reasonable doubt. Nevertheless, the jury's decision is not necessarily unreasonable. They may have made a very reasonable decision based on the evidence and arguments presented to them. Still, they could be wrong. Scientists may conclude something that later turns out to be false. Nevertheless, the scientists' decision is not necessarily unreasonable. They may have made a very reasonable decision based on the evidence before them. Journalists may report something that turns out to be false. Again, their report may have been very reasonable, given the information available to them.

On the other hand, inductive arguments may be based on values. Such arguments are notoriously difficult to reduce to deductive proofs with unquestionable premises. Here is a list of such topics. Each of these topics is likely to have contradictory arguers who believe they have reasonable grounds for accepting their position.

Is morality relative? Should drugs (abortion, euthanasia) be legalized? Should prostitution (gambling, pornography) be illegal? Should capital punishment be abolished? Is affirmative action morally right? Is killing human beings ever justified? Do rich nations have a duty to help poorer nations? Does a government have a duty to look out for the health, education and general welfare of its citizens? Is it ever justified to disobey the law? Does the ownership of a socially valued object or talent obligate one not to destroy it? Does a person have a natural right to commit suicide? Is it immoral to eat meat? Is it justifiable to kill animals for sport? or clothing? or food? Is it justifiable to capture and train animals to entertain humans? Should racist or sexist language be illegal?

The list of endlessly debatable items is endless. Nevertheless, on many of these issues we make decisions and feel comfortable with the reasonableness of our decisions. If we change our minds on a controversial issue, it need not be because we arrived at our first belief unreasonably. We may have; but we may also have arrived at our first belief reasonably. Our new belief, although contradicting our old belief, may indicate the discovery of new information. It may indicate a deeper delving into an issue. It may indicate recognition of an inconsistency with other beliefs.

Thus, when we say that a good inductive argument might have true or reasonable premises but a false conclusion, we do not mean that inductive arguments are unreasonable or flawed. We do not consider fallibility a flaw. It is a fact of the human condition. It is little more than mysticism to assert that being infallible would make us perfect. As critical thinkers we must not fret over the fact of our fallibility and lack of absolute certainty about many, if not most, of the important issues that face us. We must accept our situation and make the best of it. That is, we must determine our beliefs and actions on the most reasonable grounds we can muster.

Exercise 4-9 Self-test: true or false? (Check your answers in Answers to Selected Exercises.)

1. The statements which comprise a conditional statement are neither affirmed nor denied.
2. A sub-argument is one whose conclusion is the main conclusion of a complex argument.
3. Both the premises and the conclusion of an argument are asserted (i.e. stated or claimed)..
4. An argument requires that at least one assertion be given in support of the truth of at least one other assertion.
5. Conditional statements and arguments have in common the fact that antecedents and premises are asserted to be true.
6. All arguments have premise or conclusion indicators.
7. A conditional statement is one which joins simple statements together with the connector 'if' or the connectors 'if...then'.
8. The assumptions of an argument are the basic premises upon which the argument stands or falls.
9. Some passages are vague or ambiguous and there is no clear-cut correct interpretation of them as containing an argument.
10. A conjunction joins simple statements together, usually using the word 'or', or using the expression 'either...or'.
11. A complex statement is one which consists of two or more simple statements.
12. An assumption in an argument is a premise for which no support is given.
13. An argument is a simple statement of one's opinions, without providing any support for them.
14. All arguments involve giving reasons in support of a claim or position.
15. An argument may have ten premises and four conclusions.
16. A premise is a statement given as a reason for accepting some claim.
17. Words such as 'since', 'because' and 'for' often indicate that the next assertion is a premise.

18. Words such as 'evidence' and 'support' often mean the same thing as 'premise.'

19. Conditional statements may appear as premises or conclusions in arguments.

20. A conclusion is a statement given as a reason for accepting some claim.

21. Words which may be used as premise or conclusion indicators may also be used for other purposes.

22. A conclusion of one argument may not be used as a premise in another argument.

23. An argument is any group of statements related as premise to conclusion.

24. An argument is the presentation of at least one claim to support the truth or reasonableness of at least one other claim.

25. The conclusion of an argument is the statement made last in the argument.

26. Conditional statements are types of arguments.

27. Words such as 'therefore', 'hence', and 'thus' often indicate that the next assertion is a conclusion.

28. A premise is always preceded by an indicator such as 'because'.

29. The conclusion of an argument is sometimes the first statement in the argument.

30. For a statement to be part of an argument, it must be either a premise or a conclusion.

31. A deductive argument is one whose premises try to prove its conclusion with necessity.

32. An inductive argument is one whose premises try to prove its conclusion to some degree of probability.

33. To say that a sentence 'q' "follows necessarily from" another sentence 'p' is to say that *p implies q*.

34. To say that a sentence 'q' may be inferred from a sentence 'p' is to say that *p implies q*.

35. Many inductive arguments are about values.

Further Reading

Copi, Irving M. and Cohen, Carl. (2001) *Introduction to Logic*. 11th edition. Dark Alley.

Hurley, Patrick J. (2002) *A Concise Introduction to Logic*. 8th edition. Wadsworth.

Notes – Chapter Four

[1]Logicians distinguish disjunctions such as "Either Sheila cheated or she failed the exam" from those such as "Either Sheila cheated or she did not cheat." The latter is an *exclusive* disjunction. It asserts that one of the disjuncts is true but not both. "Either Bob Dylan is the greatest poet who ever lived or Yeats is the greatest poet who ever lived" is also an *exclusive* disjunction. This asserts that one of the disjuncts it true but not both. An *inclusive* disjunction is one where at least one disjunct is true, but both may be true. There are many disjunctions that are ambiguous; it is not clear whether they are intended to be exclusive or inclusive. If it is not absolutely necessary to treat a disjunction as exclusive, we will assume it is inclusive. Since it is possible that "Sheila cheated" and "she failed the exam" are both true, the disjunction "Either Sheila cheated or she failed the exam" will be considered as inclusive, even though a person uttering this disjunction probably believes that if she passed the exam, then she cheated and if she failed then she did not cheat.

[2]A most skeptical formulation of the problem was asserted by Gorgias, made famous by Plato's dialogue of the same name. Gorgias allegedly said that there is nothing but that even if there were something we couldn't know anything about it and even if we could know something we couldn't communicate what we knew to anyone else. Plato dismissed Gorgias's claim as self-contradictory on the grounds that Gorgias was communicating something he thought he knew.

Chapter Five - Evaluating Arguments

"Negative logic [i.e., that which points out weaknesses in theory or errors in practice without establishing positive truths]...would indeed be poor enough as an ultimate result, but as a means to attaining any positive knowledge or conviction worthy of the name it cannot be valued too highly."
--John Stuart Mill

1. Two models for evaluating arguments

In the previous chapter, we noted that logicians distinguish two kinds of arguments, inductive and deductive. Logic is also often divided into two types, *formal* and *informal*. Each uses a distinct method of analyzing and evaluating arguments. *Informal logic*—or *critical thinking* as it is usually called—focuses on the evaluation of arguments in natural language. Critical thinking methods may be used to evaluate any argument. *Formal logic*, on the other hand, evaluates argument *forms* presented in *symbols* (for statements, parts of statements, connectives, and argument indicators). The formal method is useful primarily to evaluate the *validity* of deductive argument *forms*.

2. Deductive validity

In the previous chapter, we defined deductive reasoning as reasoning that starts with some statement or set of statements (**the premises**) and asserts that some other statement follows *necessarily* from those premises. Put another way, a deductive argument is one whose premises, *if true*, are sufficient to guarantee the truth of their conclusion. Determining whether the premises of a deductive argument are true is a different task from determining whether something follows with necessity from a statement or set of statements. The latter task is concerned with the *validity* of the reasoning.

A deductive argument is **valid** if the truth of its premises is sufficient to guarantee the truth of its conclusion. The argument *"All men are mortal. Socrates is a man. So, Socrates is mortal"* is an example of a **valid deductive argument**. The truth of the statements "All men are mortal" and "Socrates is a man" would be sufficient to guarantee the truth of the conclusion, "Socrates is mortal."

To put it another way, it would be *logically impossible* for it to be true that all men are mortal and true that Socrates is a man, but false that Socrates is mortal.

A deductive argument is **invalid** if the truth of its premises is *not* sufficient to guarantee the truth of its conclusion. For example, the following deductive argument is *invalid*:

Some men are tall. Socrates is a man. So, it necessarily follows that Socrates is tall.

The truth of these premises does not guarantee the truth of this conclusion. It is true that some men are tall and that Socrates is a man, but Socrates could be a short man. (Note: Even if it happens to be true that Socrates is tall, this would still not be a good argument. Can you figure out why?)

Here is another example of an *invalid* deductive argument:

If Jon caught a fish, then we're having fish for dinner. Jon didn't catch a fish. So we're not having fish for dinner.

To say that this conclusion does not follow necessarily from its premises, and that this argument is therefore **invalid**, is to say that it could still be true that we are having fish for dinner even if these premises are true. The first premise only states what we're having for dinner if Jon catches a fish. It says nothing about what we're having for dinner if he doesn't catch a fish. Jon can always buy some fish for dinner from the local fish dealer. We might consider it *misleading* for Jon to say that if he catches a fish we'll have fish for dinner, when he intended to have fish no matter how successful his fishing expedition might be. However, it would not be logically impossible for these premises to be true and the conclusion false. Thus, the argument is not valid. In a valid deductive argument, it is logically impossible for the premises to be true and the conclusion false.

Here is an example of a **valid deductive argument**:

If Jon caught a fish, then we're having fish for dinner. Jon caught a fish. So, we're having fish for dinner.

If the premises of this argument are true, the conclusion must be true, too. The truth of these premises would be sufficient to guarantee the truth of the conclusion. It would be logically impossible for these premises to be true and the conclusion false.

2.1 Formal logic and some valid deductive argument forms

Formal logic focuses mainly on the evaluation of the validity of deductive argument *forms*. We can best see the form of an argument by presenting it in symbols. (**Formal logic** is often referred to as **symbolic logic**.) Different tests of validity have been devised for several distinct types of deductive argument forms. One type of evaluation uses **rules of inference** to evaluate arguments put into a particular type of symbolic form. In the next section, you will be introduced to four rules of inference and be given a brief introduction to a formal, symbolic logic, known as **sentential logic**. It is called sentential logic because *the sentence* (and its truth or falsity) is taken as the basic component of an argument. (Other logics, such as **predicate logic**, evaluate arguments in terms of the *components* of sentences, such as *subjects* and *predicates*.)

2.2 Some valid and invalid argument forms in sentential logic

One of the most important tasks of formal logic is to identify valid argument forms. An argument form is determined by the number and kinds of statements that make up the argument. For example, one valid form of argument is called **disjunctive syllogism**. It has the following form:

Either p or q.
Not p.
So, q.

A complete symbolic representation of this argument in sentential logic would be:

$p \lor q$
$\sim p / \therefore q$

p and **q** represent sentences used to make statements. The floating wedge, ∨, symbolizes the connective *either...or*. The tilde, ~, symbolizes negation. And the backslash, /, represents the end of the premises, while ∴ indicates that the conclusion follows.

Any argument that has the form of the disjunctive syllogism is valid. Substitute any statement for **p** (the same statement must be used for each occurrence of **p**) and another statement for **q**. The resulting argument will always be valid. For example, let **p** = 'It will snow' and let **q** = 'It will be sunny.' The following argument will be valid:

> **Either it will snow or it will be sunny.**
> **It will not snow.**
> **So, it will be sunny.**

If these premises are true, this conclusion must be true, too. The conclusion *follows necessarily* from the premises in this argument. That is what makes the argument **valid**.

Establishing *validity* is a separate issue from establishing the *truth* of the premises. The premises of a valid argument may be false. The validity of the argument depends on the *relationship* of the premises to the conclusion, not on the truth of the premises. A valid relationship, we might say, is *truth-conditional*: *if* the premises are true *then* it is necessarily the case that the conclusion is true. *A cogent or sound deductive argument must fulfill* two *conditions: it must be valid and it must have true premises.*

Probably the easiest way to learn the difference between truth and validity is to recognize that you can determine whether or not an argument is valid without knowing whether the premises are true or false. In the above example of an argument in the form of a disjunctive syllogism, you do not need to know whether it is true that it will either snow or be sunny, nor do you need to know whether it is true that it will not snow, in order to know that the argument is valid, i.e., that the statement 'it will be sunny' follows necessarily from the statements 'either it will snow or it will be sunny' and 'it will not snow.'

The argument form of disjunctive syllogism is as follows:

> Premise 1 is a disjunction;
> Premise 2 denies one of the disjuncts of premise 1;
> The conclusion is the other disjunct of premise 1.

Any argument that has the form of disjunctive syllogism is a valid argument.

Another valid form of argument is **modus ponens**, which has the form

> **If p then q.**
> **p.**
> **So, q.**

The ⊃ symbol represents *if...then*. A complete symbolic representation of **modus ponens** would be

p ⊃ q
p /∴ q

Let **p** = 'It will rain' and let **q** = 'Jones will bring an umbrella.' The following argument will be valid:

> **If it will rain then Jones will bring an umbrella.**
> **It will rain.**
> **So, Jones will bring an umbrella.**

If these premises are true, then this conclusion must be true. Again, notice that you do not have to know whether the premises are true to know that the argument is valid, i.e., to know that *if* the premises were true it would be necessary that the conclusion be true. Also, notice that the argument form of modus ponens is:

Premise 1 is a conditional statement;
Premise 2 states the antecedent of the conditional in premise 1;
The conclusion states the consequent of the conditional in premise 1.

Any argument that has the form of modus ponens is a valid argument.
 A third valid form of argument is **modus tollens.**

If p then q.
Not q.
So, not p.

(You should be able to figure out what the symbolic representation of modus tollens would look like.)

Let **p** = 'The President is honest' and let **q** = 'He is telling the truth.' The following argument will be valid:

If the President is honest then he is telling the truth.
He is not telling the truth.
So, the President is not honest.

If these premises are true, then this conclusion must be true, too. The form of modus tollens is:

Premise 1 is a conditional statement;
Premise 2 denies the consequent of the conditional statement in premise 1;
The conclusion is the denial of the antecedent of the conditional statement in premise 1.

Any argument that has the form of modus tollens is a valid argument.
 We will consider one more valid argument form: the **hypothetical syllogism**, which has the following form.

If p then q.
If q then r.
So, if p then r.

(You should be able to figure out what the symbolic representation of hypothetical syllogism would look like.)
Let **p** = 'The Dodgers traded Sax' and let **q** = 'The Giants will defeat the Dodgers' and let **r** = 'The Dodgers won't win the pennant.' The following argument will be valid:

If the Dodgers traded Sax then the Giants will defeat the Dodgers.
If the Giants (will) defeat the Dodgers then the Dodgers won't win the pennant.
So, if the Dodgers traded Sax then the Dodgers won't win the pennant.

If these premises are true, then this conclusion must be true, too. And, any argument that has the form of hypothetical syllogism is a valid argument.

Each of the valid deductive forms has in common the fact that it would be logically impossible for the premises of the argument to be true but the conclusion false. Any argument that is stated in one of these forms will always be a *valid* argument: its conclusion will follow necessarily from its premises. In short, each of these valid deductive argument forms may be used as a *rule of inference* in deductive proofs.

We will not go any deeper into this subject, but there are many excellent texts available to those who wish to pursue formal logic in depth. We will conclude our brief discussion of formal logic with a look at two *invalid* argument forms.

2.3 Two invalid deductive argument forms

An invalid deductive argument is one whose conclusion does *not* follow necessarily from its premises.

2.3.1 Affirming the Consequent

Compare the following pairs of arguments. One pair is in the valid form of **modus ponens**, while the other is in the invalid form of **affirming the consequent**. Study the invalid forms carefully. Notice how the premises of the invalid forms could be true, but their conclusions could be false. In a valid deductive argument, however, the conclusion follows necessarily from the premises: it is not possible for the premises to be true and the conclusion false in a valid deductive argument. *It is possible, however, for an* **invalid** *argument to have* **true** *premises and a* **true** *conclusion.* Remember: *validity refers to the* **inference** *of a conclusion from premises, not to the* **truth** *of the premises or conclusion.*

1. If interest rates are down, then the economy is in a recession. Interest rates are down. So, the economy is in a recession.
2. If Jones is married to Smith then Smith is an attorney. Jones is married to Smith. So, Smith is an attorney.

1. If interest rates are down, then the economy is in a recession. The economy is in a recession. So, interest rates are down.
2. If Jones is married to Smith then Smith is an attorney. Smith is an attorney. So, Jones is married to Smith.

modus ponens

(valid)

affirming the consequent

(invalid)

It may still not be clear to you how the premises could be true and the conclusion false in the invalid arguments just presented. It may help to remember that the conditional statement asserts that the antecedent provides a sufficient reason for the consequent. Thus, the conditional *if interest rates are down then the economy is in recession* asserts that the interest rates being down would be a sufficient reason for believing that the economy is in a recession. It does not say any more than that. It does not say, for instance, that interest rates *are* down. It does not say anything about the economy for the condition of interest rates being *up*. You might think that the statement logically implies that if interest rates are *not* up then the economy is *not* in a recession, but it does not. It does not say that *only if* interest rates are down are we in a recession. It leaves it open as to whether there might be other conditions besides interest rates being down which might be sufficient to warrant believing that there is a recession.

You might think that the conditional *if Jones is married to Smith then Smith is an attorney* logically implies that if Jones is *not* married to Smith then Smith is *not* an attorney. It doesn't. The conditional asserts that Jones being married to Smith is sufficient to warrant believing that Smith is an attorney. It does not say that *only if* Jones is married to Smith are we warranted in believing that Smith is an attorney. It does not say anything about Smith's occupation should it be true that Jones is *not* married to Smith. It may well be true that if Jones is married to Smith then Smith is an attorney. (Maybe Jones only marries attorneys.) However, if Jones is not married to Smith, it might still be true that Smith is an attorney.

2.3.2 Denying the Antecedent

Compare the pairs of arguments below. One pair is in the valid form of **modus tollens**, while the other is in the invalid form of **denying the antecedent**. Study the invalid forms carefully and notice how the premises of the invalid forms could be true, but their conclusions could be false.

1. If interest rates are down, then the economy is in a recession. The economy is not in a recession. So, interest rates are not down. *2. If Jones is married to Smith then Smith is an attorney. Smith is not an attorney. So, Jones is not married to Smith.*

modus tollens
(valid)

1. If interest rates are down, then the economy is in a recession. Interest rates are not down. So, the economy is not in a recession. *2. If Jones is married to Smith then Smith is an attorney. Jones is not married to Smith. So, Smith is not an attorney.*

denying the antecedent
(invalid)

Exercises 5-1

A. For each of the following arguments, identify the argument form as one of those valid or invalid forms mentioned above. [Exercises with an * are answered in Answers to Selected Exercises.]

* 1. If this house is a solar home then it is expensive. This house is not expensive, so it is not a solar home.
  2. If this house is a solar home, then it is expensive. It is expensive. So, this house is a solar home.
* 3. If this house is a solar home, then it is expensive. It is a solar home. So, it is expensive.
  4. If Jones stole the sign then he should be prosecuted. He should not be prosecuted. So, Jones did not steal the sign.
  5. If Jones stole the sign then he should be prosecuted. Jones did not steal the sign. So, he should not be prosecuted.
*6. If Jones stole the sign then he should be prosecuted. He should be prosecuted. So, Jones stole the sign.
  7. If Jones stole the sign then he should be prosecuted. Jones stole the sign. So, he should be prosecuted.
  8. Either the Republicans will win the senate election or the ambassador will resign. The Republicans will not win the senate election. So, the ambassador will resign.
  9. If Rosetta wins an academy award then MGM will reap a windfall in profits. If MGM will reap a windfall in profits then we should invest in MGM. So, if Rosetta wins an academy award, then we should invest in MGM.
  10. If the hero of this myth is superhuman then this myth is a religious myth. The hero of this myth is a superhuman hero. So, this myth is a religious myth.
  11. If the hero of this myth is superhuman then this myth is a religious myth. This myth is not a religious myth. So, the hero of this myth is not a superhuman.
* 12. If the hero of this myth is superhuman then this myth is a religious myth. The hero of this myth is not a superhuman. So, this myth is not a religious myth.
  13. If the hero of this myth is a superhuman then this myth is a religious myth. This myth is a religious myth. So, the hero of this myth is a superhuman.

* 14. If this myth involves superhuman struggles against evil, then this myth is a religious myth. If this myth is a religious myth, then its hero is superhuman. So, if this myth involves superhuman struggles against evil, its hero is superhuman.

15. Either the elephant has escaped from its cage or the zookeeper is sleeping on the job. The zookeeper is not sleeping on the job. So, the elephant has escaped from its cage.

16. If there is evil in the universe, then the maker of the universe is evil. There is evil in the universe. So, the maker of the universe is evil.

17. If the creator of the universe is evil, then there is evil in creation. The creator of the universe is not evil. So, there is no evil in creation.

18. If there is evil in the universe, then the creator is evil. The creator is not evil. So, it is not true that there is evil in the universe.

* 19. Either France will go to war with Denmark or Denmark will invade Albania. France will not go to war with Denmark. So, Denmark will invade Albania.

20. If France went to war with Denmark then Croatia went to war with Hungary. If Croatia went to war with Hungary then Italy remained neutral. So, if France went to war with Denmark, then Italy remained neutral.

B. Each of the following arguments is incomplete. Such arguments are called *enthymemes*. Some leave the conclusion unstated. Some omit stating a premise. Fit each argument into one of the four *valid* argument forms discussed above and determine the unstated premise or conclusion.

* 1. If he was drunk then he's responsible for the accident. And, he was drunk.

2. If all human beings are naturally good then God is a French wine merchant. And, God is not a French wine merchant.

3. Either Jones is lying or Fermini really does visit the sick. But, Fermini does not visit the sick.

* 4. She didn't bring her umbrella, so it's not going to rain.

5. Either inflation will cease or the sun will stop shining. And, the sun will not stop shining.

6. If an institution allows the people it serves to participate in its governance, then it is a democratic institution. This school is not a democratic institution.

* 7. If everything in the universe is made up of atomic particles, the soul must be made up of atomic particles. And everything in the universe is made up of atomic particles.

8. If all is one, then individuals are non-existent. But, individuals are not non-existent.

9. Either the universe had a beginning or it has existed forever. It's impossible for something to exist forever. So....

* 10. If I buy a car, then I'll be broke. If I am broke, then it's bye-bye education. So....

3. Critical Thinking (Informal Logic) and the evaluation of arguments

The model of argument evaluation for critical thinking is called an *informal* model, since it will *not* be concerned with evaluating argument forms for validity. This model asks whether assumptions are warranted; whether premises are relevant, weighted properly, and sufficient to support their conclusion; and whether relevant information has been omitted. We will use this model for all arguments, deductive as well as inductive.

Since inductive arguments consist of all those arguments that do not claim to prove their conclusions with necessity, the range of arguments that can be called inductive is very large indeed. More importantly, evaluating an argument that purports to provide reasonable grounds for its conclusion is quite different from evaluating the validity of deductive forms. Also, for the purposes of evaluating the arguments of daily life, including those in our courtrooms and scientific journals, reducing arguments to a deductive model is an unnecessary, and, in some cases, a misleading exercise. It is unnecessary because a critical thinker will usually be able to evaluate the connection between statements equally well with or without training in formal logic. It is misleading in some cases because one is easily deluded into thinking that one's premises are absolutely certain and thus one's necessary conclusion is true when in fact it is just as questionable as one's premises. For example, it follows necessarily

that *abortion is murder* from the premises *It is murder to kill a human being unjustly* and *abortion is the unjustified killing of a human being.* However, one need not be an expert in syllogisms or any other form of deductive argument to see that the statement *abortion is the unjustified killing of a human being* is a controversial assumption. Thus, any conclusion validly drawn from it is also controversial.

Using an informal model for argument evaluation forces us to focus our attention on the reasonableness, relevance, and sufficiency of the premises in an argument. Since the purpose of an inductive argument is to provide reasonable grounds for its conclusion, it is essential that the premises of an inductive argument be reasonable themselves. Of course, a sound deductive argument is not only valid but is also based on true premises. The emphasis on validity, however, restricts the utility of such arguments to those cases where the truth of the premises is beyond question. Such premises must be either self-evident or definitions. The perfect model of deductive reasoning would be Euclidean geometry with its deductions from definitions, axioms, and postulates. Claims about the things that matter in everyday life—in religion, politics, art, law, science, and the like are rarely beyond question. While there is little room for argument over the definition of a triangle or a circle, there will always be disagreement over definitions of such terms as 'just' and 'unjust', 'reasonable' and 'unreasonable,' 'human being,' 'honorable', and so on.

This is not to say that the study of formal logic is useless or of less value than the study of informal logic. Expertise in deductive validity evaluation is essential in mathematics and all forms of hypothetical and conditional reasoning, including, but not limited to, science and computer programming. (Hypothetical reasoning is reasoning that uses *hypotheses* as its premises. It does not assume its premises are true. Hypothetical reasoning asks *what follows if we assume such and such is true?* For example, *what follows if galaxies are moving away from each other at a constant rate?* Conditional reasoning in computer programming presents a set of conditions that must be met before some procedure or calculation is executed. The instructions the programmer gives to the computer may be in the form of elaborate deductive inferences from complex conditional statements.)

For the arguments of everyday life, however, the informal model will prove more valuable. It will prove more valuable if only for the simple reason that we can easily apply it to *all* arguments, even deductive ones. Deductive models of argument evaluation, with their focus on validity of form, cannot be applied to natural language arguments without an elaborate and sometimes questionable process of translating the natural language argument according to some deductive model. For the student of critical thinking this simply means that *you do not have to identify arguments as deductive or inductive to evaluate them.* Another way of putting this is to say that the distinction between inductive and deductive arguments does not matter, *unless testing the validity of deductive arguments is one's sole or main concern.* (For this reason, there are no exercises in this book requiring you to distinguish deductive from inductive arguments.)

4. Evaluating argumentative reasons and reasoning

An argument is the giving of reasons to support a conclusion. The *reasons* are the *premises* of the argument. The *basic* reasons or premises are the *assumptions* of the argument. No reasons are given in support of an assumption. We determine the *reasonableness* of the assumptions of an argument by consulting our knowledge and experience, the source of the information, and the kind of claim being made. We determine the *cogency* or *validity* of the reasoning of the argument by deciding whether the premises provide a sufficient reason to accept the conclusion. Premises, even if warranted, will be insufficient to support a conclusion if they are *weak* or *irrelevant*. That is, the cogency of the argument can suffer either because of the *quantity* of the evidence or because of the *quality* of the evidence. Either the evidence will be the right kind of stuff (relevant) but there won't be enough of it to justify accepting the conclusion, or the evidence will be the wrong sort of stuff (be irrelevant).

So, evaluating an argument involves more than just deciding if the assumptions are warranted or not. *To evaluate the argument is to evaluate the relationship between the premises of the argument and their conclusion.* The premises must be *relevant* to proving their conclusion and they must be *sufficient*.

In addition, a cogent argument must be *complete*: it must present *all the relevant evidence*. Arguers may give their arguments the semblance of a good argument by being very selective in the use of evidence. They omit or suppress relevant information. Thus, an argument based on true, relevant, and apparently sufficient data might not be a cogent argument. For example, a researcher on extrasensory perception might provide a very strong case for the position that ESP exists by providing only the data that supports the claim and suppressing the data that is not supportive. Of course, a skeptic might do the same: provide only the data that is not supportive of ESP and ignore the data that is supportive.

Finally, a good argument is called *valid*, *cogent*, or *sound*. The Latin *validus* means *strong*. As we have already noted above in our presentation of deductive arguments, the term *valid* is used to designate a deductive argument whose conclusion follows necessarily from its premises. Because deductive validity is distinct from the truth of statements (remember: valid deductive arguments can have true *or* false premises), formal logicians often insist that the term *valid* not be used when talking about *statements*. *Statements* are *true* or *false*; *arguments* are *valid* or *invalid*. Such restrictive use of terms avoids the confusion of having to say of some arguments that they are both valid (have good reasoning) and invalid (give bad reasons). However, the term *valid* is quite often and quite rightly used in ordinary English to describe statements and to describe good inductive reasoning. When applied to statements, *valid* means *warranted*. When applied to inductive reasoning, *valid* means *sound* or *cogent*. To avoid confusion, however, we will use 'valid' to refer to deductive arguments whose conclusions follow necessarily from their premises. We will use the term 'cogent' or 'sound' to refer to inductive arguments whose premises are adequate to support their conclusion, as well as to valid deductive arguments with warranted assumptions.

To sum up: A cogent argument is

1. **Based on clear and accurate (i.e., warranted) assumptions;**
2. **Provides relevant and sufficient support for its conclusion, giving proper weight to each premise, and**
3. **Does not omit relevant evidence.**

We will begin at the beginning, with the question of what makes an assumption warranted.

4.1 Warranted assumptions

A cogent argument is based on warranted assumptions. **An assumption is a claim that is taken for granted. A** *warranted* **assumption is an assumption that is either known to be true or is reasonable to accept without requiring an argument to support it.**

Since a good argument must be based on true or reasonable assumptions, it follows that arguments based on *false* or *questionable* assumptions are not good arguments. One of the most fundamental criticisms that can be made of an argument is that the argument is *based on false or questionable assumptions*. A *questionable assumption* is one that is controversial or debatable. Since most strongly stated opinions are debatable, they should be argued for, not given or accepted as assumptions in an argument. Questionable assumptions can be made about facts as well, however.

The assumptions of an argument are the foundations that support the main conclusion of the argument. If the foundation is weak, the conclusion will not be adequately supported. Thus, probably the most basic question we can ask in evaluating an argument is *Are the assumptions on which the conclusion is based warranted?*

How do we determine which assumptions of an argument are warranted and which ones are not? It should be obvious that many, if not most, statements can be known to be true or false only by studying the particular field in which the statements are made. If you want to know whether a statement about law is true, you have to study the field of law; if you want to know whether a particular statement about biology is true, you must study biology. Many of the claims you will run across as you read arguments—and many of the claims you will make in your own arguments—will come from experts and authorities in fields you are not knowledgeable in. We discussed the importance of knowing how to handle claims intelligently in fields beyond your own expertise in chapter three.

We determine whether or not assumptions are warranted based on our knowledge, experience, the quality of the source of our information, and the type of claim made. If we are unable to determine whether the premises of an argument are warranted, we may still be able to go on and evaluate the *reasoning* of the argument. That is, we can often determine the relevance and sufficiency of evidence *even if we do not know whether the premises are true.* We may conclude our evaluation of an argument sometimes by saying that an argument would be cogent *if* its premises are true. Or, we may conclude that an argument is not cogent even if its premises turn out to be true.

Even if we find that we cannot accept the premises of an argument, we might still find the argument instructive. The argument may clarify concepts that are fuzzy to us, or introduce new material we were ignorant of, or make us aware of material that should be included in an argument on the topic at hand. The argument may serve as a model of reasoning; for, the arguer whose premises we cannot accept might be very adept at drawing conclusions from those premises.

Finally, do not consider an assumption unwarranted simply because you do not know whether it is true. Your lack of knowledge does not make a claim questionable. Put another way, an assumption does not become questionable just because *you* question it.

4.2 Fallacies of assumption

A sound argument is free from fallacies. Fallacies are errors, mistakes, or weaknesses regarding the reasons or reasoning in an argument. There are many ways to classify fallacies and some logicians have made an art form out of naming fallacies. However, there is little usefulness in burdening ourselves with a long list of names of fallacies, especially if the list includes many obsolete Latin expressions.

There are several fallacies that are based on false or questionable assumptions.

4.2.1 Begging the question

When an argument assumes what it should be proving, it *begs the question.* If premises entail, include, or otherwise presuppose the conclusion, the argument begs the question. For example: *Abortion is murder because abortion is the unjustified killing of a human being.* The argument assumes that abortion is murder when it assumes that abortion is the unjustified killing of a human being. For, the unjustified killing of a human being *is* murder. This argument assumes not only that a fetus is a human being, but also that every killing of every fetus is unjustified. To prove that abortion is murder, the argument must provide adequate support for both of these claims.

A common form of begging the question is to use a questionable general statement as a premise to support a conclusion that follows from the premise. For example: *The government should not sell oil exploration leases to drill off the California coast because no ocean area should be dug up to look for oil.* The argument assumes that the government should not sell oil exploration leases to drill off the California coast when it assumes that *no* ocean area should be dug up to look for oil.

Begging the question has several forms. One form of begging the question is called *arguing in a circle.* When one uses a premise to support a conclusion that is then used to support the original premise, one argues in a circle. For example: *You can trust me. Ask Richard about me. He's an honest man. He'll tell you that you can trust me.* Or, *God exists because it says so in the Bible and the Bible is the word of God.*

Another form of begging the question is called the *loaded question.* A question is loaded if directly answering it traps one into implying that the truth or falsity of some claim may be taken for granted when, in fact, the truth or falsity of the claim is the issue at hand. For example: (said to a postal clerk) *Why do you overcharge for such inferior service?* Two assumptions are made here: one, that the post office overcharges, and two, that the service is inferior. Imagine trying to answer this question directly: "well, the reason we overcharge for our inferior service is . . . ."

Examples of begging the question

"How did you manage to escape undetected from the scene of the crime?" - - asked of someone when the issue to be determined is whether she was in fact ever at the scene of the crime. (loaded question)

"The United States is the freest country in the world because here alone can you find citizens who are truly freer than anywhere else."

"When are you going to get married?" -- asked of someone who has not given the slightest hint that she intends to get married. (loaded question)

Prisons are inefficient because they do not rehabilitate. They don't rehabilitate because they're not efficient. (arguing in a circle)

"Another reason judicial restraint is the best way to interpret the Constitution is that remaining true to the conceptions and words of the constitution is the best avenue to take." (from a student essay)

4.2.2 Slippery Slope

The **slippery slope fallacy** occurs when one asserts, *without providing any evidence to support the assertion*, that a chain of horrible events will follow the taking or not taking of some action. In other words, the argument *assumes* that the horrible chain of events will occur, but offers no proof. This fallacy is usually combined with an *appeal to fear*. The more horrible the chain of events is, the better the chance that this fallacy will work on uncritical minds.

Examples of the slippery slope fallacy

They're at it again. The regulators want to control our lives. Today, it's smoking. Tomorrow will it be our right to free speech? Our right to read what we want? Where will it stop? Eventually, the regulators will try to control everything. We'll have no freedom, then. So, vote NO on proposition 10. Don't let them regulate smoking today or they'll be back tomorrow and tomorrow and tomorrow....

I have to oppose handgun registration. Regulators won't stop at that. They'll be back for rifles and shotguns next. Then, they won't be satisfied with registration; they'll have to confiscate all our guns. Only criminals, soldiers, and cops will have guns, and when that war begins, I don't want to be around.

4.2.3 The gambler's fallacy

The gambler's fallacy is to assume that the odds for something with a fixed probability increase or decrease depending upon recent occurrences. This assumption is false: fixed probabilities do not change. The odds of red coming up in roulette are the same even if black has come up ten times in a row. The odds of heads coming up on a coin toss are the same each time, even if tails has come up twenty times in a row. (This assumes that the game is not fixed and the coin is not loaded, of course.) The odds of any given number being selected in a state lottery do not change from week to week. Therefore, picking numbers that have not come up for a long time, or numbers that have recently come up frequently, does not increase your chance of winning.

4.3 Relevant premises

In addition to being based on warranted assumptions, a cogent argument must have premises that are **relevant** to supporting its conclusion. To say that a premise is relevant to supporting a conclusion means that it is *appropriate* to use the premise. It means that the premise is *pertinent* or *germane* to the argument.

Likewise, to say that a premise is **irrelevant** to proving a conclusion is to say that it is *inappropriate* to use it. What makes a premise relevant or irrelevant depends on the argument. No claim is relevant or irrelevant in itself. **Relevance of premises is always relative to proving or supporting the conclusion**. Whether or not a particular claim is relevant to a conclusion depends on the subject matter and on exactly what the argument is about.

Relevance should not be confused with *significance*. Two pieces of evidence may both be relevant to a particular position but one may be more significant than the other. For example, it may be true that a killer wore an expensive set of gloves and that he left a unique and peculiar shaped footprint at the scene of the crime. The fact that the killer wore expensive gloves is relevant but not as significant as the footprint. Many people own expensive gloves but the footprint is unique and peculiar, making it more significant.

There is, however, very little specific advice to give regarding the evaluation of the relevance of premises. The best general advice is to *avoid the common fallacies of relevance,* the topic of the next section.

4.4 Fallacies of relevance

Certain types of *irrelevant* appeals often make their way into arguments. Some types of irrelevant appeals occur so frequently that they have been given names.

4.4.1 Ad hominem

One of the most common ways of trying to cast doubt on a claim or position that has been argued for by another is to criticize the *person* making the argument rather than the argument itself. The *ad hominem* fallacy is an *irrelevant assertion about a person* who has taken a position or made an argument. The assertion about the arguer is made in the belief or hope that it will be taken as relevant evidence against the argument itself. Rather than criticize a person's premises or reasoning, an *ad hominem* asserts something about the person's character, associations, occupation, hobbies, motives, mental health, likes or dislikes.

The fallacy in the *ad hominem* is due to the *irrelevant* nature of the appeal made, not its *falsity*. If what is said about the person is false, in addition to being irrelevant, two fallacies are committed, *false premise* and *irrelevant premise*. Many people are seduced by *ad hominem* attacks. The appeal of the *ad hominem* is that it puts bad doctrines (i.e., those you disagree with) into the mouths of bad people (those you dislike). The *ad hominem* allows one to feel that one's opponent is evil as well as stupid. Attacking a person, rather than the person's position or argument, is usually easier as well as psychologically more satisfying to those who divide the world into two classes of people—those who agree with them and are therefore good and right, and those who disagree with them and are therefore evil and wrong.

The *ad hominem* is attractive to lazy thinkers, who would rather ridicule or belittle a person than seriously examine an opposing viewpoint. The *ad hominem* is also a tactic of the clever manipulator of crowds, the experienced demagogue who knows how to play on the emotions of people and seduce them into transferring their attitude of disapproval for a person to disagreement with that person's position.

Examples of ad hominem appeals

"You shouldn't believe a word my opponent says about me since he is just bitter because I'm ahead in the polls."

"Of course the American Dental Association advises us to have our teeth checked twice a year. Their members stand to profit quite a bit from this advice. Don't listen to them."

"Samson's views on strategic air command are wrong; what would a former employee of Disneyworld know about such matters?"

4.4.2 Poisoning the well

Poisoning the well is a type of ad hominem fallacy that occurs when a person tries to prejudice the atmosphere against an opponent or an opposing position, thereby making it nearly impossible for the opposition to get a fair hearing. For example, "the Communist Party supports the proposed tax increase, so we can be sure it is a bad idea." Or, "Now that we've heard from the thoughtful group, is there anything any of you *bearded anarchists* have to say?" Or, "Anyone who opposes the President's deployment of troops to Saudi Arabia is a *traitor*! They should be put in a cell with Hanoi Jane Fonda. But, this is America, so go ahead and have your say." Or, "Before you begin spouting your *liberal propaganda*, let me just say...." Or, "This just in from the *femi-nazis*." Or, "And here's one from the *animal rights wackos*."

Examples of poisoning the well

"Nietzsche went insane. Hi criticisms of Christianity are just the demented ravings of a madman."

"Reagan's an actor. His economic policies are as absurd as the roles he played in the movies."

"Supporting a graduated tax is typical communist idea. A vote for this tax proposal is a vote for communism!"

"Moore has a reputation for getting the basic facts wrong. You can't trust anything he says in *Fahrenheit 9/11.*"

4.4.3 Irrelevant Appeal to Authority

An *irrelevant appeal to authority* is an attempt to get a controversial claim accepted on the basis of its being supported by an admirable or respectable person. For example, *Since the Pope thinks that capital punishment is morally justified, it must be morally justified.* Or, *Einstein believed in God, so God must exist.*

Perhaps the most frequently appealed to traditional authority is **common sense**, that characteristic which most of us feel is sufficient in ourselves but deficient in others. Unfortunately, common sense often has little of sense in it—which may account

> *"The devil can cite Scripture for his purpose."* --William Shakespeare (Antonio, The Merchant of Venice*)*

for its being so common! Appeals to common sense and to other forms of **traditional wisdom** or authority are often made in the misguided belief that such appeals will (a) convince like-minded uncritical thinkers, (b) elicit agreement because of shared emotional attachments and attitudes rather than because of reasonable evidence, and (c) allow one to avoid having to provide any evidence for one's conclusions.

On the other hand, appeals to traditional authority may be made either to exemplify a point or to establish a common ground—a basis for further discussion and communication—and, as such, amount to a *profession of faith*—a way of saying 'this is the foundation upon which I stand.' In either case, **the appeal to traditional wisdom or authority is irrelevant to providing logical grounds for accepting a conclusion.**

Appealing to persons we admire or respect, rather than to evidence or arguments, is seductive since it lets us be lazy while at the same time uniting us with attractive persons. Clever manipulators of the masses use appeals to authority knowing that most people would rather assent to a proposition they don't understand than admit ignorance. People are intimidated by experts and feel humble next to them. Clever speakers know how to seduce us by working on our insecurity and our desire to be associated with appealing persons.

Examples of irrelevant appeals to authority

"Your plan to do this research on the humpback whale is ridiculous; the idea has been rejected by both our president and personnel manager."

"If the experts at General Electric who build nuclear power plants say they are safe, then they must be pretty safe after all."

"Norman Mailer's a great writer, and if he thinks that Virgil's *Aenead* is an excellent book, then it must be."

"Man is not the aggressive, cruel animal he has been made out to be. Professor Leakey has found new evidence to disprove this erroneous view that human nature is violent."

4.4.4 Ad populum

The *ad populum* fallacy is the appeal to the **popularity** of a claim as a reason for accepting it. The number of people who believe a claim is *irrelevant* to its truth. Fifty million people *can* be wrong. In fact, millions of people have been wrong about many things: that the Earth is flat and motionless, for example, and that the stars are lights shining through holes in the sky. The ad populum fallacy is also referred to as the *bandwagon fallacy, the appeal to the mob, the democratic fallacy,* and *the appeal to popularity.*

The ad populum fallacy is seductive because it appeals to our desire to belong and to conform, to our desire for security and safety. It is a common appeal in advertising and politics. A clever manipulator of the masses will try to seduce those who blithely assume that the majority is always right. Also seduced by this appeal will be the insecure, who will be made to feel guilty if they oppose the majority and who will be made to feel strong by joining forces with large numbers of other uncritical thinkers.

Examples of ad populum appeals

"TRY NEW, IMPROVED [fill in the blank with the name of any one of innumerable commercial products]. EVERYBODY's USING IT!

"God must exist, since every culture has some sort of belief in a higher being."

"The *Bold and the Listless* must be a great book. It's been on the best seller list for 8 weeks."

"Arnold Killembetter's movie *True Garbage* is the greatest movie of all time. No movie has made as much money as it did."

"The fact that the majority of our citizens support the death penalty proves that it is morally right."

4.4.5 The argument to ignorance

The fallacy of the *argument to ignorance* occurs when one tries to argue that *something is true because it has not been proved false* or vice-versa. This fallacy might be better called 'the fallacy from lack of sufficient evidence to the contrary.' For, the fallacy does not involve claiming that any person is ignorant. Rather, its irrelevance is based on the fact that a claim's falsity must be shown by refuting evidence to the claim, not by pointing out that a proponent of the claim hasn't proved it is true. I cannot prove that Einstein's theory of relativity is true, but that is hardly relevant to the truth or falsity of the theory. I cannot prove it is false that aliens have landed on Earth and are mutilating cattle and kidnapping people for experimentation. However, my inability to disprove the claim does not have any relevance to the issue of whether the claim is true. I cannot explain how unconscious matter can give rise to consciousness, but that is irrelevant to proving that consciousness cannot be material.

If you think of ignorance as being *without knowledge*, the name of this fallacy may not be as misleading as it would otherwise be. The fallacy occurs when reasoning from the lack of knowledge that a position is true to the conclusion that an opposing position is therefore true. The argument from ignorance seems to be more seductive when it can play upon wishful thinking. People who want to believe in angels, for example, may be more prone to think that the lack of evidence to the contrary of their desired belief is somehow relevant to supporting it.

The fact that it cannot be proved that the universe is not designed by an intelligent creator does not prove that it is. Nor does the fact that it cannot be proved that the universe is designed by an intelligent creator prove that it isn't. On the other hand, the fact that many people have done many serious investigations in support of the claim that there is a monster living in Loch Ness and all have failed to produce a single bit of uncontested evidence in support of the claim make it reasonable to conclude that it is very unlikely that such a creature exists. In short, the lack of evidence for a claim may be taken as a good reason for rejecting the claim *if the claim is the kind of thing for which there should be strong evidence if it were true.*

Examples of argument from ignorance

"God must exist, since no one has yet been able to prove that God doesn't exist."

"ESP doesn't exist, since no one has yet proved it is real."

"There must be life on Mars; after all, no one has been able to prove there isn't."

"I must be innocent; since, so far no one has been able to prove that I'm guilty."

116

4.4.6 Irrelevant comparisons

Many advertisements make irrelevant comparisons; for example, comparing a relatively inexpensive single-function Minolta copier to an expensive, multi-function Xerox machine. True, both make good copies—and the ad tries to get the consumer to focus on this fact—but the Xerox machine performs a multitude of tasks (such as collating, stapling, back-to-back copying, and more) which the Minolta cannot do. These differences are ignored in the ad. Thus, even though the ad is correct in stating that copies made on the Minolta will be equal in quality to those on the Xerox but much cheaper per copy, the comparison is irrelevant. To be relevant, the Minolta should be compared to an *equivalent* Xerox machine.

Another ad that uses an irrelevant comparison is the one that compares two brands of paper towels by dropping an egg and trying to catch it with the paper towel. Since paper towels generally are not used to catch eggs, the fact that one is better than the other at this task is irrelevant.

Articles on the high cost of going to college often commit the fallacy of irrelevant comparison. It is irrelevant, for example, to compare the cost of going to a public community college with the cost of going to a major private university. Room and board costs are not included in the community college costs, but they are in the private school costs. Furthermore, the institutions are extremely different. A more relevant comparison would be to compare the costs of various private universities to one another or the costs of various community colleges with one another.

4.4.7 Irrelevant appeals to feelings or emotions

Arguers often make *irrelevant* emotive appeals when they lack logical reasons for their position or when persuasion rather than truth is their goal. Emotion is generally a much more powerful *motive* to belief and action than logical reasons are. Hence, emotive appeals are often persuasive. Some people are moved to purchase products they do not need by irrelevant appeals to their vanity, guilt, fear, or the desire for pleasure. Others are vulnerable to appeals to pity. Show them a picture of anyone crying or of an emaciated child and they open their pocketbooks. When the issue requires logical reasons, do not accept mere emotional appeals as sufficient evidence.

Of course, it is not always irrelevant to appeal to emotions. For example, one of the most powerful motivators is fear. It is a favorite not only of advertisers, but parents, sales persons, preachers, newscasters, and politicians. Often, these appeals are irrelevant, but not always. Advice not to play with guns because you might kill someone is good advice and not in the same league as warning a child not to lie because the bogeyman is keeping track and punishes liars by turning their tongues black.

4.4.8 Evading the issue (the red herring)

A tactic frequently used in argumentation—especially if one has been accused of wrongdoing—is to *divert attention to an issue irrelevant to the one at hand*, thereby attempting to *evade* the real issue. (The irrelevant diversion is sometimes referred to as a *red herring*.)

There are many reasons for evading an issue, and many ways to do it. One may not want to discuss an issue; one may not want to reveal one's position. One may be lazy, afraid, arrogant, disgusted, or the like. One may evade an issue by creating a diversion, such as telling a joke or making a humorous remark, by accusing others of wrongdoing in hopes of putting someone else on the defensive. Remember: *evasion implies a direct attempt to avoid facing an issue*. It is not accurate to accuse an arguer of **evading an issue** simply because the arguer's evidence is irrelevant or inadequate to support his or her conclusion.

Examples of evading the issue

"My opponent has accused me of bribing a witness. This accusation is absurd. For twenty years I have worked hard to build a reputation of the highest type. I am recognized as a good, decent, hard-working and honest man. I have the respect of my peers, even of those I have defeated in the past. These charges are raised by people who dislike my decency and my willingness to represent in court people whom other lawyers would not touch with a ten foot tort."

"You accuse me of embezzling funds from the Club's treasury while I served as treasurer. But how about your behavior when you were president of the club? There was much more money unaccounted for when you held office!"

4.4.9 Non sequitur

When the reasons given for a position are irrelevant to supporting it, the conclusion is said to be a *non sequitur*. Literally, this is saying that 'it does not follow.' Technically, any argument based on nothing but irrelevant reasoning is an example of a non sequitur. Fallacious arguments based on *relevant* premises are not said to commit the fallacy of non sequitur. Usually, however, the term is reserved not just to indicate that a premise is irrelevant but that the conclusion is *far removed* from the premises. For example: "Nothing is certain; so, one should follow the customs of one's country." "We have an inborn desire for immortality, so the soul must exist and be created for eternal life." "I have an innate aversion to water; therefore, I think I should take up sky diving."

I would use the term 'non sequitur' to describe any fallacy of relevance that does not fall into one of the categories listed in this section.

Examples of non sequitur

"Christians believe the Bible is the word of God. And in the Bible it says that homosexuality is a sin. Therefore, we should make it illegal to be a homosexual." [What is the relevance of the beliefs of a religious group to the issue of what should or should not be legal? These premises are relevant to a different issue, viz., the issue of whether or not a Christian may be a practicing homosexual.]

"I support property tax relief. The homeowner is being taxed out of existence and must be protected. We must pass the Hogwash-Mishmash Amendment now!" [The premises are not relevant to the conclusion given, but to another issue, viz., that some sort of property tax relief is needed. What would be relevant to the conclusion that the Hogwash-Mishmash Amendment ought to be passed would be evidence that this amendment would provide property tax relief. Note that in addition to being a non sequitur, this argument also begs the question. It assumes what ought to be proved as well as providing nothing but irrelevant premises in support of its conclusion.]

Exercises 5-2

A. Evaluate the premises of each of the following arguments. Are they warranted? Are they relevant to supporting their conclusions? Identify any fallacies.

* 1. (14 year old daughter to her mother) "You should buy me make-up; every other kid's mother buys her make-up."
2. (Bumper sticker:) CANCER CURES SMOKING

118

* 3. "No one has proved that human beings have free will. I know that all our actions are predetermined, then, and not free."

   4. The IBM personal computer must be the best one around since everybody has one.

* 5. Your advice on child rearing is useless, since you have no children of your own.

   6. "There's never been a good argument for price controls; therefore, price controls is obviously a bad idea."

   7. "The President's position is sheer non-sense....but what can you expect from someone who once shared top billing with a chimpanzee?!"

* 8. Your view on prayer in the schools is obviously wrong; after all, you're an atheist.

   9. "God can't possibly exist; since it is impossible for finite beings to prove the existence of an infinite being."

* 10. Publishers in America do not print anything which is known to be false. So, that story about the Russians deliberately and knowingly shooting down a commercial airliner must be true.

   11. Women are too emotional to be trusted in positions of power. Thus, you shouldn't vote for Ferraro.

* 12. A person of your intelligence surely sees the wisdom of my plan.

   13. "Since you can't give me any good reason why I shouldn't believe you're guilty, I'll just have to assume that you are guilty."

   14. The speaker's defense of Dr. Mill is not worth considering. Nothing she says in Mill's defense is worth counting since, after all, she and Mill are very good friends.

* 15. Of course Smith supports an amendment to give her equal rights. What else can you expect from a Woman's Libber?

   16. (Advertisement) "I use Pittenween Super Z-99 motor oil in my racing car when I'm driving the Indianapolis 500. You should use it in your car, too. If it's good for my race car, it'll be good for your Honda!"

   17. "I knew it was against the law to grow marijuana, but so is driving over 55 m.p.h., and everybody does that."

* 18. (Bumper sticker:) BETTER ACTIVE TODAY THAN RADIOACTIVE TOMORROW.

   19. Here we have another *liberal* argument in defense of gun control. Of course, Justice Doright favors gun control, since he's always supported the liberal agenda.

* 20. Children should not enter child beauty contests because photographers will make them pose for sleazy pictures and judges will give them drugs.

   21. (Advertisement) "The Fireball 500's have made it over the roughest roads in the world in the Baja 500 mile race. These roads were made in Hell! If these tires can survive the world's most rugged conditions, surely they must be good for your station wagon. Get the Fireball 500's today!"

   22. (Lawyer to a jury.) "Ask yourselves how you would feel if this young man on trial were your son. Would you want him to go to prison where he'd probably be brutally raped? Think of that when you make your decision about his guilt or innocence."

*23. (Letter to the editor:) "Are all those asbestos deaths of no value or importance? Hundreds upon hundreds of shipyard workers died from the exposure of asbestos because of their work with it....Now we read in *The Bee* that 66 percent of the schools, public and private, checked so far for asbestos hazards have failed to comply with the rules requiring them to identify and report asbestos hazards....We're dragging our feet on this issue in our school systems, and we're allowing a death sentence for our children."

B. Evaluate the premises of each of the following arguments. Are they warranted? Are they relevant to supporting their conclusions? Identify any fallacies due to irrelevant appeals.

* 1. As everyone knows, the wise person is the one who does not rock the boat during a storm. Don't be a fool: comply with your orders to report for military duty even if you think the government wants to use you as a pawn in an immoral war. Besides, since no once can really prove that the war is immoral, it seems reasonable to conclude that it is moral after all. Even the Pope thinks its a good war.

   2. A man convicted of murdering his parents pleads with the jury: "Please have mercy on me. I'm an orphan!"

   3. (After Secretary of the Interior James Watt made an insensitive remark about women, minorities and the handicapped, a reader wrote:) "We should dump Watt not because we disagree with his idea of a joke, but because he is one, and a bad one at that."

* 4. Senator Strom Thurmond supported a bill that would require the following label on all bottles whose contents are more than 24 percent alcohol: "Caution: Consumption of alcoholic beverages may be hazardous to your health, may be habit forming, and may cause serious birth defects when consumed during pregnancy." Senator Sam I. Hayakawa opposed the bill. Said Hayakawa: "Our Lord at the wedding feast at Cana changed water into wine; there is no record of His having issued any warnings against its abuse on that occasion....If Jesus found such warnings unnecessary, that's good enough for me."

5. "Slavery was ordained by God. Christ himself gave a sanction to slavery. He admonished them to be obedient to their masters; and there is not a word in the whole of his life which forbids it...." (William Smith of South Carolina quoted in The Shaping of the American Past by R. Kelly)

* 6. (A letter from the Faculty Association of California Community Colleges, urging support of a political action committee (PAC), argued the following:) "...many groups of ordinary people have formed PAC's and those groups are gaining influence as well. In recent years the nurses--who make less than we do on the average--have built one of the strongest new PACs in the State....The same story is being repeated with police officers whose State association now numbers 40,000 strong....The list goes on and on...farm workers, chiropractors, bulldozer operators. They're all building PACs...."

7. (From a letter to the editor:) "Re your editorial "Keep the UN In NY": As a newspaper of some repute in Northern California, one would suppose that the Bee would be somewhat familiar with the wishes and attitudes of most of the citizens in the area regarding the U.N. Since the publication of your editorial, President Reagan stated publicly that a great majority of the American people were in accord with the statement pronounced by Ambassador Lichenstein. It appears that the Bee's attitude and recommendation as expressed in the editorial is not a popular one. I suggest that in the future, before heralding such viewpoints, find out what people are thinking on the subject."

* 8. We ought to establish a Peace Academy to promote peace. We could get one started for about $7.5 million for the site, about $6 million in seed money and about $10 million for the next year's operating budget. The Pentagon spends more than this on a tank or airplane that often doesn't even work. The idea has the support of 53 co-sponsors in the Senate and more than 100 in the House of Representatives. (This is a paraphrase of an argument made by syndicated columnist Jack Anderson.)

9. (Student to teacher:) "I know I haven't attended any classes since the first week of the semester, but I got real busy and then my car broke down just before I caught the flu. And you have a reputation on campus for not only being the best teacher but also for being the fairest and most decent of them all. Besides, you wouldn't flunk a black man, would you? What would the newspapers think if they found out you were a racist? Give me a break. Just give me a 'C' and I'll be happy."

10. Since most people cheat on their income taxes and are basically dishonest, we ought to do away with tax forms and just charge everybody the same tax. The government just wastes most of our money anyway, so we could make the tax real low by firing most of the public serpents who lay around and sun themselves at the public trough. Nobody really cares about honesty. All they care about is themselves and their fancy cars.

* 11. It is unnecessary to know how to read or write to get ahead in this society. Idiots control everything. Power goes to those who take it, not to those who earn it through honest aggression and accepted forms of immorality. Being stupid and ignorant is what pays in this world. So, there is absolutely no reason in the world why you should want to go to college. Get a job.

12. So what if I took your car without asking. You've done a heck of a lot worse, Dad. I remember you telling me that when you were my age you used to steal your grandfather's horse and ride over to see your girlfriend in another town. Hey, and least I don't do drugs, Dad. Most kids around here stay home and get stoned. And what about my grades, huh? They're pretty good, aren't they. You just don't like me, Dad. You never have. Admit it.

13. "The inquisition must have been justified and beneficial, if whole peoples invoked and defended it, if men of the loftiest souls founded and created it severally and impartially, and its very adversaries applied it on their own account, pyre answering pyre." --Benedetto Croce

14. (William B. Kolender, director of the California Youth Authority, accused *The Sacramento Bee* of making an **irrelevant comparison** in an editorial. Analyze Kolender's reasoning and determine whether or not he was justified in his accusation.) "*The Bee*'s editorial "Prep schools for prison" repeated some of the same, tired rhetoric we have heard for years about other states' juvenile justice systems being cheaper and more effective than California's This is not supported by the facts. The editorial, for example, claimed that the "cost per juvenile" is $23,000 a year in Massachusetts and $31,000 in California. But this is a comparison of apples and oranges. Comparable information would be that it costs California $31,000 per ward in a secure institution, and it costs Massachusetts $58,000 per ward in such institutions. Massachusetts' $23,000 figure is the cost for that state's entire juvenile ward population, including those on supervised parole. The comparable figure for the California Youth Authority (CYA) is an overall cost of about $21,000 per ward. "Similarly, *The Bee* compared the six out of 10 juveniles released from the CYA who will be arrested again within four years with the reincarceration rate in Massachusetts, which is 23 percent. But rearrest is very different from reincarceration. The rearrest rate is always much higher [than the reincarceration rate]."

Exercises 5-3

1. Find three examples of irrelevant reasoning in magazine or newspaper advertisements.

2. Find three examples of irrelevant reasoning in letters to the editor in a daily newspaper.

3. Evaluate the relevance of the premises used in a newspaper or magazine editorial.

4. Find several examples of advertisements of the following types and comment on them in light of what was said in this chapter regarding the reasonable use of authorities:

  a. Ads that feature a celebrity or well-known figure;
  b. Ads that emphasize mass appeal, that you ought to get on the bandwagon, too;
  c. Ads that emphasize belonging to the in-crowd;
  d. Ads that emphasize patriotism or loyalty;
  e. Ads that emphasize tradition.

4.5 Sufficient reasons

Even if every warranted and relevant premise available were brought forth to support a conclusion, that conclusion still might not be justified. For, the premises might not be *sufficient* to support the conclusion. A conclusion based on insufficient evidence is called a **hasty conclusion**. (If the conclusion is a generalization based on insufficient evidence, it is called a **hasty generalization**.)

No doubt you have heard of a district attorney dropping the charges against someone accused of a crime on the grounds of *insufficient evidence*. Just what constitutes *sufficient* support for a conclusion?

You would think that if there are any clear criteria for determining the sufficiency of evidence it would be found in our courtrooms, where people's lives depend on other people's ability to evaluate evidence. Yet, the best our legal system has come up with is the criterion of **reasonable doubt**. Weigh the evidence, the jury is told, and if there is a *reasonable doubt* as to the guilt of the accused, then the jury is to bring in a verdict of not guilty. However, if the prosecutor proves to the jury's satisfaction *beyond a reasonable doubt* that the defendant is guilty, then the jury is to bring in a verdict of guilty. What constitutes *proof beyond a reasonable* doubt? This is a very high standard, but does not require proof that is absolutely certain.

Are there any guidelines for evaluating the sufficiency of premises to support their conclusions? Yes. First, in the area of deductive logic, very clear and precise procedures have been developed for demonstrating that conclusions do or do not necessarily follow from given sets of premises. We discussed formal logical proofs earlier in this chapter and have nothing further to say on the matter except this: for those interested in this extremely important area of reasoning, it is recommended that they take a course in symbolic logic.

Secondly, maintain a critical attitude, an attitude of open-mindedness and sincere desire to improve your beliefs. Be constantly on guard against biased or wishful thinking. Be aware of your purposes. Ask yourself why you are investigating a particular subject and how significant it is to you. Your purposes will sometimes determine how much evidence you should require.

Thirdly, become aware of contemporary standards of evidence in different subjects or areas of inquiry. You cannot judge what would be sufficient evidence to draw a conclusion in evolutionary biology if you know nothing of contemporary methods of testing claims in that science. The same is true of any other field. As you study and begin to specialize in areas, you will discover the various standards of different fields for clarity, truth, relevance, completeness, and sufficiency.

Finally, pay attention to the *strength* with which a conclusion is asserted to be supported by its premises. *A conclusion should be asserted with a degree of certainty proportionate to the evidence presented in the premises.* Conclusions may be asserted to follow with *necessity* or with some degree of *probability*. The range of strength with which conclusions may be asserted to follow from premises is very broad, indeed. Thus, an argument may sometimes be improved simply by weakening the warrant for the conclusion. That is, the same premises that are insufficient to support a *strong* conclusion may very well support a *weaker* conclusion.

4.5.1 Evaluating the significance of premises

One of the more difficult aspects of argument evaluation is deciding how much *weight* to give to premises which have been determined to be both true and relevant to supporting the position at hand. There are no clear-cut guidelines to present here, since *the significance of any premise will depend on the subject matter.* Here we can give only general advice.

One factor that ought to be considered in determining how much weight to give to a premise is its *source.* All else being equal, the more reliable the source, the more weight the premise ought to be given. Also—again, all other things being equal—*the more warranted a premise, the more weight it ought to be given.*

However, since the significance of any piece of evidence in an argument depends on the nature of the argument, it is difficult to provide useful general advice in this area. To illustrate the general point that different pieces of evidence might be given different weight, one might think of an example from a criminal trial. Some of the eyewitness testimony might be quite strong, while some of it might be weak. Some of the physical evidence might be relevant and indicate a *possible* connection of the defendant with the crime. Still other physical evidence might indicate a *probable* connection of the defendant with the crime. The circumstantial evidence might indicate a *strong probability* of guilt while the physical evidence might be exculpatory and therefore outweigh the circumstantial evidence. Discovery of a *motive* for committing a crime would indicate at least a possible connection to the crime, but in the absence of any other evidence would generally be taken as very weak evidence.

A prosecutor might present a jury with two pieces of evidence, each relevant to the argument that the defendant is guilty, yet each piece of evidence need not be of equal weight. For example, an eyewitness may have seen someone wearing a black hat leaving the seen of the crime. The defendant may own a black hat and that fact would be relevant to whether he committed the crime but it shouldn't carry much weight because black hats are common. However, the fact that the defendant's fingerprints were found on several items linked to the crime would not only be relevant but should carry much more weight than his hat ownership.

Finally, the expression 'hasty conclusion' is reserved for arguments with *truthful, relevant* premises. Hence, if an argument is unsound due to unwarranted or irrelevant premises, it is not said to commit the fallacy of hasty conclusion. In the examples below, notice how the premises are *relevant* to the conclusion but they are not sufficient to warrant accepting it. Hasty conclusions are often the result of wishful thinking, stereotyping, or other hindrances to critical thinking. In such cases, it is generally not too difficult for the critical thinker to detect this fallacy. However, there will be many cases where reasonable parties will disagree as to the sufficiency of evidence for a given conclusion. In such cases, it would be unwise to simply accuse one party of committing a fallacy of hasty conclusion. As with even the most blatant cases of hasty conclusion—for example, generalizing on the basis of single, haphazard experience—one should be prepared to present an argument in defense of the position that the evidence of a given argument is insufficient to support the conclusion asserted.

Examples of hasty conclusions

"Men are all cruel. I know; I was married to one for twenty years."

"Bonzi shoes are the best in the world. I bought my first pair last week and I really love them. You ought to get a pair, too."

"Don't buy any apples from Jinsten. I tasted one from his sample box, and it was awful!"

"I must have a brain tumor. I keep getting these terrible pains on the top of my head."

122

"My little niece just loves to play the trombone. That just goes to prove that children have an innate love of music and if given the opportunity they would all make good musicians."

"Did you see those teenagers taking the tires off that car. What's happened to kids today? Why are they all crooks and thieves?"

"This new diet technique will help anyone lose weight. I tried it for six months and I've lost twenty pounds."

4.6 Omitting relevant evidence: selective thinking and suppressed evidence

If we think of the conclusion of an argument as the roof of a building and the premises as the pillars supporting the roof, if relevant information about the pillars isn't revealed then the building might appear to be stronger than it really is. If we were to find out that some of the pillars were hollow or that they had internal structural flaws, we would not think so highly of the edifice. Similarly, an argument that omits relevant evidence can appear to be stronger than it really is. Thus, the detection of omitted or suppressed evidence is as much the job of an argument evaluator as is the detection of variations from the specifications of the blueprint is the job of the building inspector.

A cogent argument not only presents warranted, relevant premises; a cogent argument does not omit relevant evidence. It is often very difficult to detect when relevant information has been intentionally or unintentionally left out. Thus, relying upon the arguer to provide us with all the information needed to evaluate an argument is not a wise policy. On the other hand, when preparing to construct an argument of our own, we must seek out opposing views and arguments. We must include all relevant material, even if it does not support our position. We should try to anticipate objections to our arguments and respond to those objections.

It is a rare arguer who actively seeks out opposing views and treats them seriously; yet, that is exactly what a critical thinker must do. The natural tendency of the smug and lazy (most of us) is to ignore the stronger arguments of opponents and to omit from consideration any point that might make our own appear weaker. Thus, we must strive to overcome the natural tendency to commit this fallacy. We must strive to be well informed; for, obviously it will be easier to deceive us by suppressing evidence if we lack information on the subject argued about.

Besides the obvious cases of advertisements, interested-party press releases, and slanted news reports, there are other typical situations where relevant information is likely to be suppressed. Physicians often fail to inform their patients of the possible harmful side effects of a medication. Sometimes this is due to ignorance, as the number of medications is staggering; even so, it is inexcusable. Sometimes this is done out of concern for the patient's health—would the patient take the medicine if he or she knew of the potential harmful consequences? Also, employers have been known to fail to inform employees of the results of mandatory medical exams or of known health hazards associated with normal employment in an industry. The coal, asbestos, nuclear fuel, and tobacco industries have knowingly suppressed evidence regarding the health of their employees or the health hazards of their industries.

Selective thinking is common in politics, where a candidate may inform an audience that an opponent has been accused of or investigated for some wrongdoing, but will omit informing the audience that the opponent has been cleared of all charges. In parapsychology, it is common practice among some researchers to count only evidence that supports the belief in the existence of ESP, clairvoyance, remote viewing, and the like. Contrary evidence is ignored or suppressed. For example, Dean Radin's *The Conscious Universe* (1997) claims that parapsychologists have proven that psi phenomena (ESP and psychokinesis) exist. However, Radin ignores the major experiments and experimenters that have failed to find support for the psi hypothesis. He also either ignores or gives very little weight to criticisms of the work of parapsychologists.

Peddlers of alternative remedies that are supposed to cure such diseases as cancer are notorious for their ignoring evidence contrary to their claims.

Unless you know what evidence has been suppressed or omitted, you cannot detect this kind of unsoundness in an argument. The only advice one can give here is to be on guard in those types of situations where evidence is often conveniently suppressed: in advertisements, in political speeches and press releases, in editorials, in courtroom defenses and prosecutions, in medical prescriptions, in sales pitches, and in pseudoscience.

4.6.1 False dilemma

Relevant evidence is often omitted in situations where alternatives are presented. The fallacy of *false dilemma* occurs whenever one restricts the number of alternatives to fewer than there really are, thereby omitting relevant alternatives from consideration. (This fallacy is also called the *black-and-white fallacy* or the *either/or fallacy*.)

The clever manipulator of uncritical thinkers will only present alternatives for consideration that he favors. Clever writers will do the same. Beware of articles or books with "Either/Or" titles. The authors of such articles may have restricted the alternatives to just two. They will then proceed to demonstrate that one of the alternatives is unreasonable, foolish, or false. The reader is then seduced into accepting the author's claim that the alternative position is therefore reasonable, wise, or true. The fact is, however, that an alternative not even mentioned may be more reasonable than either of those presented for consideration.

Examples of false dilemma

[Wife to husband]... "Well, the budget is a mess for next month. What do you want to give up, your tennis lessons or the new dress shoes you want?"

"You are not for me; so, you must be against me."

"She's not a Democrat; so, she must be a Republican."

"America: Love it or Leave it!"

"Either we should fully support our football program so that we can compete with the best universities in the country or we should give up football altogether."

4.6.2 The straw man

A sound argument presents alternative positions and anticipates objections. The *straw man fallacy* occurs when a position one opposes is presented in a distorted way by exaggerating it or by presenting only its weakest defense. For example, if an opposing position asserts that something *could* happen, you report it as asserting that it *should* happen; if it says that something *may* be, you report it as saying that it *will* be. If your opponent says that smoking is *a health hazard*, you distort this by saying that she claims that smoking is *the worst health hazard in the history of mankind*. If your opponent advocates increasing the amount of *free medical care given to the aged*, you assert that he says that we should have *socialized medicine*. If your opponent says that we should *curtail the sale of candy in elementary schools*, you assert that she wants *to eliminate all free choice and involve the government in every aspect of our lives.*

The straw man fallacy seems to be appealing to those who would rather *distort by omission and exaggeration* than take seriously an opposing viewpoint. The arguer who resorts to straw man tactics seems to think that by

124

placing his own position next to one which is obviously weak (at least it appears weak in its distorted presentation), his position will appear stronger than it really is.

Examples of straw man

(The issue being argued below is whether to construct a nuclear power plant nearby.)

Proponent: "Unless we construct a nuclear power plant in this area within the next ten years, we will not be able to meet the significantly growing demand for power."

Opponent: "What you're saying is that you couldn't care less what happens to the wildlife and plant life or even the human lives that might be harmed by the presence of nuclear radiation in this area."
(Note how opponent distorts the proponent's position.)

(The issue being argued below is the Equal Rights Amendment.)

Proponent: "I must conclude that there is no moral, logical, or legal justification for discriminating against a person on the basis of a person's sex. Therefore, I am wholeheartedly supporting the Equal Rights Amendment."

Opponent: "Look, if you want men and women being forced to use the same rest rooms and to sleep together in trenches during wartime, then go ahead and support the ERA. It looks to me though that you women just don't want to do housework anymore.

Exercises 5-4

(Note: good arguments generally require specialized knowledge, or there is little likelihood that there will be general agreement about them. There are many good arguments in non-technical fields, but because personal values often play a major role in establishing fundamental premises as well as the importance of the issues themselves, using such arguments as examples is likely to be as misleading as illuminating. In the exercises that follow, however, some of the arguments presented are arguments I consider to be good, or at least free from any obvious fallacies. There may be disagreements about these arguments; healthy discussions ought to follow.)

A. Evaluate the following statements or arguments. For the arguments, indicate whether the premises are warranted, relevant and sufficient to support their conclusion. If you believe relevant evidence has been omitted, indicate what data should have been brought up. Identify any fallacies.

* 1. Why are bureaucrats always inefficient?
* 2. It is imperative that we prepare for war; for, either the terrorists will conquer the world or the United States will stop them with its military might.
  3. Justice can't exist for the poor because justice is nothing but the way the rich protect their interests.
  4. (Letter to the editor:) "Either we execute rapists or we let rapists have free reign over our women. What's it going to be?"
* 5. God exists; for, the world needs a Creator.
  6. Since the majority of voters think that capital punishment is morally justified, it must be morally justified. The majority can't be wrong about matters of right.
* 7. If all humans are created equal then it is not right to discriminate. All humans are not created equal. So, it is right to discriminate.
  8. We should draft women into the army because it's a good idea.
  9. A politician can't get elected unless he lies. Therefore, all elected officials are liars.
* 10. The government ought to pay for the abortions of poor women since they can't afford to pay for them out of their own funds.
* 11. Since women are smaller than men, it follows that men are stronger than women.
  12. Why can't most high school graduates read or write?
  13. (At the conclusion of a final exam, a student writes:)"Thank you for a wonderful learning experience. You are a great teacher! Of all my college classes, none has benefitted me more than yours. I really enjoyed it. Thanks again!"
* 14. If all humans are created equal, then it is not right to discriminate. It is not right to discriminate. So, all humans are created equal.

* 15. There are some philosophers who believe that someday it will be possible to develop a computer that thinks. But they are wasting their time. Computers cannot think; for, if something is a machine, then it cannot think.

16. I believe in equal rights, but the President and priests are and should be men. The first president was a man, and Jesus and his apostles were all men.

17. (Police officer to suspect.) "When were you at the scene of the crime?"

* 18. "Free speech will be abused. Every liberty is abused."

19. There is no question about it: we simply cannot afford to continue our current high lifestyle. We're either going to have to quit giving money to charity or quit going out to dinner once a week.

* 20. Since 7 is greater than 5, and 12 is greater than 7, it follows that 12 is greater than 5.

* 21. (Advertisement:) Dr. Ferriss Wheel can help you lose weight right now. No obligation. Get thin for the summer, now! No strenuous exercise required. Eat all you want and still lose weight on the fabulous, proven Ferriss Wheel 180 day Superlosers Diet.

* 22. "Meanings do not reside in the words themselves. Meanings are in the minds of the people who use and hear the words." (Richard Weaver)

* 23. Most politicians never intend to keep their campaign promises. So, don't believe anything this candidate claims he's going to do.

* 24. A California state consultant on readability, Dr. Eycanmakitsimple, claimed that any text can be rewritten to the 6th- to 7th-grade reading level without loss of accuracy or detail in its content. She graduated from Harvard *magna cum laude*. Therefore, it certainly is possible to produce a grade school edition of *Finnegan's Wake* and Kant's *Critique of Pure Reason*.

25. (From a letter to the editor criticizing a judge's decision that agreed with the University of Georgia's claim that it had a right to know how professors on a tenure committee voted.) "The ruling sounds like the beginning of a totalitarian state. Next the government will want to prohibit secret voting in unions, professional organizations, civic organizations, corporations, and finally in general elections."

26. You can be sure that Elmo Zentug is a lazy cheat with a phony back problem, since he's on welfare and most welfare recipients are able-bodied persons who are too lazy to work and who would rather cheat the government than take an honest job.

* 27. Anyone who opposes legislation that would allow abortions only when the life of the mother is endangered condones the murder of innocent children. Therefore, Melissa, you are condoning murder if you oppose this proposed law.

* 28. Children should not enter child beauty contests because photographers will make them pose for sleazy pictures and judges will give them drugs. Once they get hooked on drugs they'll turn to prostitution and pornography to support their drug habit. They'll probably get AIDS and die from dirty sex or dirty needles.

B. Evaluate the following statements or arguments. For the arguments, indicate whether the premises are warranted, relevant and sufficient to support their conclusion. If you believe relevant evidence has been omitted, indicate what data should have been brought up. Identify any fallacies.

* 1. The best counselors for juvenile delinquents are ex-convicts who were juvenile delinquents themselves. So, we ought to hire this character Smith since he's the only candidate for the job with a long history of juvenile delinquency.

2. "At the heart of the issue of abortion is the question of what America is all about. Will we continue to destroy the innocent and helpless for mere self-gratification or go back to a nation that protects its children?"

* 3. We should establish a Peace Academy to train young Americans to promote peace because a Peace Academy would definitely prove to a dubious world that the United States is serious about resolving international conflicts without resorting to military might.

* 4. (Letter to the editor: "Abortions should be made illegal because murder in any form should be unlawful. Slaughtering innocent children should never be condoned. The next thing you know, handicapped children and old people will be murdered in the name of 'freedom of choice'. Don't be fooled by the pro-choice rhetoric. Free choice is freedom to be killed if they don't like the way you look."

* 5. "Remembering, which occurs now, cannot...possibly prove that what is remembered occurred at some other time, because the world might have sprung into being five minutes ago, exactly as it then was, full of acts of remembering which were entirely misleading." --Bertrand Russell, *An Outline of Philosophy*

6. All unhappiness is due to unsatisfied desires. All happiness is due to satisfied desires. And, no one can satisfy all his or her desires. Therefore, either one must give up desires and be happy or one must resign oneself to a life of unhappiness. (This is a paraphrase of one of the teachings of the Buddha, Siddhartha Gautama.)

126

7. (Advertisement:) "Why should you take Casavetti's word for it when we tell you that we'll give you the best deal in town on a new car? That's a good question, and we'll give you an honest answer. You can take our word because you can count on us to always deal fair and square. That's the truth! Believe me!"

* 8. It is unreasonable to believe in punishment in the afterlife. For, either there is no afterlife or there is one. If there is none, then it is absurd to believe in punishment after death. If there is an afterlife, then an all-just and all-merciful God would not punish a creature for being too weak to resist desires instilled by the Creator.

* 9. You argue that we should not use American tax dollars to support the Contras in their attempt to overthrow the communist government of Nicaragua. What you are really advocating is support of communism. If we follow your line of reasoning, we should let the communists walk all over us. We should just step out of their way when they set their greedy eyes on another country to conquer.

10. [George Bush, in his closing statement during a debate with Democratic vice-presidential candidate Geraldine Ferraro, Oct. 11, 1984]: "The choice is: Do we move forward with strength and with prosperity, or do we go back to weakness, despair, disrespect?"

11. "We have two alternatives to solving the criminal problem. Either we start sentencing criminals to life in prison without possibility of parole or we institute something similar to Moslem law and begin castrating rapists and cutting off the hands of thieves."

* 12. "There are only three alternatives possible for the origin of the world: it is self-existent, or self-caused, or caused by some external agency. And each of these alternatives is really without meaning to our minds. We cannot conceive that a thing exists in its own right without any source beyond itself; we cannot conceive self-creation, for that implies that the thing exists before it exists; and to refer it to an external creator merely defers the question. For we have to ask, Whence the creator?" --William Ernest Hocking, *Types of Philosophy*.

13. (The following pleas to viewers to send in money are from the wife of a televangelist who had recently purchased a home for $449,000, a Rolls-Royce and a Mercedes Benz.) "Jim and I can't pay the bills. We've given everything we have. And literally we have given everything. I have offered to sell everything I own because things really don't mean that much when it comes to getting the gospel of Jesus Christ out."

* 14. (President Reagan)"If Congress does not pass the IBBM Bill, it is inevitable that there will be an international monetary crisis of insurmountable proportions. Not one country on the face of the earth will be left unscathed and economic ruin will be the result for hundreds of nations throughout the world.

15. All the great minds have been minds of men. The great sculptors have been men—Michelangelo, Rodin, Polyclitus, Moore—and the great painters—Vermeer, da Vinci, Rembrandt—and the great writers—Homer, Dante, Flaubert—and the great philosophers—Plato, Rousseau, Nietzsche—and so on.

16. (Letter to the editor:) "During the holidays, I was stopped in a California Highway Patrol drunk-driver checkpoint. Although the officers were very polite and the time I was stopped was very brief, I felt this checkpoint was only the beginning of things to come. If the checkpoint program is allowed to stand, by the courts and the public, then next will be a checkpoint just for drugs, or infant car seats, or driver's licenses. As a retired police officer, I can express my dislike of the drunk driver. I can understand the checkpoints as a police tool, but I think the citizens' right to free movement is more important. I think if we allow the checkpoints now we will regret them in the future."

* 17. "*The rich aren't paying their share of taxes.* That probably is the most popular of all the liberal shibboleths. The figures: In 1980, wealthy Americans (let us agree to call an American wealthy who earns $50,000 per year or more) amounted to 3 percent of the population. They paid 31 percent of the taxes collected....In sum, the top 3 percent are paying at least five times as many taxes as the bottom 50 percent. Put that in your rich-get-away-with-everything gun, aim at Reagan and pray that someone changes the subject." (William F. Buckley, from his syndicated column of October 5, 1983.)

18. (Reporter) "Mr. President, what do you think about your Secretary of State saying that American women will change their minds on South Africa once they realize they'll have to give up their diamonds if the United States imposes economic sanctions against that country in protest of its policy of apartheid?"
(President)"You guys are always trying to stir up trouble. The secretary's comments were made off the record. I'll bet you buy your lady friends diamonds. I'll bet your mother likes diamonds.

* 19. (The issue being argued is whether unreasonably obtained evidence should be excluded from use by the prosecution during a trial.)
   Proponent: "We should continue excluding illegally obtained evidence in order to protect all citizens from abuses of power on the part of the police. If there are no restrictions on how they obtain evidence--if they are permitted to violate the law at their discretion--then all of us give up a needed protection."
   Opponent: "So, you favor letting criminals go free? You would rather have murderers running around loose in the community than let police officers perform their legal duties."

20. (Letter to the editor:) "Can't you see your inconsistency? In your lead editorial of Feb. 20 you condemn Reagan's hypocritical human rights policy for not opposing human rights violations across the board. Yet you followed with an editorial giving vague endorsement to some form of draft. Isn't it apparent that the draft, by compelling involuntary servitude, is a form of slavery and thus is the greatest of all human rights violations--the right to one's own life?....To endorse a draft is to accept the basic principle of all totalitarian regimes--that the individual exists for the sake of the state. In this country, theoretically at least, isn't the government's purpose to protect the rights of the individual, not violate them?"

C. Evaluate the following statements or arguments. For the arguments, indicate whether the premises are warranted, relevant and sufficient to support their conclusion. If you believe relevant evidence has been omitted, indicate what data should have been brought up. Identify any fallacies.

* 1. (Letter to the editor, in response to Walter Mondale's opposition to a constitutional amendment which would allow organized but voluntary prayer in public schools:) "So Mondale wants to remove religious freedom from schools. This country was founded on God and prayer. We need a president who believes in prayer and the Bible."

2. (Letter to the editor:) "Marx predicted that unrestrained capitalism would destroy itself as the rich grew richer and the poor poorer. It was generally believed that the painful process of establishing restraints by the western powers held the Marxist prediction at bay. Business opposed these restraints, but adapted to them. There was enough leeway for free enterprise to contribute a variety of useful products....Now, under Reaganomics, these restraints have been torn away and unrestrained capitalism rules. All the Russian bear has to do is to sit by and watch unrestrained capitalism destroy itself. The Marxist prediction will be realized."

* 3. U.S. Supreme Court Justice William J. Brennan, Jr. argued against the death penalty many times. In a speech at Hastings College of Law on November 18, 1985, he said : "The state, even as it punishes, must treat its citizens in a manner consistent with their intrinsic worth as human beings....The calculated killing of a human being by the state involves by its very nature an absolute denial of the executed person's humanity and, therefore, violates the constitutional ban on cruel and unusual punishment."

4. "The so-called Child Care Act, which has been introduced into the U.S. Senate, ought to be defeated. It is a deceptive bill; its real aim is to replace parents with government authority. This bill is a spin-off of the declaration by the Communist dominated United Nations, which declared this year the Year of the child. As a member of Citizens for Responsible Government, I urge you to oppose this dangerous bill which, in its own words, will `provide assistance and coordination in the provision of child-care services for children living in homes with working parents and for other purposes.'"

* 5. The problems that plague nuclear power plants are serious and worth thinking about before heavy investment is made in them. Quite apart from the question of safety, there is the matter of disposing the nuclear waste produced by the plants. The wastes can be trapped and reduced to a solid form so that they do not escape into the atmosphere. But what then? Radioactive solids with a half-life of thousands of years will be an enormous burden to future generations. Unless we solve the problem ourselves, we will be creating a situation in which numerous future generations will have to assume an unfair and undeserved responsibility.

* 6. (Letter to the editor:) "What are we up against in the selection of a president? Inflation is worse than ever -- many banks have gone out of business, farmers have gone into foreclosure, warmongering about the world is common, and yet this administration claims success. At least our president doesn't lie--he just atones for it all with excuses. Does he want to be re-elected to further saddle the U.S. with another $100 billion deficit or so?...If we re-elect the present administration, this country will be at its mercy when either the U.S. will go into bankruptcy or be forced to have the highest tax rate in the world. Nobody is better off today because of present administration actions--some may be better off from only natural economic trends....The opponent to the president is sincere and honest. Let's hope the election will result with what's best for the United States."

7. (Former California State Senator John Briggs made the following argument concerning a public initiative to forbid homosexuals from teaching in the state's public schools.) "If the initiative is defeated, then all of those [homosexuals] are going to be asked to come out of the closet and declare themselves, and then what we have done is placed in front of our children those legitimized role models for our young children to emulate. And I think it just portends a period of moral decay in this country that is going to lead to the carrying out or bearing out of the prediction of Gen. MacArthur, who stated that no civilization has ever been recorded as having survived when it falls into a period of economic decline and moral decay. We are certainly in both periods right now . . . .The thrust of the gay liberation movement is to have males reject females in favor of another male and females reject males in favor of the female. Well, if you follow that to its logical conclusion, and since every group wants to multiply many times over, we would breed ourselves out of existence as a country over a long period of time."

128

* 8. (Advertisement).... The Environmental Protection Agency by promulgating--or causing to be promulgated--unnecessarily restrictive regulations, will block the burning of millions of tons of good American coal. Coal that is critical to America's energy needs. They have decided that, in implementing the Clean Air Act, the only way to protect human health from stack gas emissions is to measure the sulfur-oxides at the top of the stack--instead of at ground level where people live and breathe....Will E.P.A. accept the responsibility for the economic effect their restrictive decision will have on the country? Oh no! They'll try to wriggle off the hook by saying you can burn all the coal in America if you'll just install stack gas scrubbers....The naked truth is that there does not exist today a reliable non-polluting stack gas scrubber for electric utility use to eliminate sulfur-oxide emissions. A conclusion shared by the Federal Power Commission, T.V.A., and other respected authorities....At a time when America needs all the coal it can get, it is absolutely senseless for the E.P.A. to stubbornly insist on a particular method for meeting the ambient air standards of the Clean Air Act. It is the results that are important--not the method. ...It would be a crime if a significant portion of this vast American asset went unused because the Environmental Protection Agency could see only one way...their way...to meet the mandate of the Clean Air Act....We know their way won't work. That's what burns.

9. (Letter to the editor:) "I oppose the plan to have federal and state governments turn over our prison systems to private enterprise for the purpose of turning a profit out of inmate labor. How long will it be before political dissidents are arrested on trumped up charges and sent off to the corporate concentration camps to shut them up? How long will it be before the vagrancy laws are reintroduced to acquire cheap slave labor? How long will it be before certain inmates are hired as corporate hit-men to keep the other inmates on the job and producing? How long will it be before judges are offered commissions (i.e., bribes) by corporations for each convict they send to prison? The fact is that our government--federal and state--are rotten to the core. The private prisons idea will provide nothing but corporate slave-labor concentration camps for whatever private business is willing to pay off the government officials put in charge of running the programs. Any government official who supports this idea of prisons run by private corporations ought to be indicted for criminal racketeering."

* 10. (Letter to the editor:) "The ultimate perversion of our actions seems to be what we are doing in Nicaragua, where the Somoza family that had oppressed the country for years was ousted. By supporting Somoza's defeated mercenaries with CIA money and by threatening Nicaragua with our fleet off both the Atlantic and Pacific coasts, we are, by sabotage, trying to destroy this newly formed government. The CIA-sponsored "contras," which we have labeled, ironically, Freedom Fighters, are destroying bridges, dams and towns, and killing women and children. In this situation, it should be no surprise that the Nicaraguans turn to Cuba and the U.S.S.R. for help....What a peculiar way for us, a nation born in revolution only a little more than 200 years ago, to be acting. The greatest mistakes in policy have been made by the present administration, but previous administrations, both Democratic and Republican, have supported oppression in developing countries. We must rethink our policies. Otherwise, we will be the most hated nation in the world, and at the same time, oppressed peoples will look to the U.S.S.R. for help in breaking their chains of bondage, instead of to the U.S."

11. (Letter to the editor:) "Every month an innocent woman is put to death in a most brutal manner. The murderer, when apprehended, is treated to months of trials, fed, housed, and if not released for lack of evidence, is given an extremely short jail term. The criminal justice system has in essence stated, 'Every person has the right to take another's life, and we will in turn treat the offender as if he/she were the person who was oppressed.' We have two alternatives to solving the criminal problem in California. The first is to abolish the lenient sentencing system. If a person commits a planned murder, for example, the minimum sentence should be life with no parole. The second alternative would be something similar to Moslem law. If, for example, a thief steals, his hands would be cut off, And, a rapist would be castrated."

* 12. (Letter to the editor:) "Your paper has not been living up to its potential and it has not been doing its job. In several instances recently, your staff could have taken mundane or morbid stories and made incisive commentaries on the human condition. Instead, you opted for mediocrity. In an article on the deaths of three local youths, you could have dealt with the role of nutrition in mental illness, but you didn't. In an article on the Blues Festival, you could have discussed the music, but you didn't. And, in an article on renovating slums, you could have chided an elected official for hypocrisy, but you failed to do so."

13. (Letter to the editor, written in response to the imposition of a $50 per semester education fee for full-time community college students:) "I keep hearing all of this bilge about how the imposition of fees in community colleges will have a negligible effect. I could expect no less from an individual, Governor George, who views the current governor's salary of $49,000 a year as woefully inadequate.... Education is the great equalizer of individuals. To impose additional financial burdens on the backs of the politically disenfranchised is to further increase the disparity of economic conditions within our state. Education should be provided to all at the lowest, or no, cost....Education is expensive to provide. Nonetheless, education is crucial for the social and material development of this nation. The greater expense and travesty would be to deprive, de facto, those with scarce resources of an education....Governor George reminds me of a certain British monarch. The monarch merely taxed tea. Governor George would impose a tax on learning."

14. (Letter to the editor, in response to an editorial that complained that too much farmland is being bought up by land developers and that legislators 'ought to do something about it to protect farmland the way certain public lands are protected':) "The ownership of private property separates a free people from an enslaved people. It is not our farmland; this land belongs to the individual farmer. I own state parks, I own public property, I do not own the farmland. If we the people permit government to start owning private farmland, where will this lead us? The next step will be government owning other rights of individual citizens, such as your bank account, your choice of where you live, your choice of work and so on and so on....It is time to stop encouraging our people to refer to farmland, ranchland or any land owned by a private individual as "ours." If the American people are now ready to embrace the Communistic philosophy of government ownership of land and production, then I guess starting with farmland is the first logical step. I, for one, am not ready to hand over my rights to private property; neither am I ready to take the rights of the farmer or any other American to buy and sell his property to suit his financial or personal needs....Who knows, maybe next year government control of newspapers for the so-called "good of the people" will follow the confiscation of private land use."

* 15. (The following passage is a response to the question "Should voters enact some federal laws directly?") "The proposed national legislative initiative is a mischievous and deceptive means of centralizing, polarizing and destabilizing a tested Constitutional order. It would undermine the government of balanced power, reason and broad-based consent, prophetically advanced by our Founding Fathers. The Supreme Court, the states, Congress, political parties and the presidency would have to take a back seat to well-financed campaigns by passionate single-issue groups for simplistic national solutions to complex problems. Consider the havoc which would be caused by "yes" votes on initiatives repealing civil rights acts, or balancing the federal budget by percentage reductions in defense appropriations." [Peter G. Fish, associate professor of political science, Duke University]

Exercise 5-5 Self-test: true or false? (Check your answers in Answers to Selected Exercises.)

1. It is an irrelevant appeal to authority to try to establish the truth of a controversial point by noting that a well-known expert has taken the position you are supporting.
2. The assumptions of an argument are the basic premises upon which the argument stands or falls.
3. A non sequitur is a type of hasty conclusion.
4. The slippery slope fallacy always occurs when one asserts that a chain of horrible events will follow the taking or not taking of some action.
5. An assumption in an argument is a premise for which no support is given.
6. If the conclusion of an argument is false then that conclusion cannot follow from the argument's premises.
7. When an arguer assumes something questionable in order to support a questionable claim, she is said to be *begging the question*.
8. All else being equal, the more reliable a source for a given premise, the more weight the premise ought to be given.
9. When evaluating the testimony of others, we are evaluating their character and integrity as well.
10. When a conclusion is based upon insufficient evidence the argument is said to commit the fallacy of *hasty conclusion*.
11. A conclusion should be asserted to follow with a degree of certainty proportionate to the evidence presented in the premises.
12. If it is not certain that a premise is true, the most reasonable belief is that the premise is probably false.
13. An argument with an irrelevant or false premise should not be rejected as completely unsound if there are more significant premises that, taken together, provide adequate support for the conclusion.
14. To try to divert attention away from a charge being made against a person is called an *ad hominem*.
15. Emotive appeals are rarely persuasive.
16. Human emotions are generally much more powerful motives to action than logical reasons are.
17. If the premises of an argument are false or questionable, then the argument is unsound.
18. The *argument to ignorance* might be more accurately called 'the fallacy of lack of sufficient evidence to the contrary.'
19. The *slippery slope fallacy* is usually combined with an *appeal to vanity*.
20. Hypothetical assertions are questionable assertions assumed to be false.
21. The *non sequitur* fallacy occurs when a position one opposes is presented in a distorted way by exaggerating it or by presenting only its weakest defense.
22. The fallacy of *ad populum* occurs when one restricts the number of alternatives to fewer than three.
23. A good argument is clear and is based on relevant, warranted assumptions.
24. A question is loaded if directly answering it traps one into asserting the truth or falsity of some claim that is questionable.

130

25. Perhaps the most frequently used technique for making an argument appear stronger that it really is, is to omit relevant evidence.
26. The ad hominem fallacy occurs when the fact that large numbers of people believe something is taken as a sufficient reason for accepting the belief as true.
27. A good argument does not try to mislead, nor does it omit warranted, relevant evidence.
28. The fallacy of the argument from ignorance occurs when one tries to argue that something is true only because it hasn't been proved false or false only because it has not been proved true.
29. Whenever an arguer assumes what ought to be proved, she is said to be affirming the consequent.
30. If the premises upon which a conclusion stands are false or questionable, then the argument is said to be unsound because based on unwarranted assumptions.
31. Relevant premises are those which are germane or pertinent to proving the conclusion of the argument.

Further Reading - Chapter Five

Browne, M. Neil and Stuart M. Keeley (2003). *Asking the Right Questions: A Guide to Critical Thinking*, 7th edition. Pearson Education.

Damer, T. Edward (2000). *Attacking Faulty Reasoning: A Practical Guide to Fallacy-Free Arguments*. 4th edition. Wadsworth.

Engle, Morris S. (2000). *With Good Reason: An Introduction to Informal Fallacies*, 6th edition. Bedford Books.

Kahane, Howard. (2001). *Logic and Contemporary Rhetoric: The Use of Reason in Everyday Life*. 9th edition. Wadswordth.

Chapter Six - Evaluating Extended Arguments

Men are so made that they can resist sound argument,
and yet yield to a glance.
--Honoré de Balzac

1. Introduction

To develop your critical thinking skills you will need to read long--sometimes difficult--articles which contain arguments. We will refer to such articles as *argumentative essays* and to the arguments they contain as *extended arguments.* Analyzing and evaluating extended arguments can help you develop critical thinking skills by stimulating you to think more clearly and deeply about complex topics.

One of the more difficult tasks you will face in evaluating extended arguments will be detecting *unstated premises and unstated conclusions.* Arguers will not always explicitly state all their premises. Some premises may be unstated because they are taken for granted by the arguer; others may seem too obviously true to need stating. A conclusion may be so obviously implied that it is left unstated. For example, if you and some thirsty companions are on a hike and you come upon a waterhole, you might test the water before drinking it. Imagine that you have a water-testing kit that works this way: you put a drop of testing solution in a special container which you fill with the water to be tested; if the water turns red, it is unsafe to drink. You test a sample of the water. It turns red. Now, imagine you say to the others, "It turned red, so we'd better not drink it." You have made an argument, but you have not stated all your premises or conclusions. A complete version of your reasoning might go like this:

(1) [unstated premise]	**If the sample turns red upon adding a drop of the testing solution, then the water is unsafe to drink.**
(2) stated premise	***The sample turned red upon adding a drop of the testing solution.***
(3) [unstated conclusion and unstated premise]	**The water is unsafe.**
(4) [unstated premise]	**If we drink unsafe water, we'll get sick.**
(5) [unstated premise]	**We do not want to get sick.**
(6) stated conclusion	***We'd better not drink the water.***

The argument as stated makes two explicit claims (statements 2 and 6 above). A simple diagram might be drawn to represent the relationship of premise to conclusion (see diagram 1).

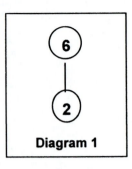

Diagram 1

That is, statement 2 is offered as a reason for accepting statement 6. (Compare the two sentences, "It turned red" and "the sample turned red upon adding a drop of the testing solution." Notice that although these sentences are not identical, they make the same claim. That is, they make the same statement. Thus, although sentence no. 2 in the reconstructed argument is not the same as the *sentence* in the example given, it is the same *premise*. Technically, the premise is the claim or statement made, not the actual sentence used to make it. Thus, I have labeled no. 2 as a stated premise, although it is not the same sentence as the one in the original example.) A diagram of the completed or filled-out argument is given in diagram 2.

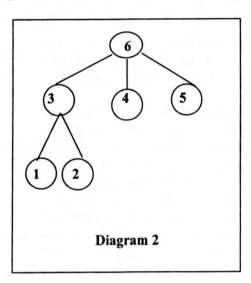

Diagram 2

Statements 1, 2 and 3 make up a sub-argument with 3 as the conclusion. Statement 3 is also a premise, along with statements 4 and 5, offered to support the main conclusion, statement 6.

The unstated premises in the above example were left out because they are so obvious. That is, in the given context it would be reasonable to assume that everybody knew how this test worked and that no one would desire to get ill. The context, in other words, will often determine what premises or conclusions will be unstated due to their obviousness.

2. Hidden assumptions

Sometimes, however, an arguer makes assumptions that many people would not take for granted. If these unstated assumptions are presumed to support a conclusion, we might call them *hidden assumptions,* to distinguish them from mere unstated premises. For example, an arguer might say, "No law should allow murder, so capital punishment should be outlawed." The arguer is assuming that capital punishment is murder--not an assumption many people take for granted.

Exercise 6-1.

Identify any unstated premises or conclusions in the following arguments. Note any hidden assumptions.

* 1. Either we don't make the car payment or we don't pay the rent. If we don't pay the rent, we'll be kicked out into the streets. So, I guess we'll pay the rent.
2. No one has a right to deprive another person of his right to life. So, abortion is wrong.
3. If everyone thought the way you do, there would be no freedom. Thank God, not everyone thinks like you.
4. Either you are lying or you've made a mistake, and you haven't made a mistake.
* 5. If the Reds came in second, then the Dodgers came in first. So, the Dodgers came in first.
6. Four murder suspects agree among themselves to each make only one statement to the police. They also agree that three of the statements will be false and one statement will be true. Abe says "I didn't kill Dr. Logico." Babe says "Dave killed Dr.

Logico." Dave says "Abe killed Dr. Logico." Ewe says "I didn't kill Dr. Logico." (So, obviously, _____ killed Dr. Logico!)

7. Exxon's management must be out of its corporate mind, since it allowed a man without a valid driver's license due to drunken driving convictions to steer a fully loaded supertanker through the environmentally fragile waters of Prince William Sound.

8. You say you don't understand why the SPCA wants to end the eating of dogs by Southeast Asians, so you must not be aware of the torture methods used by these people. They string the dogs up by their hind legs and then often skin or boil them alive. Tradition is no excuse for barbarism, especially in a society such as ours, which professes to believe in the humane treatment of pets.

9. All drugs should be legalized immediately. The present situation is ridiculous: Organized crime makes billions of dollars; turf wars kill innocent bystanders and terrorize the citizenry; burglary and muggings by drug addicts are a normal aspect of city life; police departments are understaffed and overworked; violent criminals are released because of prison overcrowding; despite billions of dollars spent on drug enforcement there are more illegal drugs available to more people than ever before.

The current "solution"--strict anti-drug laws--doesn't work at all. The only people who benefit by keeping these laws in place are organized crime, government officials (representatives who depend on hefty contributions from organized crime to fund their re-election campaigns and bureaucrats whose job status depends on the perpetuation of, not the solution to, the drug problem) and pushers of legal drugs (tobacco and alcohol kill 100 times more people annually than all the illegal drugs combined).

Also, it is nobody's business what drugs anyone takes, so long as each person pays his or her own way in society and does not harm others.

3. Analysis of extended arguments

Before evaluating an extended argument, the argument must be identified. This will involve not only recognizing premises and conclusions, but also separating the argument from the other material presented along with it in the argumentative essay. This other material will include background information, illustrations (graphs, charts, clarifying examples, etc.), and fluff. The background material serves to introduce the topic and often to indicate its significance or to explain why the author is motivated to write about that particular issue. Background material can be useful in clarifying the sense and importance of an argument. Illustrations, too, can help clarify premises. Fluff, on the other had, refers to material having no argumentative or illuminative purpose. Fluff need not simply be padding--excess verbiage--but may include such things as stories, anecdotes and jokes, which may serve a rhetorical and persuasive function.

An argument evaluation should be of the argument itself, not of the background material, illustrations or fluff. What follows is an outline of a method to follow for analyzing and evaluating extended arguments. This method is, of course, not the only possible method for argument analysis and evaluation, but it is a good one for beginners. After the student becomes more practiced at argument evaluation, she ought to modify the method to serve her needs and purposes best.

3.1 A general method for analyzing and evaluating extended arguments

Each of the steps of the method will be exemplified in detail below.

1. *Read the argument and identify the main point.* Pay attention to the title, if there is one. Try to grasp the main conclusion and the general line of argument. Do not try to analyze or evaluate the argument on the first reading.

2. ***Extract the argument from the other material in the essay***. List the reasons and arguments given in support of the main conclusion.

3. ***Evaluate the reasons and the reasoning.***

On the second reading of the argument, many students will find it useful, if not essential, to take notes. Restrict your notes to making *evaluative* comments on the premises or the reasoning in the argument. Your notes should indicate a critical reading, i.e., they should highlight the strengths (warranted, relevant, significant premises) and weaknesses (unclear language, unwarranted or irrelevant premises, omitted evidence, insufficient evidence) of the argument.

Your evaluation of the argument ought to be presented in the form of a short essay that summarizes the main strengths and weaknesses of the argument. An in-depth evaluation might also include counter-arguments, as well as anticipated criticisms of your counter-arguments. A counter-argument is a contrasting, opposing or refuting argument. For example, you might use evidence omitted by an arguer to support a conclusion contrary to the arguer's. Or you might use the same evidence as the arguer, but try to show that it leads to a different conclusion from the one made by the arguer. Finally, you might conclude your evaluation with a statement of your own view on the topic and an indication of what further information you might need in order to judge the issue more clearly and fairly.

3.2 Exemplifying the Method

To illustrate the method, we will go through each of the three steps for the following argumentative essay, "How to Stop the Violence." Read the article before going on to study the analysis and evaluation. Try to grasp the main conclusion and the gist of argument, but do not try to analyze or evaluate the article during your first reading.

How to Stop the Violence

As everybody knows, there is an epidemic of violence in our country. Every day we read about teenagers shooting other teenagers in their schools. Some people blame the Internet. They say that children can learn how to build bombs and where to buy guns by going online. But people were shooting one another long before the Internet came along.

Others blame guns. They say that only if there were more gun laws, there wouldn't be all this violence. More gun laws would just mean that when people use guns to commit crimes they would be breaking more laws, but it wouldn't reduce the number of gun deaths.

Still others think that the depiction of vivid violence in movies and in video games is the cause of the violence. People were violent long before video games and movies came along.

People are putting the blame in the wrong place. The reason there is so much violence today is because we have lost our moral character. If there had been a copy of the Ten Commandments on the walls of the classrooms at Columbine High in Colorado, those boys never would have killed all those people. If there had been required prayer every day from kindergarten on up, violence in America would be almost non-existent.

I know there will be skeptics who will say, "But Stalin was a seminarian and Hitler sang in the church choir." These claims are true, but Stalin and Hitler are exceptions that prove the rule. Slobodan Milosovic may have been raised in a religious household but that does not disprove my point. He lost faith in God at some point, as did Stalin and Hitler. Had they kept the faith, they would not have become so evil.

We need to return to the days when we all worshipped the same God on Sunday. Only then will we return to the days of peace and quiet our ancestors used to know. Science will prove me right. There have been studies that have shown that people who pray live longer than people who don't. Moreover, prayer has been shown to help the sick recover more quickly.

Thus, we must have a constitutional amendment to require prayer in our public and private schools. This notion is supported by former Vice-President Sam Snail and by Senator Leeroy Smart; both start each day with a prayer and have not shot anyone in all their days on Earth. Only when we require every school child to pray, will there be an end to the violence that plagues our nation.

§

First, look at the title of the essay. The title reveals that this essay is going to tell us how to stop the violence and the article itself tells us that the only way we can stop the violence in America is through prayer. The main conclusion of the argument is that **we must have a constitutional amendment requiring prayer in school.** What premises and sub-arguments does the author give to support this claim?

One line of reasoning *assumes* that the cause of the violence is either the Internet, lack of gun controls, the mass media (violence films and video games), or lack of moral character. This is a *questionable assumption*. In fact, it is a *false dilemma*. There are other alternatives that should be considered, such as the fact that nations often resort to violence against each other when they have a grievance. Not only is this a bad example for children, it indicates that maybe there is something violent in human nature. Also ignored, is the possibility that the violence has several causes.

The arguer also assumes that people with good moral character do not blow up their schools and shoot their classmates. This seems like a safe assumption.

The arguer dismisses the Internet and the mass media as causes of the violence because people were violent before the Internet, movies or video games arrived. This is true, but irrelevant. The Internet may well be a significant contributing factor to the violence by providing easy access to guns by mail order and detailed instructions on how to make bombs. This topic needs to be studied, not dismissed outright. There have been many studies that have found a significant, if small, correlation between exposure to violent media and violent behavior. These studies should be discussed, not ignored.

The arguer assumes that the only way to control guns is by laws. The arguer is probably correct in assuming that if there were more gun control laws, criminals would just be violating more laws when they used guns to commit their crimes. More laws may not have a significant effect on criminal activity. Yet, all laws are not the same. Some laws may make it very difficult for young people to quickly access guns and ingredients for bombs. This issue should be studied further, rather than dismissed. Furthermore, control need not be by law. Education, greater care in securing weapons and ammunition by gun owners, etc. might be effective. The issue should be investigated.

The arguer assumes that if children were required to pray in school and had such things as the Ten Commandments hanging in their schools, they would grow up with good moral character. The evidence that this assumption is false seems overwhelming. The arguer even mentions three of the most evil men in our century, all of whom were raised on the Ten Commandments and in Christian religious environments. Contrary to what the author says, the examples do not prove that being taught to pray from an early age will lead to good moral character. If anything, the examples prove that being religious while young does not necessarily mean you will grow up to be a good person.

Furthermore, many people of faith have killed and tortured others because they would not accept the "true religion" or simply because they belonged to some other religion than the ones doing the violence. Most people do not do violence to others. Thus, it is probably true that most religious people do not do violence to others, but the arguer does not provide any data that shows that a significantly greater number of those who do violence are irreligious.

The author also assumes that once upon a time there was peace in the land and it was because people worshipped on Sundays. The author produces no evidence to support these notions, most likely because there isn't any. Moreover, the references to studies connecting prayer with health, even if accurate, are irrelevant to the issue of prayer and violence. Also irrelevant are the appeals to Snail and Mart as authorities.

We can summarize the argument as

We must have a constitutional amendment requiring prayer in school because it will end violence in America. The Internet, availability of guns, and the mass media are not significant factors in the violence in America. People who learn to pray at an early age grow up to be of good moral character and people of good moral character do not commit violent crimes.

The argument is unsound. It is based upon numerous questionable and false assumptions. It also introduces irrelevant appeals to studies that have nothing to do with the issue of prayer and violence and to political authorities who support the idea.

4. Some Additional Strategies

The only way to become proficient at extended argument analysis and evaluation is to practice. This chapter will conclude with links to Internet sites where you will find several unanalyzed and unevaluated extended arguments. Apply the method outlined and exemplified above to these arguments for practice.

In addition to what we have already said, here are a few additional strategies to employ when critically evaluating extended arguments.

1. **Language**. Look for highly emotive, biased or slanted language. Some arguments are persuasive mainly because of the persuasive language used, not because of the logic of the reasoning.

2. **Either/or arguments.** Look out for those arguments which propose two alternative positions, attack one of the positions, and then, even though little or no positive evidence has been given to support the other position, lead the reader to believe that the unscathed position is warranted. This is a not-so-subtle form of false dilemma.

3. **Argument by anecdote**. Some arguments are persuasive because of the powerful anecdotes, stories, examples, etc. that are put forth to support broad generalizations already uncritically held by numbers of people. Attacks on the Welfare System, Education, Government Bureaucracy, Politics, Science, Religion, the Military, the Police, Teenagers, etc., are often persuasive though the only support for the attacks may be an anecdotal horror story--perhaps not even a true story, just one made up to "illustrate" the general point being asserted (but not proved). Such arguments inevitably beg the question and play upon people's prejudices and preconceived notions.

IV. **The Baffle-You-With-Numbers Argument**. Every fallacy mentioned and described in chapter five can be committed using statistics. In the next chapter, the use and misuse of statistics will be discussed in more detail. Here we simply warn you to look out for suppressed evidence, irrelevant comparisons, and questionable claims in arguments which try to baffle you with numbers.

5. Argument Evaluation Checklist.

1. Do I understand the main conclusion?

2. Have I separated the reasons given to support the conclusion from background material, examples, illustrations, irrelevant fluff, etc.?

3. Can I list the main premises and sub-arguments?

4. Is there any ambiguity, vagueness or obscurity that hinders my understanding of the argument?

5. Have I evaluated the truth, relevance, fairness, completeness, significance, and sufficiency of the premises to support the conclusion?

6. Are there any fallacies?

7. Is the language excessively emotive?

8. What further information, if any, do I need in order to make a reasonable judgment on the issue?

9. What is my overall evaluation of the argument?

Exercise 6-2

Find an extended argument in a newspaper or magazine. Analyze and evaluate the argument. Use the Argument Evaluation Checklist to go over your evaluation. (Note: do not just answer the questions 'yes' or 'no'! Demonstrate that you understand the premises, conclusions, and the like.)

Exercise 6-3

Visit the following WWW sites and evaluate the arguments posted there.

1. Against the Death Penalty (American Civil Liberties Union):
   http://www.aclu.org/DeathPenalty/DeathPenaltyMain.cfm
2. In support of the Death Penalty (John Stuart Mill): http://ethics.acusd.edu/Mill.html
3. Against Gay Marriage (Stanley Kurtz):
   http://www.nationalreview.com/kurtz/kurtz200402050842.asp
4. In support of Gay Marriage (Andrew Sullivan):
   http://www.andrewsullivan.com/homosexuality.php?artnum=20010813
5. Against Experimenting on Animals (Christopher Anderegg, M.D., Ph.D. et al.):
   http://www.mrmcmed.org/Critcv.html
6. In support of Animal Experimentation: http://www.curedisease.com/Altern1.html

Chapter Seven – Sampling & Analogical Reasoning

> "We come to believe that the results of opinion polls
> *are* what people believe, as if our beliefs
> can be encapsulated in such sentences as
> 'I approve' and 'I disapprove.'"
> -- Neil Postman

> "Analogies prove nothing, that is quite true,
> but they can make one feel more at home."
> --Sigmund Freud

Two of the more important kinds of inductive reasoning are sampling and analogical reasoning. Sampling is a type of simple induction that generalizes from what is known about some individuals of the same type (a sample) to others of that type. Analogical reasoning involves comparing things on the basis of similarities.

1. Surveys and Polls

Surveys and polls have become a part of everyday life in our country. How are they done and why does anyone consider them reliable sources of useful information? Let's take a close look at part of the National Annenberg Election Survey (NAES) published on May 17, 2004, by the Annenberg Public Policy Center of the University of Pennsylvania. The survey asked people for their opinion on same-sex marriages, which became legal in Massachusetts on the day the results of the poll were released. They also inquired into people's opinion on a constitutional amendment that would prohibit such marriages. Their press release began with the following statements.

> As same-sex marriage begins today in Massachusetts, Americans remain opposed to the concept but still dubious about prohibiting it by a constitutional amendment, the University of Pennsylvania's National Annenberg Election Survey shows.

> Interviewing of 3,775 adults from May 3 through 16 showed that 61 percent of the public said they opposed a law that would permit same-sex marriages in their state, while 30 percent said they favored it.

> Those findings were not significantly different from the last Annenberg measure of the question. February 14 through 23 polling found that 64 percent were opposed to a same-sex marriage law in their state while 30 percent were in favor.

> Nor was there significant change on the issue of a constitutional amendment to prohibit states from allowing same-sex marriages. In the latest polling, 42 percent supported such an amendment while 50 percent opposed one. In the February 14-23 period (which ended one day before President Bush called for an amendment), 41 percent favored an amendment and 48 percent opposed one.

The NAES asserts that *Americans* are opposed to same-sex marriage and are dubious about the constitutional amendment. We're told that 3,775 adults were interviewed. What justifies drawing a conclusion about *Americans*—who number about 300,000,000—from a **sample** of just 3,775?

First, we should note that *Americans* is short for "American adults," which is considered the **target population** for this survey. Only American adults were in the sample, so the conclusion can only be about

American adults. Even so, how could 3,775 adults be **representative** of the entire adult population? What kind of method did the Annenberg folks use to give them the confidence to **generalize** about the adult population as a whole based on their sample of fewer than 4,000? We're told

> The 2004 National Annenberg Election Survey is based on telephone interviews which began October 7, 2003 and will continue past Election Day.
>
> The sample of telephone exchanges called was randomly selected by a computer from a complete list of thousands of active residential exchanges across the country. Within each exchange, random digits were added to form a complete telephone number, thus permitting access to both listed and unlisted numbers. Within each household, one adult was designated by a random procedure to be the respondent for the survey. The interviewing is conducted by Schulman, Ronca, Bucuvalas, Inc.
>
> The results have been weighted to take account of household size and number of telephone lines into the residence and to adjust for variation in the sample relating to geographic region, sex, race, age and education.
>
> This report deals with interviewing conducted from May 2 through May 16, when 3,775 people were asked about a proposed constitutional amendment. In theory, in 19 cases out of 20 the results will differ by no more than three percentage points, up or down, from what would have been obtained by interviewing all American adults. The question about a state law allowing same-sex marriages was asked of 1,181 people, and the margin of sampling error for those answers is plus or minus three percentage points. For smaller subgroups, the margin of sampling error would be higher.
>
> In addition to sampling error, the practical difficulties of conducting any survey of public opinion may introduce other sources of error into the poll. Variations in the wording and order of questions, for example, may lead to somewhat different results.

Without getting bogged down in too many details regarding these procedures, we can see that the polling firm has a number of specific techniques it uses to get a fair and balanced cross section of the adult population in its sample. Yet, the pollsters admit that there are **sampling errors** and "practical difficulties" that mean, in effect, they can't guarantee their results. Nevertheless, they are quite confident that if someone were to repeat the interviews using their methods that 95% of the time (19 out of 20) they'd get the same results plus or minus three percentage points. *In theory*, they say, we can accept these results as what we'd have gotten had we interviewed all American adults.

We'll get to the notion of **sampling error** in due time. First, let's review the method of selecting the sample. The validity of sampling depends upon the **representativeness** of the sample, which in turn depends on *how* the sample was selected and *how many* were in the sample. A sample is likely to be representative if a method of selecting the sample is used that will result in **a good cross section of typical items in the target population.** If a **biased** method is used to select the sample, then the reasoning will not be justified. If the sample is *too small*, it is likely to be biased. We can never be absolutely sure a sample is representative, but the more unbiased the method of selecting the sample is, the more likely it will be representative. If a method is used that favors or disfavors the selection of particular items to the sample, then the sample will be biased. For example, a sample of American adults that favored the selection of Republicans over Democrats would be biased no matter how large it is.

A method of selecting a sample that gives each item in the target population an equal chance of being selected is considered the most unbiased way of sampling. Such a sample is called a **random sample**. Let's say that we manufacture widgets and want to make sure our widgets perform to our standards. We could test every widget that comes off the assembly line. Sometimes this is possible; sometimes it is necessary. This is the only

140

way we can be sure that every item performs exactly as it is supposed to perform. However, sometimes it is impossible to test every item, e.g., when the test would destroy or damage the item. Often, it is not necessary to test every item. Moreover, sometimes it is impractical to test every item, e.g., when the target population is extremely large. Testing an adequate random sample—rather than all items in a population—will be sufficient.

How do we select a random sample, and *how many* should we select? First, do not let the word 'random' mislead you. You might think that someone standing on the assembly line, whimsically selecting items, would be collecting a random sample. She wouldn't. The mark of a **random sample** is **that each item in the target population has an equal chance of being selected**. You could not be sure that the person whimsically choosing items was in fact free of bias in her method of selection. She may be unaware of her bias and you may not be able to identify any bias. To be sure that the method of selection is unbiased, we should use another method. For example, we could program a machine to select items randomly by numbering each item and having the machine select random numbers.

If a random sample is impossible or impractical, we might use the method of **systematic sampling**. For example, we could have a robot select every 10th, 100th, or 1000th widget as it came off the assembly line. We could program the computer to select a random number (under 11, 101, or 1001) to determine which widget will be the first tested. A systematic sample would *not* be a truly random sample. It might even lead to a biased sample in some cases. Imagine, for example, an assembly line running 24 hours a day, 5 days a week. The company has three different work crews, each working an 8-hour shift. If the robot is programmed so that it continually skips one shift, or significantly under-represents one shift, the sample will be biased. We can get a good cross section of the widgets using the systematic method, but we must make sure the robot selects an adequate sample from each of the three shifts.

Some very famous surveys have been biased. The Kinsey report, for example, is the source for a homosexuality statistic widely reported in both the mass media and in scientific publications, though the statistic is based on biased samples and is erroneous. Kinsey's famous studies on sexual behavior have been repeatedly cited as the basis for the claim that 10% of the population is gay. In fact, numerous studies have been done which put the percentage of *adults who describe themselves as exclusively gay* as between one and two percent.[1] The reason that the Kinsey statistic on gays was so much higher than other studies is due to the biased samples he used. (*Bias* refers to *unintentional inclination,* not to homophobia.) He gathered his data, in part, by distributing questionnaires to prisoners and to people who attended his lectures on sexuality, neither of which were likely to be a good cross section of Americans.

2. Inductive generalizations

Surveys and polls use inductive reasoning to draw conclusions about target populations based on samples taken from those populations. Justified inductive generalizations can provide us with a useful means of facing the future because they are *predictive*. They tell us not only about the people we have interviewed or the items we have observed and measured; they tell us about people we haven't interviewed and about items we have not observed or measured.

The testing of causal hypotheses in science is based, in part, on the same inductive principle as polling: We need only study a *part* of a population to gain knowledge about that population in general. A scientist does not have to study *every* virus of a certain type in order to draw justifiable conclusions about that type of virus. Since the number of individual viruses of any given type is probably extremely large, it is possible that in some cases the percentage of individuals of a type actually observed might be close to zero. The same would be true for an astronomer studying any particular type of star. No matter how many stars astronomers actually observe, that number will be an infinitesimally small fraction of all stars. The same would be true for a chemist studying human DNA. The same is true for a pollster studying the opinions or behavior patterns (beliefs and actions) of human populations. For example, there are about 300,000,000 Americans. The poll which concluded that 61% of all American adults are opposed to same-sex marriages was based on a sample of 3,775 adults, which is a very small percentage of the total population. Each person polled represents about 80,000 others. However, this sample is immensely larger than any percentage of the "population" a chemist, biologist, or physicist is likely to study in a lifetime of scientific investigation of molecules, cells, or atomic particles. The samples studied by the chemist, the biologist, and the physicist are generally homogeneous, however. Once the type of item to be studied is identified, selecting which items to study is not a major problem since "one water molecule is pretty much like any other water molecule," etc. What matters is not what *percentage* of the total target population is in the sample. **What matters is how likely it is that the sample is a good cross section of the target population.** What matters is how likely it is that the items in the sample are *typical* of the target population.

More problematic than the size of polling samples is that opinions are treated as if they were observable, measurable, and fixed qualities. The "technique of polling promotes the assumption that an opinion is a thing inside people that can be exactly located and extracted by the pollster's questions" (Postman 1992: 134). Furthermore, it promotes the assumption that we *ought* to have an opinion on the issue being polled. Maybe what we *ought* to have is information that would help us make a reasonable judgment about the issue. Maybe questions ought to stimulate thought and discussion about an issue rather than end it by gathering useless data from an uninformed populace and announcing some statistic.

3. The method of selecting the sample

To select its sample the Annenberg survey on same-sex marriages used a rather elaborate telephone survey method, involving randomly selected telephone exchanges (the first three digits of a local number) from across the country. Since the last four numbers of each person called were selected randomly, both listed and unlisted numbers were included. Finally, a random procedure was used to select which person in the household would be interviewed. As stated above, the ideal way of selecting a sample would be to use a method that gives every member of the target population an equal chance of being in the sample. This would give us a *random sample*. However, a true random sample is not possible or feasible in polling large populations. The method used in the Annenberg Poll, *telephone sampling*, is perhaps the most common method of conducting polls. Area codes and phone numbers can be randomly generated by a computer or randomly selected from lists of phone numbers, ensuring that a good cross section of the state or nation is called. It is true that such a method will *systematically exclude* large sections of the target population: people not at home, people who are home but who will not participate, and people without telephones. Ask yourself, however, whether such people are likely to be significantly different with respect to their beliefs and actions than people who are home when the pollsters call? How would you go about finding out such a thing? If people are not home, will not participate, or do not have a telephone how can you poll them to see if they are significantly different from the people who are home and do participate? The only thing we can be sure of is that people who do not have a telephone are never counted in telephone surveys.

Any other method than the telephone survey of a large target population would probably be too costly and time consuming. Door to door sampling is out of the question for a statewide survey by a polling firm. Randomly selecting addresses to poll in a town is possible and safe only in small towns. Using mailed questionnaires allows one to send out the survey to all members or a good cross section of a target population, but there is no guarantee that those who return the survey are representative. Such a method can be very costly, also. More importantly, *self-selected samples are always biased*.

Thus, at most, we should probably say that the Annenberg Poll uses a method that is likely to give us a good idea of what a good portion of society believes.

4. Size of sample and margin of error

Next, let's consider the size of the Annenberg sample. How many were in the sample, and is it large enough to give us a good cross section of the target population?

You might think that the Poll was biased because it was based on the views of only 3,375 people out of a population of 300 million. Actually, most pollsters would consider this sample to be of adequate size. How a sample of one, two, or three thousand can be representative of a population of 30,000,000 or 300,000,000 is a curious thing and worthy of concern. I'll try to explain it as best I can, though the 'real' reason has something to do with Gaussian curves, standards of deviation, probability distributions, and a few other statistical concepts best left to experts to explain. I will begin my non-expert explanation with the concept of **margin of sampling error**.[2]

The Annenberg Poll states that it has a margin of sampling error of plus or minus three percentage points. This statistic is calculated by plugging the value of the size of the sample into a statistical formula. Many news articles refer to the margin of sampling error as the *margin of error*. As a result, this statistic may give the appearance of being a measure of the poll's accuracy, i.e., representativeness, but *margin of sampling* error is completely independent of representativeness. A small margin of error (plus or minus 3 percent or less) tells us that the researchers are extremely confident that if they were to repeat the telephone survey one hundred times, in 95 of those times they would get the same results *plus or minus the margin of sampling error*. In other words, the Annenberg pollsters are extremely confident that there is a high probability that the percentage of American adults who oppose same-sex marriage is between 58% and 64%.

If the poll were repeated, no one would expect each sample to result in exactly the same statistics. There would be some variation due to chance. The margin of sampling error gives us a good indication what that chance variation is likely to be. The statistical formula that measures margin of error measures only a statistical probability of chance differences among individual items in a random sample. It does not measure errors due to biased data, erroneous calculations, or inappropriate application of the statistical data. I repeat that it can therefore be a very misleading statistic. A small margin of error might be taken to indicate that a sample is very representative of its population. However, the margin of error is dependent solely on the *size* of the sample. If the *method* of selecting that sample is biased to begin with, a small margin of error won't help. In other words, a low margin of error might be said to mean that *if the sample is not representative, that fact is not likely due to the sample size being too small!*

In addition, the margin of error does not decrease by a one-to-one factor with sample size. Margin of error varies with the square root of the sample size. Thus, to increase the reliability of a properly done statistical study 10-fold, one would have to increase the size of the sample 100-fold (Langley 1970: 45).[3] Often, increasing the accuracy of a properly done study by two or three percent would be extremely costly; hence, researchers commonly use samples of under 1,000. In fact, it is probably safe to say that the size of most public opinion polls is determined in large part by *cost*. If one can get a margin of error of about plus or minus 3% with a sample of about 1,200 why spend the money, time, and effort to double or triple the sample size, when the decrease in margin of error would be barely noticed or appreciated?

Another thing to consider is that when pollsters divide their sample into sub-groups, the sample sizes for each sub-group must be smaller than the sample of all those polled. Therefore, the margin of sampling error for sub-groups will be *greater* than the margin of error for all those polled. For example, in the Annenberg poll, the strongest opposition to same-sex marriage laws comes from those who attend church frequently and from the elderly. Among those who go to religious services more than once a week, 82 percent are opposed to same sex-marriage and 81 percent of those 65 and older oppose. The margin of sampling for the frequent church goers and the elderly is greater than plus or minus three percentage points.

Intuitively, each of us would recognize that if the Annenberg Poll surveyed only a half dozen Americans, the sample size would be too small to warrant justifying any beliefs about the target population as a whole. In addition, it might seem obvious that the greater the number of people interviewed, the greater the probability that a sample is representative of the entire population. A closer examination will reveal, however, that what seems obviously true is actually obviously false in most cases.

Remember what we said above about most scientific samples. No matter how large the sample gets when we are studying DNA, viruses, stars, etc., it will always equal a negligible percentage of all DNA, viruses, stars, etc. Many human populations are also very large, and pollsters will never be able to survey any more than a very small fraction of the target population. Increasing the size of the Annenberg sample to 10,000, for example, would increase its percentage of the total population by a negligible percentage. It is generally pointless to try to get a sample that would be the size of a large percentage of the target population. In fact, such large samples would defeat the purpose of sampling! We sample in order to be able to study only a small part of a population to gain useful information about the whole population. If a target population is so small that we could realistically study nearly all the members of the population, then sampling would be unnecessary.

It might seem that there is a major difference between studying human populations for their opinions and studying DNA or stars for their properties. The objects of scientific study are homogeneous; whereas human beings are a rather heterogeneous lot when it comes to their opinions. Random differences among homogeneous items are statistically unimportant (Werkmeister 1948: 479). Pollsters study a very heterogeneous aggregate in studying the opinions and behaviors of human groups. Even so, if we select the sample properly, the large random differences expected in the opinions and behaviors of a human population should tend to cancel out one another. If the method of selecting the sample is proper, a relatively small sample can give reliable results. A poll with a sample as small as about 1,200 taken from a target population of 300,000,000 can have a margin of error of about plus or minus 3%. In fact, whether the target population has 3 million, 30 million or 300 million, the margin of error would be the same. The margin of error depends on the *size of the sample*, not on the size of the sample in proportion to the total target population. An example might help clarify this.

Imagine that you have a computer data bank with 30,000,000 items. The items are *numbers.* They are either *even* or *odd*, but are not sequential. Your task is to figure out how many of the items are even and how many are odd. If the numbers were sequential, you would not need to do any sampling. You would know that 50% are even and 50% are odd. However, since the numbers are not sequential, you can either examine 30,000,000 items or do a random sampling. Even if it only took one second to examine each item and record the results, it would take you about four years, working eight hours a day, five days a week, to complete your task. Your computer could examine each item in much less time, of course, but we need not overwork the computer, either. We could program it to select items randomly from the data bank and keep track of the oddness or evenness of each item.

After ten items had been selected, would you feel confident that the percentages of odds and evens selected is representative of the data bank? You shouldn't. Ten would be too few to base our judgment on. How about 100? Would that be enough? Well, it would clearly be better than ten. In fact, the margin of error would be reduced from about plus or minus 30% for a sample of 10, to about plus or minus 10% for a sample of 100. But a sample of 100 is still too small. How about a sample of 1,000? Wouldn't you feel confident that a computer randomly selecting items from the data bank would give you a good cross section of those items when it had selected 1,000 items? In fact, the margin of error is now down to about plus or minus 3%.

You might think that things would be a bit more complicated if the items in the data bank had more than two properties (*odd* or *even*). However, it would not make any difference to the representativeness of our sample. We could have had our computer identify not only whether the sample items were odd or even, but whether the sum of their digits was odd or even, and whether they were prime numbers, and whether they ended in 5, etc. A random sample of 1,000 examined for two properties will be as representative as a sample of 1,000 examined for more than two properties. So, whether we are sampling opinions with only two variables (e.g., *yes* or *no*) or several variables (e.g., *extremely concerned, somewhat concerned, not too much concerned, not at all concerned*), we can be equally confident of similarly sized samples selected by similar methods.

Obviously, a very small sample is likely to be unrepresentative, even if the population from which the sample is taken is very small. For very small populations, the safest method is to study all the members of the population. For example, if you had a box with three marbles in it and you picked out one black marble, even though the one marble represents one-third of the population, the probability that the next marble you select will be black is impossible to tell without more information. On the other hand, if you had 30,000,000 marbles in the box, you could make a very accurate prediction about the percentages of different colors after randomly selecting a very small percentage of the total. As noted above, with a sample of 1,000 the margin of error would be about plus or minus 3%. How much could you reduce the margin of error by doubling your sample? Maybe about plus or minus

144

1%. Would it be worth it? It might be very costly to increase the size of a poll to 2,000 from 1,000. Would the small reduction in margin of error be worth it?

4.1 The *Literary Digest* fiasco

A classic example of fallacious sampling occurred in 1936 when *Literary Digest* magazine concluded on the basis of a sample of 2,376,000 that Landon would defeat Franklin D. Roosevelt by 57% to 43%. Roosevelt won by a landslide, getting 62% of the votes. How did the pollsters err? Their sample was *biased*. The poll selected its sample from readers of the magazine, lists of registered automobile owners, and those with telephones. It systematically excluded the poor, a significant stratum of society, many of whom voted Democratic.

> **"A question, even of the simplest kind, is not and can never be unbiased."** --Neal Postman

The *Literary Digest* poll could have been improved only by improving its *method of sample selection*. Increasing the *size* of a poorly designed survey will not improve its reliability. The pollsters should have used an unbiased method. Selected properly, the poll could have included only about 1,500 people and been much more reliable than the one with over 2,000,000 in the sample.

The pollsters might have used a **stratified random sample**, which takes into account various characteristics known to be relevant to the matter being polled. We know, for example, that a person's voting behavior is related to characteristics such as gender, race, age, income, education, geographical habitation, and political party affiliation.

If the target population is known to be differentiated according to factors such as political party, income, education, occupation, age, gender, religion, geographic location, etc., then the method of selecting the sample should ensure that the relevant social strata are adequately represented. The researcher should control the study to ensure that relevant sub-groups are neither over- nor under-represented. "Thus, every important or relevant social stratum within a given population must be present in proper proportion in the sample if the latter is to be an adequate representation of the [target population]. The greater the number of important characteristics which the sample has in common with the aggregate or the group as a whole the more representative and, therefore, the more reliable the sample will be" (Werkmeister 1948: 477).

The *Literary Digest* sample could have included a representative number (relative to those who vote) of democrats, laborers, women, southerners, college graduates, farmers and any other group whose interests or characteristics would be significantly related to their vote.

5. The questions asked

The Annenberg pollsters noted that "variations in the wording and order of questions… may lead to somewhat different results." To evaluate an opinion poll properly, you must consider what questions were asked by the pollster. The questions must be clear and they must be fair. Some polls ask the questions in different order to different people, to offset any bias that might occur because of the order of asking the questions. If you are told only the results of the poll, you cannot be sure it is unbiased, even if the method of selection was unbiased and the size of the sample is satisfactory. The questions asked might be leading or misleading questions. The questions might be asked in such a way as to suggest a particular response. The questions might be loaded, be based on false dilemmas, make subtle appeals to authority, popularity, etc. Certain words might tend to evoke positive responses, while other words might tend to evoke negative responses.

Here are the questions asked in the Annenberg survey:

Would you favor or oppose an amendment to the U. S. Constitution saying that no state can allow two men to marry each other or two women to marry each other?

Would you favor or oppose a law in your state that would allow two men to marry each other or two women to marry each other?

These questions seem clear enough, but are they fair? They seem straightforward enough. The wording isn't obviously leading or biased. (Note: some polls allow respondents to answer "no opinion.")

Asking unbiased questions about controversial issues is very difficult. For example, what questions would you ask about *abortion*? Would you ask: *Are you for or against abortion?* What kind of question is that? Is it even meaningful? How can a person be *for* abortion? How can anyone be *against* abortion? If you are *for* abortion does that mean you do not want anyone to have a baby or that you want all pregnant women rounded up and brought in to abortion clinics? Does it mean that you are for not interfering with a woman's decision to have an abortion? If so, then that is quite a different matter from being *for* aborting all fetuses. Does it mean that you would have an abortion if you got pregnant? Does it mean that the more abortions there are the happier you are? Does it make sense for a male to say he is *for* abortion? Does it make sense to ask a pregnant woman if she is for or against having an abortion? The pregnant woman who is trying to decide whether to have an abortion would have her decision trivialized by reducing it to being *for* or *against* abortion. How could anyone be *for abortion* in general? You might say that one is either for or against having a specific abortion but not for or against abortion in general.

Would you ask: *Should abortion be illegal*? That seems like a straightforward enough question, but is it? The question assumes that all abortions are the same. Imagine asking *Should firearms be illegal?* Most of us would at least want to make a distinction between firearms used by the military and the police in their efforts to protect society, and firearms used by gangsters and thugs in their efforts to harm society. The question forces us to treat all firearms, used by anyone for any purpose, as equal. Likewise, for the question *should abortion be illegal?* The question forces us to treat all abortions, done at any time for any reason by anyone, as equal. It forces us to treat the abortion performed in order to try to save the pregnant woman's life as equal to the abortion performed in order to take advantage of a free cruise. It forces us to treat an abortion in the first days or weeks of pregnancy as equal to an abortion in the seventh or eighth month of pregnancy. It forces us to treat an abortion of a rape victim as equal to an abortion of a woman who tried to get pregnant and then changed her mind about having a baby. Some people who have done some deep thinking about abortion think these distinctions are important. However, the question forces the respondent to take an all or nothing stance.

Would you ask: *Should the decision to have an abortion be up to the pregnant woman?* This question, too, seems straightforward enough. Yet, is it suggesting that either a pregnant woman be given total control over her pregnancy or be forced to carry her fetus to full term? Is the question forcing us to focus our attention on the power struggle for control over the woman's body? If so, it is leading us to say *yes*, for most of us are trained from birth in the U.S. to value the individual and privacy against the incursions of governmental power.

Sometimes, it is obvious that a question is biased. For example, if people are asked if they favor "affirmative action" they respond more positively than if asked if they favor "preferential treatment." On the other hand, overall results differ when people are asked if they "favor" something rather than if they "are opposed to" the same thing. As noted by the Annenberg pollsters, even the order in which questions are asked can influence the responses. For example, in 1939 two polls asked whether the U.S. should allow its citizens to join the German army. In one group, 31% said "yes." In the other, only 22% said "yes." The first group was first asked *Should the U.S. permit its citizens to join the French and British armies.* The second group was first asked *Should the U.S. permit its citizens to join the German army.*

In 1996, the National Democratic Party sent out a nationwide poll, allegedly to get input for the Democratic platform. Respondents were asked, "Which position to you believe the Democrats should adopt regarding Medicare?" The choices were (A) "To make the Medicare program more financially stable, we should make deep cuts in Medicare spending—even if it means higher premiums and a lower standard of care." (B) "Some spending reductions are necessary but they should focus on controlling health care costs. The best way to fund future Medicare spending is to cancel the proposed Republican tax breaks for Americans making more than $100,000 per year." (C) We should not cut Medicare spending. We should cancel the proposed Republican tax break for the rich and reduce spending in other areas." (D) No opinion or none of the above. The likelihood is slim that many would choose higher premiums and lower quality of care. Some might have no opinion. The majority will choose either B (some spending reductions) or C (no reductions), but in either case they must also choose to favor something that has nothing to do with Medicare: a proposed Republican tax reduction. However, the whole point of this question may have been to poison the well against the Republican proposal by characterizing it as a "tax break for the rich."

Another question in the survey asked "Do you favor or oppose Republican efforts to eliminate the 100,000 new police positions funded under the President's 1994 Crime Bill?" How many citizens will oppose hiring new police officers? (It depends on how you ask the question! *Do you favor hiring twenty new police officers even if it means closing down the City Park & Recreation programs and the local high school?*)

Finally, even if the questions are unbiased the pollster can bias the answers by priming the subjects. For example, early in 1999, Juanita Broaddrick claimed that President Clinton sexually assaulted her 21 years ago. A CNN/Gallup/*USA Today* poll found that 34% believed the claim was true and 54% did not believe her. A Fox News/Opinion Dynamics poll, however, found that 54% believed her and only 23% thought her claim was not true. An editorial in the *Wall Street Journal* explained the difference as due to the fact that the CNN poll used the word 'rape' in its question, while Fox used 'sexual assault.' CNN asked "Do you think Broaddrick's allegation (of rape) is true?" Fox asked "Based on your knowledge of Bill Clinton, are the allegations (of sexual assault) more likely to be true or not true?" On the surface, this might seem like a plausible explanation. However, the *Wall Street Journal* intentionally omitted from its editorial some crucial information. *The two polls were done at different times.* The Fox poll was done *before* an NBC *Dateline* interview with Broaddrick. The CNN poll was done *after* the interview. Before the *Dateline* interview, she had not used the word 'rape' to describe the incident; during the interview, the incident was repeatedly referred to as *rape*. So, the two polls used different words because those were the words Broaddrick was using at the time the polls were done. The pollsters were not trying to bias the results by using different words.

In addition to not informing its readers that one poll was done *before* the television interview and the other *after*, the *Wall Street Journal* failed to report that Fox had primed its subjects with a set-up question: *"Last week The Wall Street Journal published 20-year-old sexual assault allegations by Juanita Broaddrick against Bill Clinton. Broaddrick says while forcing her to have sex, Clinton tore her pantyhose, held her down, and bit her lips. She also says that Clinton tried to apologize 13 years later, just before announcing his campaign for president. Have you heard about Broaddrick's allegations against Clinton?"* Compare this question with the set-up question asked by CNN: *"A woman from Arkansas named Juanita Broaddrick has recently stated that Bill Clinton raped her in 1978. Clinton has denied the allegation. Have you heard the news about this allegation before now, or not?"*

By the way, Peter Hart and Robert Teeter of the *Wall Street Journal* did their own poll *after* the editorial appeared, using the word 'rape' in their question, and found that 50% did not believe the allegation by Ms. Broaddrick. Thus, it seems that it was the timing and the priming done by the pollsters, not the words used in the question that led to the different results.[4]

6. Public Opinion Polls

A variant of managing or faking the news, discussed in chapter three, is the use of opinion polls to create news where none existed before the poll was done. Just as advertisers use imagery to involve the audience, TV stations and newspapers try to connect with their audiences by using gimmicks like taking an opinion poll on such issues as whether there should be abortion on demand or whether viewers are for or against a constitutional amendment to prohibit desecration of the flag or whether they think we should get out of Iraq. The polls are unscientific and their results have no meaningful news value. Yet, the results are often presented in news stories as if they were accurate measurements of the community's pulse.

On the other hand, television stations and newspapers have marketing directors whose job is to do viewership or readership surveys. Such surveys not only determine what pretty boy or girl stays hired (on TV) but what kind of news and information will be presented to the public.[5]

> 59% percent of Americans can name the Three Stooges, but only 17% can name three U.S. Supreme Court justices.--Washington Post Poll, *Washington Post*, October, 12 1995

Of course, any political adviser or consultant, whose job is to create news which would work in their candidate's or boss's favor, is very familiar with manipulating the press or the public through opinion polls. Selective release of poll data enables political managers to manipulate the media and public opinion about candidates or office holders. The news media can hardly be a reliable source of information about government and special interest blocs if the government and special interest groups themselves are managing information that might affect our opinion of them.

Public opinion analysis has been an integral part of presidential politics for the past 20 years.[6] Robert Teeter, a pollster and adviser to George Bush, used polls to find out what issues Bush should push and which ones he should avoid or go lightly on. He focused on political issues on which the Democrats were presumed to be vulnerable, such as crime and taxes.[7]

The problem with public opinion is that it is ephemeral. It is inherently unstable and shifts with changing winds of information and events. "Change the wording of a question, and you change the opinion. Change the order of questions, and you change the opinion. Change the time of day you conduct the poll, and you change the opinion."[8] "Journalists, trained to seek out fact, increasingly have failed to make a distinction between objective, quantifiable fact and opinion. The result has been that ephemeral opinion has, all too often, begun to substitute for objective fact in the diet of information the media provide."[9] What we would like journalists to do is inform us of what is going on. What we are getting is journalists informing us of our *opinion* of what we think is going on.[10] Norman Bradburn, director of the National Opinion Research Center at the University of Chicago, calls these non-scientific polls *SLOP surveys*. SLOP is an acronym for *self-selected listener opinion polls*. He compares them to radio talk shows: they attract a slice of America that is not representative of the country as a whole. "As a result, SLOP surveys litter misinformation and confusion across serious policy and political debates, virtually wherever and whenever they are used."[11] The inaccuracy of such polls should be obvious. Those who call in to give their opinion are self-selected rather than randomly selected. It appears that people who are willing to call in their opinion once will sometimes call in their opinion more than once. For example, in a *USA Today* call-in poll 81 percent of the more than 6,000 respondents said that "Donald Trump symbolizes what made the U.S.A. a great country." However, 72 percent of the favorable calls came from two telephones in one insurance company office. Another call-in poll, conducted by *Parade* magazine in August 1990, found that the "overwhelming majority of the nearly 300,000 respondents who participated ... were opposed to abortion." (Scientifically done national surveys consistently find that a majority of Americans favor allowing abortion.) Parade later admitted that 21 percent of the callers "may have voiced their opinions more than once."

CBS tried the gimmick of call-in polling in "America on the Line," which featured two surveys conducted immediately after President Bush's State of the Union speech. There were 314,786 self-selected callers in one survey and 1,241 adults previously selected by a more scientific method in the other survey. The latter was to act as a check on the call-in survey. CBS's Dan Rather commented on the similarity of results in the surveys, a sentiment that was echoed the next day in the *Washington Post*, which wrote, "by and large, the two polls produced the same or similar results." The facts, however, do not support this judgment. "On two of the nine questions asked in both polls, the results differed by more than 20 percentage points. On another five, the differences were 10 percentage points or more."[12] Kathy Frankovic, director of surveys at CBS, said that "the important thing is that we are engaging people." What kind of news can we expect when the purpose is *to engage people* rather than to inform them?

7. Evaluating polls: another example

Many newspaper and television stories focus on polls that are scientifically done but which provide little useful information. An Associated Press (AP) story appeared in a local newspaper that is typical of the statistical amusements often reported on by journalists.

The article had a headline that read **MANY WOMEN CONFESS THEY MARRIED WRONG MAN.** The opening line of the article read: "Only half of all women who have been married one time say they would marry the same man if they had it to do over again, according to a new survey." We are told that the survey was based on more than 56,000 questionnaires taken from *Women's Day* magazine. Pollsters Yankelovich, Skelly & White chose 3,009 of the forms at random and tabulated the results. "The resulting statistics have a margin of error of plus or minus 1.8 percent, according to the magazine," said the AP story. Of course, the pollsters found many other interesting things. For example, they found that *only* 38 percent said they would *not* marry the same man again. They also found that of those married more than once, 63 percent said they *would* marry their present husbands again; *only* 24 percent said they wouldn't. Thus, the headline does not quite fit the data. Yet, how many people would read a story with the headline MANY WOMEN SAY THEY WOULD MARRY SAME MAN AGAIN.

To begin our evaluation of the poll, we ask: *how? how many?* and *what? How* was the sample selected. *How many* were in the sample? *What questions* were asked? We are told that 3,009 questionnaires (out of 56,000) were evaluated. We are told that the sample was a random sample. We have no reason to doubt that a reputable firm, which makes its living by its reputation, would not have selected a random sample. In any case, it would be quite simple to get a random sample from this population of 56,000 questionnaires. All we need to do is devise a method that will give each respondent an equal chance of being selected for the sample. For example, we might assign a number to each questionnaire and have a computer randomly generate three thousand numbers between 1 and 56,000. The point is that we do not have to examine each of the 56,000 questionnaires in order to arrive at valid statistical generalizations about the target population. Nevertheless, when examining the *Woman's Day* poll we discover that although the method of selecting the sample is proper and the sample size is more than adequate, the poll's data is completely misused.

First, what is the population about which the conclusions of the article are drawn? The population is said to be *women*. But the population from which the sample was drawn was a group of 56,000 women who answered a questionnaire published in *Women's Day*. How likely is it that the readers of this magazine who responded to the questionnaire are typical of women in general?

Who conducted the survey? We do not know who wrote the questions, nor do we know what the questions were, for they are not mentioned in the AP article. We know that *Women's Day* published both the survey questions and the analysis of the results. We know that the analysis was done by Yankelovich, Skelly and White (a reputable polling firm). It is not possible to evaluate the questions for bias, since the newspaper article does not list them. In any case, the magazine may have done the study to find out about its readers, not about women in general. However, the newspaper article presents the results as if the survey had a more general application.

Since the population from which the sample was taken is likely to overrepresent certain kinds of women and underrepresent others, the sample is likely to be biased. This is true if the sample is used to draw conclusions about women in general. It is even doubtful that this method justifies conclusions about readers of the magazine.

Finally, note the claim that "the resulting statistics have a margin of error of plus or minus 1.8 percent, according to the magazine." This statistic seems to give the study an aura of respectability and accuracy. However, it is misleading. It only means that if they took a random sample from the questionnaires, 95 out of 100 times they would get the same results plus or minus 1.8 percent. That is, it is highly probable that they would get the same useless results—regarding women in general—no matter how many times they repeated the sampling.

8. The Nielsen ratings

The A.C. Nielsen company (Nielsen Media Research) probably wields more power over television programming than any other entity. The basis for their power is the acceptance of their rating system, a system of surveying television viewers and estimating how many people watch particular programs. Many advertisers agree to base their rates on the Nielsen data. Since television programs exist mainly to provide advertising, a Nielsen rating can make or break a program.

> There are an average of 50 ads for "junk food" during Saturday morning cartoon shows.--Center for Science in the Public Interest report, Washington DC, 1991.
>
> The average child views some 30,000 commercials a year. —*Consumer Reports*, February 1998.

A.C. Nielsen uses several methods of surveying television viewers. Unlike most companies that do polling and surveying of opinions and behaviors, Nielsen does not rely on telephone surveying. They do about two million questionnaires a year by mail in the country's 211 media markets. Prospective participants are asked to keep a diary of their TV viewing for the week. This is done four times a year during what is known as "sweeps week." However, their most well known method involves attaching a box to the television sets of those selected to be Nielsen participants. This box monitors the set, letting the Nielsen folks know when the set is on and what channel it is tuned to. They even monitor the recording of programs on VCRs. Nielsen also provides about 5,000 homes with a "people meter," an electronic pad for data input by anyone who watches TV in the home. Each person in the home is assigned a button on the pad, which they are supposed to punch whenever they are watching TV. Even visitors have a button to punch. Participants are asked to punch out whenever they are leaving the TV area, even if only to go the kitchen for a snack or to the bathroom. If the TV is tuned to the same channel for 70 uninterrupted minutes, a light flashes on the meter. If a viewer does not push the "yes" button (to indicate he or she is still watching TV), the Nielsen box stops registering TV input.

The Nielsen box is connected to a telephone line. During the middle of the night it uploads data to Nielsen's computers in Dunedin, Florida. About twelve hours later, the data has been analyzed and is ready for publication, though Nielsen press reports are generally issued weekly.

The 5,000 homes with the box and the meter agree to participate for two years. Nielsen researchers select a stratified random sample of households from across the nation. New participants are added at a rate of several hundred a month, as current participant's terms expire. The first week of data from the home is ignored, to give the family time to adjust to the setup. Nielsen also hooks up about 500 homes for five-year periods. These homes do not have the "people meter" and they are selected from the 36 largest media markets, rather than from across the country. Any participant who publicly acknowledges that they are a Nielsen home is disconnected.

> The American Psychological Association estimates that the average American child will view 8,000 murders and 100,000 other acts of violence on television before finishing elementary school.

One Nielsen rating point is the equivalent of some 970,000 households, i.e., about 1% of all households, or about two million viewers. The Nielsen people provide a number of statistics regarding our television habits. For example, in 1988 they reported that the average American watches 3 hours and 46 minutes of TV each day. That translates into more than 52 days of nonstop TV-watching per year. By age 65 the average American will have spent nearly 9 years watching TV. The television is on for an average of 7 hours and 12 minutes a day in the typical American home. That's a lot of electricity. Two-thirds of us watch TV while eating dinner. That's a lot of indigestion. The final episode of NBC's 11-year hit sitcom "Cheers" in May, 1993, attracted 93.1 million viewers (64% of all viewers), with a 45.5 Nielsen rating. Ten years earlier, the last episode of M*A*S*H had a rating of 60.2 (some 77% of all TV viewers were tuned in).

Primarily, however, the Nielsen ratings are used to decide how much to charge advertisers. Over a year, a difference of one rating point could mean as much as $100,000,000 in advertising revenue. Television programs are cancelled because their Nielsen ratings are too low. How accurate are the ratings? It is difficult to know, since there is no **standard** to measure the ratings against. However, some things we do know. For instance, we know that Nielsen **does** not measure TV viewing in hospitals, hotels, bars, college dorms, airports, prisons, and other

150

public places. There is no way to monitor how diligent the participants are in using the people meters, and no way to know how honest they are in filling out the diaries. Equipment failures, which apparently are significant, affect the ratings. Many of the complaints about Nielsen accuracy come from the major networks, which have seen their ratings decline steadily with the advent of cable television. There have been two important responses by the major networks ABC, NBC, and CBS: (1) they have bought or started their own cable networks and (2) they are funding a rating system of their own. The system called SMART (for Systems for Measuring and Reporting Television) is run by Statistical Research, Inc. It may offer competition to Nielsen in the future, but it is being criticized as a system designed mainly to increase network ratings.

9. Statistics and tricks with numbers

When evaluating statistical studies it is important to know who did the study, how it was conducted, the size of the sample, and the questions asked of those polled. Many polls and surveys are done by self-interested groups or individuals; they're self-serving and rarely do they inform the public of how they were conducted or how many individuals were studied. I am referring to polls taken by political candidates and their organizations, and polls taken by commercial companies and the advertising firms they hire to sell their products. Such polls and surveys generally have little news value. The fact that you are not told how a study was conducted and how many were in the study is a good sign that the study is not trustworthy.

It is easy to be misled by statistical studies. Precise numbers make conclusions seem accurate. Sometimes, however, their very precision should make us skeptical. For example, a magazine article reported that "a record 577,357 criminals now crowd the nation's jails."[13] Since the number of jail inmates changes continuously, claiming to know the exact number of inmates is ridiculous.

Numerical data can be presented in misleading ways, too. For example, if you were told that 60 percent of those polled favored a particular consumer product, you might be impressed. However, if the sample included only five members of a very large population, the large percentage is meaningless.

Statistics do not always tell the whole story, either. If evidence is omitted, a story can be misleading. For example, the *Washington Post* published a story by reporter Cheryl Thompson on March 10, 1999 in which she gave some statistics about a federal program that detained those accused of crimes in pretrial halfway houses. She noted that a number of those detained had escaped and that "at least 83 of those 226 pretrial inmates who absconded—some more than once—were rearrested on new charges, including manslaughter and armed robbery, according to District [of Columbia] and court records." She was correct, but she did not mention that 63 of the 83 when rearrested were charged only with escaping from the halfway house. Thus, she gave the impression that the escapees had gone on a crime spree. Only one escapee was charged with manslaughter and one with armed robbery.[14]

Insurance companies often cite studies that show that more deadly accidents occur among young drivers (age 16-25) than among any other age group. They charge young people a correspondingly higher rate for insurance. Many times such studies fail to consider the number of drivers in the various groups or the number of miles driven on average by members of the various age groups (to establish that the young drivers are not disproportionately represented). Another example is the seemingly annual article on the high cost of college. Writers project that by the year two thousand it will cost $25,000 a year to go to college, but they omit that they are assuming that inflation will continue at a certain rate and they fail to note that the value of those dollars in the next century won't be quite the same as their current value. Such articles also tend to omit consideration of costs that a student would have even if he or she did not go to college, such as the cost of food and housing.

Finally, a word of caution about the term *average*—a very frequent term in statistical studies—ought to be given. There are several different meanings of the term 'average', and it is possible to be misled by a statistical study which uses 'average' ambiguously. One meaning of 'average' is the *arithmetic mean*. This is the figure one gets when a set of numbers are added up and divided by the number of items in the set, e.g., finding the class average on a test by adding up the scores of each student and dividing the sum by the number of students who took the test. The arithmetic mean is a good measure of the average if there are no extremely low or high values that would skew the results.

Another way of determining the average is to determine the *median*. To compute the median, a list of values must be composed in either increasing or decreasing order. If the number of values is odd, then the median is the value that falls in the middle of the list. If the number of values is even, then the median is the arithmetic mean of the two middle values. Thus, if we wanted to find the median of (70, 75, 76, 85, 90) we would find the middle value, namely, 76. If the list were (70, 75, 76, 80, 85, 90), then the median would be 78, i.e., the arithmetic mean of 76 and 80. The median represents the average of the majority of values in the list. It is especially useful if there are extremely low or high values in the list that would skew the results. A person buying a house in a neighborhood might want to know what the median cost of a house in that neighborhood is.

Another kind of average is known as the *mode*. The mode represents the value that occurs most frequently in a set of values. For example, a shoe store owner might say that the average size shoe he sells is 9½, meaning that he sells more shoes of that size than any other size. It is important that one know which 'average' is being referred to in a statistical study in order to properly evaluate it.

Exercise 7-1 Self-test: true or false? (Check your answers in Answers to Selected Exercises.)

1. Justified inductive generalizations can provide us with a useful means of facing the future because they are *predictive*.
2. Telephone sampling is the most common method of conducting polls for the mass media.
3. Very large samples are always representative samples.
4. A *stratified random sample* is one that randomly selects strata of society to poll.
5. Samples that are self-selected are rarely biased.
6. If the sample is *too small*, it is likely to be biased.
7. Even if the questions are unbiased, the pollster can bias the answers by priming the subjects
8. A representative sample is one that will give us a good cross section of typical items in the target population.
9. The *margin of sampling error* in a poll is a measure of the poll's accuracy and representativeness.
10. Someone standing on an assembly line, whimsically selecting items to be tested, would be collecting a random sample.
11. If a sample is a truly representative sample, then the larger the sample the more likely it is representative of the target population.
12. The term *target population* refers to the whole aggregate from which a sample is taken.
13. The margin of sampling error is a measure of errors due to biased data, erroneous calculations or inappropriate application of the statistical data.
14. The mode represents the value that occurs most frequently in a set of values.
15. A *random sample* is one selected in such a way as to give each item in the target population an equal chance of being selected.
16. A small margin of error indicates that if the sample is biased it's not because the size of the sample is too small.
17. Opinion polls are never used to manage the news.
18. Call-in polls are unscientific and although they have no meaningful news value, they are often presented in news stories as if they were accurate measurements of the community's pulse.
19. According to Kathy Frankovic, director of surveys at CBS, the important thing about call-in polls is that they engage people not that they provide any useful or reliable information.

Exercise 7-2

Discuss the following questions asked by a pollster.

1. *Do you favor retaining loud-mouthed, pro-terrorist, racial agitator Andrew Young as U.S. ambassador to the United Nations?*
2. *Do you favor stronger punishments for criminals or do you favor the current lenient system of punishment?*

152

3. *What is your political affiliation? (Assume the answer is 'Democrat'.) Which of the currently running democratic nominees do you favor?*

4. *Do you support your constitutional right to own and bear arms?*

5. *Do you agree with most American women that abortion should be a woman's choice?*

6. *Do you agree with the Supreme Court that women should be allowed to murder their babies at will?*

7. *Are you for or against capital punishment?*

8. *Do you support American intervention in Kosovo even if it means many American soldiers will be killed?*

9. *Do you favor releasing dangerous criminals from prison, even if they have served their full sentence?*

10. *Have you ever experienced a period of time of an hour or more, in which you were apparently lost, but you could not remember why, or where you had been?*

Exercise 7-3

There are 3,000 guests at a party. One hundred are interviewed at random and it is discovered that 70 are registered Democrats, 20 are Republicans and 10 are Independents. The margin of error is ±12%. Discuss each of the following statements as if they were independently drawn conclusions.

1. It is highly probable that the majority of guests are democrats.
2. 70 percent of the guests are democrats.
3. It is probable that at least 60 percent of the guests are democrats.
4. It is highly probable that about 70 percent of the guests are democrats.
5. It is highly likely that the Republicans are in a minority at this party.
6. It is highly probable that most people are democrats.

Exercise 7-4

Evaluate the following arguments. [Exercises with an * are answered in Answers to Selected Exercises.]

*1. The democrats will win the election by a landslide, according to a survey taken today at Farmer's Market in downtown San Francisco. Two hundred people were interviewed during the lunch hour and 75 percent said they plan to vote democratic in the upcoming state and federal elections.

2. To find out what percentage of their income a family of four spends on food, a pollster goes through the phone book of a major city and randomly selects 1,500 different names to call. Three hundred and twenty five of those called identify themselves as families of four. Three-fourths of these say they spend at least 30 percent of their income on food. The pollster concludes that in the United States 75 percent of the people spend 30 percent of their income on food.

3. "The more sexual activity married women have, the more highly they think of themselves--a phenomenon that does not hold true for men. These are two of the many conclusions from a small study of 11 couples in marriage counseling and 11 couples who responded to an ad requesting 'happily married' couples to participate in a research project." *Psychology Today*, February, 1980

4. "People on welfare are a bunch of lazy cheats--parasites living off the labor of us hardworking folks. Last week I saw this lady at the grocery store. She was all dressed up in a nice outfit, wearing nice rings and an expensive watch. She bought steaks and expensive roasts, while all I could afford was chicken! And what did she pay for her food with? Food stamps!"

* 5. "Men are basically insecure babies. I know; I was married to one for twenty years."

6. The majority of working class Americans supports the government's import quotas on foreign automobiles, as is evidenced by a recent poll taken outside of General Motor's plant in nearby Dearborn. More than 90 percent of the 47 General Motor's employees polled believe that "it is fully consistent with capitalism's ideal of free enterprise" to restrict the importation of foreign automobiles in order to help bolster sales of American-made cars.

Exercise 7-5

The following consists of a base argument. Look at the base argument and get a general notion of the sufficiency of the premises for the stated conclusion. Following each base argument is a list of statements. The statements either change the strength with which the conclusion is asserted to follow from the evidence or they offer alternative premises. Treating each additional statement separately, determine whether it strengthens, weakens or has no effect on the argument. Give reasons for your views.

BASE ARGUMENT: A newspaper reports that a recent study showed that persons who were registered Democrats were 75 percent more likely to vote for a Democratic candidate than for a Republican candidate. The study was a telephone survey of six hundred registered Democrats. The margin of error was ±5%.

a. The survey was done by a firm known to have done business with Democrats.
b. Only San Diego was included in the study.
c. The study was done in such a way as to insure that the sample included representatives of several geographical areas of the country.
d. All of those in the study were women.
e. Those conducting the study are all married.
h. The study sample is a good cross-section of persons, i.e., is a stratified random sample.

Exercise 7-6

Find two or three articles based on polls in newspapers or magazines and evaluate them. Comment on the method of selecting the sample, the size of the sample, the fairness of the questions asked and the margin of error. Is the sample likely to be representative? Why or why not? Is there anything not mentioned in the article about the study which should have been mentioned?

10. Analogical reasoning

Sampling involves studying a part of a population (the sample) and drawing a conclusion about the whole population. It is both *empirical* and *predictive*. The justification of sampling depends on the representativeness of the sample, which depends on how the sample was selected and how many were selected.

Sampling is a type of **simple induction**. When we generalize from several particular items or experiences, we are doing in a non-systematic way what the pollster is doing. For example, when we conclude that "General Motors makes great trucks" based upon a few experiences with their trucks, we are using simple induction. If the items we have experienced are typical and we have experienced a sufficient number of them, then our conclusion is a sound one.

Another type of inductive reasoning we commonly engage in is **analogical reasoning**, which involves comparing one thing or group of things with similar things or groups. Like sampling, analogical reasoning is both empirical and predictive. However, *the justification of analogical reasoning depends on the relevant similarities outweighing the relevant dissimilarities of the items being compared.* If the relevant similarities are more significant and more numerous than the dissimilarities, then the analogy is a sound one.

The basic structure of analogical reasoning is as follows:

1. X and Y have strong relevant and significant similarities.

2. If X & Y have strong relevant and significant similarities, then what is true of X is probably true of Y and vice versa.

3. 'a' is known to be true of X.

4. So, 'a' is probably true of Y.

154

The letter 'a' represents some quality or relation, such as *earns over $50,000 a year*. 'X' and 'Y' may represent an individual—such as *Jane Woe*—or some individuals—such as *40 percent of the adults in Woeville*—or all individuals of the same type—such as *all the adults in Woeville.*

Below are three examples of analogical reasoning.

---

1. Humans and rodents have strong, relevant & significant similarities in their reproductive systems.

2. If humans and rodents have strong, relevant & significant similarities in their reproductive systems, then what is true of human reproduction is probably true of rodent reproduction and vice versa.

3. Human females sometimes produce an enzyme that prevents spermatozoa from penetrating her eggs.

4. So, it is probably true that female rodents sometimes produce an enzyme that prevents spermatozoa from penetrating her eggs.

Example 1 – analogical reasoning

---

1. The philosophy class I am taking this semester has strong, relevant and significant similarities to the philosophy class I am enrolled in for next semester.

2. If philosophy classes have strong, relevant and significant similarities, then what is true of one of the classes is probably true of the other.

3. I really enjoyed the philosophy class I am taking this semester.

4. So, I probably will enjoy the philosophy class I will take next semester.

Example 2- analogical reasoning

---

1. Double-celling of criminals has strong, relevant and significant similarities to forcing children to sleep in bunk beds.

2. If double-celling of criminals has strong, relevant and significant similarities to forcing children to sleep in bunk beds, then what is true of double-celling is probably true of double-bunking.

3. Double-celling of criminals is cruel.

4. So, forcing children to sleep in bunk beds is probably cruel.

Example 3 – analogical reasoning

Justifiable analogical arguments must be based on *strong* analogies. That is, it must be true that the relevant and significant similarities outweigh the relevant dissimilarities. In addition, as with sampling, we must make sure that the conclusion is stated with the appropriate strength. The stronger the analogy, the stronger the conclusion should be.

To see the difference between simple induction and analogical induction, compare the reasoning of **Example 2** above with non-analogical reasoning to the same conclusion. Suppose that a person took a philosophy class and found it to be extremely rewarding. In planning her schedule for the next semester she decides to take another philosophy course, fully expecting it to be rewarding also. We might reconstruct her reasoning as follows:

---

1. The philosophy course I took was extremely rewarding.

2. So, all philosophy courses are extremely rewarding.

3. Therefore, the philosophy course I take next semester will be extremely rewarding.

Example 4 – simple induction to a hasty generalization and a valid deduction

---

If the student were to reason this way, we would find fault in the process of drawing a conclusion about *all* philosophy courses based on a single experience. She would be making a **hasty generalization**. There are too many variables to justify a universal generalization about the "rewardingness" of philosophy courses based on one person's single experience.

Now compare the reasoning in **Example 4** with that of **Example 2**. In the case of **Example 2**, no generalization is made about philosophy courses. Instead, an *analogy* is drawn between the course already taken and the course offered next semester. The adequacy of the reasoning depends on the relevant similarities between the two courses outweighing the relevant dissimilarities between them.

Generally speaking, the greater the number of characteristics that different items or types of items share, the greater the likelihood those items or types of items will share some further characteristic. Also, generally speaking, the fewer the characteristics that items or different types of items share, the less likely it is that they will share some further characteristic. However, the *number* of shared characteristics is not nearly as important as their *relevance* and *significance* to the issue at hand. In **Example 2**, the issue is whether the philosophy course the student enrolled in for next semester will be rewarding. What characteristics of a philosophy course are relevant to its being rewarding or not? Does the proposed course share in common many of these characteristics with the course already taken? Are any of these characteristics known *not* to belong to the proposed course?

We will assume that the following list of characteristics is made up by the student in response to the first question.

Characteristics relevant to a philosophy course being rewarding

Course content.	Course requirements.
The instructor.	Where the course is to be taught.
The text book(s).	Hour at which the course is offered.
Interest in the subject.	

If the instructor for the two courses is the same, that strengthens the argument. If the instructors are different persons but very similar in their styles and personalities, that would also strengthen the argument, but not quite as much as if the instructor were the same for each course. If the instructors were not only different, but also very different in personality and teaching style, that would weaken the argument.

What about the course content? If the course taken was in the history of philosophy and the proposed course is in mathematical logic, would that strengthen or weaken the argument? What if both courses were in the history of ancient philosophy? What if the text book in both courses was identical (different chapters being read in each course)? What if the books were different?

What if the requirements for the course taken were all in the form of take-home essays and papers, but the proposed course will have only in-class essays and/or true/false questions on exams?

In short, relevant similarities strengthen the argument; relevant dissimilarities weaken the argument. Whether or not the student reasoned well in the example depends on the strength of the relevant similarities outweighing the strength of any significant dissimilarity.

Finally, many characteristics that are similar or dissimilar about the two courses are *irrelevant*. For example, each course will require the same registration fee, the classrooms will have doors, the teachers will be short, tall, blue-eyed, and so on, but these are irrelevant. Thus, you need not consider them.

11. False analogies

Example 3 reveals an interesting characteristic of many analogies. Two *concepts* are compared: *double-celling of criminals* and *forcing children to sleep in bunk beds*. An argumentative analogy is a good one if the relevant similarities of the items being compared outweigh the relevant dissimilarities, which is not the case in this argument. While it is true that there are some similarities to forcing a criminal to share a cell with another criminal and forcing children to sleep in the same room in bunk beds, there are so many relevant and significant dissimilarities between the two that any argument based on an analogy between the two will be a **false analogy**. False analogies are often seductive, and a critical thinker must remember to consider relevant *dissimilarities* not likely to be brought up by the one making the argument.

Here is another example of a *false analogy*:

Since people are like vines, they will grow up unhealthy, unruly and wild, if they are not disciplined and cared for when they are very young.

Example 5 – a false analogy

There are too many relevant and significant dissimilarities between vines (or any other kind of plant) and human beings with respect to the issue of growth for this analogy to be relevant. Similarities by themselves are not sufficient to prove any conclusion in an analogical argument. Thus, while it is true that raising vines and raising children share some things in common, the relevant and significant differences between the two outweigh any similarities they might have. If this were not so, then it would make perfect sense to buy a book on raising vines to help you figure out the best way to raise your child. Likewise, it would be wise to buy a book on child care before starting your garden.

12. Analogies in illustrations

Not all analogies are argumentative. Many analogies compare very dissimilar things in order to try to *exemplify* or *illustrate* a point. For example,

---

People are like vines. If they are not disciplined and cared for when they are very young, they will grow up unhealthy, unruly and wild.

Example 6 - an illustrative analogy

In **Example 6**, the analogy tries to *illustrate* a point. This is a perfectly good use of an analogy. **Example 6** uses the same analogy as **Example 5**; however, in **Example 5** the analogy tries to *prove* a point. Since their function is different, the analogies must be evaluated differently. An illustrative analogy is a good one if it clarifies or helps makes a point more vivid. An argumentative analogy is a good one if its premises adequately support its conclusion, i.e., if the relevant and significant similarities outweigh the dissimilarities.

13. A famous analogy: argument or illustration?

One of the most famous analogies in the history of law is the analogy used by Oliver Wendall Holmes in *Schenk v. United States*. Holmes compared passing out anti-draft leaflets during war time and falsely yelling "Fire!" in a crowded theater. The analogy, however, was *not* an *argumentative* analogy. It was an *illustrative* analogy. Holmes was trying to illustrate his point that passing out anti-draft leaflets during war time was a "clear and present danger" to the national interest and was no more protected by the First Amendment than "falsely shouting fire in a theater and causing a panic." Attorney Allen Dershowitz calls it an "inapt analogy" because the

> example of [falsely] shouting 'Fire!' obviously bore little relationship to the facts of the Schenk case. The Schenk pamphlet contained a substantive political message. It urged its draftee readers to *think* about the message and then--if they so chose--to act on it in a lawful and nonviolent way. The man who [falsely] shouts 'Fire!' in a crowded theater is neither sending a political message nor inviting his listener to think about what he has said and decide what to do in a rational, calculated manner. On the contrary, the message is designed to force action *without* contemplation."[15]

Holmes was not trying to *prove* that passing out anti-draft leaflets during war time is not protected by the First Amendment *because* such activity is just like falsely yelling "Fire!" in a crowded theater. He was not saying that the two examples are so similar that since the one is not protected speech neither should the other be. Holmes was trying to illustrate what most of us would probably accept as a truism: whether speech is protected by the First Amendment depends on the circumstances. Nevertheless, his analogy is inapt because it did not do what *illustrative* analogies are supposed to do. It did not clarify the issue. In fact, Holmes muddled up the point so badly, says Dershowitz, that most of the frequent references to it since have made it into "little more than a caricature of logical argumentation." One of the most frequent uses of the analogy, says Dershowitz, is in arguments against censorship. The Rev. Jerry Falwell, for example, argued

> Just as no person may scream 'Fire!' in a crowded theater when there is no fire, and find cover under the First Amendment, likewise, no sleazy merchant like Larry Flynt [publisher of *Hustler*

> magazine which had been sued by Falwell] should be able use the First Amendment as an excuse for maliciously and dishonestly attacking public figures, as he has so often done.

Even judges have cited the Holmes' analogy to justify restricting pornography, picketing, and marching. Dershowitz cites numerous other examples of misuse of the Holmes' analogy. He agrees that there are exceptions to the First Amendment's exhortation that the "Congress shall make no law...abridging freedom of speech, or of the press." However, Dershowitz denies that any of the exceptions bear any meaningful resemblance to falsely shouting "Fire!" in a crowded theater.

14. Analogical arguments in law

One field where analogical arguments abound is law. Judges and lawyers often defend their positions by appealing to precedents analogous to the case at hand. For example, In *Stanley* v. *Georgia* the court wrote, "If the First Amendment means anything, it means that a State has no business telling a man, sitting alone in his house, what books he may read or what films he may watch." Several years later, a lawyer cited *Stanley* and argued that viewing pornography at home was analogous to committing sodomy at home. His client had been charged with violating the Georgia sodomy statute by committing that act with another adult male in the privacy of his own bedroom (Bowers v. Hardwick, 478 U.S., 106 S. Ct. 2841, 1986). The attorney argued that since the Court recognizes that States have no business in telling a person what to read in the privacy of his own home, they have no business in telling a person what sex acts he can perform in the privacy of his own home. However, Justice Byron White noted some significant differences in the two cases. White argued that just because the two cases involve acts done in private isn't sufficient to make them so analogous that a State has no business in telling a person what sex acts they can perform in privacy. Reading books is a First Amendment issue (freedom of speech, freedom of the press); having sex is not. White also pointed out that there are many other acts which, though done in the privacy of one's own home, does not protect them from State legislation: "...the possession and use of illegal drugs do not escape the law where they are committed at home." In other words, there is a strong disanalogy between the two cases.[16]

An even more telling example is the analogical reasoning used by the court to decide *People* v. *Duglash*, 41 N.Y.2d 725 (1977). The court cited *United States* v. *Thomas*, 13 U.S.C.M.A. 278 (1962).[17] Duglash was charged with attempted murder. The person Duglash shot, however, was already dead when Duglash fired his pistol. Since it is not logically possible to murder a dead person, it seemed plausible that Duglash could not have attempted to murder that person. To do so would be to attempt to commit a crime that is factually impossible to commit. The court ruled that the Duglash case was analogous to an earlier case, the Thomas case. Thomas had been charged with attempted rape but it was established that his victim had died before he had sex with her. The court ruled that since the defendant *believed* his victim was alive, he could be charged with *attempted* rape. Thus, the court ruled, since Duglash *believed* his victim was alive, he could be charged with *attempted* murder. It had been established in the Thomas case that all that is necessary to *attempt* to commit a crime is the *belief* that you are doing so. If your actions demonstrate that you *intended* to kill the victim, you can be said to have *attempted* to commit murder, even if the victim is dead before your action, thereby making it factually impossible to commit the crime you intend.

It is perhaps worth noting that analogical reasoning by precedent is based upon non-analogical reasoning. For example, the Thomas case was decided without precedent. How was it decided? By analysis of the concepts of 'attempted act,' 'belief,' 'intent,' and so on. It seems reasonable to think that even if Thomas had never existed, the same reasoning that was valid in that case would be valid in the Duglash case. Thus, it seems that argument by precedent, which plays such an immense role in legal reasoning in the United States, is ultimately a search for *authoritative support* of one's position. However, deciding similar cases in similar ways is a requirement of consistency and fairness. Reliance on precedent also reminds us that judges must give reasons for their opinions; and those reasons must not be personal, whimsical, or arbitrary.

15. Analogical arguments in philosophy

Philosophers are also fond of analogical arguments. One of the most celebrated arguments from analogy in the history of philosophy is William Paley's "analogy of the watch" argument for the existence of God. Paley (1743-1805), the Archdeacon of Carlisle, writes in his *Natural Theology* (1802):

> **In crossing a heath, suppose I pitched my foot against a *stone* and were asked how the stone came to be there, I might possibly answer that for anything I knew to the contrary it had lain there forever; nor would it, perhaps, be very easy to show the absurdity of this answer. But suppose I had found a *watch* upon the ground, and it should be inquired how the watch happened to be in that place, I should hardly think of the answer which I had before given, that for anything I knew the watch might have always been there.**

The reason, he says, that he couldn't conceive of the watch having been there forever is because it is evident that the parts of the watch were put together for a *purpose*. It is inevitable that "the watch must have had a maker," whereas the stone apparently has no purpose revealed by the complex arrangement of its parts.

One could, of course, attack Paley's argument at this point and say, as Clarence Darrow did, that some stones would be just as puzzling as a watch; for, they are complex and could easily have been designed by someone for some purpose we are unaware of. It may well be that "on close inspection and careful study the stone...is just as marvelous as the watch."[18] Be that as it may, Paley's point was not that watches are inherently more interesting than stones. His point was that a watch could be seen to be analogous with the creation of the universe. The design of the watch implies an intelligent designer. This fact, says Paley, would not be diminished even if we discovered that the watch before us was the offspring (no pun intended) of another watch. "No one," he says, "can rationally believe that the insensible, inanimate watch, from which the watch before us issued, was the proper cause of the mechanism we so much admire in it--could be truly said to have constructed the instrument, disposed its parts, assigned their office, determined their order, action, and mutual dependency, combined their several motions into one result, and that also a result connected with the utilities of other beings."

Paley then goes on to claim that "every manifestation of design which existed in the watch, exists in the works of nature, with the difference on the side of nature of being greater and more, and that in a degree which exceeds all computation." The implication is that the works of nature must have had a designer of supreme intelligence who contrived to put together the magnificent mechanism of the universe. According to Darrow, this 'implication' is actually an *assumption*.

> **To say that a certain scheme or process shows order or system, one must have some norm or pattern by which to determine whether the matter concerned shows any design or order. We have a norm, a pattern, and that is the universe itself, from which we fashion our ideas. We have observed this universe and its operation and we call it order. To say that the universe is patterned on order is to say that the universe is patterned on the universe. It can mean nothing else.[19]**

The problem with Paley's analogy is that the belief that the universe shows orderliness and purpose is an *assumption*. One quality of a good analogical argument is that the characteristics cited as shared characteristics must be truly shared characteristics. If there is doubt that one item (the universe) has a most significant characteristic (being designed and purposive), then the analogical argument is not a sound one.

Another philosopher, David Hume (1711-1776), took up the design analogy a few years before Paley, in his *Dialogues Concerning Natural Religion*. One of the characters in Hume's dialogue, Philo, suggests that "If the universe bears a greater likeness to animal bodies and to vegetables than to the works of human art, it is more probable that its cause resembles the cause of the former than that of the latter, and its origin ought rather to be ascribed to generation or vegetation than to reason or design" (Book VII). "The world," says Philo, "plainly resembles more an animal or a vegetable than it does a watch or knitting-loom. Its cause, therefore, it is more probable, resembles the cause of the former. The cause of the former is generation or vegetation. The cause, therefore, of the world we may infer to be something similar or analogous to generation or vegetation."

Exercise 7-7 Self-test: true or false?

1 In an analogical argument, generally speaking the greater the number of relevant similarities between items being compared, the greater the probability they will share some further related characteristic.

2 Some analogies are made to illustrate, not prove, a point.

3 In analogical reasoning, the *number* of shared characteristics between items which are compared is more important than the *relevance* of the characteristics to a given conclusion.

4 A false analogy is an analogy used to prove a point when there are no relevant differences between the items being compared.

5 Since there are many dissimilarities between humans and other mammals such as laboratory rats, any conclusion drawn for humans based on studies of rats is unsound and improbable.

6 Analogical arguments are rarely used in law.

7 Common sense is all that is necessary to detect whether or not a characteristic is relevant in an analogical argument.

Exercise 7-8

Analyze the following analogical arguments according to the guidelines discussed in this section: compare the relevance, strength, and significance of the similarities with the dissimilarities, and determine whether the conclusion is stated with the appropriate strength or is too strong.

*1. "...Among these countless planets there are conditions of heat and light equivalent to those we experience on earth; and if this is the case, and the planet is near our age and size, there may very likely exist human beings like ourselves, probably with strange costumes and still stranger manners." (Robert Goddard, "The Habitability of Other Worlds," unpublished paper cited in *Broca's Brain* by Carl Sagan (New York: Random House, 1979), p. 225n.)

2. Since eating only one kind of food would drive you to hate that food, it follows that having only one wife will lead you to hate that person eventually.

3. "The one and only film I saw which was directed by Wertmuller disgusted me; so, her new film will probably disgust me, too."

4. It is absolutely necessary to force atheists to accept our religious beliefs. A reasonable person would not think twice about using force to prevent a deluded person from jumping off the edge of a steep cliff. Force is sometimes necessary when dealing with children and barbarians.

5. I wouldn't give that rotten food to my dog. If it would make me sick, it will probably make my dog sick, too.

6. "I've been buying NEW IMPROVED DRUDGERY laundry detergent for years. Each box of detergent has been great, so I expect the next box I buy will be great, too."

7. People should live together before getting married because you shouldn't buy a pair of shoes without trying them on.

8. I don't think we should drink from this water hole, Mo. There are an awful lot of horse and cow carcasses lying at the water's edge. I think it's poisoned, and if it can kill a horse it can probably kill us, too.

9. Crime is like a cancer in the organism of the body politic. And like a cancer, unless it is completely excised, it will spread and eventually destroy the whole organism. The criminal, therefore, if allowed to live amongst the rest of us, will eventually spread his or her disease throughout the entire society, and we will all perish.

*10. A lawyer for the Becton Regional High School board of trustees in East Rutherford, N.J., defended a school plan to require all students to submit to a blood and urine test administered by the school nurse or doctor, or, if the students choose to do so, by a family physician. The tests would be used to determine drug usage. The drug testing, said the lawyer, "would be no different from screening for communicable diseases, such as tuberculosis or lice."

11. It is probable that there are other minds and that I am not the only person with a mind. I don't know this for certain, but I see many other creatures who look like me, talk like me, act like me, who give signs of having a mind. That is, I know that when I talk as they do and act as they do it is because I have a mind capable of thought and intelligent discourse and action. So, I conclude that these bodies I observe driving cars and making change at the grocery store are most likely persons with minds and not robots or androids.

12. 'As President, I am the captain of the Ship of State. And, as on a ship it is *mutiny* to disobey the captain's order, so too in matters of the common good, when your President gives an order, to disobey is mutiny, that is to say *treason*!'

*13. President Harry Truman once argued something to the effect that the United States never should have stopped atmospheric testing of nuclear bombs. 'Where would the world be today,' reasoned Truman, 'if Thomas Edison had stopped doing his experiments with the electric light bulb?'

14. (Letter to the editor:) "In all of the news media the litany of doom is prevalent. Churches and schools are full of it: 'If there is atomic war everything ends, nothing survives.' I would almost swear that there are thousands of people going about their business in Hiroshima and Nagasaki."

15 (Letter to the editor:) My neighbor leaves his doors and windows unlocked; also, he considers a burglar alarm too costly. Is he not careless? My doors and windows are locked; I have installed a burglar alarm. Furthermore, I have a gun to use in the event an intruder manages, somehow, to attack me. Which house is more likely to be entered? Does this mean I want a confrontation? ...President Reagan has no desire for war. He is only 'protecting the house.' Nuclear war is out. I refuse to believe the whole world wants to commit suicide."

16. "[Educated people] bought their education just like I buy my land and I pay taxes on the land, but they don't have to pay taxes on their knowledge and that irks me....I use the land to earn my living and they use their knowledge to earn theirs. If the government can tax my investment, then it should tax their knowledge." (Dairyman Earl E. Chapman, cited in Robert Baum, *Logic*, 2nd ed., (New York: Holt, Rinehart & Winston; 1980), p. 431.

*17. (Letter to the editor:) "Superior Court Judge Beverly B. Savitt has proclaimed that the double-celling of criminals is cruel and unusual punishment. Does this mean that children who are forced to sleep in bunk beds because their tax-burdened parents cannot afford larger houses can now sue their parents for cruel and unusual punishment?"

18. In a debate on spankings in school, Paul V. Armstrong, president-elect of the West Virginia Association of Elementary School Principals, said that with proper controls, corporal punishment can be an effective disciplinary tool. "I do not believe administering corporal punishment for fighting teaches aggression any more than I believe receiving a speeding ticket teaches you to be a race car driver," Armstrong told a U.S. Senate Judiciary subcommittee on juvenile justice.

19. "All the conspicuous features on the surface of the moon are the result of impacts. These features include not only the craters, which plainly advertise their origin, but also the great maria, or "seas," which are craters that filled with lava following the impact of very massive objects. Most of the impacts took place during a relatively brief period about four billion years ago, when debris left over from the formation of the solar system was swept up by the planets and their satellites. The earth probably received as heavy a pelting as the moon did, and it therefore must have been densely cratered. ("Science and Citizen," *Scientific American* June 1976.)

20. Several experiments have shown that the life span of mice can be significantly increased by a diet which includes certain toxic substances in small amounts. It is therefore highly probable that human beings could significantly increase their life spans by following a diet which includes small amounts of toxic substances.

21. "We judge a man's intelligence by his words and deeds. The core of the argument for artificial intelligence lies in the fact that computer systems can be observed, by their words and deeds, to behave in similar ways. A machine can learn. It can respond (when programmed with sufficient sophistication) to a new situation. It can solve problems. It can direct conduct (as in oil refineries and space explorations; all astronauts are guided in the first, critical miles of take-off by computers that observe and correct the trajectory of the space vehicle). It can even answer certain questions from standard intelligence tests. In these matters, the observed behavior of computers and men differ not in kind, but in degree." (Donald G. Fink, *Computers and the Human Mind*)

*22. (Letter to the Editor:)"Reading your article on Sacramento's deplorable welfare situation brings to mind my college history professor's lecture on the 'Rise and Fall of the Roman Empire.' He allowed as how the Roman Empire became so liberal and supportive of the poor that finally everyone wanted to be "poor" and live off the government. The government gave the people no incentive to support themselves. The liberal lawmakers wanted to control the people's minds and lives. They did this by doling out most of the taxpayers' money to welfare. The empire's military might, which had brought about its rise, was now sorely neglected, which in turn brought about its fall.... could it be that Sacramento and the nation are experiencing the very same thing that happened in Rome several centuries ago?....I can only conclude that our legislators, like those of the Roman Empire, want to control our lives and our votes to the extent they are jeopardizing the freedom of this nation by spending our taxpayers' money too freely for welfare and too little for defense."

*23. "An electron is no more (and no less) hypothetical than a star. Nowadays we count electrons one by one in a Geiger counter, as we count the stars one by one on a photographic plate. In what sense can an electron be called more unobservable than a star: I am not sure whether I ought to say that I have seen an electron; but I have just the same doubt whether I have seen a star. If I have seen one, I have seen the other. I have seen a small disc of light surrounded by diffraction rings which has not the least resemblance to what a star is supposed to be; but the name 'star' is given to the object in the physical world which some hundreds of years ago started a chain of causation which has resulted in this particular light-pattern. Similarly in a Wilson expansion chamber I have seen a trail not in the least resembling what an electron is supposed to be; but the name 'electron' is given to the object in the physical world which has caused this trail to appear. How can it possibly be maintained that a hypothesis is introduced in one case and not in the other?" (Sir Arthur Eddington, *New Pathways in Science*)

*24. The writer Alice Walker was awarded a statuette by the California state legislature for being a "state treasure." The legislature wanted to honor Walker for her novels and short stories, and probably atone for the fact that one of her short stories was removed from a state reading test after objections to the story were made by Christian conservatives. The Christian conservatives objected to "Roselily" being required reading for a state aptitude test on the grounds that it promoted unwed motherhood (the story presents the thoughts of a pregnant young woman just before her marriage).

Walker objected to the statuette of a nude woman's torso. She called it an embodiment of society's acceptance of the mutilation of women. David Link, a Los Angeles attorney, wrote an article arguing that Walker's reaction to a statuette was very similar, if not identical, to the reaction to her story by the Christian conservatives. Link also argued that since the Christian conservative reaction was an "aggressive act of interpretative violence, worthy of the strongest condemnation," so too was Walker's reaction to the statuette designed by "one of the most gifted sculptors of our time, Robert Graham." [in "Alice Walker isn't that easy to honor," *L.A. Times* reprinted in *The Sacramento Bee*, April 30 1994, p. B7.]

25. "Anybody who wants to repeat an experiment in modern subatomic physics has to undergo many years of training. Only then will he or she be able to ask nature a specific question through the experiment and to understand the answer. Similarly, a deep mystical experience requires, generally, many years of training under an experienced master and, as in the scientific training, the dedicated time does not guarantee success. If the student is successful, however, he or she will be able to 'repeat the experiment.'

"A mystical experience, therefore, is not any more unique than a modern experiment in physics. On the other hand, it is not less sophisticated either, although its sophistication is of a very different kind. The complexity and efficiency of the physicist's technical apparatus is matched, if not surpassed, by that of the mystic's consciousness--both physical and spiritual--in deep meditation. The scientists and the mystics, then, have developed highly sophisticated methods of observing nature which are inaccessible to the layperson. A page from a journal of modern experimental physics will be as mysterious to the uninitiated as a Tibetan mandala. Both are records of inquiries into the nature of the universe" (Fritz Capra, *The Tao of Physics*).

Exercise 7-9

In the 19th century, many temperance societies were formed in the U.S., Great Britain, and Europe in response to increasing alcoholism (e.g., the Woman's Christian Temperance Union). Temperance workers such as Susan B. Anthony (1820-1906), Lucretia Coffin Mott (1793–1880), and Carry Nation (1846-1911) organized efforts to induce people to abstain from alcoholic beverages. The temperance movements urged prohibition, and the Prohibition Party made it a national issue in 1869. The temperance movement gained impetus during World War I, when conservation policies limited liquor output. In the U.S., temperance advocates worked for and, in 1919, secured federal prohibition through the 18th amendment to the U.S. constitution. But enforcement, through the Volsted Act, which prohibited the sale, manufacture, and transportation of all alcoholic beverages, failed to abolish bootlegging and the widespread lawbreaking associated with it. The illegal production and distribution of liquor during prohibition became a large industry dominated by gangsters. Its association with graft and violence was a major factor in Prohibition's repeal in 1933.

An analogy has been drawn between this era and the current drug situation, Drug sale and production is dominated by criminals and associated with violence and corruption said to be analogous to what happened during prohibition. Thus, it has been argued that we should repeal all laws which absolutely forbid the sale, manufacture and transportation of drugs. Just as the repeal of Prohibition ended the gangster era of Al Capone, so too would the repeal of drug laws end the street crime, violence and corruption associated with illegal drugs.

Is this a good analogical argument?

Further Reading – Chapter Seven

Giere, Ronald (1996). *Understanding Scientific Reasoning*. 4th ed. Wadsworth.

Langley, Russell (1970). *Practical Statistics Simply Explained*, rev. ed. Dover Publications, Inc.

Postman, Neil (1992). *Technopoly*. Alfred A. Knopf.

Werkmeister, W. H. (1948). *An Introduction to Critical Thinking - A Beginner's Text in Logic*. Johnsen Publishing Company.

Notes – Chapter Seven

[1] "Homosexuals and the 10% Fallacy," J. Gordon Muir, *Wall Street Journal*, March 31, 1993.

[2] I would recommend that every college student take a course in statistics. Statistical methods are used in most scientific and sociological fields. They are also the basis for the incessant polling and surveys done to discover and, sometimes, to sway public opinion. The material in this chapter is being presented in a simplified way in order to provide a foundation to the beginning college student for further study. No statistical formulae will be presented and all mathematical concepts will be presented in a simplified way. For the student who has not taken a course in statistics, I recommend Ronald Giere's *Understanding Scientific Reasoning*, 2nd ed.(New York, Holt Rinehart, Winston: 1984), chapters 10 and 11.

[3] For most TV, newspaper and magazine polls, if the samples were selected in such a way as to get a representative cross section of the target population, the margins of sampling error for various sample sizes would be approximately as follows: about plus or minus 4% for a sample of 500; about plus or minus 3 % for a sample of 1,000; about plus or minus 2% for a sample of 1,500.

[4] "Making Sense of the Polls," Warren J. Mitofsky in *Brill's Content*, May 1999.

[5] "The media: How opinion polls start to replace facts," Bill Kovach, *Sacramento Bee*, September 23, 1989, p. B9. Kovach is a former editor of the *Atlanta Journal-Constitution*, and is curator of the Nieman Foundation, a Harvard program for journalists.

[6] "Bush's cautious alter ego," *U.S. News & World Report*, March 26, 1990, p. 26.

[7] *ibid.* Richard Wirthlin, an adviser to Ronald Reagan, was nicknamed "Numbers" because his usual support for policy matters came from polls which showed that the majority agreed with Reagan on most policy issues. "Public opinion was all he talked about, largely ignoring political strategy."

[8] "The media: How opinion polls start to replace facts," Bill Kovach, *Sacramento Bee*, September 23, 1989, p. B9.

[9] *ibid.*

[10] Cable News Network (CNN) announced on July 23, 1990, that during its evening news broadcasts it would poll viewers to determine which stories they wanted to see. While the anchors read the news, viewers are shown a menu of topics. Viewers can call a '900' number to vote for the story they're most interested in seeing. The top two vote-getters are the stories that viewers will see that evening. Which would you rather see: a story about rich people defaulting on loans or a story about housewives who moonlight as prostitutes? Which would be your choice: a story on problems with nuclear waste disposal or a story on priests with mistresses? This feature is sure to be just as popular as CNN's nightly polling of viewers for the opinions on such things as 'Do you think the stock market is a good way to invest your money?' Why don't we get an investigative report on investing in the stock market? Are we really enriched by hearing the truck driver from Nantucket who thinks the stock market is just like gambling? Do we really benefit by the call from the Detroit stockbroker who assures us that his clients are doing real well by investing in stocks?

Fortunately, CNN realized the error of their ways and has discontinued both of these practices.

[11] "Call in polls: Pseudo-Science debases journalism," by Richard Morin, *Sacramento Bee*, Feb. 12, 1992, p. B11. Morin is the director of polling for the *Washington Post*.

[12] *ibid.*

[13] "Punishment Outside Prisons," *Newsweek*, June 9, 1986, p. 82.

[14] "The Story Behind the Stat," Robert Schmidt, in *Brill's Content*, May 1999, p. 38.

[15] "Shouting 'Fire!'," Alan M. Dershowitz, *Atlantic Monthly*, (January 1989), pp. 72-74, reprinted in *The Art of Reasoning - Readings for Logical Analysis*, Stephen R. C. Hicks and David Kelley (New York: W.W. Norton & Co.: 1994), pp. 258-264.

[16] A few years later (2003) in Lawrence v. Texas, the United States Supreme Court overturned Bowers in a 6-3 decision. Justice Anthony Kennedy, writing for the majority, said that in Bowers the Court had viewed the liberty at stake too narrowly. He wrote that intimate consensual sexual conduct is part of the liberty protected by substantive due process under the Fourteenth Amendment. Homosexuals, according to Kennedy, have "the full right to engage in private conduct without government intervention."

[17] See *Reasoning and Writing*, Kathleen Dean Moore (New York: MacMillan, 1993), pp. 166-167.

[18] "The Delusion of Design and Purpose," Clarence Darrow, from *The Story of My Life* (New York: Scribner and Sons, 1932), cited in *Philosophy and Contemporary Issues*, 6th ed., edited by John R. Burr and Milton Goldinger (New York: MacMillan Publishing Co., 1992), pp. 123-130.

[19] *ibid.* p. 124.

Chapter Eight- Causal Reasoning

> At the root of the whole theory of induction is the notion of physical cause. To certain phenomena, certain phenomena always do, and, as we believe, always will, succeed. The invariable antecedent is termed the 'cause,' the invariable consequent, the 'effect.' Upon the universality of this truth depends the possibility of reducing the inductive process to rules.
> --John Stuart Mill

> In reality, all arguments from experience are founded on the similarity which we discover among natural objects, and by which we are induced to expect effects similar to those which we have found to follow from such objects.
> --David Hume

The International Agency for Research on Cancer, an arm of the World Health Organization, labels a substance as a *probable human carcinogen* when at least two animal studies indicate a substance causes cancer.[1] This agency gives little or no weight, however, to studies indicating that substances do *not* cause cancer. Thus, crystalline silica, the main ingredient in beach sand and rocks, is declared as a substance "known to cause cancer," even though several studies have found no evidence of such a causal connection.

We read or hear in the media many stories about causes of cancer and other diseases. Often the stories seem to contradict one another. One story says that a study found that eating broccoli reduces cancer risk. Another story says that a new study casts doubt on the protective effects of broccoli. What are we to make of such studies and reports? How reliable are they?

While it would go beyond the limits of this book to try to resolve the issue of how to apply to humans the results of studies done on animals, we can shed some light on how to evaluate the animal tests themselves. And we can review the kinds of things to consider when evaluating causal reasoning. We'll begin by clarifying what we mean when we say that something is a **cause** or a **causal factor** of something else.

1. Causes as necessary and sufficient conditions

Whenever we say that *some x causes some y*, we are saying that *x* is a significant factor in bringing about *y*. Furthermore, when we think we know the *cause* of something, we think we have explained it. Though it is possible, of course, to know that, say, *smoking causes cancer* and not have a clue as to the actual mechanisms by which the chemicals in cigarette smoke bring about cell damage. Even if we cannot understand how chemicals in smoke turn normal cells into cancerous ones, the knowledge that smoking causes cancer can be applied by us. This gives us some control over the effects of smoking. In short, knowing *that* smoking causes cancer is not the same as knowing *how* smoking causes cancer. Our concern here is with claims *that* something is a cause of something else. The *how*, the actual causal mechanisms, cannot be our concern. Those studies must belong to the different disciplines studying the causes of diseases, the causes of bridges or buildings collapsing, the causes of hurricanes or earthquakes, and so on.

Sometimes, when we say that *x* is a *cause* or *causal factor* of *y*, we mean that *x* is a *necessary condition* for *y.* To say, for example that *smoking cigarettes is a significant causal factor in the development of lung cancer* is to say not only that (1) smoking is a significant factor in bringing about lung cancer but that (2) it is necessary for one to smoke to develop the lung cancer caused by smoking and that (3) if one does not smoke one cannot get the lung cancer caused by smoking. So, even if we don't understand *how* smoking causes cancer, we can control the effects of smoking by not smoking.

Still, we all know that even if it is true that smoking causes cancer, there are people who have smoked for many years, lived to be old, and never developed cancer. So, how could smoking cause cancer if it is possible to smoke and not develop cancer? The answer is that smoking is *not* a **sufficient condition** for cancer. Not all causal events involve causes that are sufficient conditions. For example, some viruses are *necessary*, but *not sufficient*, conditions for getting the flu. Thus, for example, if a particular type of virus had not been present in Grimes' body, Grimes would not have contracted the flu. But had Grimes' immune system been working better or had Grimes been vaccinated (had his flu shot), he would not have gotten the flu even though the virus that causes the flu would still have been present in his body.

Had the virus been a **sufficient condition** for getting the flu, then Grimes would have gotten the flu no matter how well his immune system was working and no matter whether he did or did not have his flu shot. **If a causal factor is a sufficient condition for an effect, then that causal factor is sufficient to bring about its effect.** Smoking is not a sufficient condition for cancer. So, it is possible to smoke and not develop cancer, even though smoking is a significant causal factor in the development of lung cancer.

A third sense of 'cause' is that of a condition that is **both necessary and sufficient**. For example, the spirochete *Treponema pallidum* is both a necessary and a sufficient condition for syphilis. You cannot get syphilis if the spirochete is not present, and if the spirochete is present, you have syphilis. Thus, when we say *smoking causes cancer, a virus causes the flu*, and *a spirochete causes syphilis*, we do not mean exactly the same thing by 'causes' in the each case.

To say *x is a cause of y* is to say that *x* is a *necessary condition*, a *sufficient condition*, or *both a necessary and a sufficient condition* for bringing about *y*.

2. Causal claims: individuals and populations

We know that there are certain patterns to the behavior of both humans and natural phenomena. Some of these patterns involve variables (aspects that can change) which are complex, numerous, and difficult to control or measure. For example, cancer and heart disease seem to be related to many factors: genetic make-up, smoking, exercise, diet, weight, stress, etc. Finding the cause or causes of heart disease is not a matter of finding a single condition or lack of a single condition. Predicting who will get cancer or heart disease is usually difficult. We can be very sure that a person subjected to high doses of certain kinds of radiation will soon develop cancer. However, most cancer predictions will have to be couched in terms of *statistical probabilities*. Thus, instead of saying that a certain smoker is likely to die because of the effects of smoking, we say that *the death rate for smokers is 1.57 times the death rate for non-smokers* or that *the relative death rate from lung cancer is over 10 times greater in smokers than in non-smokers*.

It is difficult to translate a statistical probability into a specific prediction regarding any particular individual. Nevertheless, it seems clear from the data that smokers run a *greater risk* of harming their health and shortening their lives than non-smokers do. How much of a risk each individual smoker runs cannot be precisely determined. For some, the risk may be insignificant; for others, it may be enormous.

It is one thing to know that a study found that smokers died of lung cancer at a rate ten times higher than expected. In itself, this statistic does not prove that smoking is a significant causal factor in the development of lung cancer, but it supports the hypothesis that it is. But, even if smoking is a relevant and significant factor in the development of lung cancer *in general*, what does this relevance and significance mean for any given individual who now smokes but does not have lung cancer?

Determining that smoking causes lung cancer is not like establishing that if a baseball is thrown at a typical window in a typical house, the window will break. We can measure the fragility of the window and the force of the thrown object with sufficient accuracy to be able to predict which particular window will break when hit by the thrown ball. But we cannot measure a given individual's susceptibility to lung cancer with anything near the same kind of accuracy, even though we know that if the individual smokes his or her susceptibility to lung cancer is greater than it would be if the individual did not smoke. Thus, even if we can accurately say that smoking causes lung cancer, we cannot accurately say that any given individual who smokes will contract lung cancer due to smoking. We can accurately say, however, that if one smokes, then one runs a considerably higher risk of contracting lung cancer than one would if one did not smoke.

3. Sequences, correlations, and causes

Causal relationships are regular patterns in nature that are characterized by **sequences of events** and **correlations**. Thus, if there is a causal relationship between smoking and lung cancer, then the smoking must precede the development of lung cancer and there must be a *correlation* between smoking and lung cancer. If there is a correlation between smoking and lung cancer, then there must at least be a significant difference between the percentage of smokers with lung cancer and the percentage of non-smokers with lung cancer. A significant difference is one that is not likely due to chance.[2] In a later section, we will discuss methods of testing causal hypotheses. There we will explain in more detail how one establishes whether a correlation is significant.

4. Causal fallacies

It is obvious that many events occur in sequences without any causal connection between them. A car passes by and a leaf falls from a nearby tree, for example. Moreover, not all correlated events are causally related. A correlation may be due to **chance** or **coincidence**. For example, correlations exist between batting averages of major league ball players and presidential election years (the averages are usually lower during election years). Correlations have been established between sex crimes and phases of the moon and between hair color and temperament. Finally, there is the story of the jungle natives who beat their drums every time there is an eclipse. It never fails—the sun always returns after the ceremony: a case of *perfect correlation but no causality. To conclude that one thing must be the cause of the other solely because the two things are correlated is to commit the fallacy of false cause or questionable cause.*

    Another characteristic of causally related events is that the cause precedes the effect. However, *simply because one event precedes another does not mean that there is a causal relationship between the two events.* To reason that one thing must be the cause of the other solely because it preceded the other is to commit the **post hoc fallacy**, a type of *false cause* reasoning. The name is taken from the Latin *post hoc ergo propter hoc* (after this, therefore because of this). Just because the pain in your wrist went away after you started wearing your new magic copper or magnetic bracelet, does not mean that the bracelet caused the pain to be relieved. Just because the patient died right after the priest gave the patient a blessing, does not mean the blessing caused the death! Just because you thought of your mother right before she telephoned, does not mean your thoughts caused her to call!

4.1 The regressive fallacy

Things like stock market prices, golf scores, and chronic back pain inevitably fluctuate. Periods of low prices, low scores, and little or no pain are followed by periods of higher prices and scores, and greater pain. Likewise, periods of high prices and scores, and little pain are followed by periods of lower prices and scores, and more severe pain. This tendency to move toward the average away from extremes was called "regression" by Sir Francis Galton in a study of the average heights of sons of very tall and very short parents. (The study was published in 1885 and was called "Regression Toward Mediocrity in Hereditary Stature.") He found that sons of very tall or very short parents tended to be tall or short, respectively, but not as tall or as short as their parents. To ignore these natural fluctuations and tendencies often leads to self-deception regarding their causes and to a type of post hoc fallacy. The **regressive fallacy** is the failure to take into account natural and inevitable fluctuations of things when ascribing causes to them (Gilovich 1993: 26).

For example, a professional golfer with chronic back pain or arthritis might try a copper bracelet on his wrist or magnetic insoles in his shoes. He is likely to try such gizmos when he is not playing well or is not feeling well. He notices that after using the copper or the magnets that his scores improve and his pain diminishes or leaves. He concludes that the copper bracelet or the magnetic insole is the cause. It never dawns on him that the scores and the pain are probably improving due to natural and expected fluctuations. Nor does it occur to him that he could check a record of all his golf scores before he used the gizmo and see if the same kind of pattern has occurred frequently in the past. If he takes his average score as a base, most likely he would find that after a very low score he tended to shoot a higher score in the direction of his average. Likewise, he would find that after a very high score, he tended to shoot a lower score in the direction of his average.

Many people are led to believe in the causal effectiveness of worthless remedies because of the regressive fallacy. The intensity and duration of pain from arthritis, chronic backache, gout, and the like, naturally fluctuates. A remedy such as a chiropractic spinal manipulation, acupuncture, or a magnetic belt is likely to be sought when one is at an extreme in the fluctuation. Such an extreme is naturally going to be followed by a diminishing of pain. It is easy to deceive ourselves into thinking that the remedy we sought caused our reduction in pain. It is because of the ease with which we can deceive ourselves about causality in such matters that scientists do controlled experiments to test causal claims.

4.2 The clustering illusion

The clustering illusion is the intuition that random events occurring in clusters are not really random events. The illusion is due to selective thinking based on a false assumption. For example, it strikes most people as unexpected if heads comes up four times in a row during a series of coin flips. However, in a series of 20 flips, there is a 50% chance of getting four heads in a row (Gilovich). "In a random selection of twenty-three persons there is a 50 percent chance that at least two of them celebrate the same birthdate."[3] What are the odds of anyone dreaming of a person dying and then that person actually dying within 12 hours of the dream? A statistician has calculated that in Britain this should happen to someone every two weeks (Blackmore 2004: 301). It may seem unexpected, but the chances are better than even that a given neighborhood in California will have a statistically significant cluster of cancer cases.[4]

What would be rare, unexpected, and unlikely due to chance would be to flip a coin twenty times and have each result be the alternate of the previous flip. In any series of such random flips, it is more unlikely than likely that short runs of 2, 4, 6, 8, etc., will yield what we know logically is predicted by chance. In the long run, a coin flip will yield 50% heads and 50% tails (assuming a fair flip and fair coin). But in any short run, a wide variety of probabilities are expected, including some runs that seem highly improbable.

Finding a statistically unusual number of cancers in a given neighborhood--such as six or seven times greater than the average--is not rare or unexpected. Much depends on chance and much depends on where you draw the boundaries of the neighborhood. Clusters of cancers that are seven thousand times higher than expected, such as the incidence of mesothelioma (a rare form of cancer caused by inhaling asbestos) in Karian, Turkey, are very rare and unexpected. The incidence of thyroid cancer in children near Chernobyl in the Ukraine was one hundred times higher after the disaster in 1986.[5] Such extreme differences as in Turkey and the Ukraine are never expected by chance.

Sometimes a subject in an ESP experiment or a dowser might be correct at a higher than chance rate. However, such results do not indicate that an event is not a chance event. In fact, such results are predictable by the laws of chance. Rather than being signs of non-randomness, they are actually signs of randomness. ESP researchers are especially prone to take streaks of "hits" by their subjects as evidence that psychic power varies from time to time. Their use of optional starting and stopping (counting only data that supports their belief in ESP) is based on the presumption of psychic variation and an apparent ignorance of the probabilities of random events. One would expect, by the laws of chance, that occasionally a subject would guess cards or pictures (the usual test for ESP) at a greater than chance rate for a certain run. Combining the **clustering illusion** with **confirmation bias** is a formula for self-deception and delusion.

A classic study on the clustering illusion was done regarding the belief in the "hot hand" in basketball.[6] It is commonly believed by basketball players, coaches, and fans that players have "hot streaks" and "cold streaks." A detailed analysis was done of the Philadelphia 76ers shooters during the 1980-81 season. It failed to show that players hit or miss shots in clusters at anything other than what would be expected by chance. The researchers also analyzed free throws by the Boston Celtics over two seasons and found that when a player made his first shot, he made the second shot 75% of the time and when he missed the first shot he made the second shot 75% of the time. Basketball players do shoot in streaks, but within the bounds of chance. It is an illusion that players are 'hot' or 'cold'. When presented with this evidence, believers in the "hot hand" are likely to reject it because they "know better" from experience.

In epidemiology, the clustering illusion is known as the **Texas-sharpshooter fallacy**. The term refers to the story of the Texas sharpshooter who shoots holes in the side of a barn and then draws a bull's-eye around the bullet holes. Individual cases of disease are noted and then the boundaries are drawn.[7] Kahneman and Tversky called it "belief in the Law of Small Numbers" because they identified the clustering illusion with the fallacy of assuming that the pattern of a large population will be replicated in all of its subsets.[8] In logic, this fallacy is known as the **fallacy of division, assuming that the parts must be exactly like the whole.**[9] For example, just because the leukemia rate for children is such that, say, six children in your city would be expected to contract the disease in a given year, there is no immediate cause for alarm if two or three times that number are diagnosed this year. Such fluctuations are expected due to chance. However, if your area consistently has several times more new cases than the national average, there could well be an environmental factor causally related to the cancers. Of course, it might also be due to the fact that there is good treatment in your area and people are moving there with their sick children because of it.

4.3 Correlation and causality

When two events (call them *x* and *y*) are significantly correlated, that does not necessarily mean that they are causally related. The correlation could be spurious and coincidental. Even if the correlation is not coincidental, it is possible that *x* causes *y* or *y* causes *x* or that *z* causes both *x* and *y*. We may find a significant correlation between the rise in sex education classes and the rise in teenage pregnancy. The classes may be stimulating the teens to experiment sexually, leading to the increase in teen pregnancies. Or, the classes may have been instituted in response to the rise in teen pregnancy. Or, it may just be a coincidence. There may be a significant correlation between hip size and grade point average among sorority sisters, but it is unlikely that either factor causes the other. Perhaps the larger sisters study more, while their thinner ones are socializing when they should be studying. Perhaps it's just coincidence. The moral is simple: Correlation does not prove causality. Yet many scientists seem to be on a quest to do nothing more than find statistically significant correlations and conclude that when they find them they have evidence of a causal connection.

Many defenders of psychic phenomena, for example, think very highly of Robert Jahn's experiments with people trying to use their minds to affect the random output of various electronic or mechanical devices. Jahn was an engineering professor until he got interested in the paranormal. The work took place at Princeton University in the Princeton Engineering Anomalies Research (PEAR) lab. In 1986, Jahn, Brenda Dunne, and Roger Nelson reported on millions of trials by 33 people over seven years of trying to use their minds to override random number generators (RNG). (Think of these devices as randomly producing one of two variables, a 0 and 1, for example. Your task is to try to will more 0s than 1s, or vice versa.) In 1987, parapsychologist Dean Radin and Nelson did a meta-analysis of the RNG experiments and found that they produced odds against chance beyond a trillion to one (Radin 1997: 140). This sounds impressive, but as Radin says "in terms of a 50% hit rate, the overall experimental effect, calculated per study, was *about* 51%, where 50% would be expected by chance" [emphasis added] (141). Similar results were found with experiments where people tried to use their minds to affect the outcome of rolls of the dice, according to Radin.

However, according to psychologist Ray Hyman, "the percentage of hits in the intended direction was only 50.02%." And one 'operator' (the term used to describe the subjects in these studies) was responsible for 23% of the total data base. His hit rate was 50.05%. Take out this operator and the hit rate becomes 50.01% (Hyman 1989: 152). This reminds us that statistical significance does not imply importance. Furthermore, Stanley Jeffers, a physicist at York University, Ontario, has repeated the Jahn experiments but with chance results (Alcock 2003: 135-152).

Based on the results of these experiments, Radin claims that "researchers have produced persuasive, consistent, replicated evidence that mental intention is associated with the behavior of …physical systems" (Radin 1997: 144). He also claims that "the experimental results are not likely due to chance, selective reporting, poor experimental design, only a few individuals, or only a few experimenters" (Radin 1997: 144). Radin is considered by many as a leading parapsychologist, yet it is difficult to see why anyone would find these correlations indicative of anything important, much less as indicative of psychic powers.

An even more problematic area of scientific research that seeks statistically significant correlations is the area of healing prayer. Several scientists have tried to prove that praying for somebody can heal them by the intercession of some spiritual force. Some have found significant correlations between prayer and healing. Some critics have accused these researchers of fraud. But my concern is that these scientists are assuming that finding a statistic that is not likely due to chance is evidence for supernatural intervention. They also don't seem to realize what it would mean if supernatural beings (SBs) could cause things to happen in the natural world. This might sound like a good thing. After all, who wouldn't like to be able to contradict the laws of nature whenever it was convenient to do so? However, if SBs could contravene the laws of nature at will, human experience and science would be impossible. We are able to experience the world only because we perceive it to be an orderly and lawful world. If SBs could intervene in nature at will, then the order and lawfulness of the world of experience and of the world that science attempts to understand would be impossible. If that order and lawfulness were impossible, then so would be the experience and understanding of it. Finally, if spirits could intervene in our world at will, none of the tests for causal claims, which we will turn to now, would even be possible.

5. Testing causal claims

There are several ways we can test causal claims. Three of the most important empirical methods are (1) **the controlled experiment,** (2) **the prospective study,** and (3) **the retrospective study.**

Each of the empirical methods of testing causal claims presupposes certain *logical methods of analysis* as well. The logical methods were systematically presented by John Stuart Mill in the nineteenth century, and thus are known as *Mill's Methods.*

5.1 Mill's methods

The first of Mill's methods is called the **method of agreement**. If six people at a dinner party get sick and the only food they all ate was the salmon, then the salmon probably caused the sickness, all else being equal. When only 'C' is shared in common by instances of 'E', then 'C' is probably the cause of 'E'. (Of course, the difficulty is in knowing that 'C' is the only thing besides 'E' that the instances have in common.)

The second method is called the **method of difference**. If two people have dinner, one having steak and the other salmon, and the one having salmon get sick, then the salmon probably caused the sickness, all else being equal. When 'E' occurs where 'C' is present but does not occur where 'C' is not present, then 'C' is probably the cause or a significant causal factor of 'E'. (Again, the difficulty is in knowing that 'C' is the only significant difference between the items.)

The third method is the **joint method of agreement and difference**. If a group of laboratory rats is randomly divided into two groups that are treated exactly alike except that one group is given a large dose of arsenic while the other is not, and all those given the arsenic die shortly thereafter, while none of those not given the arsenic die shortly thereafter, then the arsenic probably caused the deaths. When two groups differ only in 'C' and the group which has 'C' also develops 'E' but the group with no 'C' does not develop 'E', then we reason that 'C' is the cause or a significant causal factor of 'E'. (Everything here depends on knowing that everyone in one group got 'C' and no one in the other group got 'C' and that the only significant difference between the two groups is 'C'.)

A fourth method is the **method of concomitant variation**. If 'C' and 'E' are causally related there ought to be a correlation between them such that 'E' varies directly with the presence or absence of 'C'. For example, if lead causes lung cancer, then there should have been proportionately fewer cases of lung cancer as the amount of lead in the atmosphere decreased, as it did during the gasoline shortage during World War II and in the period following the removal of lead from gasoline in the U.S. Also, there should have been a proportionate increase in lung cancer as gasoline usage increased after the war.

Mill's methods are not tests of causal hypotheses but they are presupposed to some degree by the empirical tests we will now consider.

5.2 Controlled experiments

The preferred scientific way to test a causal claim is by doing a **controlled experiment**. If, for example, we want to test the causal claim that *crystalline silica causes lung cancer*, we might (1) randomly assign mice to two groups; (2) introduce crystalline silica into one group (the **experimental group**) but not the other (the **control group**), and otherwise treat the two groups identically for a specified length of time; and then (3) determine if there is a significant difference in the lung cancer rates of the two groups. If *crystalline silica causes lung cancer*, we should observe a significantly higher incidence of lung cancer in our experimental group. A significant difference would be one that is not likely due to chance. If we found that the lung cancer rate in the experimental group was 8.4 percent and in the control group was 7.9 percent, it is possible that the 0.5 percent difference is due to chance. That is, it is possible that had we studied two groups of mice, neither of which had been given the silica, we might have gotten similar results. However, if our study results in twice as many lung cancers in the experimental group as in the control group, we would be justified in concluding that silica is probably a cause of lung cancer. Such a huge difference in groups is not likely due to chance and is probably due to the silica.

If we did not use a **control group**, we would have no way of knowing whether an 8.4 percent rate of lung cancer among the mice we gave the silica to was significant or not. For all we know, that might be a typical rate among mice in general. By having a control group, we can compare the rate of the experimental group to a group that has *not* been affected by the substance we are testing. If silica is *not* a cause of lung cancer, then we should not see a rise in lung cancer rate among mice that have ingested silica. Thus, if our study resulted in the two groups having very similar lung cancer rates, we would be justified in concluding that silica is probably not a cause of lung cancer.

To justify thinking that a difference in effect observed between an experimental and a control group is indicative of a causal event, it is necessary that the groups be of adequate size and that the study go on long enough for the effects, if any, to reveal themselves. If the control and experimental groups are too small, we cannot be sure that any difference we observe is not due to chance. One advantage to mice studies is that the mice can be bred to be nearly identical. If the mice were not nearly identical, much larger groups of mice would have to be studied. Studies that can now be done with *hundreds* of mice would require *thousands* instead. Nevertheless, it is important that the mice be *randomly* assigned to their groups, to reduce the chances of any unknown bias entering the process.

Why study mice, you might ask? If we are interested in whether silica causes lung cancer in humans, should we be studying humans instead of mice? Yes and no. We couldn't in good conscience do a controlled experiment with humans that requires us to give the experimental group members a substance that is potentially lethal. Animal studies do introduce, however, analogical issues that must be dealt with.

5.2.1 Animal Studies

Much scientific reasoning is based upon research done on animals such as rats and mice. The reasoning depends upon drawing comparisons between humans and rodents. Obviously, there are many dissimilarities between humans and rodents. There are also many physiological, anatomical, and structural similarities. As an example of the difficulty in evaluating such reasoning, we will look at some comments that were frequently heard regarding a study done on the effects of saccharin on laboratory animals.

A group of 183 laboratory rats was randomly divided into an experimental group of 94 and a control group of 89. The experimental group was fed the same diet as the control group with the exception of saccharin. Saccharin was given to 78 first-generation and 94 second-generation rats. (The rats were observed for two generations; the second-generation experimental rats were fed saccharin from the moment of conception.) The amount of saccharin given the rats varied. The maximum dose of saccharin amounted to 7 percent of the rats' diet. In the experimental group, cancers developed only in the rats given the 5 percent dose: in the first-generation, 7 male rats and 0 female rats developed bladder cancers; in the second-generation 12 males and 2 females developed bladder cancers. In the control group, only one rat—a first-generation male—developed bladder cancer. The differences are not likely due to chance and indicate a causal relationship between saccharin and bladder cancer in rats.[10]

Many well-informed scientists concluded from this study that saccharin probably causes cancer in humans. Some non-scientists criticized the study because they believed that since the quantity of saccharin given to the rats (about 7 percent of their daily diet) was the equivalent of the amount of saccharin in about 800 12-ounce cans of diet soda, the study had little relevance for humans. These critics felt that the *quantity* of saccharin given the rats was obviously *relevant* to whether or not it would cause cancer in humans. They thought that since the amount humans are likely to ingest was significantly different, it invalidated any conclusion regarding the carcinogenic effect of saccharin on humans. On the surface, the critics appear to be quite reasonable. A bit of critical thinking, however, reveals that the critics were not thinking very critically. It might turn out to be correct that giving high doses of substances to animals is not a very good way to determine the potential carcinogenic effects of those substances on humans. However, this cannot be known a priori or intuitively; it can only be discovered empirically.

A critical thinker knows that in areas outside of his or her own area of expertise, authorities or experts in those fields must be consulted and trusted beyond non-experts, provided that the area of the field of expertise at issue is not controversial among the experts themselves. The field of cancer research is well established, and there are things known by these researchers that may not be understood by the public. In any case, before assuming that the quantity of saccharin given the rats invalidates the study, a critical thinker would investigate the issue. A little research would reveal that at the time the saccharin studies were done most researchers agreed that anything that had been found to cause cancer seemed to cause it without regard to the quantity of the carcinogen. Quantity seemed only to affect the *speed* of the development of cancer. Giving high doses allowed researchers to discover potential carcinogens much more quickly and with much smaller samples than would otherwise be needed. Instead of a few hundred mice studied for a short period, the saccharin study would have gone on for years and would have required about 85,000 mice at dosages close to normal human exposure.[11] Scientists give large doses of suspected carcinogens to speed up and streamline their studies, not because they are ignorant as to what a relevant dosage would be. Most cancer researchers, in other words, did not believe that the massive doses given rodents invalidated their studies.

On the other hand, a little research on why scientists use large doses would also have revealed that there is some controversy in this area. Not all researchers agree with the practice of giving massive doses of chemicals to the animals. For example, Bruce Ames, a professor of molecular and cell biology at the University of California at Berkeley, and Lois Gold, a cancer researcher at Lawrence Berkeley Laboratory, think that many chemicals described as hazardous may actually be harmless at normal human exposures.[12] However, even though Ames and Gold think that the method of giving massive doses of substances to mice is bankrupt, they do *not* claim either that the analogy between mice and humans is a bad one or that common sense tells them that the quantity of dosage makes the analogy irrelevant. Rather, they base their conclusion on recent evidence that they believe shows that "tumors are induced by the high doses themselves, because they tend to stimulate chronic cell division."

A 1992 report by the National Institute of Environmental Health Sciences, the branch of the National Institute of Health that directs animal studies, states that many of the assumptions driving rat and mouse research "do not appear to be valid."[13] The report claims that the practice of giving rodents the maximum dosages they can tolerate (M.T.D.) produces about two-thirds "false positives." "In other words, two-thirds of the substances that proved to be cancerous in the animal tests would present no cancer danger to humans at normal doses."[14] In addition, there is also evidence that some substances that are *not* carcinogenic in animal studies nevertheless cause cancer in humans, e.g., arsenic.

A new research method, based on an *analogy* between animal cells and human cells, looks promising. However, it is "costly and time consuming," according to Dr. Robert Maronpot, who has used the method in a study of oxazepam, a direct chemical relative of Valium, one of the most-often prescribed drugs in America. The method involves examining frozen DNA sections from animals given varying dosages of substances. Dr. Maronpot found that the rats and mice in M.T.D. studies develop cancer because of the high doses of oxazepam. "Oxazepam would not be a problem even for a mouse at normal human dosage levels," he said.

What this means is not that animal studies are irrelevant for drawing conclusions about humans. Nor does it mean that massive doses of substances should *never* be given in animal studies. It does seem to indicate, however, that reliance on statistics in animal studies to establish probabilities of cancer-causing substances will be diminished.[15]

5.2.3 Control Groups

Comparing experimental to control groups is useful for discovering causal connections only if the two groups are alike in all relevant respects except for the characteristic being tested. For example, it would be irrelevant to compare a group of smokers to a group of non-smokers in order to study the effects of smoking on a person's health if the smokers are sedentary, overweight, under extreme stress, eat vast quantities of fried foods, are alcoholics and have family histories of heart disease, while the non-smokers are active, of average or below average weight, lead calm lives, eat healthful foods, drink alcoholic beverages in moderation and do not have family histories of heart disease. The differences between the two groups would make the comparison irrelevant; for, any of the differences in weight, activity, health history, and the like, could account for the differences in health between the two groups. *In short, all potentially relevant causal factors should be identical between the experimental and control groups except for the factor being tested.*

Likewise, our controlled experiment to test the claim that silica causes lung cancer would have been invalidated if the two groups of mice were significantly different to begin with. For example, the experiment would be invalid if one group consisted of mice bred to be clones and to be used for scientific experimentation, while the other group consisted of field mice. Any significant difference in lung cancer rates we might observe between the two groups might be due to significant differences they had before the experiment began.

How can one tell whether one has controlled for all potential causal factors except the one we are testing? You cannot, at least not with absolute certainty. There is always the possibility that you have overlooked something, or are ignorant of the real cause of the effect being studied. Again, it requires *background knowledge* in order to be able to judge competently what is or is not potentially relevant in a given situation. Moreover, there is always some possibility of error. Hence, as with all inductive reasoning, conclusions regarding causes must be stated as being to some degree *probable*.

On the other hand, if one were not to use a control group, one could not know that any effect observed was due to the suspected cause. For example, you might think a particular acne medication is a miracle worker at getting rid of pimples because you put it on for a week and your blemishes went away. However, if you had done nothing at all, your blemishes might have gone away. On the other hand, perhaps you also did something else that week (e.g., gave your face a nightly ice bath), which was actually the cause of the blemish reduction. However, if you put the acne medication on one side of your face but not the other and treat both sides of your face equally during the week, then if there is a difference in effect, it is probably due to the medication. Without a control, you cannot be sure what caused the effect.

5.2.4 Controlled studies with humans

One of the benefits of working with animals is that one doesn't have to worry about their beliefs or demeanors affecting the outcome of the study. The beliefs and demeanors of humans, both researchers and subjects in experiments, can affect the outcome of a controlled study.

Robert Rosenthal has found that even slight differences in instructions given to control and experimental groups can affect the outcome of an experiment. Different vocal intonations, subtle gestures, even slight changes in posture, might influence the subjects.

The **experimenter effect** is the term used to describe any of a number of subtle cues or signals from an experimenter that affect the performance or response of subjects in an experiment. The cues may be unconscious nonverbal cues, such as muscular tension or gestures. They may be vocal cues, such as tone of voice. Research has demonstrated that the expectations and biases of an experimenter can be communicated to experimental subjects in subtle, unintentional ways, and that these cues can significantly affect the outcome of the experiment (Rosenthal 1998).

Many researchers have found evidence that people in experiments who are given inert substances (**placebos**) often respond as if they have been given an active substance (the **placebo effect**). The placebo effect may explain, in part, why therapies such as homeopathy, which repeatedly fail controlled testing, have many satisfied customers nonetheless (Carroll 2003: 293).

Double-blind experiments can reduce experimenter and placebo effects. In a **double-blind** experiment, neither the subjects of the experiment nor the persons administering the experiment know certain important aspects of the experiment. For example, an experimenter who works for a drug company that is trying to produce a new drug for depression would be wise to have another experimenter randomize the participants into the group getting the new drug and the group getting a placebo. The subjects should not be told what group they are in; their expectations might affect the outcome. The experimenter who does the randomization should keep to himself any information regarding who is in which group and should not be the one to distribute the pills/placebos to the subjects. The one who hands out the pills/placebos and keeps records of who gets which should not be the one who records the effects on the participants. In this way, any bias on the part of the experimenters is minimized. Only after the experiment is concluded should the members of the groups be unblinded. There should be an exception, of course, if something bizarre began happening, such as several patients dying of heart attacks. In such cases, the experiment might be halted and the participants unblinded to examine the possibility that the new drug might be killing people (Carroll: skepdic.com/experimentereffect.html).

The experimenter effect may explain why many experiments can be conducted successfully only by one person or one group of persons, while others repeatedly fail in their attempts to replicate the results. Of course, there are other reasons why studies cannot be replicated. The original experimenter may have committed errors in design, controls, or calculations. He may be deceived himself about his ability to avoid being deceived. Or he may have committed fraud. While the experimenter effect does not discriminate among sciences, parapsychologists maintain that their science is especially characterized by the ability of believers in psi (ESP and psychokinesis) to get positive results, while skeptics get negative results. Many parapsychologists also believe that subjects in their card-guessing experiments who believe in psi produce above chance results, while those who are skeptics produce below chance results (the **sheep-goat effect**). Skeptics note that in any card-guessing experiment there should be some who score above chance and some who score below. What is not expected is that one person should consistently and repeatedly score significantly above chance. Some parapsychologists who have subjects that seem to perform psychic tasks such as bending metal with their minds or guessing correctly 20 out of 25 cards whose faces they can't see have found that when they institute tighter controls on their subjects, the subjects lose their ability to perform. Rather than admit that the apparent success of psychic ability was due to poor controls, these scientists claim that psi diminishes with increased testing (the **decline effect**) or that psi only works when the experimenter shows absolute trust in the subject. Having rigorous controls to avoid cheating or sensory leakage (unconscious and inadvertent communication between the subject and others) shows distrust, they argue, and destroys psychic ability. Skeptics think these are **ad hoc hypotheses**; that is, claims created to explain away facts that seem to refute their belief in psi.

5.2.5 Replication

Since there are so many variables that can affect the outcome of a controlled study, it is important that we not put too much faith in a single study. If we or others are unable to replicate the results of a controlled study, it is likely that the results of our study were spurious. If, on the other hand, our results can be replicated by ourselves and by others, that is an indication that the results were not spurious, but genuine. However, if the original study design was flawed in some way or our control protocols were not adequate, then replication is meaningless. For example, when Fleischmann and Pons announced that they had successfully produced cold fusion, they were greeted with both skepticism and with attempts by others to duplicate their experiments. (This was difficult, since they didn't publish all the details of their experiment.) Even when others seemed to duplicate the results of their experiments, many remained skeptical. Further inquiry determined that the results that seemed so promising were due to faulty equipment and measurements, not cold fusion.

One of the traits of a cogent argument is that the evidence be sufficient to warrant accepting the conclusion. In causal arguments, this generally requires—among other things—that a finding of a significant correlation between two variables, such as magnets and pain, be reproducible. Replication of a significant correlation usually indicates that the finding was not a fluke or due to methodological error. Yet, the news media and research centers often create the illusion of importance of single studies. For example, the *University of Virginia News* published a story about a study done on magnet therapy to reduce fibromyalgia pain. The study, conducted by University of Virginia (UV) researchers, was published in the *Journal of Alternative and Complementary Medicine*, which asserts that it "includes observational and analytical reports on treatments outside the realm of allopathic medicine...."

The only people who refer to conventional medicine as *allopathic* are opponents of conventional medicine. So, they may not be the most objective folks in the world when it comes to evaluating anything "alternative." Be that as it may, the study must stand or fall on its own merits, not on the biases of those who publish it. Furthermore, the study must be distinguished from the press release put out by UV. The headline of the UV article states that Magnet Therapy Shows Limited Potential for Pain Relief. The first paragraph states that "the results of the study were inconclusive." Even so, the researchers claimed that magnet therapy reduced fibromyalgia pain intensity enough in one group of study participants to be "clinically meaningful." (Perhaps UV considers 'limited potential' as the middle ground between 'inconclusive' and 'clinically meaningful.')

The UV study involved 94 fibromyalgia patients who were randomly assigned to one of four groups. One control group "received sham pads containing magnets that had been demagnetized through heat processing" and the other got nothing special. One treatment group got "whole-body exposure to a low, uniformly static magnetic field of negative polarity. The other...[got]...a low static magnetic field that varied spatially and in polarity. The subjects were treated and tracked for six months."

"Three measures of pain were used: functional status reported by study participants on a standardized fibromyalgia questionnaire used nationwide, number of tender points on the body, and pain intensity ratings." One of the investigators, Ann Gill Taylor, R.N., Ed.D. stated: "When we compared the groups, we did not find significant statistical differences in most of the outcome measures." Taylor is a professor of nursing and director of the Center for Study of Complementary and Alternative Therapies at UV. "However, we did find a statistically significant difference in pain intensity reduction for one of the active magnet pad groups," said Taylor. The article doesn't mention how many outcome measures were used.

The study's principal investigator was Dr. Alan P. Alfano, assistant professor of physical medicine and rehabilitation and medical director of the UV HealthSouth Rehabilitation Hospital. Alfano claimed that "Finding any positive results in the groups using the magnets was surprising, given how little we know about how magnets work to reduce pain." Frankly, I find it surprising that Alfano finds that surprising, since it is unlikely he would have conducted the study if he didn't think there might be some pain relief benefit to using magnets. His statement assumes they work to reduce pain and the task is to figure out how. Alfano is also quoted as saying that "The results tell us maybe this therapy works, and that maybe more research is justified. You can't draw final conclusions from only one study." This last claim is absolutely correct. His double use of the weasel word 'maybe' indicates that he realizes that one shouldn't even make the claim that more research ought to be done based on the results of one study, especially if the results aren't that impressive.

Not knowing how many outcome measures the researchers used makes it difficult to assess the significance of finding one or two outcomes that look promising. Given all the variables that go into pain and measuring pain, and the variations in the individuals suffering pain (even those diagnosed as having the same disorder), it should be expected that if you measure enough outcomes you are going to find something statistically significant. Whether that's meaningful or not is another issue. A competent researcher would not want to make any strong causal claims about magnets and pain on the basis of finding one or two statistically significant outcomes in a study that found that most outcomes showed nothing significant.

But even if most of the outcomes had been statistically significant in this study of 94 patients, that still would not amount to strong scientific evidence in support of magnet therapy. The experiment would need to be replicated. Given the variables mentioned above, it would not be surprising if this study were replicated but found different outcomes statistically significant. Several studies might find several different outcomes statistically significant and some researcher might then do a **meta-study** (a study that combines the data of several studies and treats them as if they were part of one study) and claim that when one takes all the small studies together one gets one large study with very significant results. Actually, what you would get is one misleading study.

If other researchers repeat the UV study, looking only at the outcome that was statistically significant in the original study, and they duplicate the results of the UV study, then we should conclude that this looks promising. But one replication shouldn't seal the deal on the causal connection between magnets and pain relief. One lab might duplicate another lab's results but both might using faulty equipment manufactured by the same company. Or both might be using the same faulty subjective measures to evaluate their data. Several studies that showed nothing significant for magnets and pain might be followed by several that find significant results, even if all the studies are methodologically sound. Why? Because you are dealing with human beings, very complex organisms who won't necessarily react the same way to the same treatment. Even the same person won't necessarily react the same way to the same treatment at different times.

So, a single study on something like magnets and pain relief should rarely be taken by anybody as significant scientific evidence of a causal connection between the two. Likewise, a single study of this issue that finds nothing significant should not be taken as proof that magnets are useless. However, when dozens of studies find little support that magnets are effective in warding off pain, then it seems reasonable to conclude that there is no good reason to believe in magnet therapy (Carroll 2003: 209).

5.3 Prospective studies

Another way to test the causal claim that *crystalline silica causes lung cancer* would be to study a large random sample of humans. Divide the sample into two groups: those who have been exposed to significant amounts of silica and those who have not. Compare the lung cancer rates of the two groups over time. If *crystalline silica causes lung cancer*, we should find that the lung cancer rate is significantly higher in the exposed group.

This type of study is called a **prospective study,** and it can only be done to test a substance that is already present in the population. Thus, we could not do a prospective study on a new drug or chemical. Only substances that have been present in an environment long enough to have an effect can be tested by the prospective method.

One drawback to the prospective study is that there is no control over potentially relevant causal factors other than the one being tested. For example, we already know that smoking, coal dust, and environmental pollution are significant causal factors in lung cancer. In a controlled experiment, one has the advantage of being able to systematically control for such factors, called **X-factors**, which might be causing the effect being studied. We make sure that our control and experimental groups are alike in lifestyle, age, family health history, weight, etc. However, in a prospective study, our sample is chosen at random. Thus, it is possible that we could get a disproportionate number of smokers in the group that has ingested silica. If so, any difference in lung cancer rates between that group and the one which has not ingested silica might be due to smoking, not silica. However, this drawback can be mitigated by using a very large random sample. In a very large random sample, potential causal factors other than silica (**X-factors**) are likely to be evenly distributed amongst those exposed to silica and those not exposed to silica. If there were only 100 people in the sample, by chance they might all be coal miners or all live in heavily polluted industrial areas or be smokers. If I study 100,000 randomly selected people, the odds are that not all those in the silica group live in heavily polluted areas or smoke, while all those in the non-silica group live healthy lives in pristine countryside villages. It is more likely that potential X-factors will be evenly distributed among both the silica and non-silica populations in a very large random sample.

Having to study very large samples has some obvious disadvantages besides not being able to control for X-factors. Such studies may be time-consuming and costly, as it may take years to collect and analyze the data. However, there are some advantages to a prospective study over the controlled experiment. One advantage is that it allows us to study the effects of substances on human beings without doing experiments on humans or other mammals. In addition, for substances suspected of being health hazards, which have been in use for many years, prospective studies can be done in a relatively short time. The effects of smoking may take 20 or more years to develop. A controlled experiment on humans to study the effects of smoking would be very difficult and lengthy, as well as immoral. Whereas, the American Cancer Society's famous prospective study (1952) on the effects of cigarette smoking took only a few years to complete because large numbers of men had been long-term smokers (i.e., had smoked for 20 years or more). In that study, the sample included about 200,000 men between the ages of 50 and 69. Women were not included in the sample because it was believed that there would not be very many women who had been long-time smokers. The study found that the mortality rate from lung cancer for persons who smoke one to two packs of cigarettes a day is 11.5 times greater than for those who do not smoke. Although women were not included in the sample, it would have been reasonable to conclude that similar results would be

178

obtained from a large sample of long-term women smokers. Why? Reasoning analogically, we would argue that since women are like men in many relevant respects regarding the issue at hand, namely, in having the same kind of respiratory system, we would expect that it is probable that what is true of men for smoking and lung cancer will also be true of women. Nevertheless, it was less certain, from this study, that women who smoke run the same risks as men who smoke—simply because women were not included in the study. For all we know, there may be some relevant difference in lifestyle or physiology of women that would make a difference. In fact, however, later studies of the effects of smoking on women have demonstrated that women are susceptible to the same kinds of health hazards from smoking as men are.

A later and larger prospective study (685,748 women and 521,555 men, begun in 1982) by the American Cancer Society found mortality risks among current smokers are higher than those among nonsmokers. In all, it is estimated that cigarette smoking causes approximately 23 percent of all cancer deaths in women and smoking is responsible for 42 percent of all male cancer deaths (Shopland et al. 1991). The risk of developing any of the smoking-related cancers is dose-related; that is, the more cigarettes consumed daily, the younger the age at which one initiates smoking, and the more years one smokes, the greater the risk. This kind of data strengthens the case against smoking. Among male cigarette smokers, the risk of lung cancer is more than 2,000 percent higher than among male nonsmokers; for women, the risks were approximately 1,200 percent greater.

Prospective studies are useful in testing causal hypotheses regarding substances that have been widely used for many years. However, for substances that have only recently been introduced into human populations, many years will have to go by before the effects on humans can be known by prospective studies. Since an experiment on laboratory animals can yield results in a relatively short time, it seems inevitable that such experiments will continue to be used to test the potential harmful effects of new substances introduced into the human ecological system.

Mill's Method of **concomitant variation** is often used in designing a prospective study. For example, suppose you wanted to test the claim that *lack of calcium is a cause of leg cramps*. One could do a prospective study, which would involve getting a very large random sample from the general population. We would need dietary information and the incidence and severity of leg cramps of those surveyed. From the dietary information, we could determine the amount of calcium a person ingests. We would predict that if lack of calcium causes leg cramps there would be a correlation between the amount of calcium people ingest and the incidence of leg cramping. We would expect that as the amount of calcium in the diet increases the amount of leg cramps would decrease and as the amount of calcium in a diet decreases, the amount of leg cramping should increase. On a graph, our predicted data would look like this:

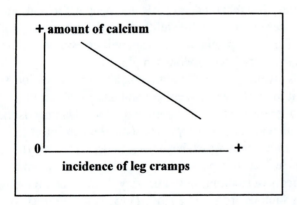

If the data matches our prediction, we can say we have *confirmed* our hypothesis, but we should not assert that we have proved that lack of calcium causes leg cramps. A single study should not be taken as proof of anything. We need replication under critically examined conditions.

5.4 Retrospective studies

Retrospective studies *are those done on populations already demonstrating the effect whose cause is being sought.* In a retrospective study, we compare a group demonstrating the effect to a group which does not demonstrate the effect. We must have some idea as to what is the cause of the effect, and we test our idea by looking to see if there is a significant difference in the presence of the suspected cause between the two groups. The significance of the study depends heavily upon the two groups being similar in relevant respects.

For example, imagine that it is known that the lung cancer rate among workers at a granite-quarry is very high. We might suspect that silica is the cause of many of the lung cancers. After all, such workers are exposed to silica dust and some animal studies have indicated that silica causes lung cancer. To do a retrospective study, we must first find a comparable group of people who do not have lung cancer (that is, they do not show the effect). This comparable group must be like the group showing the effect in all relevant ways except for having lung cancer. They should be in the same age group, have the same kind of smoking rates, live in similar environments, have similar family health histories, and the like. If *silica causes lung cancer*, we should find that the group with no lung cancer has been exposed to significantly less silica than the lung cancer group. If it turns out, that the no lung cancer group has been exposed to similar quantities of silica as the lung cancer group, then it is probably the case that silica does not cause lung cancer. Also, if we were to compare workers at the quarry who have lung cancer with those who don't and were to find that all of those who have lung cancer also smoke, while none of those who don't have lung cancer smoke, this would indicate that smoking, not silica, is likely the cause of the lung cancers.

One advantage of the retrospective study is that often it can be done much more quickly than an experimental or a prospective study. One drawback with the retrospective method is that samples are not randomly selected, leaving open the possibility of a variety of X-factors as potential causes.

For example, imagine that 35 people out of 100 at a company picnic get food poisoning. To discover whether it was the potato salad, for example, that caused the illness, we couldn't take a group of people and feed them the salad and compare them with those who don't eat any potato salad. To do so would be impractical as well as immoral. We could, however, poll each of the 100 people and ask them what they ate. If we discovered that there were a total of six different food items at the picnic and that only people who ate the potato salad got sick, we might justifiably conclude that the potato salad was the causal factor of the illness. By Mill's joint method of agreement and difference we reason that if something is a cause of something else, we expect the cause to be present where the effect is present—the agreement—and we expect to find that the effect is not present in a different group where the cause isn't present—the difference. We could be wrong, of course, in concluding that the potato salad was the causal factor of the illness. Something unknown to us could have caused the sickness.[16] Nevertheless, I think under such circumstances we would be wise to dispose of the potato salad.

Another example of a retrospective study is discussed in Giere's *Understanding Scientific Reasoning* (1996: 297-303). A few years after the use of birth control pills became widespread in the United States and England, it was noticed that blood clots among young women seemed to be on the rise. To determine whether or not there was a significant or chance correlation between taking birth control pills and blood clotting would have taken years using either the experimental or the prospective design method. Therefore, a retrospective study was made of young married women who had recently been hospitalized for blood clots. It was found that 45 percent of them had been taking the pill. This group was compared to a control group of married women matched for age, number of children and a few other things thought to be possibly relevant to developing blood clots. Each of the control group women had been recently admitted to a hospital for a serious medical problem other than blood clotting. It was found that only 9 percent of the control group were on the pill. The difference between the two groups seems significant but it isn't. The researchers failed to consider the smoking habits of each group. The difference between the two groups turned out to be due more to smoking than to the birth control pill.

Scientists use specific methods to test causal hypotheses to avoid self-deception and false cause reasoning. Yet, even experts sometimes forget that correlations by themselves do not prove causal connections and that *experimental and control groups must be alike in all relevant respects except for the tested factor*. In the 1970's the U.S. Government issued a warning to women using birth control pills. The warning asserted that studies had shown that for women between the ages of 40-44 the death rate from heart attacks was 3.4 times higher for women on birth control pills than for those not on the pill. Since smoking was known at the time to be a relevant causal factor in heart attacks, it should have been controlled for. In fact, when the women were divided into smokers and non-smokers, something quite startling was discovered: Smokers on the pill die from heart attacks at a rate 3.4 times greater than women smokers not on the pill and smokers on the pill die from heart attacks at a rate 8.4 times greater than women non-smokers either on or off the pill. Taking the pill does not seem to be a causal factor in death by heart attack *unless a woman also smokes*, in which case the risk of dying of a heart attack is 4.2 times as great as for sister smokers not on the pill. (Note: later studies have not found that women who smoke and use birth control pills are at any higher risk of heart attack than women who only smoke.)

In another study, it was found that 84 granite-quarry workers in Vermont had died of lung cancer. Those who did the study concluded that exposure to silica caused the lung cancers. However, other researchers obtained smoking histories of those in the study and found that all 84 of those who died from lung cancer were smokers. Thus, perhaps none of those who got lung cancer got it from exposure to silica.[17]

6. Importance of testing under controlled conditions

Anybody can claim their product works wonders. But not everybody puts their product to the test. In fact, many new products that promise relief from pain or instant happiness are never tested at all. The money behind the product has all gone into marketing. Little, if any, is spent on research. That is why it is important before investing your money in a new product to find out if the product has been tested, how it was tested, and what were the results. For example, the DKL LifeGuard Model 2, from DielectroKinetic Laboratories, was advertised as being able to detect a living human being by receiving a signal from the heartbeat at distances of up to 20 meters through any material. This would be a great tool, if it really works, for law enforcement agencies. Sandia Labs tested the device using a double-blind, random method. (Sandia is a national security laboratory operated for the U.S. Department of Energy by the Sandia Corporation, a Lockheed Martin Co.) The causal hypothesis they tested could be worded as follows: *the human heartbeat causes a directional signal to activate in the Lifeguard, thereby allowing the user of the LifeGuard to find a hidden human being (the target) up to 20 meters away, regardless of what objects might be between the LifeGuard and the target.*

The testing procedure was quite simple: five large plastic packing crates were set up in a line at 30-foot intervals and the test operator, using the DKL LifeGuard Model 2, tried to detect in which of the five crates a human being was hiding. Whether a crate would be empty or contain a person for each trial was determined by random assignment. This is to avoid using a pattern that might be detected by the subject. The tests showed that the device performed no better than expected from random chance. The test operator was a DKL representative. The only time the test operator did well in detecting his targets was when he had prior knowledge of the target's location. The LifeGuard was successful ten out of ten times when the operator knew where the target was. It may seem ludicrous to test the device by telling the operator where the objects are, but it establishes a baseline and affirms that the device is working in the eyes of the manufacturer. Only when the operator agrees that his device is working should the test proceed to the second stage, the double-blind test. For, the operator will not be as likely to come up with an ad hoc hypothesis to explain away his failure in a double-blind test if he has agreed beforehand that the device is working properly.

If the device could perform as claimed, the operator should have received signals from each of the crates with a person within but no signals from the empty crates. In the main test of the LifeGuard, when neither the test operator nor the investigator keeping track of the operator's results knew which of five possible locations contained the target, the operator performed poorly (six out of 25) and took about four times longer than when the operator knew the target's location. If human heartbeats cause the device to activate, one would expect a significantly better performance than 6 of 25, which is what would be expected by chance.

The different performances—10 correct out of 10 tries versus 6 correct out of 25 tries—vividly illustrates the need for keeping the subject blind to the controls: it is needed to eliminate self-deception. The evaluator is kept blind to the controls to prevent him or her from subtly tipping off the subject, either knowingly or unknowingly. If the evaluator knew which crates were empty and which had persons, he or she might give a visual signal to the subject by looking only at the crates with persons. To eliminate the possibility of cheating or evaluator bias, the evaluator is kept in the dark regarding the controls.

The lack of testing under controlled conditions explains why many psychics, graphologists, astrologers, dowsers, paranormal therapists, and the like, believe in their abilities. To test a dowser it is not enough to have the dowser and his friends tell you that it works by pointing out all the wells that have been dug on the dowser's advice. One should perform a random, double-blind test, such as the one done by Ray Hyman with an experienced dowser on the PBS program *Frontiers of Science* (Nov. 19, 1997). The dowser claimed he could find buried metal objects, as well as water. He agreed to a test that involved randomly selecting numbers which corresponded to buckets placed upside down in a field. The numbers determined which buckets a metal object would be placed under. The one doing the placing of the objects was not the same person who went around with the dowser as he tried to find the objects. The exact odds of finding a metal object by chance could be calculated. For example, if there are 100 buckets and 10 of them have a metal object, then getting 10% correct would be predicted by chance. That is, over a large number of attempts, getting about 10% correct would be expected of anyone, with or without a dowsing rod. On the other hand, if someone consistently got 80% or 90% correct, and we were sure he or she was not cheating, that would confirm the dowser's powers.

The dowser walked up and down the lines of buckets with his rod but said he couldn't get any strong readings. When he selected a bucket, he qualified his selection with words to the effect that he didn't think he'd be right. He was right about never being right! He didn't find a single metal object despite several attempts. His performance is typical of dowsers tested under controlled conditions. His response was also typical: He was genuinely surprised. Like most of us, the dowser is not aware of the many factors that can hinder us from doing a proper evaluation of events: self-deception, wishful thinking, suggestion, unconscious bias, selective thinking, and communal reinforcement (Carroll 2003: 82).

7. A word about statistical significance and meta-analyses

I noted above in the discussion of the Jahn PEAR studies that statistical significance is not necessarily important. Let me explain. The most common meaning of 'statistical significance' when applied to the results of a scientific study is "according to an arbitrary statistical formula, the results obtained are not likely due to chance." Most of the time, a formula is used that translates into layman's terms as: *One out of twenty such tests will yield spurious results.* However, scientists never put it that way. They will tell us that **p<0.05** (p = the probability of the results being spurious) or that "We observed a decrease of 5.1 percent (95 percent **confidence interval**, 1.5 to 8.7 percent; p = 0.02)." What they really mean is that 5 percent of the time, doing exactly the same study in exactly the same way, one can expect to get results that look significant when they're not. In short, one out of twenty scientific studies is wrong (Brignell 2000: 52).

How did scientists land upon this magical 95 percent confidence interval? The idea came from R. A. Fisher, one of the pioneers of statistics as a science. How did he land upon the significance of a probability of 0.05? There isn't any profound reason for it. He just found the number convenient (Brignell 2000: 52). Many scientists consider it to be the gold standard. Finding a statistical correlation that is significant at the 95 percent confidence level has become the goal of some researchers. And why wouldn't it, since anything less is unlikely to get published in many journals. Although, it is becoming more frequent to see studies claiming significance at the 90 percent confidence level, which means that one in *ten* such studies is likely to yield spurious results. The Environmental Protection Agency, for example, was willing to declare that secondhand smoke causes 3,000 lung cancer deaths a year on the basis of a study that used the 90 percent confidence interval.

182

If you think about this for a short time, you will see that there are some significant problems with this standard. A scientist who does ten or twenty experiments can expect at least one of them to yield significant results according to some arbitrary statistical formula. Guess which study the scientist writes up and submits to a scientific journal for publication? Not the nine or nineteen that found no significant correlation. Those get filed in the drawer. This is known as the *file-drawer effect* or *publication bias*. Also, the media tend to publish stories about studies that show positive results. This explains in part why we rarely see a follow-up to all the stories about the latest wonder drugs or cures that are hyped when someone publishes a paper after having found a statistically significant correlation. It also explains why we should not put too much faith in the results of any single study. Publication bias also makes it possible for some drugs to get marketed that have scientific support that they work, when in fact they may be little more than placebos.

Finally, when one combines the trend among scientists to do *meta-studies* (combining the results of several studies done by different scientists and treating them as if they comprised one large study) with the file-drawer effect, one has a recipe for exaggerated significance as well as exaggerated importance. Considering the fact that there may be many studies on a particular subject that have never been published because they got negative results, it is likely that a meta-study of that subject will have a disproportionate and unrepresentative collection of studies to analyze. And, even though researchers try not to mix heterogeneous studies, it is very difficult to find dozens of studies that all used the same subject selection criteria, employed the same treatments, and used the same statistical methods.

As scientist and author John Brignell says, "The safest thing to do with meta-analyses is take them with a large pinch of salt."

Exercise 8-1 Self-test: true or false? (Check your answers in Answers to Selected Exercises.)

1. A controlled experiment has the advantage of allowing us to systematically control for factors that could be causing the effect being studied.
2. One drawback to the prospective design is that it takes many years to perfect.
3. A necessary condition is one that necessarily produces an effect.
4. A sufficient condition is one that is sufficient to produce an effect
5. Publication bias refers to the tendency of scientific journals to publish articles that fit with the editors' biases and prejudices.
6. In a retrospective study, we compare a group demonstrating the effect to a group that does not demonstrate the effect.
7. To divide a large random sample into a group that has been exposed to a substance that might be carcinogenic and a group that has not been exposed to the substance, would be done if one were using the prospective method.
8. An experimental group is one that is introduced to the suspected causal factor, to be compared with another identical group not introduced to it.
9. If a sample from a very large human population is selected properly, the large random differences of opinions and behaviors one would expect to find in that population should tend to cancel out one another.
10. Causal relationships are regular patterns in nature that are characterized by sequences of events and significant correlations.
11. If a single study finds a statistically significant correlation between two variables, we should take that as proof of a causal connection between the variables.
12. It is impossible for non-causally related phenomena to exhibit patterns of regularity of behavior.
13. Each of the empirical methods of testing causal claims presupposes certain logical methods of analysis as well.
14. To say that something is a relevant causal factor in the development or production of something is to say that it is either part of or wholly a necessary condition, a sufficient condition, or both a necessary and sufficient condition for the effect to occur.
15. The *post hoc* fallacy is a type of sampling error due to carelessness after the fact.
16. All perfectly correlated events are causally related.
17. All causally related events are significantly correlated.
18. One disadvantage to the retrospective study is that samples are not randomly selected.

19. In causal reasoning, if done scientifically, there is little possibility of error and conclusions regarding causes are almost absolutely certain.
20. Replication of a scientific study proves the original results were correct.
21. Correlation proves causality.
22. Double-blind studies are done to minimize experimenter and test subject bias.
23. A single study demonstrating a significant correlation is rarely sufficient to justify belief that a causal connection has been established.
24. The results of studies on animals such as mice are completely irrelevant for humans.
25. An ad hoc hypothesis is a claim created to explain away facts that seem to refute one's belief.

Exercise 8-2

Each of the following consists of a base argument. Look at the base argument and get a general notion of the sufficiency of the premises for the stated conclusion. Following each base argument is a list of statements. The statements either change the strength with which the conclusion is asserted to follow from the evidence or they offer alternative premises. Treating each additional statement separately, determine whether it strengthens, weakens, or has no effect on the argument. (Note: while each of the following passages is based on an actual experiment, the data have been changed for the purposes of this exercise.)

*1. Over a period of several years, 100 rats were fed a diet which consisted of 7 percent saccharin (the experimental group). Another 100 rats were fed the same diet except for the saccharin (the control group) . The offspring of each group were put on the same diet as their parents. The rats used in the experiment were all carefully bred laboratory rats (i.e., nearly identical "twins"). Both male and female rats we used in equal numbers in the first generation. Bladder cancer was discovered in 3 percent of the first-generation experimental group. No first-generation control group rat developed bladder cancer. In the second generation, 14 percent of the experimental group and 2 percent of the control group developed bladder cancer. Therefore, saccharin very likely causes cancer in humans.

1.1 CONCLUSION: Saccharin causes cancer in rats.
1.2 PREMISE: The rats were collected from sewers and fields.
1.3 PREMISE: The experimental group members were from the sewers, but the control group members were carefully bred laboratory rats.
1.4 PREMISE: All the experimental rats developed bladder cancer.
1.5 PREMISE: One thousand rats were used in each group.
1.6 CONCLUSION: More studies should be done to determine if there is any causal link between saccharin ingestion and bladder cancer in humans.
1.7 PREMISE: Different lab technicians fed the rats different diets on different days, except for the saccharin, which was always kept at 7 percent of the experimental group's diet and was absent from the control group's diet.
1.8 PREMISE: The experimental group members were frequently x-rayed to see if any tumors were developing.
1.9 PREMISE: The 30 or so substances known to cause cancer in humans are all known to cause cancer in laboratory animals when given in high doses.
1.10 CONCLUSION: Pregnant women should be advised that using saccharin during pregnancy may increase the risk that their child will develop bladder cancer.

2. One hundred weanling rats on a diet of 20 percent Brazilian peanut meal showed liver damage after 9 weeks. After 6 months, 9 of 11 rats developed multiple liver tumors, and two of these rats had lung metastases (i.e., the malignancy spread). Therefore, peanuts are carcinogenic (i.e., cancer-causing).

2.1 CONCLUSION: Peanut meal may cause cancer in humans.
2.2 PREMISE: A control group fed the same diet as the weanling rats, except for the peanut meal, developed no tumors.
2.3 PREMISE: Several experiments, using peanuts from several different countries, produced the same results.
2.4 PREMISE: 800 of 1000 young turkeys died of liver lesions within two weeks of being fed a substance which contained the Brazilian peanut meal.

184

2.5 PREMISE: Peanut meal often contains aflatoxin and 20 millionths of a gram of aflatoxin will kill a day old duckling in 24 hours; and CONCLUSION: Studies should be done to determine the frequency of aflatoxin in peanuts and peanut-based foods. Note:This issue is discussed in detail in *Man Against Cancer*, Bernard Glemser (New York: Funk & Wagnalls, 1969).

3. A group of 50 sterile laboratory rats were being kept as pets by a lab technician. No consistent diet was   given to the rats, but what each individual rat ate each day was recorded. 25 of the rats developed liver cancer. An analysis was made of each rat's diet, and it was discovered that each of the cancerous rats had consumed .5 milligrams of sodium nitrite each day for a year. Therefore, sodium nitrite probably causes liver cancer in humans.

3.1 PREMISE: The 25 non-cancerous rats consumed no sodium nitrite during the year.
3.2 PREMISE: Excluding water, ground rice and spinach, the only substance each of the cancerous rats ingested in common was the sodium nitrite.
3.3 PREMISE: Other studies have linked sodium nitrite to liver cancer in laboratory animals.
3.4 PREMISE: In another study, an experimental and a control group are fed the same diet, except for .5 milligrams of sodium nitrite given daily to each of the members of the experimental group. 40 percent of the experimental group develop cancer, while only 38 percent of the control group develop cancer.

Exercise 8-3

Evaluate the causal reasoning in the following passages. If reasonable, suggest at least one experiment to test the conclusion made in each argument (i.e., treat the conclusion as a hypothesis).

*1. I know Vanish-X Cream eliminates acne because last night I used some and today my skin is much clearer.
2. Leg cramps are caused by lack of calcium. I know because last year when I had leg cramps I started taking calcium supplements and within two weeks my cramps were gone.
3. Friends, do you want to get rich like Brother Billy Bob? Just send a card with your contribution to the Reverend I. Am Greedy like our listener Mrs. Goodfaith did. She writes, "Dear Brother Billy Bob: On the very day I sent you my check for $100, I found a $1000 check that I had misplaced months ago." Praise the Lord!
4. In our neighborhood, a recent survey revealed that 75 percent of the men who had lost their jobs in the last year had quit going to church before losing their jobs. That should prove to even the greatest skeptic that it does not pay to leave the church.
5. I never shave before I pitch a ball game because the last time I shaved before a game, I gave up 14 runs in the first inning!
*6. It's all those food additives that are causing the crazy criminal acts to increase. You check it out. There is a direct correlation between the increase in the use of food additives and the increase in senseless crimes of violence.
7. The inflation rate went down after President Reagan took office, so his economic policies must have caused it.
8. Since Senator Rodda has been in office the crime rate has gone up 10 percent a year. It's time to elect someone who will do something positive about crime!
9. Andy, Beth, Carol, Dave, Edie and Frank had dinner together. All six developed violent stomach cramps within 30 minutes of finishing their meal. The meal consisted of salad with vinegar and oil dressing, baked potatoes with sour cream and chives, broccoli, broiled sirloin steak, and red wine. Edie is on a diet and refused the potato, but she put sour cream on her steak. Andy and Beth don't drink wine. Carol is a vegetarian. Dave and Frank hate broccoli. Therefore, the sour cream was a causal factor in their stomach cramps.
*10. In the 18th century, millions of people died from smallpox. Edward Jenner, a country doctor of Gloucestershire, spent 20 years investigating the cause of small pox and trying to establish that inoculation with cowpox immunizes a person from smallpox. Cowpox is a much milder disease than smallpox. Jenner heard from local folk that those infected with cowpox never got smallpox. He documented about 20 cases of people infected with cowpox who, when inoculated with smallpox were unaffected. It was well-known that others who were infected with smallpox were always affected unless they had already had the disease. He concluded that cow-pox immunizes human beings against smallpox. See *A History of the Sciences*, Stephen F. Mason (New York: Collier Books, 1962), p. 519; see also Langley, *op. cit.*, pp. 93-94.
11. "Joyce Kenyon, a San Jose, Calif., computer-systems manager, thanks her [Zuni] hummingbird fetish for saving her neck on more than one occasion. Recently, in an `intuitive hit', it cautioned that she might want to assure that a backup to her company's computer system was in place. `It's a good thing I did the backup work because the computer crashed the next day.' she said." (L. A. Winokur, "Pushing Their Luck: Zuni Indians Peddle `Magical' Charms," *The Wall Street Journal*, April 28, 1993.)

12. A recent study found that men under 5-foot-7 had about 70 percent more heart attacks than those over 6-foot-1. The study was based on a survey of 22,071 male doctors from across the United States. It was found that for every inch of height a person's heart attack risk goes down 3 percent. This means that someone 5-foot-10 is 9 percent less likely than someone 5-foot-7 to suffer a heart attack. The researchers found that shorter men were more likely to be overweight and to have high cholesterol and blood pressure. but even when these factors were taken into consideration, their risk of heart attacks was still higher than taller men's. Another study found a similar link between height and heart attacks in women. Short people might be at risk because their blood vessels are skinnier, so they are more prone to becoming clogged.

13. "Criminals convicted of murder, rape and other violent crimes have significantly higher levels of the metal manganese in their hair, say brain researchers with the University of California, Irvine. The finding might indicate that such prisoners suffer from a metabolic disorder that affects the brain, said Dr. Monte Buchsbaum, a professor of psychiatry and one the study researchers. People who suffer manganese poisoning from industrial exposure develop a syndrome similar to Parkinson's disease, he said. That disease causes shaking of the hands and loss of fine motor control consistent with damage to the brain's basal ganglia, a switchboard-like area that coordinates movement with sensory information.

"Either the prisoners are being exposed to higher level of manganese or they could have a disorder that results in higher levels of manganese," Buchsbaum said.... "Whether the finding is related to the environment might be significant for the general population because manganese is the metal that has been used to replace lead in gasoline. This alerts us not to an immediate danger but to the need to know more about the neurological effects of manganese," Buchsbaum said.

The study initially looked at prisoners at Deuel Vocational Institution in San Joaquin County who had been convicted of violent crimes. Guards and townspeople were also tested as comparison groups. Although all had fairly low level of manganese, the prisoners had seven times the amount in their hair as townspeople and five times that of guards.

Two more groups of prisoners, guards and locals were then studied. The second group included convicts in San Bernardino County Jail. The third group included recently arrested inmates awaiting trial in Los Angeles County Jail in an effort to rule out long-term exposure to the jail environment as a factor. While the Los Angeles inmates had substantially lower levels than the other prisoners, they still had double the amount found in guards and local residents.

The scientists said they needed to do more studies, perhaps with other aggressive people who have not been jailed, such as boxers or other athletes. ("Metal found in criminal's hair," by Susan Peterson, *The Sacramento Bee*, April 12, 1992. The article first appeared in the *Orange County Register*.)

14. For some young men, clinical depression--a state of feeling sad and without hope--"may have more to do with drug abuse than with deep psychological problems or a genetic predisposition to depression." Psychiatrist Marc Schuckit of the University of California at San Diego studied 964 men between the ages of 21 to 25 who were affiliated with the university. He found that while 82 percent had never been depressed, 11 percent had been. An additional 7 percent had depression that seriously interfered with their lives....Schuckit reported that only 30 percent of the never-depressed young men had problems connected with drug or alcohol use (job loss, arrest, ill health, marital disruption), compared with half of the most seriously depressed group. Moreover, a majority of the depressed men said that their drug-related problems had preceded their depression. (Only about a quarter said that they had become depressed first.) ....[S]tudents would do well to consider changing their drug habits before they come to the conclusion that they are hopelessly depressed." (Phillip Shaver, *Psychology Today*, May 1983, p. 16)

15. Public school administrators across the country have been cutting costs by increasing the number of pupils per class, citing studies that assert such changes will not harm the quality of education. Teachers cite other studies that show just the opposite. An exhaustive new survey of all the research to date shows mixed results for both sides. Achievement levels, it seems, increase significantly in classes with fewer than 20 students to each adult, but for classes larger than 20, achievement levels remain relatively constant even if classes swell to over 60....Gene Glass and Mary Lee Smith, psychologists with the Laboratory of Educational Research at the University of Colorado at Boulder, turned up 80 different controlled studies of the effects of class size....Classes in those studies ranged from tutorials for just a few students to packed classrooms of more than 60. Teachers' aides were counted as teachers in determining the ratio of students to adults. Glass and Smith found that both the negative and positive effects of class size were slightly greater in secondary school than in elementary school; the subject matter also made little difference....Other things being equal, pupils in a class of 15 will achieve more than those in a class of 30. Reducing class size from 30 to 25, however, will barely bring a noticeable change, according to the research.

*16. "[Dr. Ian James of the Royal Free Hospital in London wanted to find out whether oxyprenolol, a member of the beta-blocker group, might possibly alleviate anxieties and thus allow otherwise competent drivers [of automobiles] to perform to their full capabilities [during driving tests, which they had failed because of excessive nervousness]....
Beta-blockers do exactly what the name implies. They block the beta receptors on the surface of cells, preventing adrenaline from binding on these sites--a reaction that prolongs and intensifies the effects of a stressful situation....Thirty-four healthy young string players (not selected for undue nervousness) performed on separate days after receiving oxyprenolol or a placebo

186

[an inert compound]. Their playing was then assessed by two experts who did not know which of the two compounds the musicians had received. The aim of the experiment was to determine the effect of what Dr. James termed 'stage fright'--the natural anxiety and stress of performing in public. He chose string players because he felt the adverse effects of tremor would be more noticeable in them....As reported in *The Lancet* [1977, Vol. II, p. 952], the outcome was striking. Musical quality improved significantly--especially on the first occasion when players took oxyprenolol. All aspects of their playing improved: right- and left-hand dexterity, intonation, and control of tremor. Although the overall mean improvement was only 5 percent, some subjects registered 30 percent, and one registered 73 percent. As the musicians were not selected for being particularly prone to anxiety, the results suggest that some people might benefit greatly from such medication." [Dr. Bernard Dixon, "Ill-Defined Parameters," in *Omni*, July 1979, pp. 29-35.]

17. Irwin K.M. Liu, associate professor of reproduction at the University of California, Davis, School of Veterinary medicine, was searching for a method to prevent infertility in domestic horses when he came upon an alternative solution to the problem of wild horse overpopulation which is leading to overgrazing of public range lands. Currently, the government either slaughters the horses or lets people adopt them. Liu was aware that "a naturally occurring antibody found in some women blocks penetration of an egg by sperm." He reasoned that the same phenomenon might well occur in horses. He developed a vaccine which stimulates the antibody in horses. "The horses were turned loose with a fertile stallion, and when they were recaptured almost a year later, nine out of the ten mares had not conceived. The tenth was in the very early stage of pregnancy, Liu said, indicating the antibody had worn off." ("Davis professor invents, test birth-control vaccine for horses," by Kathryn Eaker Perkins, *The Sacramento Bee*, Aug. 1, 1984, B1.)

18. "A study of 900,000 Americans confirmed that the 40% to 50% of adults who have quit smoking sharply cut their risk of dying of lung cancer." Researchers at the University of Michigan analyzed health and lifestyle data of the group over a period of six years. "About half of [the 900,000] had never smoked tobacco, another quarter had quit smoking and the remaining fourth continued to smoke....The analysis showed that among each 100,000 persons in the population, fewer than 50 of those who had never smoked died of lung cancer by the age of 75. Among those who continued to smoke, the death rate from lung cancer by age 75 was about 1,250 per 100,000 men and 550 per 100,000 women....Among the men who quit smoking in their 30's, the death rate from lung cancer by age 75 was about 100 per 100,000 persons in the population, or only 7% of that of men who continued to smoke. Among women who quit in their 30's, the lung cancer death rate by age 75 was about 50 per 100,000, or about 10% that of smokers....If the smoker waited until his or her early 60's to quit smoking, the chances of dying of lung cancer by age 75 were about half those of smokers. Specifically, of every 100,000 persons in the population, about 550 men and 250 women who waited until their early 60's to quit smoking died of lung cancer by age 75....But, ...even those who quit in their 30's have a risk approximately twice that of those who have never smoked, a difference that does not decrease with age." ("When a Smoker Quits May Determine Chances of Dying From Lung Cancer," by Jerry E. Bishop, *The Wall Street Journal*, March 17, 1993, B7.)

19. A study by the Drug Safety Research Unit in Southampton, England, studied 448 women between the ages of 16 and 44 who had suffered heart attacks. They matched them by age and region with 1,728 women who had not had heart attacks. 13 percent of those who had heart attacks used birth control pills. 15 percent of those who did not have heart attacks used birth control pills. 80 percent of those who had heart attacks smoked, while only 30 percent of those who did not have heart attacks smoked. The study concluded that "there is no increased risk [of heart attack] associated with taking the oral contraceptive." The researchers also found that "among those who smoked, taking the pill did not further increase the chance of heart attack." ("Study: Birth control pills not linked to heart attacks," by Emma Ross, Associated Press, *Sacramento Bee*, June 11, 1999.)

20. "In a study of more than 1,700 North Carolina adults age 65 or older, Duke University researchers found that those who attend religious services at least once a week have healthier immune systems than those who don't." The study measured blood samples for levels of interleukin 6 (IL6) and other substances that regulate immune and inflammatory responses. (Those with AIDS, Alzheimer's, osteoporosis, and diabetes have high levels of IL6, which is also associated with stress and depression.) Those who attended religious services once a week were about half as likely as those who didn't to have elevated levels of IL6.

Dr. Harold Koenig, director of Duke's Center for the Study of Religion/Spirituality and Health, was the lead author of the study. Koenig is a psychiatrist and family doctor. The study was funded by the National Institute on Aging and was published in the *International Journal of Psychiatry in Medicine*. Said Dr. Koenig: "Maybe believing in [a] higher power...could be a strong key to people's health. We can actually show that these immune systems are functioning better." He thinks that people who go to church are "probably able to handle stress better. They are significantly less likely to be depressed." He also said, "We think that both the social aspects and the faith aspects of having a belief system help them cope." Dr. Koenig cautioned that the results might show a regional influence, since participants are from the Bible Belt South, "where religion is ingrained in the social fabric."

Chaplain David Carl claimed that the study supports the notion that "our beliefs show up, right now, in our biology." ("Attending church boosts immune system, study says," by Karen Garloch, Knight-Ridder Newspapers, *Sacramento Bee*, October 24, 1997.)

Holly Nelson, in a letter to the editor, asked, "Was it ever considered that these people [attending church] already have healthier immune systems, or lead healthier lives, than those who cannot attend?" She also questioned whether the important thing was getting up and moving about, rather than faith or belief. "This incomplete study said almost nothing of importance," she wrote.

Exercise 8-4

Find several articles from newspapers or magazines that are based on causal reasoning. Evaluate the reasoning in the articles. Before you begin your evaluation, you might find it useful to state the main conclusion(s) of the article and the main premises. Evaluate the size of samples and the methods of selecting samples.

Further Reading - Chapter Eight

Alcock, James E. et al. (2003). Eds. *Psi Wars – Getting to Grips with the Paranormal*. Imprint Academic.

Brignell, John (2000). *Sorry, Wrong Number! The abuse of measurement*. Brignell Associates.

Carroll, Robert T. (2003). *The Skeptic's Dictionary: A Collection of Strange Beliefs, Amusing Deceptions, and Dangerous Delusions*. Wiley & Sons.

Hyman, Ray (1989). *The Elusive Quarry – A Scientific Appraisal of Psychical Research*. Prometheus Books.

Giere, Ronald (2004). *Understanding Scientific Reasoning*. 5th ed. Wadsworth.

Gilovich, Thomas (1993). *How We Know What Isn't So*: The Fallibility of Human Reason in Everyday Life. The Free Press.

Radin, Dean (1997). *The Conscious Universe – The Scientific Truth of Psychic Phenomena*. HarperSanFrancisco.

Rosenthal, Robert (1998). "Covert Communication in Classrooms, Clinics, and Courtrooms," *Eye on Psi Chi*. Vol. 3, No. 1, pp. 18-22.

Shopland, D.R., Eyre and Pechacek (1991). "Smoking-attributable mortality in 1991. Is lung cancer now the leading cause of death among smokers in the United States?" *Journal of the National Cancer Institute*. 83(16):1142-1148.

Notes – Chapter Eight

---

[1] "Cancer scare: How Sand on a Beach Came to Be Defined As a Human Carcinogen," by David Stipp, *Wall Street Journal*, March 22, 1993, p. A4.

[2] Establishing whether a correlation is likely due to chance depends, in part, on the size of the sample, the method of selecting the sample, and the statistical formula one uses. This text is intended as an introduction to the material presented and is purposely non-technical. However, I suggest you do further reading on the matter of statistically significant correlations in either a statistics text book or in an excellent book on critical thinking in the sciences: *Understanding Scientific Reasoning*, 5th ed., Ronald N. Giere (Wadsworth, 2004).

[3] Martin, Bruce. "Coincidences: Remarkable or Random?" in *Skeptical Inquirer*, September/October 1998.

[4] Gawande, Atul. "The Cancer-Cluster Myth," *The New Yorker*, February 8, 1999, pp. 34-37.

[5] *ibid.*

[6] Gilovich, T., R. Vallone, and A. Tversky, "The hot hand in basketball: On the misperception of random sequences," *Cognitive Psychology*, 17, 295-314.

[7] Gawande, loc. cit.

[8] Tversky, A. and D. Hahneman (1971). "Belief in the law of small numbers," *Psychological Bulletin*, 76, 105-110.

[9] To assume that the whole must be exactly like the parts is to commit the *fallacy of composition*. For example, just because a part of a person's brain is not functional, it does not follow that the person's brain itself is not functional. Just because the individual players on a basketball team are exceptional does not mean that the team is exceptional. Likewise, just because a team is exceptionally good does not mean that each of the players is exceptionally good.

[10] An analysis of this study is given in the Congressional Office of Technology Assessment report *Cancer Testing*, and is discussed in Giere, op. cit., pp. 274-284.

[11] "Berkeley study doubts value of cancer tests in mice," Deborah Blum, *The Sacramento Bee*, August 31, 1990.

[12] *ibid.*

[13] "Animal Tests as Risk Clues: The Best Data May Fall Short," Joel Brinkely, *The New York Times*, March 23, 1993,

[14] *ibid.*

[15] *ibid.*

[16] As a farfetched possibility, we might imagine that just the 35 who got ill also drank from a public water fountain which was contaminated. Or, maybe 20 of them were suffering from food poisoning, 10 from intestinal flu, and 5 from psychosomatic symptoms--in which case our assumption that there was a single cause would be in error. The point is that there are numerous possibilities we are likely to overlook.

[17] "Cancer scare: How Sand on a Beach Came to Be Defined As a Human Carcinogen," by David Stipp, *Wall Street Journal*, March 22, 1993, p. A4.

Chapter Nine - Science and Pseudoscience

*"We are living at a time of rising interest, on the part of an uninformed public,
in wild beliefs which the entire science community considers close to zero in credibility."*
--Martin Gardner

*"The most common of all follies is to believe passionately
in the palpably not true. It is the chief occupation of mankind."*
--H. L. Mencken

Many of our students emerge after years of compulsory education with no grasp of the nature of science. Polls done for the National Science Foundation have repeatedly found that many Americans are scientifically illiterate. Millions of Americans believe that the sun goes around the earth, that it takes one day for the earth to orbit the sun, that an electron is larger than an atom, and that sound travels faster than light. Most Americans could not tell you what a molecule is.

The great majority of American high school graduates have not had a day's instruction in algebra, physics, or chemistry. In one survey, 75 percent said they believe antibiotics are effective against viruses. In another, one in six could not identify DNA. One study even found that about 19 percent of high school biology teachers erroneously believe that dinosaurs and humans lived at the same time. Dr. Raymond Eve, director of the study, was most surprised by the finding that 95 percent of the teachers surveyed seemed to misunderstand what science is all about. Given the statement, "Scientists seek facts, but sometimes the best they can do is theories," only 5 percent correctly answered "definitely false."

Only about one-fourth of the biology teachers responding to Eve's study have degrees in biology. A study on physics instruction found the same statistic for high school physics teachers: only a fourth hold degrees in physics. According to a promotional piece for the chemistry department at Jarvis Christian College "a high percentage of our nation's students are learning chemistry from teachers who have no degree in chemistry."

Some blame our scientific illiteracy on our education system. Others blame the media. Some blame politicians who promote science only when it accords with their own religious views. Whatever the reason may be, many scientists and defenders of science are convinced that America is becoming less and less rational. We may be living in an age of science, but it is also very much an age of wild beliefs.

1. Wild beliefs in the age of science

Despite the fact that scientists almost universally agree that astrology has no scientific credibility, belief in astrology increased from 25% to 28% over the last decade of the 20th century, according to a Gallup poll. According to the same poll, belief that some people can get messages from the dead has increased from 18% to 26%. This number has probably increased recently due to the popularity of self-proclaimed psychics like James Van Praagh. He claims he has a special gift that enables him to receive messages from anyone who has died. He appears frequently on entertainment talk shows such as *Larry King Live*, where he says he hears voices of spirits who want him to pass on a message to his host or to members of the audience. He even claims to get messages from the dead pets and from the spirits of those who telephone the show. He passes on information such as, "It's nice over here" and "I forgive you." Or he throws out cryptic

> The National Opinion Research Council reports that 42 percent of American adults believe they have been in contact with someone who has died (up from 27 percent a decade earlier). And two-thirds of American adults say they have experienced extrasensory perception (ESP). Twenty-three percent believe in reincarnation.
> -- John Dart, "The 'New Age' Christians : Parapsychology comes out of the closet in theological circles," San Francisco Chronicle, March 8, 1987.

190

messages such as "There is a Miss Piggy involved here" or "Your dog is upset that you gave away his favorite food bowl." There is a two-year wait for those who want a private reading from Mr. Van Praagh. Similar stories can be told about others who have found a large market for the bereaved, such as John Edward, Silvia Browne, George Anderson, and a host of others. The list of pet psychics is also growing, led by Sonya Fitzpatrick, who always asks the pet owner for the pet's name before proceeding to tell the owner that the pet wants him or her to know this or that.

Millions of people believe psychics have a special gift that brings them into direct contact with the spirits of the dead, even dead animals. This belief not only supports their hope that there is life after death, it gives them hope that they might be able to make contact with a loved one who has died, even a beloved spaniel. These hopes are so strong in some people that they lead to irrational behavior. Take this example from Sylvia Browne and Larry King on the Larry King Live show (December 5, 2003):

KING: Shizuoka, Japan. Hello.

CALLER: Oh, hi.

KING: Hi.

CALLER: I'd like to ask about my mother. We had some unresolved issues.

BROWNE: Yes. But I don't know if you could have had any resolved issues with your mother because she was so very difficult to deal with. And I'm not saying that to be cruel. So, you see, the thing that you got to realize is when somebody goes to the other side, everything is OK.

CALLER: But she's -- you can definitely see her on the other side?

BROWNE: Yes. Little. She's little.

CALLER: Yes, well, the last time I spoke to her, she was alive.

BROWNE: Yes, but see, I don't -- she's not alive now.

CALLER: She's dead.

BROWNE: Yes.

CALLER: You're telling me my mother has died?

BROWNE: Yes.

CALLER: You're sure about this?

BROWNE: I'm positive.

CALLER: OK. Well, I'll have to get back to you after I've called her.

BROWNE: All right.

CALLER: Thank you.

KING: OK, now, what -- she doesn't know, hasn't heard from her mother.

BROWNE: No.

KING: And she's trying to reach her, hasn't heard from her.

BROWNE: That's right.

KING: You saw her as gone.

BROWNE: That's right.

KING: OK. And you were truthful enough to say that.

Of course, the caller was never heard from again. Neither King nor Browne will give it another thought. They are not going to follow up and see if the mother is dead or not. Why? They don't have to. The woman's dead. Sylvia "saw her as gone." That's all you need to know. Next caller, please. It doesn't matter that Browne just says whatever pops into her head, no matter how silly or stereotypical. She's little! She's Japanese so she must be little. Even in death the Japanese are little. Everybody else who called wanted to contact the dead, so why would Sylvia assume this lady from Japan was any different? A mother and daughter have unresolved issues and the daughter wants to make contact. What would Browne do if she was confronted with the fact that the mother is alive. She said she was positive the mother had died. She could always say: I never claimed to be infallible. Sometimes I get it wrong. Let's move on. This is a win-win situation for the psychic. If the client can make sense out of what you say, you're right. If the client can't make sense out what you say, you're also right. And if the client can make sense out of what you say and find you in error, you're still right because you never said you were always right. Therefore, whether you're right or wrong, you're right!

Belief in psychic phenomena is widespread, though the scientific evidence for such beliefs is scant. The Gallup poll mentioned above found that belief in ghosts has increased in recent years from 25% to 38%. Belief in ESP has remained steady at 50%. Yet, more than one hundred and fifty years of research has produced little of significance in parapsychology, the science that studies ESP and psychokinesis. As mentalist and author Milbourne Christopher put it: "Many brilliant men have investigated the paranormal but they have yet to find a single person who can, without trickery, send or receive even a three-letter word under test conditions" (Christopher 1970: 37). We still await the first person to move even a pencil across a table without blowing it or pulling it by a thin thread. And we implore all the many self-promoting psychic detectives and clairaudients to use their powers to please tell us where a terrorist will strike next.

Bizarre psychotherapies, with no empirical studies to support their validity, sprout up like mushrooms in the wild. In 2001, two psychotherapists went on trial for smothering a 10-year-old girl to death during "rebirthing therapy." The 70-minute therapy-killing was videotaped. Jurors wept as they watched. The prosecutor called it "torture" not therapy. The therapists were unlicensed, but so is every other psychotherapist in Colorado. They were also unregistered, which is illegal in Colorado. The victim, Candace Newmaker, was found not breathing and with no pulse when she was unwrapped after the procedure. Prosecutors say she asphyxiated on her own vomit. The two therapists were found guilty of "reckless child abuse resulting in death," which carries a mandatory minimum prison sentence of 16 years in Colorado. Rebirthing therapy is now illegal in that state. But many other unorthodox and unproven therapies are not illegal in Colorado or anywhere else.

So-called "alternative" medicine has been joined by "alternative" history and "alternative" science. In each case, "alternative" seems to mean "we don't have to follow traditional rules of evidence and argumentation. We can substitute imagination and desire for proof. We have satisfied customers; that's all that matters." Alternative medicine is often based upon metaphysical beliefs and is frequently anti-scientific. Because truly alternative medical practices would be ones that are known to be equally or nearly equally effective, most alternative medical practices are not truly alternative.

Some of our most popular television programs feature alien visitations, spirits, angels, psychics, healing prayer, and government conspiracies to cover up each of the above. Daily newspapers feature stories on astrology, graphology, or personology, a revitalized version of physiognomy, a 16th century pseudoscience. One is more likely to see a biography of Michel Nostradamus, a 16th century French astrologer, or Edgar Cayce (d. 1945), an American psychic who predicted California would sink into the ocean and who recommended "bedbug juice" as a remedy for dropsy, than one is to see a biography of Albert Einstein, Sir Isaac Newton, or Carl Sagan.

It is not just avid readers of *The National Enquirer* or *The Star* who are likely to be attracted to tales of alien abductions or of children who can read newspapers by sitting on them. Numerous educated and intelligent people believe and advocate equally incredible claims.

Why is it that occult, paranormal, and pseudoscientific claims are so popular in this Age of Science?

On the other hand, are the critics of *wild beliefs* simply close-minded skeptics who will not give an idea a chance if it does not fit with their preconceived notions of a tidy, scientifically explicable universe? Are the disagreements over alien abductions, channeling, ESP, biorhythms, psychics, apparitions, healing prayer and the like, nothing more than what we would expect when reasonable people tackle complex issues? Are the skeptics too skeptical?

We should note that skeptics of pseudoscience are not all atheists who believe that only scientific claims are meaningful. Many skeptics are religious. Many recognize the *limits* of science and do not restrict themselves to belief in only empirical, scientific matters. On the other hand, believers in pseudoscientific, occult, or paranormal claims are not all ignorant and uneducated. They are not all gullible to the point of intellectual disablement, resenting anyone smarter than they are. Many believers are highly educated, intelligent people, with no axes to grind. Because of the varied natures of skeptics and believers, it is not possible to determine whether an idea is a legitimate scientific idea or a crackpot idea simply by determining *who* holds the idea. Thus, we will not be able to identify *pseudoscience* solely by a set of characteristics that apply to all believers. Nor can we identify something as *science* by a set of characteristics that apply to all scientists. There are distinguishing features of scientists and pseudoscientists, but these features are to be found in their *methods of investigation*, in their *treatment of evidence*, and, to some extent, in the areas they believe are open to scientific discovery. We will consider each of these features, but first let me give the reader some more examples of what Gardner means by *wild beliefs*.

One current *wild belief* is the belief in **channeling**, a process whereby an individual (the "channeler") claims to be invaded by a spirit entity. The spirit allegedly speaks through the channeler. Actress Shirley MacLaine and the ABC television network gave credibility to this modern version of ghosts speaking through a medium.[1] Channeling has become big business. In 1987 in the San Francisco Bay area, $15 would get you in to hear "Michael", an entity said to have had 1,050 beings over time, give personal advice to enthusiastic young professionals. After the show, customers were offered *Acu-Kinetic Repatterning*. For $520 anyone could become a "certified practitioner," and for $150 anyone could purchase the program "Change Your Life Through Colors." The latter was usually $275, but this was a special introductory offer.[2] According to the Gallup poll mentioned earlier, about 15% of adult Americans believe in channeling.

In Tacoma, Washington, people spend thousands of dollars to attend sessions by J.Z. Knight. She claims to channel Ramtha, a 35,000 year-old warrior spirit who once lived in the mythical land of Atlantis. Another *wild belief* is the belief in **alien abductions**. The popularity of books such as Whitley Strieber's *Communion: A True Story* or movies such as *Fire in the Sky* indicates the attractiveness of the idea of humans being abducted by aliens. Yet, the idea has little or no scientific backing. There are many such ideas that are very popular today, even among educated and intelligent people. John E. Mack, a professor of psychiatry at the Cambridge Hospital, Harvard Medical School, has published an account of his patients who claim to have been abductees.[3] After four years of treating some twenty people, Mack says "it became clear to me that I was dealing with a phenomenon that could not be explained psychiatrically, yet was simply not possible within the framework of the Western scientific worldview." In other words, 'I don't think my patients are crazy and there is no way they could be telling the truth unless we abandon all the laws of nature and rules of scientific evaluation of evidence we've developed these past two millennia. Therefore, they are probably telling the truth.' This is not very good logic, but it may make Mack rich and famous. (It was reported that he received a $200,000 advance for his first book about the abductions.) He has recently published another book, *Passport to the Cosmos: What the Alien*

Visitations Are Teaching Us (Crown Publishing, 1999), to prepare us for the new millennium.

Another *wild belief* is the belief in **dianetics**, the so-called "modern science of mental health" created by L. Ron Hubbard. *Dianetics* is a text that has zero credibility in the scientific world, yet it has sold millions of copies and is the foundation of a very lucrative organization, Scientology. Another popular *wild belief* is the belief in **biorhythms**. Like astrology, biorhythm theory holds that your fate is determined by your time of birth. Unlike astrology, however, biorhythm theory is based on alleged natural cycles, rather than on the positions of celestial phenomena at the time of birth. The numbers 23, 28, and 33 are all you need to know. Where the moon, sun, stars, planets, and the like were at the time of your birth are unimportant. What little scientific study there has been of biorhythms has indicated that the theory is false, yet its adherents remain undaunted.

Finally, there is the popularity of belief in **apparitions**, such as the case of Audrey Santo. A steady stream of letters and visitors pour into the Santo home in Worcester, Massachusetts, where Linda Santo has set up a kind of shrine to her daughter. Many people believe that Audrey has the power of healing the sick. Since 1987, Audrey has been in a coma-like state known as akinetic mutism because of a swimming accident. She was three years old when she nearly drowned. Her mother took her comatose daughter to Medjugorje in the former Yugoslavia, where pilgrims have been going since some young children in the village claimed that the Virgin Mary had appeared to them. (The local bishop investigated the matter and declared that the story was a fraud, but that did not deter the pilgrims.) According to Mrs. Santo, the Virgin Mary appeared to Audrey and asked her if she would agree to become a "victim soul," someone who takes on the sufferings and ailments of other people. According to her mother, the four-year-old, comatose Audrey agreed. How even a healthy child at age four could understand the concept of a 'victim soul' is a mystery. What is not a mystery is that while on the pilgrimage Audrey suffered cardiac arrest and had to be evacuated to the U.S. so she could receive proper medical care. Her mother did not see the cardiac arrest as Audrey's first experience as a victim soul, however. Instead, she blamed it on being near an abortion clinic. A documentary has been made about Audrey, and she has been featured on the ABC news magazine program *20/20* several times. (For more on wild beliefs, see my *Skeptic's Dictionary* published by John Wiley & Sons (2003) or my website at **www.skepdic.com**).

Of course, not all *wild beliefs* are equally wild. Furthermore, not all *wild beliefs* claim to be supported by empirical evidence. When we refer to **pseudoscientific** beliefs, we are not referring to every wild belief imaginable. We are referring only to those that falsely claim to have scientific or empirical validity. Thus, *we do not classify metaphysical or religious beliefs as pseudoscientific, no matter how wild those beliefs may be, as long as they are not claimed to be scientific beliefs.* If a person's religion requires her to believe that the souls of women are inferior to the souls of men, we do not call that belief *pseudoscientific* unless the believer claims it is a scientific fact. If he believes it on *faith* in some text he holds sacred, it is a **metaphysical** belief, not a pseudoscientific belief. In any case, it is not really the *beliefs* we should be interested in so much as *the methods of arriving at and supporting those beliefs.* After all, there are some *wild beliefs* that are generally accepted by the scientific community as having very strong probability, such as *the theory of evolution of species* and *the Big Bang Theory.* We should not disconnect beliefs from how they were acquired and how they are supported. Scientific methods of testing and evaluating claims are an integral part of scientific claims. When those methods are misunderstood, misapplied, or ignored, the beliefs based on them lose whatever scientific integrity they might otherwise have had. The result is not science but **borderline science, junk science,** or **pseudoscience**. I prefer the term **pseudoscience**, and will use it in this chapter to describe *those endeavors to defend a claim or theory as scientific when either* (1) *the methods used to defend the belief are misapplied or misunderstood scientific methods;* (2) *the belief itself is not capable of being scientifically tested; or (3) the belief is capable of being scientifically tested and has been falsified, but its adherents refuse to give up the belief.*

Before examining some *wild beliefs*, we will first outline what is required of a scientifically credible claim. This should help us understand some important features of scientific reasoning. Then, we will go on to examine some examples of pseudoscience.

194

2. Scientific facts and theories

Science presupposes a regular order to nature and assumes there are underlying principles according to which natural phenomena work. It assumes that these principles or laws are relatively constant. Science systematically gathers facts about the empirical world and proposes theories to explain those facts. But this process is more complex than, say, gathering flowers in a basket and then going home to categorize them.

A scientific theory is a unified set of principles, knowledge, and methods for explaining the behavior of some specified range of empirical phenomena. Non-scientists commonly use the term 'theory' to refer to a speculation or guess based on limited information or knowledge. However, when we refer to a scientific theory, we are not referring to a speculation or guess, but to *a systematic explanation of some range of empirical phenomena*. Scientific theories attempt to understand the world of observation and sense experience. They attempt to explain how the natural world works. A scientific theory must have *some logical consequences* we can test against Nature by making predictions based on the theory. The exact nature of the relationship of a scientific theory making predictions and being tested is something about which philosophers widely disagree, however (Kourany 1997).

It is true that some scientific theories, when they are first developed and proposed, are often little more than guesses based on limited information. On the other hand, when mature and well developed, scientific theories systematically organize knowledge and allow us to explain and predict wide ranges of empirical events. In either case, however, one characteristic must be present for the theory to be *scientific*. The distinguishing feature of scientific theories is that they are "capable of being tested by experience" (Popper 1959: 40). To be able to test a theory by experience usually means to be able to predict certain observable or measurable consequences from the theory. For example, from a theory about how physical bodies move in relation to one another, one predicts that a pendulum ought to follow a certain pattern of behavior. One then sets up a pendulum and tests the hypothesis that pendulums behave in the way predicted by the theory. If they do, then the theory is **confirmed**. If pendulums do not behave in the way predicted by the theory, then the theory is **falsified**. This assumes that your predicted behavior for the pendulum was correctly deduced from your theory and that your experiment was conducted properly.

The fact that a theory passed an empirical test does not *prove* the theory, however. The greater the number of severe tests a theory has passed, the greater its **degree of confirmation** and the more reasonable it is to accept it. However, to *confirm* is not the same as to prove logically or mathematically. No scientific theory can be proved with absolute certainty.

The more tests that can be made of the theory, the greater its empirical content (Popper 1959: 112, 267). A theory from which very few empirical predictions can be made will be difficult to test and generally will not be very useful. A useful theory is **rich**, i.e., many empirical predictions can be generated from it, each one serving as another test of the theory. Useful scientific theories lead to new lines of investigation and new models of understanding phenomena that heretofore have seemed unrelated (Kitcher 1983). For example, Darwin's theory of natural selection enormously increased our understanding of biology when it was joined with the new field of genetics (Larson 2004).

However, even if a theory is very rich and even if it passes many severe tests, it is always possible that it will fail the next test. It is always possible that a new hypothesis will be derived from the theory. An experiment may be set up to test the new hypothesis and it may turn out that what *should* follow from the theory does not occur.

Evolution "is a scientific theory only, and it has in recent years been challenged in the world of science and is not yet believed in the scientific community to be as infallible as it was once believed." --Ronald Reagan
There are at least three errors in this quote from Mr. Reagan: 1. Evolution is a fact *and* a theory (such as Darwin's theory of natural selection); 2. Natural selection has been challenged but the scientific community has rejected the challenges; and 3. The scientific community has never thought of natural selection or any other theory as infallible.

Karl Popper calls this characteristic of scientific theories "falsifiability." A necessary consequence of scientific claims being falsifiable is that they are also **fallible**. For example, Einstein's special theory of relativity is accepted as "correct" in the sense that "its necessary inclusion in calculations leads to excellent agreement with experiments" (Friedlander 1972: 41). This does not mean the theory is infallibly certain.

Scientific facts, like scientific theories, are not *infallible certainties*, either. Noted paleoanthropologist and science writer Stephen Jay Gould reminds us that in science 'fact' can only mean "confirmed to such a degree that it would be perverse to withhold provisional assent" (Gould 1983: 254). However, facts and theories are different things, notes Gould, "not rungs in a hierarchy of increasing certainty. Facts are the world's data. Theories are structures of ideas that explain and interpret facts." In Popper's words, "Theories are nets cast to catch what we call 'the world': to rationalize, to explain, and to master it. We endeavor to make the mesh ever finer and finer."

For many people, 'theory' means *uncertain*. To the uninformed public, facts contrast with theories. However, scientific theories vary in degree of certainty from the highly improbable to the highly probable. That is, there are varying degrees of evidence and support for different theories. Some are more reasonable to accept than others. But even the most reasonable scientific theory is not absolutely certain. On the other hand, so-called 'facts' are not absolutely certain, either. Facts involve not only easily testable perceptual elements; they also involve interpretation.

One sign that an idea is not scientific is the claim that the idea is infallibly certain and irrefutable. Claims of infallibility and the demand for absolute certainty characterize not science but pseudoscience. The idea of **creationism** is a good example of a non-scientific theory because its adherents claim it is absolutely certain and cannot be falsified. Creationism is the doctrine that God created the universe and all species that have ever existed one by one. Although Karl Popper's falsifiability notion has been much attacked by philosophers of science (Kitcher 1983), it seems undeniable that there is something profoundly different about such theories as creationism and natural selection. It also seems undeniable that one profound difference is that the metaphysical theory is consistent with every conceivable empirical state of affairs, while the scientific one is not (Carroll 2003: 88). "I can envision observations and experiments that would disprove any evolutionary theory I know," writes Gould, "but I cannot imagine what potential data could lead creationists to abandon their beliefs. Unbeatable systems are dogma, not science." Some creationists consider the theory of creation described in *Genesis* to be a *scientific* account, and the Big Bang theory and the theory of evolution to be false.[4] In this debate, creationists have asserted such things as *evolution is not a fact, it is just a theory*. Some scientists, such as Carl Sagan, on the other hand, have asserted that *evolution is a fact, not a theory*. Stephen Jay Gould claims that evolution is *both* a fact *and* a theory. *That* evolution has occurred is a fact; the mechanism by which it occurred is theoretical. Darwin, notes Gould, "continually emphasized the difference between his two great accomplishments: establishing the fact of evolution, and proposing a theory—*natural selection*—to explain the mechanism of evolution." Darwin's proposed theory initiated a very fruitful debate. Creationists, mistaking the *uncertain* in science for the *unscientific*, see the debate among evolutionists as a sign of weakness. Scientists, on the other hand, see uncertainty as simply an inevitable element of scientific knowledge. They regard debates on fundamental theoretical issues as healthy and stimulating. Science, says Gould, is "most fun when it plays with interesting ideas, examines their implications, and recognizes that old information may be explained in surprisingly new ways." Thus, through all the debate over evolutionary mechanisms no biologist has been led to doubt that evolution has occurred. "We are debating how it happened," says Gould (1983: 256). What makes so-called "scientific creationism" a pseudoscience is that it attempts to pass itself off as science although it shares very little in common with scientific theorizing. Creationism will remain forever unchanged as a theory. It will engender no debate among scientists about fundamental mechanisms of the universe. It generates no empirical predictions that could be used to test the theory. It is considered irrefutable by its advocates, who will not consider any evidence that might falsify their beliefs.

The history of science, however, clearly shows that *scientific* theories do not remain forever unchanged. The history of science is not the history of one absolute truth being built upon other absolute truths. Rather, it is, among other things, the history of theorizing, testing, arguing, refining, rejecting, replacing, more theorizing, more testing, and so on. It is the history of theories working well for a while, anomalies occurring at times (i.e., new facts being discovered that do not fit with established theories), new facts being discovered that invigorate old theories (like genetics did for natural selection), and new theories being proposed and eventually replacing the old ones partially or completely.

Of course, it is possible for scientists to act unscientifically, to be dogmatic and dishonest. However, the fact that one finds an occasional oddball or charlatan in the history of science (or a person of integrity and genius among pseudoscientists) does not imply that there really is no difference between science and pseudoscience. Because of the public and empirical nature of scientific debate, the charlatans will be found out, errors will be corrected and the honest pursuit of the truth is likely to prevail in the end.

We should remember that science, as Jacob Bronowski put it, "is a very human form of knowledge....Every judgment in science stands on the edge of error.... Science is a tribute to what we can know although we are fallible" (Bronowski 1973: 374). "One aim of the physical sciences," he said, "has been to give an exact picture of the material world. One achievement of physics in the twentieth century has been to prove that aim is unattainable" (Bronowski 1973: 353).

Bronowski made his point about the *human* quality of scientific knowledge in a most poignant manner. For the televised version of his *Ascent of Man*, he went to the concentration camp and crematorium at Auschwitz. Millions of Jews, homosexuals and other 'undesirables' were murdered and cremated there during World War II. Some of those executed were Bronowski's relatives. Standing in a pond where the ashes were dumped, and grabbing a handful of muck, he said

> It is said that science will dehumanize people and turn them into numbers. That is false, tragically false. Look for yourself. This is the concentration camp and crematorium at Auschwitz. This is where people were turned into numbers. into this pond were flushed the ashes of some four million people. And that was not done by gas. It was done by ignorance. When people believe that they have absolute knowledge, with no test in reality, this is how they behave. This is what men do when they aspire to the knowledge of gods (374).

Scientific knowledge is *human* knowledge and scientists are human beings. They are not gods, and science is not infallible. Yet, the general public often thinks of scientific claims as *absolutely certain* truths. They think that if something is not certain, it is not scientific and if it is not scientific, then any other non-scientific view is its equal. This misconception seems to be, at least in part, behind the general lack of understanding about the nature of scientific theories.

Another common misconception is that since scientific theories are based on human perception, they are necessarily relative and therefore do not really tell us anything about the real world. Science, according to certain "postmodernists" cannot claim to give us a true picture of what the empirical world is really like; it can only tell us how it appears to scientists. There is no such thing as scientific truth. All scientific theories are mere fictions. However, just because there is no one, true, final, godlike way to view reality, does not mean that every viewpoint is as good as every other. Just because science can only give us a *human* perspective, does not mean that there is no such thing as scientific truth. When the first atomic bomb went off as some scientists had predicted it would, another bit of truth about the empirical world was revealed. Bit by bit we are discovering what is true and what is false by empirically testing scientific theories. To claim that those theories that make it possible to explore space are "just relative" and "represent just one perspective" of reality is to profoundly misunderstand the nature of science and scientific knowledge.

3. Non-scientific or conceptual theories

There is wide disagreement as to what can be a subject for scientific theorizing. The behavior of gasses or particles can be a subject for science, but can *human behavior* be a subject for science? There is much disagreement here among philosophers and practitioners of the social sciences such as psychology, sociology, history, and related fields. Is human behavior reducible to a set of principles or laws, just as the behavior of particles or waves is? Is human behavior reducible to observable phenomena or to the observable effects of lawful and regular phenomena? If so, human behavior can be the subject of scientific theorizing. If not, then no matter how empirical the study of human behavior is, it cannot be scientific. If human will, desire, and motivation cannot be reduced to principles of regularity, then human behavior is essentially different from the behavior of anything else in nature and cannot be the subject of scientific theorizing. But even if there can be no science of human behavior, there can still be explanations and theories of human behavior, whether they are psychological, sociological, or historical. Those explanations can be very heavily empirical, but because such theories are not falsifiable or testable in any way, they are non-scientific.

Can spiritual phenomena be a subject for scientific theorizing? Some scientists think so. Several articles claiming to have scientific evidence of the healing effects of intercessory prayer have been published over the past few years in reputable medical journals. A scientist at the University of Arizona has written a book called *The Afterlife Experiments: Breakthrough Scientific Evidence of Life After Death* (Atria Books 2002). Yet, most scientists believe that science is limited to explanations of the *natural* world and that *supernatural* matters should be left to the philosophers and theologians.

On the other hand, some non-scientific theories attempt to explain *non-empirical* concepts or values. Others do not try to explain anything; they are *prescriptive* in nature. A prescriptive theory, such as a theory of justice, prescribes what *ought to be* rather than describes what is. Aesthetic theories, ethical theories, literary theories and metaphysical theories are non-scientific. As theories, they are not inferior to scientific ones, but they are different and must be evaluated differently. As we shall see, each type of theory has its proper place in the human quest for knowledge and understanding of the world we live in.

Non-scientific theories—sometimes called **conceptual theories**—are characterized, in part, by not being falsifiable or empirically testable. Generally speaking, a non-scientific theory is tested by its *utility*, its *logical coherence* (i.e., the compatibility of the concepts which make up the theory), and *its consistency with what we know about the world and with our beliefs.* Thus, while it is possible to point out that certain empirical facts can be predicted from some non-scientific theories, such predictions are not tests of the theory. Non-scientific theories, if they are coherent, are *consistent with every imaginable state of affairs in the universe.* It is not surprising, then, that many non-scientific theories are put forth dogmatically. They are not offered to be tested, but to be accepted as infallibly true.

The metaphysical theory of **materialism** is an example of a conceptual or non-scientific theory. Materialism is the theory that the nature of all reality is physical. Materialism denies the existence of a non-corporeal God and it denies the existence of immaterial souls. If a materialist believes in God, it is a belief in a physical being: one who occupies space, is tangible, and the like. If a materialist believes in souls, it is a belief in physical beings. There are no spirits, or non-physical realities, according to the materialist. When a materialist tries to explain the *mind,* he or she generally claims that the mind is a function of the brain and that all mental phenomena are reducible to brain states.

How would one go about testing the theory of materialism? Like all conceptual theories, *materialism cannot be empirically tested.* It is not falsifiable. It is logically coherent. That is, there are no logical contradictions in believing that everything real is physical. It is consistent with what we know about the world. That is, everything that can be explained by spirits or non-physical realities can be explained by materialism. Furthermore, a materialist would find the theory to be compatible with science, atheism, biochemical theories of mental illness, neurological explanations for apparent paranormal experiences, and so on. A believer in materialism would no doubt find the theory useful for explaining all kinds of phenomena. Nonetheless, materialism cannot be empirically tested; thus, it cannot be empirically confirmed in any meaningful way. On the other hand, it cannot be refuted, either. There is no way one could prove that materialism is false by appeal to empirical evidence. Furthermore, everything that could be said about the value and validity of materialism applies equally to the theory of **immaterialism** (also called **metaphysical idealism**), the theory that only spiritual or non-physical reality exists, and that the material world is an illusion.

4. Pseudoscientific theories

A **pseudoscientific theory** is not another *kind* of theory, to be evaluated along with scientific and conceptual theories. A pseudoscientific theory is *not* scientific but its proponents claim that it is. The defenders of a pseudoscience will claim that their belief is based on empirical evidence. They may even use scientific methods,

198

but often they misapply or misunderstand those methods. Their theory is either essentially *not falsifiable*, or it is falsifiable and has been falsified but the adherents refuse to accept the evidence against their theory.

Pseudoscientists are fond of pointing out the *consistency* of their theories with the known facts or with predicted consequences, but they do not recognize that such consistency is not proof of anything. For example, "the truth of the hypothesis that plague is due to evil spirits is not established by the correctness of the deduction that you can avoid the disease by keeping out of the reach of the evil spirits" (Beveridge 1957: 118). The fact that a dowser finds water does not prove he is using paranormal powers. The fact that someone performs better than chance in a card-guessing experiment is not proof of ESP, even though parapsychologists claim that it is.

Several characteristics of pseudoscientists and pseudoscience seem to stand out (Radner and Radner 1982: ch. 3):

Characteristics of pseudoscience and pseudoscientists

1. The tendency to propose as scientific theories that cannot be empirically tested in any meaningful way;

2. The dogmatic refusal to give up an idea in the face of overwhelming evidence that the idea is false, and the use of *ad hoc hypotheses* to try to save the theory;

3. Selective use of data: the tendency to count only confirming evidence and to ignore disconfirming evidence; [5]

4. The use of personal anecdotes as evidence;

5. The use of myths or ancient mysteries to support theories, which are then used to explain the myths or mysteries; and

6. Gullibility, especially about paranormal, supernatural, or extraterrestrial claims.

A critical thinker should recognize the difference between scientific and non-scientific theories, and differentiate between the methods appropriate for the investigation and evaluation of each. A critical thinker ought not to claim that a belief or theory is scientific when it is actually non-scientific or pseudoscientific. The following accounts of pseudoscientific theories will provide examples of some of the above traits.

4.1 Applied Kinesiology: refusal to give up an idea in spite of the evidence against

The practitioners of applied kinesiology (mostly chiropractors) believe that muscles reflect the flow of chi ("energy") and that by measuring muscle resistance one can determine the health of bodily organs and nutritional deficiencies (Carroll 2003: 28-29). These are empirical claims and have been tested and shown to be false (Hyman 1999; Kenny et al. 1988). Some chiropractors who believe in this bogus therapy maintain that if presented with glucose (which they consider to be a "bad" sugar) and fructose (which they believe is a "good" sugar), they can detect which is which by muscle resistance. This claim was put to the test by Dr. Wallace Sampson and several others, including psychologist Ray Hyman. A baseline was established, so that the chiropractors could demonstrate in a clear fashion just what they were claiming to be able to do.

The chiropractors had volunteers lie on their backs and raise one arm vertically. They then would put a drop of glucose (in a solution of water) on the volunteer's tongue. The chiropractor then tried to push the volunteer's upraised arm down to a horizontal position while the volunteer tried to resist. In almost every case, the volunteer could not resist. The chiropractors stated the volunteer's body recognized glucose as a "bad" sugar. After the volunteer's mouth was rinsed out and a drop of fructose was placed on the tongue, the volunteer, in just about every test, resisted movement to the horizontal position. The body had recognized fructose as a "good" sugar. (Hyman 1999).

The experiment involved a number of test tubes that had been filled with either fructose or glucose and had been coded by an experimenter who was not present during the testing.

The arm tests were repeated, but this time they were double-blind—neither the volunteer, the chiropractors, nor the onlookers was aware of whether the solution being applied to the volunteer's tongue was glucose or fructose. As in the morning session, sometimes the volunteers were able to resist and other times they were not. We recorded the code number of the solution on each trial. (Hyman 1999).

The experimenter with the code then revealed what was in each tube. The researchers found that "there was no connection between ability to resist and whether the volunteer was given the "good" or the "bad" sugar. Rather than admit that the theory seemed to have been shown to be false, one of the chiropractors said to Hyman: "You see, that is why we never do double-blind testing anymore. It never works!" Hyman thought he was joking, but the man was completely serious. The pseudoscientist would rather abandon one of the best scientific techniques we have than admit his theory is wrong.

4.2 Dianetics: claims to be scientific but is not testable

In 1950, Lafayette Ronald Hubbard published *Dianetics:The Modern Science of Mental Health.*[6] The book is the "Bible" for Scientology, which calls itself both a Church and a religion. Hubbard tells the reader that dianetics "...contains a therapeutic technique with which can be treated all inorganic mental ills and all organic psycho-somatic [sic] ills, with assurance of complete cure...." and that he has discovered and demonstrated "The single source of mental derangement..."(6). However, in a disclaimer to the reader on the frontispiece of the book, we are told that "Scientology and its sub-study, Dianetics, as practiced by the Church...does not wish to accept individuals who desire treatment of physical illness or insanity but refers these to qualified specialists of other organizations who deal in these matters." The disclaimer seems clearly to have been a protective mechanism against lawsuits for practicing medicine without a license; for, the author repeatedly insists that dianetics can cure just about anything that ails you. He also repeatedly insists that *dianetics is a science.* Yet, anyone knowledgeable of scientific texts will be able to tell from the first few pages of *Dianetics* that the text is no scientific work and the author no scientist. Dianetics is a classic example of a pseudoscience.

On page 5 of his book Hubbard tells us that a science of mind must find: "A single source of all insanities, psychoses, neuroses, compulsions, repressions and social derangements." It should provide "invariant scientific evidence as to the basic nature and functional background of the human mind." And, it should find the cause and cure of all psycho-somatic ills." He also notes that it would be unreasonable to expect a science of mind to be able to find a single source of all insanities, since some are caused by "malformed, deleted or pathologically injured brains or nervous systems" and some are caused by doctors. Hubbard is undaunted by the blatant contradiction in saying a science of mind must find a *single* source of all mental problems *and* that such a source can't be found. He claims that this science of mind "would have to rank, in experimental precision, with physics and chemistry." Dianetics, he says, is just such a science. It is "an organized science of thought built on definite axioms: statements of natural laws on the order of those of the physical sciences" (6).

There are broad hints that this so-called science of mind isn't a science at all. The empirical sciences are not built on axioms and they do not claim *a priori* knowledge of the number of causal mechanisms that must exist for any phenomena. A real science puts forth *tentative* proposals to account for observed phenomena. Scientific knowledge of causes, including how many kinds there are, is a matter of discovery not stipulation.

According to Hubbard, the **engram** is the single source of insanity and psychosomatic ills. Engrams are in your *engram bank*, which is in your *reactive mind*. "The reactive mind is that portion of the mind which files and retains physical pain and painful emotion and seeks to direct the organism solely on a stimulus-response basis. It thinks only in identities" (39). The reactive mind, he says, "can give a man arthritis, bursitis, asthma, allergies, sinusitis, coronary trouble, high blood pressure and so on down the whole catalogue of psycho-somatic ills, adding a few more which were never specifically classified as psycho-somatic, such as the common cold" (51). One searches in vain for evidence of these claims. "These are scientific facts," he says. "They compare invariably with observed experience" (52).

He defines an *engram* as "a definite and permanent trace left by a stimulus on the protoplasm of a tissue. It is considered as a unit group of stimuli impinged solely on the cellular being" (60 note). Engrams are only recorded during periods of physical or emotional suffering. During those periods, the analytical mind shuts off and the reactive mind turns on. The analytical mind has all kinds of wonderful features, including being incapable of error. It has standard memory banks, in contrast to the reactive bank. These standard memory banks are recording all possible perceptions and, says Hubbard, they are perfect, recording exactly what is experienced by the senses.

What is the evidence that engrams exist and that they are "hard-wired" into cells during physically or emotionally painful experiences? Hubbard does not say that he has done any laboratory studies, but he says that

> in dianetics, on the level of laboratory observation, we discover much to our astonishment that cells are evidently sentient in some currently inexplicable way. Unless we postulate a human soul entering the sperm and ovum at conception, there are things which no other postulate will embrace than that these cells *are* in some way sentient (71).

Despite Hubbard's claim, this explanation is not "on the level of laboratory observation." Furthermore, the theory of souls entering zygotes has at least two advantages over Hubbard's own theory: it is not deceptive and is clearly metaphysical. Hubbard tries to clothe his metaphysical claims in scientific garb.

> The cells as thought units evidently have an influence, as cells, upon the body as a thought unit and an organism. We do not have to untangle this structural problem to resolve our functional postulates. The cells evidently retain engrams of painful events. After all, they are the things which get injured....

> The reactive mind may very well be the combined cellular intelligence. One need not assume that it is, but it is a handy structural theory in the lack of any real work done in this field of structure. The reactive engram bank may be material stored in the cells themselves. It does not matter whether this is credible or incredible just now....

> The scientific fact, observed and tested, is that the organism, in the presence of physical pain, lets the analyzer get knocked out of circuit so that there is a limited quantity or no quantity at all of personal awareness as a unit organism (71).

Why are these claims "scientific facts," but the claim that souls enter zygotes is not? No reason is given. Hubbard asserts that these are scientific facts based on observations and tests, despite the fact that there has not been any real work done in this field![7]

If you are still wondering how engrams work, here is Hubbard describing "an example of an engram":

> A woman is knocked down by a blow. She is rendered "unconscious." She is kicked and told she is a faker, that she is no good, that she is always changing her mind. A chair is overturned in the process. A faucet is running in the kitchen. A car is passing in the street outside. The engram contains a running record of all these perceptions: sight, sound, tactile, taste, smell, organic sensation, kinetic sense, joint position, thirst record, etc. The engram would consist of the whole statement made to her when she was "unconscious": the voice tones and emotion in the voice, the sound and feel of the original and later blows, the tactile of the floor, the feel and sound of the chair overturning, the organic sensation of the blow, perhaps the taste of blood in her mouth or any other taste present

there, the smell of the person attacking her and the smells in the room, the sound of the passing car's motor and tires, etc. (60).[8]

What does this have to do with insanity or psychosomatic ills?

The engram this woman has received contains a neurotic positive suggestion.... She has been told that she is a faker, that she is no good, and that she is always changing her mind. When the engram is restimulated in one of the great many ways possible [such as hearing a car passing by while the faucet is running and a chair falls over], she has a 'feeling' that she is no good, a faker, and she *will* change her mind (66).

Therefore, not only do we learn how engrams work, we find out that changing one's mind is a symptom of neurosis!

Hubbard tells us that enormous amounts of data have been collected and not a single exception has been found (68). We are to take his word on this, apparently, for all the data he presents are in the form of anecdotes or made-up examples.

Another "scientific fact" is that the most harmful engrams occur in the womb. The womb turns out to be a terrible place. It is "wet, uncomfortable and unprotected."

Mama sneezes, baby gets knocked "unconscious." Mama runs lightly and blithely into a table and baby gets its head stoved in. Mama has constipation and baby, in the anxious effort, gets squashed. Papa becomes passionate and baby has the sensation of being put into a running washing machine. Mama gets hysterical, baby gets an engram. Papa hits Mama, baby gets an engram. Junior bounces on Mama's lap, baby gets an engram. And so it goes (130).

We are told that people can have "more than two hundred" prenatal engrams and that engrams "received as a zygote are potentially the most aberrative, being wholly reactive. Those received as an embryo are intensely aberrative. Those received as a foetus are enough to send people to institutions all by themselves." What is the evidence for this nonsense? "All these things are scientific facts, tested and rechecked and tested again" (133). You must take L. Ron Hubbard's word for it.

Furthermore, to get cured of your illnesses you need a dianetic therapist, called an *auditor*. Who is qualified to be an auditor? "Any person who is intelligent and possessed of average persistency and who is willing to read this book [viz., *Dianetics*] thoroughly should be able to become a dianetic auditor" (173). The auditor must use "dianetic reverie" to cure you. The goal of dianetic therapy is to bring about a "release" or a "clear." The former has had major stress and anxiety removed by dianetics; the latter has neither active nor potential psychosomatic illness nor aberration (170). The 'reverie' used to achieve these wonders is described as an intensified use of some special faculty of the brain that everyone possesses but which "by some strange oversight, Man has never before discovered" (167). Yet, when Hubbard describes this 'reverie' in terms we can all understand, he simply says that it is like a man sitting down and telling another man his troubles (168). Therefore, he says, it "falls utterly outside all existing legislation," unlike psychoanalysis, which "may in some way injure individuals or society" (168-169). It is not clear, however, why auditors could not injure individuals or society.

Dianetics exhibits several classical traits of a pseudoscience. While much lip service is given to providing supportive facts and observations, little in the way of actual evidence is provided. Most, if not all, of the basic explanatory claims of dianetics are untestable. In fact, Hubbard advises auditors: "Don't evaluate data....don't question the validity of data. Keep your reservations to yourself" (300). This does not sound like a scientist giving proper advice to his followers. This sounds like a guru giving orders to his disciples or a con man giving instructions to his gang.

4.3 Parapsychology: tested, refuted, but adherents refuse to give it up

A good scientific theory ought to be testable; it should be capable of making *specific* predictions, not vague ones. If an explanation is sound, we demand that it be self-consistent, and that it be consistent with our experience and observations. Furthermore, we ought to expect certain things to follow from a scientific theory. If our predictions do follow from our theory, then our explanation is **confirmed**. Moreover, if there is enough support for our theory for it to pass the most rigorous tests of experience we can devise, then our theory is said to be worthy of belief. If, however, our predictions are consistently frustrated, if our theory consistently fails to pass experiment after experiment devised to test the theory, then the reasonable thing to do is to admit that the facts refute the theory. In the view of many psychologists and historians of science, *parapsychology* has been refuted beyond a reasonable doubt. A century and a half of experimentation has not provided a single unambiguous piece of evidence in support of ESP (extra sensory perception) or PK (psychokinesis). What has been unambiguously provided by most parapsychologists is fraud and incompetence (Gardner 1957, 1983; Hansel 1989; Hines 2003; Randi 1982; Radner and Radner 1982, and Stein 1996).

The one exception seems to be the **ganzfeld** and **autganzfeld** studies done by Charles Honorton, William Braud, and Adrian Parker from the mid-1970s to the mid-1980s. There are three phases to these tests of telepathy, the ability of the mind to send and receive information without the use of the ordinary senses.

Phase 1. Preparing the receiver and the sender. The receiver is placed in a comfortable chair. She wears headphones which play continuous white noise. [White noise is a type of noise that is produced by combining sounds of all different frequencies together. If you took all of the imaginable tones that a human can hear and combined them together, you would have white noise. This masks any distinguishable sounds and virtually eliminates sensory input from sounds.] Over her eyes are halves of ping-pong balls. A red light shines on her face. Before the test begins, a relaxation tape is played to put her in a relaxed state.

After several minutes of the unchanging sensory field, the receiver allegedly achieves a state similar to being in a sensory isolation chamber. Hallucinations are commonly reported in this state. Before being sealed in the ganzfeld chamber, the receiver is asked to say out loud what she is feeling or "seeing." She does this for about 20 minutes before being sealed in.

Phase 2. Sending the target. In another room, an assistant has already selected one picture from a target pack out of a large pool of packs. Each pack has four pictures or videos that are very unlike each other. The target is in an opaque envelope. The experimenter is blind to the target. The assistant gives the experimenter the target envelope and the experimenter gives it to the sender and seals him in the room. The sender tries to telepathically communicate the target to the receiver. Breaks are taken and the sending process is repeated several times.

In many of these experiments (the autoganzfeld), the selecting of the target is automated. (This was in response to psychologist Ray Hyman's criticisms about randomization of the targets. Receivers tend to select the first or second choice offered them.) The experimenter has a direct communication to the receiver's room and can hear and record everything she says, as well as communicate with her. The sender's room is equipped to hear what the receiver is saying. This is considered "feedback" and is supposedly helpful in guiding the sender to alter his method of telepathic sending.

Phase 3. Judging the outcome. The whole process lasts from 15 to 30 minutes. The receiver is relieved of her headphones and eye covers and is shown the four possible targets. She is asked to rank them 1 to 4, according to how well each matches her impressions during the ganzfeld stimulation period. The sender then reveals which target he was given. If the receiver ranks the actual target 1, then the trial is considered a hit; otherwise it is a miss. If the hit rate is significantly above chance (25%), the researchers take this as evidence of telepathy. If not, they take it as evidence of what you'd expect from just guessing.

A meta-analysis of 28 ganzfeld studies was done by Honorton and Daryl Bem, 23 of which had resulted in greater than chance hit rates, and the results were, according to parapsychologist Dean Radin, "odds against chance of ten billion to one." A further analysis by Honorton recalculated the odds against chance as being 10,000 to one, with replication in eight other labs besides Honorton's own. No obvious fatal design flaws could be found by skeptics, though Ray Hyman took issue with some of the randomization procedures. Radin claims that the hit rate of 37% for 25 studies corresponds to odds against chance of about a trillion to one (Radin 1997: 84).

From 1983 onward, Honorton and others began doing computer controlled ganzfeld studies (autoganzfeld) with the same kind of results as the earlier studies. Radin concludes: "We are fully justified in having very high confidence that people sometimes get small amounts of specific information from a distance without the use of the ordinary senses. Psi effects do occur in the ganzfeld" (Radin 1997: 88). (*Psi*—pronounced *sigh*—is a term used by parapsychologists to refer to either ESP or psychokinesis.

However, all we are truly justified in having a very high confidence in is that when ganzfeld studies are done, receivers are likely to guess correctly a one-in-four target at significantly greater than chance odds. It is still a leap to assume that information has been transferred and that the transfer was done by paranormal means. To say that you can't think of any other explanation for the data and that a skeptic can't provide a naturalistic explanation for it, does not justify high confidence that telepathy has been established.

Even if we are confident that our controls eliminate such things as cheating, sensory leakage (non-verbal communication to the receiver), inadequate randomization, lucky guess, unconscious pattern recognition, etc., how can we be sure that the only reasonable explanation is that what appears to be a transfer of information is in fact a genuine transfer of information? And how can we be sure that some other factor that we have not controlled for, either because we didn't think of it or because we *couldn't* think of it, is not responsible for the anomaly? In short, it doesn't follow logically that the anomaly is likely due to telepathy simply because it is not likely due to sensory input that we've controlled for. As psychologist James Alcock points out, the anomaly may not represent a genuine transfer of information. For all we know, Zeus might be responsible for it.

> The departure from chance expectation could be due to any number of influences—a non-random 'random generator', various methodological flaws, or...Zeus. (I could posit that Zeus exists and likes to torment parapsychologists, and thereby gives them significant outcomes from time to time, but does not allow replication outside parapsychology. The significant outcome would provide as much support for my hypothesis that Zeus exists as it does for the Psi hypothesis that the human subject's volition caused the results.) (Alcock 2003: 43)

Thus, even if odds against chance are achieved, it is always possible that this has nothing to do with telepathy. It may have nothing to do with Zeus, either. But it is possible that it has to do with something naturalistic that has not been accounted for. Nevertheless, says Radin, we must admit that "something interesting was going on" (1997: 79). But is it telepathy or clairvoyance? I don't know. Is it Zeus? I doubt it, but I also doubt it is telepathy or clairvoyance. However, my doubts are irrelevant as to what is really going on. The best we can say is that we do not know why some subjects perceive targets at a non-random rate. It might be worthwhile to study such subjects, not to see if they can transfer information, though we could do that, but we already know the results would show no transfer of information. We know this because if it were possible for anyone to transfer information telepathically in an unambiguous manner, it would have been done already.

Parapsychologists display another characteristic of pseudoscience: the introduction of **ad hoc hypotheses** to cover up failures to confirm their theories. The ad hoc hypothesis tries to explain away apparently contradictory or falsifying evidence. For example, rather than admit that an experiment could not be duplicated because the ESP it was supposed to confirm couldn't be confirmed, experimenters have been known to blame the hostile thoughts of onlookers for unconsciously influencing pointer readings on sensitive instruments. Of course, if this objection is taken seriously, then no experiment on ESP or PK (psychokinesis) can ever fail: Whatever the results, one can always say they were caused by paranormal psychic forces, either the ones being tested or others not being tested. This kind of ad hoc hypothesizing reached a ludicrous peak with paraphysicist Helmut Schmidt. He put cockroaches in a box where they could give themselves electric shocks. One would assume that cockroaches do not like to be shocked and would give themselves shocks at a chance rate or less (if cockroaches can learn from experience). The cockroaches gave themselves more electric shocks than predicted by chance. Schmidt concluded that "because he hated cockroaches, maybe it was *his* PK that influenced the randomizer!" (Gardner 1983: 59).

One key element of the ad hoc hypothesis is that it cannot be independently tested. In the example above, there is no independent way to test for the effect of hostile vibes. Thus, if a hypothesis appears to be ad hoc, one should always ask: Can this be tested independently of the theory it is trying to save? For example, when William Herschel discovered the planet Uranus in 1781 by telescopic observation and its orbit did not fit with predictions made using Newton's laws of planetary motion, it was proposed that another planet must exist further out from the sun than Uranus. This hypothesis could be independently tested. Its size and orbit could be calculated based on how much it perturbed the motion of Uranus. Thus was Neptune discovered. When the math for Neptune's orbit didn't work in accordance with Newton's laws, it was proposed that still another planet awaited discovery. Both of these hypotheses could be independently tested, albeit with some difficulty given the state of knowledge and technology at the time.

> "The popularity of borderline science is a rebuke to the schools, the press and commercial television for their sparse, unimaginative and ineffective efforts at science education; and to us scientists, for doing so little to popularize our subject."
> –Carl Sagan

Perhaps an even more ludicrous peak was reached with Joseph Banks Rhine, sometimes called the father of American parapsychology. Rhine once declared that a horse (Lady Wonder) had ESP. When he later tested the horse under more controlled conditions, the horse couldn't perform. Rather than conclude that the better controls made it impossible for the horse to pick up non-verbal cues from her mistress, Rhine declared that the horse had lost its psychic powers. Rhine also maintained that **the decline effect** explained why some subjects in his card-guessing experiments would do better than chance for awhile but then the number of correct guesses would start going down. Psychic power wanes with use, he declared, rather than admit that in the long run, if chance is operating on guessing what card someone is trying to telepathically send to a receiver, then you expect regression toward the mean. Rhine even went so far as to declare that subjects who consistently scored below chance gave proof of psychic powers. He called it **psi missing** and claimed it was done intentionally by subjects who were hostile to him or to belief in the paranormal. Other analysts might think that in the long run, one should expect to find some subjects scoring above chance and others below chance, and some performing above chance for awhile and then below chance for awhile. Why? Because in the long run the correct and incorrect guesses would approach chance rates, all things being equal.

Defenders of alleged psychic Edgar Cayce provided a classic ad hoc hypothesis to explain away their hero's failures. For example, Cayce and a famous dowser named Henry Gross set out together to discover buried treasure along the seashore and found nothing. Their defenders suggested that their psychic powers were accurate because either there once was a buried treasure where they looked but it had been dug up earlier, or there would be a treasure buried there sometime in the future. One wonders why Cayce did not discern this with his psychic powers.

Ad hoc hypotheses are not limited to pseudoscientists. Another type of ad hoc hypothesis occurs in science when a new scientific theory is proposed that conflicts with an established theory and which lacks an essential explanatory mechanism. An ad hoc hypothesis is proposed to explain what the new theory cannot explain. For example, when Wegener proposed his theory of **continental drift** (discussed below) he could not explain *how* continents move. It was suggested that *gravity* was the force behind the movement of continents, though there was no scientific evidence for this notion. In fact, scientists could and did show that gravity was too weak a force to account for the movement of continents.

Parapsychology is unique in that it is a discipline that devotes most of its energy to trying to prove the existence of something it cannot explain. *Most sciences try to explain observable phenomena. Parapsychology tries to observe unexplainable phenomena.* Furthermore, its practitioners do not seem to be the least bit interested that from the standpoint of physics an explanatory mechanism for alleged psychic phenomena is not likely to be forthcoming. All psi researchers have found that *spatial distance is irrelevant to the exercise of* ESP. Three of the other four known forces in nature weaken with distance. Thus, as Einstein pointed out, "This suggests...a very strong indication that a nonrecognized source of systematic errors may have been involved [in ESP experiments with favorable results]."[9]

All the other sciences have led us *away from* superstition and magical thinking. Parapsychology is alone among the sciences in its quest to find a scientific basis for divination, magical powers, and spirits. It is true that parapsychology has moved out of the séance room into the laboratory, where it seeks quantifiable and replicable data. However, parapsychologists now quest for statistical anomalies. It's simply exchanged stories of weird experiences for studies with weird statistics.[10]

Also, believers ignore or dismiss out of hand such things as the year-long study done by the United States Air Force Research Laboratories, which was unable to verify the existence of ESP. The VERITAC study, named after the computer used, is considered insignificant by psi researchers because it did not support their viewpoint. Other negative result studies, such as the one done by Richard C. Sprinthall and Barry S. Lubetkin published in the *Journal of Psychology* (vol. 60, pp. 313-18), are also rejected by psi advocates.

Researchers who claim to have found positive results systematically ignore or rationalize their own studies that do not support their claims. They also allow *optional starting* and *optional stopping*. In many tests of psychic powers, the researcher allows the subject to start or stop whenever he or she feels like it. For example, a subject may go through some warm-ups at predicting

> "The mystery of horoscopes, psychic phenomena, and biorhythm cycles never vanishes, no matter how much you delve into the 'research' on the subject. There are no underlying principles to understand."
> –Radner and Radner

numbers or card suits or whatever other silly thing is supposed to be psychically transmitted and received. The responses of the warm-ups are recorded, however, and if they look good (i.e., if they look like the psychic is revved up and getting good vibes) then the responses are counted in the experimental data. If not, then the warm-up data is discarded. Likewise, if the psychic has had a good run at guessing numbers or card suits and starts to have a bad run, he can call it quits and the researcher discards the negative data. Any reasonable test of psychic powers should have a protocol that specifically determines *before the experiment begins* exactly when the experiment will begin and when it will end.

Most psi researchers seem to limit their research to investigating either parlor tricks, like guessing a simple picture on a card, or parlor tricksters like Ingo Swann and Uri Geller. On the other hand, when they do claim to have proof of a real psychic, they cannot get the psychic to duplicate the amazing results of the study that allegedly was the final proof of paranormal phenomena. For example, J.B. Rhine claimed that Hubert Pearce, who later became a Methodist minister, correctly identified 25 ESP cards in a row after having been promised $100 for each card he could correctly identify. The only use to which Pearce ever put his alleged powers was in another test done by Rhine and J.G. Pratt, another believer. Not only did Rhine and Pratt not take precautions to make sure that Pearce did not cheat, when they had a magician independently test Pearce, he performed at the level expected by chance guessing. Rather than admit that tighter controls made it more difficult for Pearce to cheat, Rhine and other parapsychologists determined that instituting tighter controls shows lack of trust and this diminishes the ability of psychics to perform. Much of the literature on this topic deals with *integrity*: skeptics proposing that cheating was possible and Rhine and Pratt taking offense that anyone would challenge their integrity or competence, much less the integrity of their subject, Mr. Pearce. There would not have been any controversy if Pearce had gone on to demonstrate publicly his psychic powers. I suspect Pearce did not publicly demonstrate his psychic powers because he did not have any. I suspect, too, that Pearce was not an accomplished magician like Uri Geller, another star witness for the ESP defense, who did demonstrate his powers to the public: He can bend spoons and keys. He claims he can do so using his psychic powers, but another magician, James Randi, performs the same tricks and demonstrates how to do it the easy way.

Of course, many believers in ESP have not done any experiments, nor have they read the studies of J.B. Rhine, Charles Tart, Russell Targ and Harold Puthoff, Dean Radin, and the like. They base their belief upon personal and authoritative anecdotes. The personal anecdote takes the form of Aunt Daisie's dream about her father dying right before he did die, and how the dream was so vivid and accurate that it could not possibly be explained by ordinary means. Therefore, some sort of supernatural or paranormal event must have occurred. *How else could the dream be explained?* What are the odds of anyone dreaming of a person dying and then that person actually dying within 12 hours of the dream? A statistician has calculated that in Britain this should happen to someone every two weeks (Blackmore 2004: 301).

Most people know nothing about probability odds and this affects their misconceptions as to what is or isn't likely to be a coincidence. For example, the odds of being dealt any particular bridge hand are over 635 billion to one. So what? The next time you are dealt a hand are you going to declare: Do you know what the odds are of me being dealt just this hand? 635 billion to one! How weird is that? The odds of four perfect hands being dealt in bridge are staggering. The odds of it happening again are ridiculous. Even if everybody on earth played 120 hands a day the odds of a second perfect deal would be something like 2,000 billion to one. Yet, every year, cases of perfect deals are reported. It need not be paranormal. It need not involve cheating, either. And it's certainly not due to chance! All it requires is two perfect shuffles of a new deck of cards, an event that Las Vegas card dealers have shown to be not that rare or difficult.

> Two "perfect" shuffles (in which the deck is divided exactly into two halves, and perfect interleaving of the two halves is accomplished) followed by any number of simple cuts (which have no effect on the cyclic order of the cards, merely changing the starting point) will invariably generate a "perfect" bridge deal. (Alcock 1981: 152)

Finally, there are billions of dreams a night on this planet and it would be pretty odd if none of them corresponded in vague or precise ways to actual events past, present, or future. Yet, most dreams about people dying, airplanes crashing, buildings collapsing, and so on, do not correspond to future events. If a significant number of dreams of a single person corresponded to future events, then I would be the first to try to get close to the clairvoyant and recommend government funding to try to find out what mechanism was at work here. Maybe this power could be harnessed for the good of the human race. Most of us have many anxieties and concerns about people we know and love, and have frequent dreams of both good and harm befalling our loved ones. If we are honest with ourselves, I think we will admit that most of these dreams belie very real present fears and concerns. We forget most of these dreams, but if you have a dream of your mother dying and she dies the next day, there will be a natural tendency in many people to think that somehow their dream was an omen. Furthermore, as noted in chapter one, we know from many studies done on memory that many of our memories are filled in after the fact, i.e., we remember things that we learn of after the event we witnessed or experienced and incorporate those later experiences into our memories of earlier events. It is likely that memories of dreams would follow the same pattern. The striking precision of clairvoyant dreams may well come from data supplied *after* the dream but remembered as being part of the dream itself.

One thing that defenders of psychic phenomena have in common is *faith*. This alone accounts for why they pursue and provide reams of empirical data to support their claims but disregard or trivialize all empirical evidence that indicates their claims are in error. Their faith is not complete irrational fideism—belief without regard for and totally in spite of the evidence. Their faith is the kind of controlled faith that marks some religious persons. Evidence counts, but only if it supports one's beliefs. This trivializes the concept of evidence and explains, in part, why so many of the empirical tests for *psi* are inadequately designed, controlled, and administered. It explains, too, why so much ad hoc hypothesizing and rationalization goes on to explain away failures to confirm psychic events.

5. Scientific theories

The purpose of a scientific theory is to organize, unify, and make sense out of some range of natural phenomena. In short, scientists are trying to understand and, to some extent, control Nature. We have seen that pseudosciences, such as dianetics and parapsychology, also try to explain and make sense out of observations and experience. The differences between science and pseudoscience, however, outweigh their similarities. Pseudoscientists either believe untestable theories or they refuse to accept results that falsify their claims. They misuse scientific methods, as parapsychologists do when they search for an anomalous statistic and claim when they find one that they have proof of ESP. The same can be said for those who seek anomalous statistics in their healing prayer studies. Pseudoscientists tend to be selective in their use of evidence. They tend to be dogmatic and to act as if they are in search of disciples instead of critically thinking followers.

We will now examine two theories from the history of science, each exemplifying important differences between science and pseudoscience. The examples were chosen because they might erroneously be thought to be examples of science *not* at its best.

5.1 Continental drift

In commenting on the distinction between science and pseudoscience, the Radners note that there is a fine line separating speculative science from pseudoscience. Scientists, they say, recognize when their theories are sketchy, superficial, or unsupported; pseudoscientists do not (1982: 91). As an example of the difference between the practitioners of science and pseudoscience, the Radners cite the case of Alfred Wegener's *The Origin of Continents and Oceans* in which Wegener proposed the theory of **continental drift** against the prevailing theory that the earth was formed by cooling from a molten state and contractions. "Wegner's mode of reasoning lent itself to criticisms and counter-arguments. Wegener made assertions that could be checked and refuted as further evidence came in. He left room for his speculations to be superseded" (Radner and Radner 1982: 92). Wegener did not have disciples, but sympathizers who "acted like scientists."

Yet, Wegner's idea that continents move was rejected by most scientists when it was first proposed. Stephen Jay Gould notes that when the only American paleontologist defending the new theory spoke at Antioch College (where Gould was an undergraduate at the time), most of the audience dismissed the speaker's views as "just this side of sane" (Gould 1979: 160). A few years later, all the early critics of the new idea would accept it as true. Why? Was it simply a matter of Wegener and a few others jumping the gun by accepting a new idea before the evidence was sufficient to warrant assent? Were the latecomers 'good' scientists, waiting for more facts to confirm the theory? Gould's view is that dogmatic adherence to the view that the ocean floor is solid and unchanging was the main stumbling block to acceptance of the new theory. Most scientists rejected continental drift because it did not fit with their preconceived ideas about the nature of the earth's crust. They assumed that if continents did drift they would leave gaping holes in the earth. Since there were no gaping holes in the earth, it seemed unreasonable to believe that continents move. The theory of continental drift, says Gould, "was dismissed because no one had devised a physical mechanism that would permit continents to plow through an apparently solid oceanic floor." Yet, "during the period of nearly universal rejection, direct evidence for continental drift— that is, the data gathered from rocks exposed on our continents—was every bit as good as it is today."

Continental drift was considered *theoretically impossible* by some, even if it was physically possible for continents to move. The new theory could not be made to fit the theoretical model of the earth universally accepted at the time. Then, the theory of plate tectonics was proposed—the idea that the continents ride on plates that are bounded by areas where new crust is being created from within the planet and old crust is falling into trenches. This provided a mechanism for explaining how continents could drift. Continental drift, according to Gould, came to be accepted not because more facts had been piled up, but because it was a necessary consequence of the new theory of **plate tectonics**.

More facts were piled up, though—facts for the new theory of plate tectonics, of which the theory of continental drift is an essential element. Today it is taken as a fact that continents move. Yet, the exact mechanism by which plates move is still incompletely understood. This area of science will no doubt generate much debate and theorizing, testing of hypotheses, rejection and refinement of ideas. It is, as Gould says, a good example of how science works. To someone who does not understand the nature of science, the early rejection of the idea of continental drift might appear to show how dogmatic scientists are about their pet theories. If scientists had not been so devoted to their belief that the earth's crust is solid and immovable, they would have seen that continents can move. However, the fact that Wegener's theory turned out to be correct does not mean that he and his few early followers were more reasonable than the rest of the scientific community. After all, Wegener did not know about plate tectonics and he had not provided an acceptable explanation as to how continents might move. Wegener argued that gravity alone could move the continents. Gould notes: "Physicists responded with derision and showed mathematically that gravitational forces are far too weak to power such

208

monumental peregrination." Alexis du Toit, a defender of Wegener's theory, argued for radioactive melting of the ocean floor at continental borders as the mechanism by which continents might move. "This ad hoc hypothesis added no increment of plausibility to Wegener's speculation," according to Gould (1979: 163). It is true that the idea that the earth's crust is solid and immovable has been proved wrong, but Wegener didn't prove that. What the new theory could explain (about rocks and fossils, for example) other theories could explain equally well.

However, in the end, the idea of continental drift prevails. It prevails because the dogmatism of science—the tendency to interpret facts in light of theories—is not absolute but relative. What distinguishes science from pseudoscience is not that scientists are not dogmatic while pseudoscientists are. It is that scientists stand ready to give up one dogma for another should the evidence warrant it. Most pseudoscientists refuse to give up their dogmas regardless of the evidence against them. Gould notes with obvious admiration that a distinguished stratigraphy professor at Columbia University (where Gould did graduate work), who had initially ridiculed the theory of drifting continents, "spent his last years joyously redoing his life's work" (Gould 1979: 160). It is hard to imagine a comparable scene involving a pseudoscientist.

The Wegener episode demonstrates an essential difference between science and pseudoscience. That difference is to be found not in the correctness or incorrectness of proposed ideas, but *in the method used to gain acceptance for the ideas*. The difference is not to be found in the personality of the theorizer or in his stubborn adherence to an idea. It is to be found in the pseudoscientist's dogmatic refusal to give up an idea for which there is contrary evidence or for which there is not, nor ever could be, any test in experience.

5.2 Piltdown man

Piltdown was an archaeological site in England where fossil remains of humans, apes, and other mammals were found in 1908 and 1912. In 1913, an ape's jaw with a canine tooth worn down like a human's was found at a nearby site. To make a long story short, papers were published and the general community of British paleoanthropologists came to accept the idea that the fossil remains belonged to a single creature with a human cranium and an ape's jaw, the so-called "missing link." In 1953, Piltdown 'man' was exposed as a forgery: The skull was modern and the teeth on the ape's jaw had been filed down. How had so many scientists been duped? Gould offers several reasons, among them *wishful thinking* and *cultural bias*, which no doubt played a role in the lack of critical thinking among British paleoanthropologists. However, as with the Wegener episode, the Piltdown forgery demonstrates the *fallibility* and *human* quality of scientific knowledge. It demonstrates, too, the way theories and facts are related in science. Theories precede facts; they are the filters through which facts are interpreted. Yet, facts also precede theories; they are the events that theories try to explain and make sense of. Gould notes that today a human cranium with an ape's jaw would be considered extremely implausible and far-fetched. But in the early part of this century, anthropologists were imbued with the cultural prejudice that considered man's big brain to be his ticket to rule and the key to understanding all his other unique features. There was a pre-conceived notion that the human brain must have developed to its human size before other changes occurred in human structure. So, a human cranium with an ape's jaw didn't rouse as much suspicion as it would today, when the fossil evidence clearly shows a progression from small-brained but upright (hence, non-simian) hominids, to larger-brained upright humans. Scientists "modeled the facts" instead of modeling their theory to fit the facts. This was "another illustration," says Gould, "that information always reaches us through the strong filters of culture, hope, and expectation" (Gould 1982: 118). Once committed to a theory, people see what fits with the theory. Even scientists are guilty of **confirmation bias**.

The main reason Piltdown was not spotted as a fraud much earlier was that scientists were not allowed to see the actual bones, which were kept securely locked in the British Museum. Instead of focusing their attention on examining the "fossils" more closely with an eye to discovering the fraud, scientists were not allowed to examine the physical evidence at all! They had to deal with plaster molds and be satisfied with a quick look at the originals to justify the claim that the models were accurate.

The moral of Piltdown is that science is fallible, a human activity that does not always take the most direct route in fulfilling its aim of understanding nature. When an **anomaly** such as the discovery of a human cranium with an ape's jaw occurs one must either fit it into a new theory, re-examine the evidence for error in discovery or interpretation, or show that the so-called anomaly is not really an anomaly at all but in fact fits with current theories and knowledge.

As noted above, scientists can sometimes appear to be dogmatic. They resort to seemingly ad hoc hypotheses to save their theories, as in the case of not abandoning Newton's laws when it was discovered that the motion of Uranus didn't fit with what was predicted by the laws. Herschel proposed that there was another planet beyond the orbit of Uranus that would

> An anomaly is something abnormal and not easily classified. In science, an anomaly is something that cannot be explained by currently accepted scientific theories.

account for the apparent anomalous orbit of Uranus. This idea could be independently tested. It was, and Neptune was discovered. However, it too had an anomalous orbit, that is, one not in accord with Newton's laws. Again, rather than abandon Newton's laws, which worked so well in explaining numerous natural phenomena, it was proposed that there must be another planet beyond Neptune. This, too was an independently testable hypothesis. Eventually, Pluto was discovered. However, its orbit is also anomalous. Should we abandon Newton's laws or keep looking for other bodies or groups of bodies on the outer edges of the solar system that might account for this discrepancy? Should we abandon Newton's laws or look for some previous error we might have made regarding the mass of the other planets? Is there anything that scientists would accept as falsifying Newton's laws? Is there anything that would lead the community of biological scientists to give up the neo-Darwinian synthesis (natural selection in light of genetics)? It is questions such as these that have led some philosophers of science to declare that Popper's notion of falsifiability is untenable. Has Popper's theory been falsified? Perhaps, but his theory is a *philosophical* one, not a scientific theory. It's a philosophical theory *about* scientific theories— a *metascientific theory*, if you will. Hmm. Maybe we should leave this one to the philosophers to work out.

6. Scientific, metaphysical, and pseudoscientific cosmological theories

A **cosmological theory** is a theory about the origin and nature of the universe. Such theories may be scientific, **metaphysical**, or **pseudoscientific**. Some theories are so broad or vague that they are consistent with just about any state of affairs, even apparent contradictions. They cannot be refuted, even in principle. For example, Freud's theory of the Oedipus complex postulates that there is an attraction on the part of a child toward the parent of the opposite sex. This attraction supposedly leads to jealousy, rivalry, and hostility toward the parent of the child's own sex. If the child doesn't behave in overtly jealous and hostile ways toward the parent of the same sex, then the theorist can declare that the child is repressing his feelings or sublimating them into socially acceptable behaviors. Or, the believer might declare that the child is asexual. Or, if the child shows anger toward both parents, the child might then be labeled as bisexual. And, if the child is hostile to the parent of the opposite sex, the child will grow up to be gay. Any behavior, friendly or hostile against either parent, can be made to fit the theory. No behavior could ever falsify the theory of the Oedipus complex.

A religious cosmology, such as that offered in *Genesis* and accepted as a literal account of the origin of the universe by fundamentalist Jews and Christians, is an *irrefutable* type of cosmological theory. Other theories allow definite predictions to be made from them; they can, in principle, be refuted. They can be tested by experience and observation. The Big Bang Theory, for example, is a *refutable* cosmological theory. There are events that, if discovered, would falsify the theory. The religious cosmology is non-scientific and *metaphysical*; the Big Bang theory is *scientific*. Metaphysical theories are "airtight" if they are self-consistent, i.e., contain no self-contradictory elements. No scientific theory is ever airtight.

A cosmology held by a religious group may be scientific, however. For example, if a Young Earth theory says that the world was created in 4004 B.C., but the evidence indicates that the earth is several billions of years old, then the theory is a scientific one *if it is thereby taken to be refuted by the evidence*. But if, for example, the ad hoc hypothesis is made that God created the world in 4004 B.C. complete with fossils, which makes the earth look much older than it really is, then nothing could refute it.[11] It is airtight. It is pseudoscience.

If the age or dating techniques of fossil evidence is disputed, but considered relevant to the truth of the Young Earth theory, and is prejudged to be consistent with the theory, then the theory is a pseudoscientific one. If the religious cosmologist denies that the earth is billions of years old on the grounds that scientific tests prove the earth is very young, rather than very old, then the burden of proof is on the religious cosmologist to demonstrate that the standard scientific methods and techniques of dating fossils are erroneous. No reasonable person should consider such an unsupported claim to be reasonable. To maintain it would require us to believe that the entire scientific community is in error about dozens of different dating techniques.

The unscientific nature of pseudoscientific religious cosmologies is evident not just in their overriding concern to make facts fit a preconceived theory. As we have seen, this is a human tendency that affects scientists, too.[12] Rather, the unscientific nature of pseudoscientific religious cosmologists is evident in the belief that the absolute truth has already been revealed and inquiry is not needed to search for the truth. To the pseudoscientific mind, truth is not something that must be constantly open to question, refined, and, possibly, rejected. To the pseudoscientific creationist mind, scientific truth is something eternal and unchanging that is recorded in the Bible. Compare this attitude to that of the leading European creationists of the 17th century who had to admit eventually that the Earth is not the center of the universe and that the sun does not revolve around our planet. They did not have to admit that the Bible was wrong, but they did have to admit that human interpretations of the Bible were in error (Carroll 2003: 87).

In recent years, creationism has been replaced by something called **intelligent design theory (ID)** as an alternative to Darwin's theory of natural selection. ID is a classic example of a pseudoscience: The theory is said to be scientific but it isn't. The theory says that some observable phenomena could not have evolved piecemeal. Some things require that several parts must have been produced simultaneously; otherwise, they would not work together as they do. Thus, some things require an intelligent designer or, in other words, a **miracle**.

If we grant that the universe or some discoverable part of it—such as the flagellum of a bacterium or the production of protein in a human cell—is possibly or even probably the result of intelligent design, what follows from that? Certainly no scientific research program will follow; for, the theory doesn't direct us anywhere. It does us no good to throw up our arms and yell "it's a miracle" every time we come upon some biological mechanism that we can't *at present* explain by natural selection.

Let's assume a particular eco-system is the creation of an intelligent designer. Unless this intelligent designer is human-like and unless we have some experience with the creations of this and similar designers, how could we proceed to study this system? If all we know is that it is the result of ID, but that the designer is of a different order of being than we are, how would we proceed to study this system? We would be limited in always responding in the same way to any question we asked about the system's relation to its designer. The most we could ever say is *It is this way because of ID* or *To be this way requires a miracle; it couldn't have happened naturally.* Furthermore, we would have to assume that since God is the intelligent designer and has designed everything, then everything is due to intelligent design. The theory explains everything but illuminates nothing (Carroll 2003: 182).

There are many believers in religious cosmologies, such as that given in *Genesis,* who do not claim that their beliefs are scientific. They do not believe that the Bible is to be taken as a science text. To them, the Bible contains teachings pertinent to their *spiritual* lives, not their scientific endeavors. The Bible expresses spiritual ideas about the nature of God and the relationship of God to humans and the rest of the universe. Such people do not believe the Bible should be taken literally when the issue is a matter for scientific discovery. The Bible, according to this metaphysical cosmology, should be read for its spiritual messages, not its lessons in biology, physics, or chemistry. Amen to that.

7. The popularity of pseudoscience

Why is pseudoscience so popular? Two factors have been repeatedly cited: the irresponsible portrayal of science and scientific matters in the mass media and the poor quality of science education. It should be a matter of national embarrassment that it is not uncommon to see stories in *The New York Times* with headlines that read

"Biology teaching flunks panel's test." The story tells us that biology, the first science presented to most students, is taught so poorly that the experience seems designed to snuff out interest in all science education at an early age. The panel was comprised of biologists and educators convened by the National Research Council. It was not hopeful for the future, said Dr. Timothy Goldsmith of Yale, chairman of the committee that did the three-year study. Most proposals for overhauling the education system, he said, focused on managerial or administrative solutions, such as lengthening the school day or requiring more standardized tests, rather than looking at the learning process in the classroom. Bill Aldridge, executive director of the National Science Teachers Association, concluded that the state of science education in this country is disastrous.

F. James Rutherford, director of Project 2061, a science curriculum reform project of the American Association for the Advancement of Science (AAAS), laments that "much of what's done in schools focuses on facts and information, on separate disciplines and subject matter that is often unconnected." The AAAS report states that "Today's overstuffed curriculum places too much emphasis on memorizing countless formulas and generalizations, which severely hinders students' abilities to learn and understand materials....students should spend more time learning how science touches their lives and less time memorizing facts." More and more studies are calling for hands-on methods of science instruction, which include interdisciplinary approaches to current issues such as global warming, famines, earthquakes, volcanoes, and the like. However, because many parents oppose the teaching of evolution or even the teaching of science that might be applied to politically sensitive areas such as global warming, we can expect a great deal of opposition to any meaningful change in our science curricula. An enormous amount of wasted energy in school boardrooms has been spent in recent years quibbling about whether to allow intelligent design into the biology classroom. This is likely to continue, especially since an increasing number of politicians and a large vocal part of the citizenry are concerned that secular education is promoting atheism and materialism by not bringing God into the educational picture.

Rutherford gives an example of good and bad science education in teaching about cells. High school texts list 120 technical words about the cell, and students are often required to memorize the words. "We found that 11 of the words were sufficient," he said. "If you concentrate on what goes on in the cell, how it relates to the system, you come out with a deeper understanding." The committee doesn't want to eliminate learning facts, just reduce the workload so time can be spent on understanding what the terms are about. It seems, then, that unless we change the way science is taught to our young people, it is unlikely that many of them will come away with an understanding of the nature of science, much less with a desire to scientifically understand the world they live in.

According to Martin Gardner, poor science instruction is only one of several reasons for the rise in pseudoscience. In his view, there are several main reasons for the increase in wild beliefs: "The decline of traditional religious beliefs among the better educated, the resurgence of Protestant fundamentalism, the disenchantment with science for creating a technology that is damaging the environment and building horrendous war weapons, and the increasingly poor quality of science instruction on all levels of schooling...." An overlooked factor, according to Gardner, is "the role of the media as feedback," especially movies and television. He writes, "just as mild porn stimulates a demand for pornier porn, and mild violence a demand for more violent violence, so does crazy science create a demand for crazier science." Television and movies "rapidly accelerate any trend." In Gardner's view, the mass media has a moral obligation not to contribute to "the growing inability of citizens to tell good science from bad" by programs such as *Exploring the Unknown,* which present numerous 'paranormal' events claimed to be on the new frontiers of modern science, when in fact everything shown is "considered rubbish by the entire science community." Such shows far outnumber scientifically grounded programs such as *NOVA* or *Scientific American Presents.*

On the other hand, wishful thinking and human gullibility should not be discounted as essential explanatory factors in understanding why pseudosciences continue to have widespread appeal even in an Age of Science. Human beings seem to be very uncomfortable in the face of what seems inexplicable. We seem to have a need to make sense out of everything. We also like mysteries and seem to prefer supernatural or paranormal explanations to scientific ones, especially if the non-scientific explanations are not too technical and fill us with a sense of excitement and wonder. Many fear that science is telling us that there is no meaning to our lives, that we are just so much 'dirt' that will pass back into the universe of wandering atomic particles when our time is up. They want hope; belief in things spiritual and paranormal gives them that hope.

The following is an extreme example of the lengths to which some people will go to maintain their wild beliefs, yet it exemplifies a common problem: rationalization to maintain even obviously false beliefs. Marian Keech was the leader of a UFO cult in the 1950s. She claimed to get messages from extraterrestrials known as The Guardians, through automatic writing. Like the Heaven's Gate folks forty years later,[13] Keech and her followers, known as The Seekers or The Brotherhood of the Seven Rays, were waiting to be picked up by flying saucers. In Keech's prophecy, her group of eleven was to be saved just before the earth was to be destroyed by a massive flood on December 21, 1954. When it became evident that there would be no flood and the Guardians weren't stopping by to pick them up, Keech

> became elated. She said she'd just received a telepathic message from the Guardians saying that her group of believers had spread so much light with their unflagging faith that God had spared the world from the cataclysm…Most disciples not only stayed but, having made that decision, were now even more convinced than before that Keech had been right all along….Being wrong turned them into true believers (Levine 2003: 206).

Rather than give up their belief in the face of strong evidence of its falsehood, their belief became even stronger. Why? Why do people believe obvious falsehoods? According to H. L. Mencken, believing in the "palpably not true" is the "chief occupation of mankind." Maybe he's right.

Michael Shermer, publisher of *Skeptic* magazine, and author of *Why People Believe Weird Things*, says: "More than any other, the reason people believe weird things is because they want to….It feels good. It is comforting. It is consoling." Weird beliefs also offer "immediate gratification." People like weird beliefs because they are simple. Weird beliefs also satisfy the quest for significance: They satisfy our moral needs and our desire that life be meaningful. Finally, he says, people believe weird things because weird things give them hope.

We might add *ignorance* to Shermer's list. Ignorance seems to be the main reason many people believe weird things. They simply do not know any better. If they had some knowledge about physics, chemistry, biology, memory, the brain, the body, and the like, they would not even consider many of the crackpot ideas put forth for their consideration. Only a person ignorant of physics and neurology, for example, could consider it reasonable to wear a takionic headband to improve thinking.

Also, many weird beliefs are the beliefs of *groups*, not isolated individuals. They are perpetuated and spread like viruses because of mechanisms such as communal reinforcement. It is always easier to believe something, no matter how wild or weird, if others believe it, too.

Finally, some weird beliefs are empowering. Some people's beliefs make them feel special. They set them apart from the crowd and the ordinary people who just don't get it.

8. The Hidden Persuaders

In 1957, social scientist Vance Packard published a book called *The Hidden Persuaders*, in which he chronicled the many methods that advertisers and marketing experts use in their quest to manipulate the thoughts and actions of consumers. Many years later, two psychologists, Geoffrey Dean and Ivan Kelly (2003), used the expression 'hidden persuaders' to describe perceptual and cognitive illusions that lead us to erroneous beliefs. In this book, we have explored a number of logical fallacies and cognitive illusions—*hidden persuaders*, if you will—that lead people to believe in "the palpably not true."

Hidden persuaders originate in quite useful adaptations. Seeing patterns, especially causal patterns, is quite beneficial to our species. Recognizing how data support our beliefs and having others share those beliefs are also beneficial. Drawing inferences quickly may mean the difference between life and death. Having hope, reducing tension caused by conflicting ideas, and even deceiving ourselves can be psychologically advantageous. But all of these positive tendencies can become perverted and lead us into error if we are not careful.

Hidden persuaders sometimes seem to affect people in proportion to their intelligence: the smarter one is the easier it is to develop false beliefs. There are several reasons for this: (1) the hidden persuaders affect everybody to some degree; (2) the smarter one is the easier it is to see patterns, fit data to a hypothesis, and draw inferences; (3) the smarter one is the easier it is to rationalize, i.e., explain away strong evidence contrary to one's belief; and (4) smart people are often arrogant and incorrectly think that they cannot be deceived by others, the data, or themselves.

If you have learned nothing else from reading this book, I hope you will have learned, as Michael Novak put it: "Our capacity for self-deception has no known limits."

214

Exercise 9-1 Self-test: True or false? (Check your answers in Answers to Selected Exercises.)

1 Non-empirical, non-scientific theories attempt to explain concepts or values, or are prescriptive in nature, or they attempt to explain natural phenomena in ways that are not empirically testable.

2 To be likely, a scientific explanation usually must be in accordance with current knowledge, beliefs, laws and principles of the field in which the explanation is made.

3 Every test a scientific theory passes confirms it, but only thousands of passed tests will prove with absolute certainty a scientific theory.

4 The mass media, especially television, have historically shown a great concern for presenting accurate scientific information.

5 The best scientific and metaphysical theories have nothing in common.

6 Pseudoscientists are rarely motivated by an overriding commitment to religious dogma or mythology.

7 Scientific theories connect directly to experience and observation in an essential and profound way.

8 Metaphysical theories can be empirically confirmed to a lesser degree than scientific theories.

9 What distinguishes science from pseudoscience is that scientists are not dogmatic while pseudoscientists are.

10 A critical thinker must try to establish a complete set of *a priori* conditions which a theory must meet before any reasonable person should accept it.

11 There are many believers in a religious cosmology such as that given in *Genesis* who do not claim that their beliefs are scientific.

12 One sign that an empirical idea is not scientific is the claim that the idea is absolutely certain and irrefutable.

13 Any good theory must be free from self-contradictions, consistent with experience, and free of *ad hoc* hypotheses to patch up holes or weaknesses.

14 Any reasonable test of psychic powers should have a protocol that specifically determines *before the experiment begins* exactly when the experiment will begin and when it will end.

15 The moral of Piltdown is that science is fallible, a human activity that does not always take the most direct route in fulfilling its aim of understanding nature.

16 Scientists seek facts, but sometimes the best they can do is theories.

17 Many people, including the highly educated, may be attracted to pseudoscience because of ignorance regarding the nature of science.

18 The proponent of a novel idea in science must provide very good reasons for rejecting established principles because the established views are considered infallible.

19 The dogmatism of science—the tendency to interpret facts in light of currently accepted theories—is not absolute but relative.

20 When a pseudoscientist says that he or she believes in astrology or biorhythms or dianetics, etc., because it *works*, he or she usually means that there is anecdotal evidence the theory fits some data.

21 The ganzfeld studies prove beyond any reasonable doubt that telepathic communication does happen.

22 If a metaphysical theory is not self-contradictory and is consistent with the evidence of experience, it cannot be shown to be false.

23 Good scientists generally back up their theories with appropriate anecdotes.

24 The more intelligent a person is the less likely she is to be negatively affected by the hidden persuaders.

25 Sciences are built on axioms and claim *a priori* knowledge of the number of causal mechanisms that must exist for any phenomena.

26 Parapsychology, astrology, and dianetics are pseudosciences.

27 Pseudoscientific theories are put forth as if they are scientific when they are not.

28 If a scientific cosmology is inconsistent with a metaphysical cosmology, an empirical test must be done to determine which is the better theory.

29 The distinguishing feature of non-scientific theories is that they are not capable of being tested by experience.

30 To be a reasonable scientific explanation, it is enough that the explanation be a possible and consistent account of phenomena.

31 Intelligent design theory is considered a reasonable alternative to the theory of natural selection by most biologists; that is why the National Science Foundation insists it be part of the biology curriculum.

32 To be able to test a theory by experience means to be able to predict certain observable or measurable consequences from the theory.

33 To say of a scientific theory that it *works* means that it is empirically rich: many specific predictions have been deduced from it with accuracy; it is compatible with other scientific theories; it explains a great deal.

34 Parapsychology tries to observe unexplainable phenomena.

35 A good scientific theory ought to be capable of being used to make *specific* predictions, not vague ones.

36 The history of science is the history of one absolute truth being built upon other absolute truths.

37 To say that a scientific theory is "very rich" is to say that many empirical hypotheses can be generated from it, each one serving as another test of the theory.

38 The greater the number of severe tests a scientific theory has passed, the greater its degree of confirmation and the more reasonable it is to accept it.

39 If a metaphysical theory is inconsistent with the evidence of experience, it is not a good theory.

40 Pseudoscience is distinguished by its refusal to be guided by factual evidence and logical reasoning because its commitment is to dogma itself, not to evidence or fallible truth.

41 Facts are used to test scientific theories.

42 All scientific theories attempt to make sense out of the phenomena they are put forth to explain.

43 A necessary consequence of scientific claims being falsifiable is that they are also highly improbable.

44 Pseudoscience is characterized by its theories being false.

45 Scientific theories vary in degree of probability from the highly improbable to the highly probable.

46 A sign that a theory is not scientific is the fact that the theory is not falsifiable.

47 Scientific theories are explanations of events.

Exercise 9-2

Evaluate the following theory. Can you come up with a better theory than the one given? Why is yours better?

The Dreams of College Students

The three most frequently occurring kinds of dreams of college students are (1) dreams of falling, (2) dreams of being pursued or attacked, and (3) dreams of attempting to perform a task but failing.

Dreams of falling obviously originate with our tree-dwelling ancestors. Any miscalculation or neglect of the laws of gravity could mean death. If you wanted to survive, you had to stay aware of where you were. Ever present throughout the day, this awareness naturally made its way into dreams at night, where it continued to serve its purpose. The falling dream was an evolutionary mechanism to keep the primate in a tree from tossing and turning in its sleep, a habit that could be fatal.

Being pursued or attacked also originated with our ancient ancestors. There is little difficulty in imagining how the early hominids felt about saber-toothed tigers. The fear of being eaten was a formidable anxiety. If you weren't alert, you perished. Anxiety about being eaten made early man a light sleeper. The horror of attack-and-pursuit nightmares would have occurred quite often, keeping early man alert and awake.

Finally, attempting a task and repeatedly failing symbolizes the struggle of man's intelligence against the forces of nature. If a hominid tried to invent a new weapon during his waking hours but continually failed, he would be likely to dream about his efforts. He might dream about throwing stones at animals and recognize how inefficient the practice is. He might dream that during one hunt he had been jabbed by a sharp stick while running through the forest, and then he might see that a spear could be invented.

Exercise 9-3

Research and evaluate one or more of the following theories. Determine if the theory is scientific or not.

1 The theory of evolution
2 The theory of determinism
3 The global warming theory
4 The Big Bang theory
5 The virus theory of contagious diseases
6 The retributive or utilitarian theory of punishment
7 The theory of intelligent design
8. Auras
9. Psychic photography (thoughtography)
10. The psychological theory of "repression"

Exercise 9-4

Invent a pseudoscientific theory regarding (a) the healing power of color; (b) math anxiety; (c) romantic love; (d) sexism; (e) I. Q. enhancement through power breathing; or (f) some phenomenon of your own choosing.

Bibliography - Chapter Nine

Beveridge, W. I. B. (1957). *The Art of Scientific Investigation.* Vintage Books.

Beyerstein, Barry and Dayle F. Beyerstein (1991). Editors. *The Write Stuff - Evaluations of Graphology, the Study of Handwriting Analysis.* Prometheus Books.

Bronowski, Jacob (1973). *The Ascent of Man.* Little, Brown and Company.

Carroll, Robert Todd (2003). *The Skeptic's Dictionary: A Collection of Strange Beliefs, Amusing Deceptions, and Dangerous Delusions.* Wiley & Sons.

Dawes, Robyn M. (1994). *House of Cards - Psychology and Psychotherapy Built on Myth.* The Free Press.

Dean, Geoffrey and Ivan Kelly (2003). "Is Astrology Relevant to Consciousness and Psi?" *Journal of Consciousness Studies.* Volume 10, No. 6-7, June-July.

Friedlander, Michael W. (1995). *At the Fringes of Science.* Westview Press.

Friedlander, Michael W. (1972). *The Conduct of Science.* Prentice-Hall.

Gardner, Martin (1983). *The WHYS of a Philosophical Scrivener.* Quill.

Gardner, Martin (1981). *Science: Good, Bad and Bogus.* Prometheus Books.

Gardner, Martin (1957). *Fads and Fallacies in the Name of Science.* Dover Publications, Inc.

Ronald, Giere. (2004). *Understanding Scientific Reasoning,* 5th ed. Wadsworth.

Gould, Stephen Jay (1983). "Evolution as Fact and Theory," in *Hen's Teeth and Horse's Toes*. W.W. Norton & Company.

Gould, Stephen Jay (1982). "Piltdown Revisited," in *The Panda's Thumb*. W.W Norton and Company.

Gould, Stephen Jay. (1979). *Ever Since Darwin*. W.W. Norton & Company.

Hansel C.E.M. (1989). *The Search for Psychic Power: ESP and Parapsychology Revisited*. Prometheus Books.

Hines, Terence (1990). *Pseudoscience and the Paranormal*. Prometheus Books.

Keene, Lamar M. (1997). *The Psychic Mafia*. Prometheus Books.

Kourany, Janet A. (1997). *Scientific Knowledge: Basic Issues in the Philosophy of Science*, 2nd ed. Wadsworth Publishing Co.

Larson, Edward J. (2004). *Evolution: The Remarkable History of a Scientific Theory*. Modern Library.

Levine, Robert (2003). *The Power of Persuasion - How We're Bought and Sold*. John Wiley & Sons.

Popper, Karl R. (1959). *The Logic of Scientific Discovery*. Harper Torchbooks.

Radner, Daisie and Michael (1982). *Science and Unreason*. Wadsworth Publishing Co.

Randi, James, (1982). *Flim-Flam! Psychics, ESP, Unicorns, and Other Delusions*. Prometheus Books.

Sagan, Carl (1995). *The Demon-Haunted World: Science as a Candle in the Dark*. Random House.

Sagan, Carl (1979). *Broca's Brain*. Random House.

Shermer, Michael (2002). *Why People Believe Weird Things: Pseudoscience, Superstition, and Other Confusions of Our Time*. 2nd rev. ed. Owl Books.

Stein, Gordon (1996). Editor, *The Encyclopedia of the Paranormal*. Prometheus Books.

Notes – Chapter Nine

[1] The ABC television network showed a mini-series based on MacLaine's book *Out on a Limb*. It depicts MacLaine conversing with spirits through channeler Kevin Ryerson. One of the spirits who speaks through Ryerson is a contemporary of Jesus called "John." This "John" doesn't speak Aramaic--the language of Jesus--but a kind of Elizabethan English. "John" tells MacLaine that she is co-creator of the world with God. MacLaine, a consummate egoist, becomes ecstatic to find out that she is right about a belief she'd expressed earlier, viz., that she IS God. Cf. Martin Gardner, "Isness Is Her Business," *New York Review of Books*, April 9, 1987.

[2] Alice Kahn, "Channeling for Dollars," *The San Francisco Chronicle*, April 19, 1987. Kahn's article was based on her attendance at one of the sessions. She also notes that for $125 anyone could attend the 3rd annual Michael Retreat at Harbin Hot Springs for "shamanic rituals, dream-sharing, breakfast and dinner."

[3] *Abduction: Human Encounters with Aliens* (New York: Scribners, 1994) by John E Mack.

[4] One of the main leaders of 'scientific creationism' is Duane T. Gish, author of *Evolution, the Challenge of the Fossil Record* (San Diego, Calif.: Creation-Life Publishers, 1985) and *Evolution, the Fossils Say No* (San Diego, Calif. : Creation-Life Publishers, 1978).

[5] Carl Sagan wrote to a parapsychology institute to tell of a precognitive dream he had which did not pan out. They ignored him. Imagine, he asks, what kind of treatment they would have given him had he claimed that his dream had coincided with some future event. "The hits are recorded, the misses are not" (Sagan 1979: 45).

[6] Published by the American Saint Hill Organization, Los Angeles. All page references are to this hardback edition.

[7] To his credit, Hubbard recognized that the belief "no recordings can take place in the mind until the nerves are sheathed depends upon a theoretical postulate," i.e., it is a metaphysical not an empirical claim. However, his criticism of this notion because it "has never been subjected to scientific research" indicates that he doesn't recognize one key difference between metaphysical and empirical claims: only the latter can be subjected to scientific research. (p. 127)
  Also, in 1961 Hubbard set up an academic laboratory in East Grinstead, England. He is said to have "examined in depth the entire body of his work with the intention of systematizing auditing procedure." According to Tom Joyce, a former member of the Church of Scientology, this was probably the first time Hubbard "conducted himself as a scientist, *albeit one unencumbered by peer review*." [Italics added.] "Hubbard's Ladder," in *Gnosis Magazine*, 1989.

[8] Martin Gardner notes that throughout *Dianetics*, "Hubbard reveals a deep-seated hatred of women....When Hubbard's Mama's are not getting kicked in the stomach by their husbands or having affairs with lovers, they are preoccupied with AA [attempted abortion]--usually by means of knitting needles." *Fads & Fallacies in the Name of Science* (New York: Dover Publications, 1957), p.267. Gardner devotes chapter 22 to exposing the pseudoscientific traits of dianetics.

[9] From a letter to Dr. Jan Ehrenwald, 13 May 1946, translated and reprinted in Martin Gardner's *Science Good Bad and Bogus*, p. 153.

[10] A good example of this quest for the weird statistic is the work of Robert Jahn at Princeton University in the Princeton Engineering Anomalies Research (PEAR) lab. See the description of this work in the previous chapter.
  [11] Philip Henry Gosse made this claim in Darwin's time in a work entitled *Creation (Omphalos): An Attempt to Untie the Geological Knot*, published in 1857.

[12] The pseudoscientist often invents a theory to fit his beliefs and then uses the beliefs to support the theory. This type of circular reasoning is common among those who use ancient myths to support their theories and their theories to explain the ancient myths. See the work of Erich von Däniken (*Chariots of the Gods?*), Immanuel Velikovsky (*Worlds in Collision*), and Zecharia Sitchin (*Earth Chronicles*).

[13] In March 1997, 39 member of the UFO millennium cult known as Heaven's Gate committed suicide. They were promised by their leader, Marshall Applewhite, that a space ship would pick up their bodies and deliver them to a "higher level."

ANSWERS TO SELECTED EXERCISES

CHAPTER ONE - INTRODUCTION TO CRITICAL THINKING

No answers are given for the exercises in chapter one. These exercises are best used as the focus of essays and discussions to get the class members involved in the course process and to make sure they understand what the course is about and what they can expect to gain from a course that emphasizes critical thinking.

Chapter one self-test

1 T	7 T	13 F	19 F	25 F	31 T
2 T	8 T	14 T	20 T	26 F	32 T
3 F	9 F	15 F	21 T	27 F	33 F
4 T	10 F	16 F	22 F	28 T	34 T
5 F	11 F	17 F	23 F	29 T	35 F
6 T	12 F	18 F	24 F	30 T	

§

CHAPTER TWO - LANGUAGE AND CRITICAL THINKING

EXERCISES 2-1

A. 2. (old): 'dilapidated', ' antiquated', or 'aged' (more negative); and 'patriarchal', 'seasoned', or 'antique' (more positive). 7. (plan): 'scheme' or 'plot' (more negative); 'organize' or 'devise' (more positive). 10. (take): 'steal' (more negative); 'appropriate' (more positive).

B. 1. (stink): odorous; 4. (shy): restrained; 6. (murder): 'termination'.

EXERCISES 2-6 C

1. This ad makes it sound as if 'chemicals' cannot be used for bad purposes, like making napalm or other chemical weapons.
6. What could it possibly mean for a cigarette to taste as good as it looks? The expression here has no cognitive meaning, but it sounds like a good thing.
11. Why should hair *shine*?

EXERCISES 2-7

1. 'Brutality' is vague because there is no clear and definite boundary separating acts of brutality from acts which do not involve brutality. The expression 'police brutality' might be made clearer by providing some criteria as to what constitutes police brutality. However, most criteria--such as "the use of unnecessary force causing pain or discomfort to one being arrested"--will probably lead to other vague terms--such as 'unnecessary force'--needing clarification. Best might be a partial list of the kinds of cases which constitute brutality, such as the use of deadly force on an unarmed suspect or the breaking of a suspect's arm while putting on handcuffs. Any criteria, however, are bound to be vague to some extent.

220

4. This kind of claim is frequently made by government officials. 'Near future' is the kind of expression which could be replaced with a more specific one, such as one which gives a date or range of dates (e.g., 'by next December 1st' or 'between next June and next October').

EXERCISES 2-8

1. This is a good definition of 'cetacean'.
2. This definition is too broad. It would include in its denotation many persons who are not demagogues, namely, those with charisma who do not use their charm and powerful personality to play upon the basest fears and prejudices of people, which is what a demagogue does.
3. On one level, this definition may be good, namely, on the level of the novel: if the definition fits the character giving it, then the definition is a good one. However, as a definition considered in and of itself, this one is too narrow. It excludes from its denotation what most people would consider to be essential to free speech, namely, speech which criticized the government.
4. This definition would be both too broad and too narrow. It is too broad because it includes in its denotation people who drink two or more beers a day and are not alcoholics (such as sumo wrestlers). It is too narrow because it excludes from its definition those who drink other kinds of alcoholic beverages besides beer but are alcoholics. It also excludes those who are alcoholics and who drink no alcohol!
5. This definition is packed with theoretical assumptions and implications. It excludes human fetuses and comatose humans from its denotation. This may be acceptable to some people, but it is a consequence of the definition which might lead others to reject it.
6. This is a common, but greatly flawed definition of 'spirit'. It is too vague because it tells us what a spirit is NOT rather than what a spirit is.
7. Many students will find this definition obscure. A careful examination of it, however, reveals that it is a humorous way of saying that the word 'depression' has such great negative emotive content that economists and politicians would rather use a milder word, 'recession.' (By the way, Galbraith is aware that economists give technical definitions of the two terms and consider a recession and a depression to be distinct.)
9. This definition of 'aggression' is too narrow; it excludes *verbal* attacks, for example.
18. This definition is too vague. What is *a reasonable man in present-day Western society*?

EXERCISE 2-9

1. Stated as a fact and is a strong claim.
2. Stated as a fact and is a very strong claim
4. Stated as a fact and is a very strong claim.
5. Stated as a fact and is a very strong claim.
6. Stated as an opinion and is a strong claim.
7. Stated as a fact and is a very strong claim.
9. Stated as a fact and is a very strong claim.
11. Stated as an opinion and is a strong claim
15. Stated as an opinion is a weak claim
16. Stated as facts and stated weakly. (Don't be misled by the use of *will*, which seems to indicate a strong claim. The weasel words *as much as* make the claim a weak one.)
17. Stated as an opinion and is a weak claim
21. Stated as a fact and stated very strongly
25. Stated as an opinion and stated weakly
30. Stated as a fact and stated very strongly

EXERCISE 2-10

1. F	9. T	17. T	25. T	33. F
2. F	10. T	18. T	26. T	34. T
3. T	11. T	19. F	27. F	35. T
4. T	12. T	20. T	28. T	
5. F	13. T	21. F	29. T	
6. F	14. T	22. T	30. T	
7. T	15. T	23. F	31. T	
8. T	16. T	24. T	32. T	

§

CHAPTER THREE - SOURCES

EXERCISES 3-1

1. What president hasn't made such claims? Such claims are about as trustworthy as long range weather forecasts. The subject matter is very controversial, very complex, and what is being predicted is on shaky grounds. Most presidents are not economists (so this source is probably not an expert), but even if an economist made this prediction, it would be wise to take it with a grain of salt (i.e., suspend judgment). Note that these weakly Stated empirical evaluations are couched in vague language: 'as much as' leaves room for everything from 0 to the percentages Stated. Furthermore, no deadline is Stated. When are these effects on inflation and unemployment supposed to be felt? Finally, the likelihood of being able to show that any change in inflation or unemployment was caused by the president's policies is slim, indeed. The claims are practically meaningless.

3. Expert; biology is a non-controversial field (experts agree on fundamental facts and methodologies); she is stating her opinion and it is a weak one, a statement of *mere possibility,* so I would accept it based upon the general knowledge that environmental pollution is a common problem in our society; it seems reasonable to believe that the state of California requires that its biologists have the proper degrees and credentials; to know more about this particular state biologist's reliability I would need to know her reputation in the field.

6. No special expertise is needed for this claim. If the newspaper is reliable, there would normally be no reason to doubt this claims which are put forth as facts. (Note: there are 2 facts claimed here: (1) that there were 3 stabbings; and (2) that inmates stabbed inmates. Either of the claims could be inaccurate, of course; and, barring any special need to believe one way or the other on this issue, it might be wise to suspend judgment until there is further corroboration from other reports; if the story has a byline you can tell who authored it and you would need to know that writer's track record on accuracy to determine his or her reliability; otherwise, you must consider only the reputation and track record of the newspaper itself.

8. Non-expert; Stated as a fact and Stated strongly; his claim is credible (it is, unfortunately within the realm of possibility that our government would do such a thing) but I would suspend judgment on it because the source should be considered unreliable due to the strong possibility that it is propaganda; I would not concern myself with this source any further but would seek out more objective parties for further information.

11. Expert; controversial field; his claim is Stated as a fact but it is a metaphysical claim; thus, even after determining the reputation of this philosopher, I should study other equally reputable philosophers with different views on the subject before making up my mind on this issue.

13. Non-expert. It seems to me that Mr. Coleman ought to seek other means of employment if he thinks comets are causing teenage suicides and airplane crashes. Mr. Coleman's opinions about the connection between Halley's comet and teenage suicides and airline crashes are incredible and ought to be rejected. He may be an expert on suicide prevention, but his claims are well outside of that field. These tragic events also coincide with the fall from first to last place of the Chicago Cubs and with Ronald Reagan's term of office (and with many other things as well). I would not concern myself further with this source on astrological or paranormal matters.

15. You are told the source is an expert; the field of economics is controversial; the claim is clearly this person's

222

opinion Stated as a fact, but it is Stated weakly (note the weasel words "as much as"). The expert is saying that interest rates will not drop by more than ten percent in the next six months--a pretty safe claim under most conditions. I would say that if one has no knowledge of interest rates that one should suspend judgment on the claim. But anyone knowing the history of interest rates in recent years would know that the expert is asserting something about as extraordinary as claiming that the average price of a new home will not drop by more 10 % next month. That would be a very weak claim, indeed. One shouldn't reject it. To suspend judgment seems unnecessary. A knowledgeable person would not ask for proof of such a claim and would accept it because it is a pretty safe bet. To determine this person's reliability, one would have to establish that he or she is really a qualified economist. One would also want to know his or her track record in the area of predications about interest rates and other related matters.

19. Most likely a non-expert (journalist) is reporting on the claims of experts (the doctors and scientists). Both the non-expert and the experts are putting forth their claims as facts. Medicine is a mixed field; some areas are controversial and other areas are not. There would normally be no reason to doubt the report that the doctors made the claim they are said to have made about the over-use of antibiotics. The fact that the doctors issued statements in several cities around the world indicates their belief in the urgency of the message. But should one believe--solely on the basis of this report--that antibiotics are being overused throughout the world, and because of this are losing their disease-fighting power? Having no reason to doubt their claim and having some experience with antibiotics becoming ineffective because of extended use, I would accept the claim as probably true. If you have no knowledge of antibiotics, you should suspend judgment until you learn a little more. You would not likely be able to determine the reliability of each of these expert sources. See the answer to number 6 above for determining the reliability of the journalist.

23. Expert; controversial field; Stated as a fact but the claim is a self-assessment of her evidence and is a strongly asserted opinion. One ought to suspend judgment, regardless of the reliability of the source, until one sees the evidence. There is no reason to suspect that the source here is unreliable. Her degrees, credentials, reputation should be considered, but opposing experts should also be considered.

25. Woodford is presented as an expert speaking in his field. The claim he makes about melanin and marijuana having a similar chemical structure is stated as a fact and is not likely to be in a controversial area of chemistry, since it involves only comparing the chemical structure of two substances. It would therefore be reasonable to accept it as probably true. Woodford is also an expert in drug abuse court cases. His conclusion—that drug urinalysis *may* be inaccurate for dark-skinned—people is equally reasonable, as it is a weakly Stated empirical opinion by an expert. The reliability of a chemist would be determined by degrees, credentials, experience and reputation.

EXERCISE 3-3

	10 T	20 T	30 T	39 F
1 T	11 F	21 F	31 F	40 T
2 T	12 T	22 T	32 T	41 T
3 F	13 F	23 T	33 F	42 T
4 T	14 F	24 T	34 T	43 F
5 T	15 T	25 T	35 T	44 T
6 T	16 F	26 F	36 T	45 F
7 F	17 T	27 T	37 T	
8 T	18 T	28T	38 T	
9 T	19T	29 T		

CHAPTER FOUR - IDENTIFYING ARGUMENTS

EXERCISE 4-1

1. This is a complete sentence which makes a statement, so it could be used as premise or a conclusion in an argument.

5. This is a fragment of a sentence; it does not make a statement, so it could not be a premise or a conclusion in an argument.

8. This sentence makes a statement. It could be used as a premise or a conclusion.

12. This is a fragment of a sentence. It does not make a statement. It cannot be used as a premise or a conclusion.

15. This sentence makes a statement. It could be used as a premise or a conclusion.

EXERCISE 4-2

1. Premise   : Justice is nothing but the way the rich protect their interests.
Conclusion: Justice can't exist for the poor.
Premise indicator: because

5. Premise: Size is irrelevant to intelligence.
Conclusion: You are wrong in stating that women must be less intelligent than men.
Premise indicator: because
Conclusion indicator: it is necessarily the case that

10. Premise: He died before his twentieth birthday.
Conclusion: King Tutankhamen was not a great king.
Premise indicator: because

14. Premises: Astronomy was born of superstition; eloquence of ambition, hatred, falsehood and flattery;
geometry of avarice; physics of an idle curiosity and even moral philosophy of human pride.
Conclusion: The arts and sciences owe their birth to our vices.
Conclusion indicator: Thus

EXERCISE 4-3

There are several correct formulations for each of these.

1. Since immorality has to stop somewhere and because decent people have to start standing up for their rights, nude bathing should not be allowed.

6. There is nothing in the Bible which forbids slavery. The Bible is the word of God. Therefore, slavery was ordained by God.

EXERCISE 4-4

1. Premise: "Such a law would allow government to substitute its laws for our freedom to make individual decisions."
Premise: "It didn't work with liquor prohibition"
Premise: "it won't work with smoking prohibitions."
   Conclusion: "There should be no law which regulates when and where an individual may smoke."

6. Premise: "My first four husbands were insecure babies"
   Conclusion: "Men are all insecure babies"

9. Premise "As Superintendent of Schools, you have a vested interest in the funding bill before this legislative committee."
   Conclusion: "Your arguments for increased funding of the public school system may be justifiably ignored."

12. Premise: No one ever did anything he or she did not want to do.
   Conclusion: If Smith robbed that bank, then he wanted to do it.

224

15. Premises: If fatalism is true, then everything that happens has to happen. If no one can change what must happen, then there is no sense in worrying about what happens, whether it is good or bad.
  Conclusion: Fatalism should take away our worries.

EXERCISE 4-5 A

1. Premise: It might lead to psychosomatic illness or it might result in anti-social behavior"
Conclusion: "Holding in one's feelings in not healthy"
Premise indicator: "since"

7. Premise: "Either it will rain or it will snow."
Premise: "It will not snow."
Conclusion: "it will rain."
Conclusion indicator: "Therefore"

11. Premises: If the President is telling the truth then the Russians will not invade Poland. The Russians will invade Poland.
  Conclusion: The President is lying.
  Conclusion indicator: So

12. Premises: Either the Germans not will quit the United Nations or the moon will turn to green cheese. The moon will not turn to green cheese.
  Conclusion: The Germans will not quit the United Nations.
  Conclusion indicator: it follows that

EXERCISE 4-5 B

1. The conclusion of this argument is 'There must be simple substances.' 'Because' and 'for' are indicators. 'There are composites' and 'a composite is nothing else than a collection or aggregate of simple substances' are premises.
  2. This is not an argument.
  3. This is not an argument; it is a conditional statement.
  4. This is not an argument.
  8. The conclusion of this argument is 'memory should not be trusted as the sole judge of the truth of any claim.' The premise is 'memory is fallible and memory sometimes is constituted by later acts.' 'Since' is a premise indicator.
  13. The premise of this argument is 'She did well on the exam.' The word 'so' is a conclusion indicator. The conclusion is 'she will graduate.'
  16. This is a question. It is neither an argument, nor an explanation.
  19. The conclusion of this argument is '[W]e ought mutually to tolerate one another.' 'Because' is a premise indicator. 'We are all weak, irrational, and subject to change and error' is a premise.
  21. This is not an argument; it is a conditional statement.
  25. This is not an argument.
  27. The conclusion of this argument is 'there must be life on Mars.' 'Since' is a premise indicator. The premise is 'nobody has been able to prove there isn't life there.'

EXERCISE 4-7

In the answers to this set of exercises, premise indicators are *italicized*, conclusion indicators are **boldfaced**.

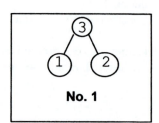

No. 1

1. "*Since* [1][beauty] is no creature of our reason...[and] *since* [2]it strikes us without reference to use...**we must conclude that** [3] beauty is, for the greater part, some quality in bodies acting mechanically upon the human mind by the intervention of the senses."

6. This is not an argument.

7. [1] Women are directly fitted for acting as the nurses and teachers of our early childhood *by the fact that* [2] they are themselves childish, frivolous and short-sighted;[3]in a word, they are big children all their life long....

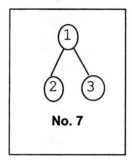

No. 7

12. [1]No educated man stating plainly the elementary notions that every educated man holds about the matters that principally concern government could be elected to office in a democratic state, save perhaps by a miracle. [2]His frankness would arouse fear, and those fears would run against him; [3] it is his business to arouse fears that will run in favor of him.

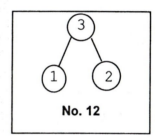

No. 12

19. [1]I just don't see why multicultural education is so popular or why people think it is value-free. [2]Multicultural education is not value-free, despite what its proponents say. [3]It teaches children to respect and accept the evil values and practices of other cultures such as genital mutilation of young girls in Africa and handing out death sentences for blasphemy in Iran.

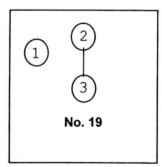

No. 19

226

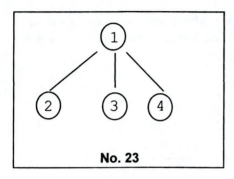

No. 23

23. [1]Restitution, rather than imprisonment should be required in those cases where property damage is the issue; *for*, [2]sending a person to prison ought to be avoided whenever possible and [3]the victim of a property crime is likely to be much more satisfied with our criminal justice system if he or she is repaid. [4]If a criminal goes to prison, he is not going to be able to make restitution. {Note that this argument assumes that the victim of property crime is due some sort of satisfaction.}

28. This is not an argument.

EXERCISE 4-8

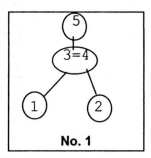
No. 1

1.1= a;   1.2 = a;   1.3 = c;   1.4 = c;   1.5 = b;
1.6 = c ('therefore' is a conclusion indicator; 'since' is a premise indicator).
Note: Statements 3 and 4 are identical. Thus, here the same statement is used as both a premise and a conclusion.

2.1 = d;   2.2 = b;   2.3 = a   2.4 = a ('for').
Note: Statement 1 is neither a premise nor a conclusion, so it is not diagrammed as being linked to statements 2 and 3.

No. 2

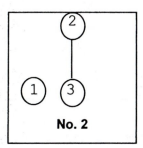

No. 4

4.1 c (statement 2 supports 1 and 1 supports 3); 4.2 = a; 4.3 = c (statement 3 is supported by statement 1 and supports statement 5); 4.4 = a; 4.5 = b (this is the main conclusion); 4.6 = a; 4.7 = c ('for' is a premise indicator; 'so' is a conclusion indicator)

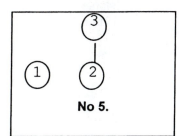
No 5.

5.1= d;   5.2= a;   5.3 = b; 5.4 = b ('therefore') Note: This argument has an unstated premise (UP): "There is disagreement about the Truth in the Holy Book."

228

11. There are two arguments in this passage. Argument
1 consists of statements 1,2 and 3.
11.1 = a; 11.2 = a; 11.3 = b;
Argument 2 consists of statements 4,5 and 6.   11.4 =
b;   11.5 = a;   11.6 = a; 11.7 = c (`thus' is a
conclusion indicator; 'since' is a premise indicator)

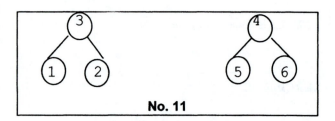

No. 11

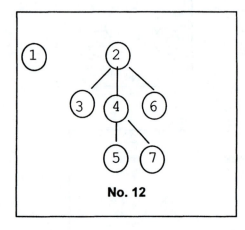

No. 12

12.1 d;   12.2 = b;   12.3 = a;   12.4 = c; 12.5 = a; 12.6 = c; 12.7 =
a;   12.8 = a (`for').
 Note that statement 1 is background information necessary for
understanding the meaning of statement 2.

15. There are two arguments
in this passage. Argument 1 consists of statements 1, 2 and 3.
15.1 = b; 15.2 = a;   15.3 = a;

Argument 2 consists of statements 4,5 and 6.
15.4 = b; 15.5 = a;   15.6 = a;
15.7 = a (both arguments use 'for')

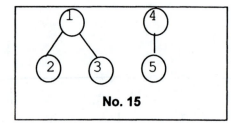

No. 15

EXERCISE 4-9

1 true	8 true	15 true	22 false	29 true
2 false	9 true	16 true	23 true	30 true
3 true	10 false	17 true	24 true	31 true
4 true	11 true	18 true	25 false	32 true
5 false	12 true	19 true	26 false	33 true
6 false	13 false	20 false	27 true	34 true
7 true	14 true	21 true	28 false	35 true

CHAPTER FIVE - EVALUATING ARGUMENTS

EXERCISE 5-1 A

1. Valid by modus tollens.
3. Valid by modus ponens.
6. Invalid; affirming the consequent.
12. Invalid; denying the antecedent.
14. Valid by hypothetical syllogism.

19. Valid by disjunctive syllogism.

EXERCISE 5-1 B

1. 'He is responsible for the accident' is the implied conclusion, derived by applying modus ponens to the two Stated claims.
4. The conclusion, "it's not going to rain," could be validly inferred by modus ponens, assuming as an unstated premise 'If she didn't bring her umbrella then it's not going to rain.' This conclusion could also be validly inferred by disjunctive syllogism, assuming as an unstated premise 'Either she brought her umbrella or it's not going to rain.'
7. 'The soul must be made up of atomic particles' is the implied conclusion, derived by applying modus ponens to the two stated claims.
10. 'If I buy a car, it means bye-bye education,' derived by applying hypothetical syllogism to the two Stated claims.

EXERCISES 5-2 A

1. Ad populum and appeal to guilt
3. Argument from ignorance
5. Ad hominem
8. Ad hominem
10. Questionable assumption
12. Appeal to vanity
15. Poisoning the well
18. Appeal to fear
20. Questionable assumptions
23. This is an irrelevant comparison. The shipyard workers were exposed to large quantities of asbestos fibers in the air. The asbestos in insulation or tile is not free floating *until one tries to remove it!*

EXERCISE 5-2 B

1. Ad populum, poisoning the well; argument from ignorance and irrelevant appeal to authority
4. Hayakawa evades the issue by making an irrelevant comparison and an irrelevant appeal to authority.
6. Ad populum
8. Ad populum and appeal to authority (also, it is irrelevant to the issue to bring up what the Pentagon spends on tanks and airplanes)
11. Questionable assumptions

EXERCISE 5-4 A

1. Loaded question
2. False dilemma
5. Begging the question
7. Invalid by denying the antecedent
10. Non sequitur; though, perhaps the arguer is making the questionable (and unstated) assumption that the government should pay for whatever medical services an individual can't afford on her own.
11. The truth of the stated premise depends upon its meaning. If it means that the average height of women is less that the average height of men, then the statement is true. If it means that every woman is smaller than every man, then it is false. There is an unstated premise here--that whoever is larger is stronger--and this is a questionable premise.
14. Invalid by affirming the consequent
15. Begging the question
18. Begging the question

20. These premises are warranted, relevant and sufficient to support their conclusion..
21. Suppressed evidence
22. False dilemma (perhaps meanings don't reside anywhere and aren't in anything. Maybe meanings are a function of the usage of words.)
23. Begging the question. The arguer has assumed that this candidate is like most politicians, in addition to assuming that most politicians can't be believed.
24. Appeal to authority
27. The arguer begs the question as well as poisons the well. He assumes what should be proved, viz., that abortion is murder.
28. Slippery slope

EXERCISE 5-4 B

1. Questionable assumption; begging the question
3. Questionable assumption; hasty conclusion
4. Questionable assumption (that abortion is the slaughtering of children); questionable claims; slippery slope
5. The premise is a statement of *logical* possibility. It would be false only if it contained a self-contradiction (such as 'round square' or 'married bachelor'). The assumption is relevant to proving the conclusion and is sufficient as well. Thus, this is a sound argument.
8. The first premise—'either there is no afterlife or there is one'—is a tautology; it is necessarily true. The second premise --'if there is none, then it is absurd to believe in punishment after death'--follows necessarily from the tautology and its implications and is therefore also true. But the third premise--that 'an all-just and all-merciful God would not punish a creature for being too weak to resist desires instilled by the Creator'--is a metaphysical claim and is questionable. It assumes that if there is a God, God is all-just and all-merciful. It assumes, in fact, the very issue that ought to be proved, viz., that God won't punish anyone. Thus, the argument begs the question.
9. Poisoning the well and straw man. To argue against giving the Contras money is not to advocate communism; so the refutation distorts the view of his opponent. And the refutation tries to associate the opponent with something considered evil.
12. Good argument, though it would be better if it were clearer what is meant by without *meaning to our minds.* I take Hocking to mean that each of the alternatives is inconceivable. The premises seem true, relevant and sufficient.
14. Questionable claims; slippery slope
17. The premises seem clear enough, relevant to demonstrating that the 'liberals' are wrong about the rich paying their fair share of taxes, but the evidence isn't sufficient because Buckley suppresses relevant evidence. Buckley doesn't reveal either what amount or what percentage of the earned income the 3 percent account for. If those 3 percent account for 62 percent of the nation's earned income, then they're only paying half as much in taxes as they should. Or if 97 percent of the people account for 35 percent of all earned income but are paying 69 percent of all taxes, then the rich are paying a lot less than their share in taxes than the rest of us.
19. Poisoning the well and straw man. The opponent distorts proponent's view and tires to associate it with evil.

EXERCISE 5-4 C

1. Straw man; the letter distorts Mondale's position.
3. Begging the question (Brennan assumes that executing a person denies their humanity, but that is the issue he should be proving, along with the assumption that denying a person's humanity while punishing that person constitutes cruel and unusual punishment.)
5. Seems like a reasonable argument to me
6. This rambling letter in support of the candidate not in office contains some warranted claims but it also makes some questionable claims (e.g., *if we re-elect the president we'll either go bankrupt or have the highest tax rate in the world* and *nobody is better off today...* Also, even if it is true that the president's opponent is sincere and honest (which might be questionable), it wouldn't be a sufficient reason to vote for him or to believe that things will be any better under his administration. Finally, the concluding claim is a bit ambiguous. If the president were re-elected, his

supporters would agree that the election resulted with "what's best for the United States"!

8. The sponsors of this ad wrongly accuse the EPA of demanding an unreasonable procedure: measuring pollutants as they come out of a smoke stack. If they were measured on the ground, what would be measured? The ad seems to say that it is irrelevant what measurements are made at the top of the stack. I don't think so. What would be irrelevant would be to provide data about pollution at the bottom of the stack on the ground or on the ground in the next town over. The only way to know what the source of the pollution is would be to measure it at the source! Imagine trying to convince someone doing a smog check on your car to put the measuring device across the street instead of up your exhaust pipe!

10. This is about as good an argument as one should reasonably expect in a letter to the editor. Of course, the letter writer assumes the reader has some basic background knowledge--a reasonable assumption, since the reader of the letter is a newspaper reader.

12. Questionable assumptions about what a newspaper is supposed to be doing; begs the question

15. Loaded language, suppressed evidence, questionable claims, and appeal to fear

EXERCISE 5-5

1 true	7 false	13 true	18 true	23 true	28 true
2 true	8 true	14 false	19 false	24 true	29 false
3 false	9 true	15 false	20 false	25 true	30 true
4 false	10 true	16 true	21 false	26 false	31 true
5 true	11 true	17 true	22 false	27 true	
6 false	12 false				

CHAPTER SIX - EVALUATING EXTENDED ARGUMENTS

EXERCISE 6-1

1. Unstated: "We don't make the car payment," and "We don't want to get kicked out into the streets."
2. Unstated: "The Reds came in second."

CHAPTER SEVEN – SAMPLING AND ANALOGICAL REASONING

EXERCISE 7-1

1. false	11. true
2. true	12. true
3. false	13. false
4. false	14. true
5. false	15. true
6. true	16. true
7. false	17. false
8. true	18. true
9. false	19 true
10. false	

232

EXERCISE 7-4

1. Unrepresentative sample. The method used is not likely to give a good cross-section of the voting population.

5. Hasty generalization.

EXERCISE 7-7

1 true
2 true
3 false
4 false
5 false
6 false
7 false

EXERCISE 7-8

1. This argument is based on the assumption that there are countless planets, an assumption itself based on analogical reasoning. For, these countless planets have not been observed. But, given our knowledge of the origin and nature of our own solar system, it seems reasonable to assume that of the countless stars in the countless galaxies, there are countless planets, some about the age and size of earth and in relation to a star as we are to our sun. If this assumption is granted--and it seems reasonable to assume so, otherwise we would need to justify believing that our solar system's origin and nature is unique and not likely to be representative of the rest of the universe--then the conclusion is a sound one. Note the language used to express the degree of probability of the conclusion: "there may very likely exist...." The language is appropriate for the evidence.
10. The lawyer ignores a relevant and highly significant difference between the two kinds of testing. The one is to prevent epidemics of contagious diseases; the other is to catch criminals and punish them. Thus, the fact that tuberculin testing is justifiable in no way implies that drug testing is justifiable. The defense of drug testing will have to come from other grounds. The argument is based on an irrelevant comparison.
13. This is a false analogy..
17. This is a false analogy.
22. This is a false analogy.
23. This is a good analogical argument. 4
24. These kinds of analogies often have a further point. In this case the author is trying to persuade us that Walker "has given aid and comfort to those seeking to dismantle the greatness of art by turning it into a particularly pernicious branch of advertising, the better to control it through the politics of the marketplace." I think what Link is trying to say is that art should not be seen as propaganda, as a set of commercials for ideas. He doesn't think art or society is served very well if every work of art is reduced to an offensive idea in the eyes of its interpreters. It is a dangerous practice to interpret every work of art as a "message" about every topic it touches, or can be stretched to touch, by an imaginative interpreter. Every work of art becomes just more grist for the mill for the perpetually offended. The Venus de Milo offends one feminist for its glorification of the mutilation of women; the Mona Lisa offends the cross-dresser who feels the artist is portraying in a demeaning way a man dressed as a woman; the whole Sistine chapel--nay, most of Italy--becomes an offensive commercial for religious fantasies and the evil which has come of them (according to some non-Christians); etc.

Finally, Link has one further point: Walker has no right being indignant at those who interpret her art using the same reductionist method of interpretation she used regarding the award she was given. I don't think he is calling Walker a hypocrite. I think he is suggesting she rethink her views on art and propaganda. He also, of course, takes it for granted that art shouldn't be propaganda. The state of California thinks differently. It not only lifted Walker's story from its test, it lifted another story which had a vegetarian character in it. The state's reason: it was lifted on the grounds that it might upset some meat eaters!

Link's comparison of Walker's reaction to the statuette to the Christian conservatives' reaction to her short story is relevant and a sound one. Good analogy.

CHAPTER EIGHT - CAUSAL REASONING

EXERCISE 8-1

1 true	6 true	11 false	16 false	21 false
2 false	7 true	12 false	17 true	22 true
3 false	8 true	13 true	18 true	23 true
4 true	9 true	14 true	19 false	24 false
5 false	10 true	15 false	20 false	25 true

EXERCISE 8-2

1.1. This is a weaker conclusion than the original one. The argument is therefore strengthened. (Generally speaking, the weaker the conclusion, the less evidence needed to support it; and the stronger the conclusion, the more evidence needed to support it.)
1.2. This would eliminate being able to control for relevant causal factors. It would weaken the argument.
1.3. The control group and experimental group must be alike in all relevant respects except for the factor being tested. This would weaken the argument.
1.4. The increase in the number of cases showing the effect would increase the strength of the argument.
1.5. The increase in the number of rats would strengthen the argument, providing the percentages of rats showing the tumors remained the same. However, using ten times as many rats will not strengthen the argument ten times!
1.6. This is a weaker conclusion than the original; it strengthens the argument.
1.7. This introduces a loss in control over potential factors being introduced which might be causing the difference in effects. It weakens the argument.
1.8. Same as 1.7. Perhaps the x-rays are a significant causal factor in the development of the tumors.
1.9. If you did not know this, it would increase the number of significant similarities between humans and laboratory animals from your point of view and would thus strengthen the argument.
1.10. This conclusion actually is two conclusions. One is that saccharin may increase the risk of bladder cancer for the offspring of women who use it during pregnancy. That conclusion may appear to be weaker than the original one, but it is actually stronger, since the original study involved offspring who were fed a saccharin diet--a very unlikely parallel for humans. The other conclusion is that pregnant women should be given a warning that using saccharin during pregnancy "may increase the risk that their child will develop bladder cancer." Whether this warning is warranted or not is debatable.

EXERCISE 8-3

1. Post hoc fallacy. Because of the difficulty in controlling for potential causal factors, a prospective study on large numbers of people with different degrees of acne might be best.
6. False cause. Correlation does not prove causality. It probably would be more sensible to produce a counterargument than to do a scientific study to determine whether or not there is a causal connection between food additives and violent crime. Also, 'food additives' covers a wide variety of substances.
10. In testing the claim *cowpox causes immunity to smallpox* by inoculating human beings is unimaginable today. A controlled experiment would have meant inoculating with smallpox another group of humans who had *not* been infected with cowpox. Since the test is for *immunity*, both the experimental and control groups get inoculated. The experimental group is infected with smallpox; the control group is not. Such an experiment would probably have led

to the deaths of most, if not all, of those in the control group. A prospective study would have gathered a large random sample, divided the sample into two groups: one which had been infected with cowpox and one which had not. Over time, the incidence of smallpox should be significantly greater in the group not infected with cowpox, if it is true that *cowpox causes immunity to smallpox.* Apparently, Jenner was reasoning by a retrospective analysis. A number of people don't die of smallpox but they are just as exposed to it as those who do die. Comparing those who show this effect with others like them who don't show the effect, it was common knowledge that dairymaids were all in the first group. Being a dairymaid exposes one to cowpox. So, Jenner reasoned it was the cowpox which was the causal factor in the dairymaid's not getting smallpox.

16. Why Dr. James did not study nervous drivers rather than string players is beyond me. Why introduce an analogy when you don't have to? The differences between playing a string instrument on stage and driving a car during a driving test would seem to outweigh any similarities they might have. Thus, even if the oxyprenolol helped the string players, it would be a stretch to conclude that it would help nervous drivers pass their driving test.

I must confess that I did not find the outcome very striking. For one thing, we are not told what the mean improvement for the control group was, so we do not know whether a 5 percent improvement is significant. Furthermore, since the samples were small, the one player with a 73 percent improvement and those with 30 percent not only could account for the entire 5 percent group improvement, but they indicate that a good number of the experimental group must have deteriorated.

Note the way the conclusion is worded: "the results *suggest* that *some* people *might* benefit greatly from such medication." Sure, and some might *not* benefit greatly. In any case, the proper way to have done this study would have been to have taken two groups of people who had failed their driving tests because of nervousness. Oxyprenolol is given to the experimental group and a placebo is given to the control group. Neither the subjects nor the driving evaluators should know who has been given the oxyprenolol. Such a study is called a *double blind study.* The study should be a double blind study to eliminate any psychological effects on the part of subjects (if one *thinks* she's been given a beta-blocker, she might relax) and any bias on the part of the evaluator (if she knows the subject has been given a beta-blocker she might evaluate him differently). If oxyprenolol is a significant causal factor in reducing nervousness of drivers being tested, then we should see a significantly higher percentage of the experimental group passing their driving tests.

CHAPTER NINE - SCIENCE AND PSEUDOSCIENCE

EXEERCISE 9-1

1 true	9 false	17 true	25 false	33 true	41 true
2 true	10 false	18 false	26 true	34 true	42 true
3 false	11 true	19 true	27 true	35 true	43 false
4 false	12 true	20 true	28 false	36 false	44 false
5 false	13 true	21 false	29 true	37 true	45 true
6 false	14 true	22 true	30 false	38 true	46 true
7 true	15 true	23 false	31 false	39 true	47 true
8 false	16 false	24 true	32 true	40 true	

Glossary

A

ad hoc hypotheses. An hypothesis created to account for a specific case or situation, especially a case which seems to refute ones theory, e.g., claiming that an esp experiment failed because it was observed by someone who does not believe in esp and their hostile vibes interfered with the subjects powers.

ad hominem. A critical remark about a person rather than about the persons argument.

ad populum. Irrelevant appeal to the popularity of a belief to justify it. Also known as the bandwagon fallacy, the appeal to the mob, the democratic fallacy and the appeal to popularity.

ambiguity. Lack of clarity due to a word or expression being reasonably open to more than one interpretation.

analogy. Similarity in some respects between things otherwise dissimilar. A comparison based on similarities.

analytic statement. A statement whose predicate is included in its subject. Statement which is true by definition. For example, A bachelor is an unmarried male.

analysis. A separation of material or an abstract entity into its constituent parts. To analyze an argument is to separate the premises and conclusions from background material, fluff, examples, illustrations, etc., in order to evaluate the argument.

antecedent. The *if* statement in a conditional statement.

apophenia. Perceiving patterns where there are none.

applied kinesiology. The belief that muscles reflect the flow of chi ("energy") and that by measuring muscle resistance one can determine the health of bodily organs and nutritional deficiencies.

a priori claims. Non-empirical claims which are taken to be necessarily true but which are not matters of definition.

arguing in a circle. To use a statement to prove itself.

argument. Any set of statements where at least one statement (a premise) is put forth to support the truth or reasonableness of another statement (a conclusion) or the reasonableness of an action.

argument from ignorance. Arguing that something is true on the ground that it hasn't been proved false, or that something is false on the ground that it hasn't been proved true.

assumption. Something taken for granted; believed or asserted without providing any proof or support. Every argument is based on assumptions, premises put forth or presupposed without proof.

autokinetic effect. Perceiving a stationary point of light in the dark as moving.

B

begging the question. Assuming what ought to be proved in an argument.

C

class. A group of items which share something in common.

classify. To group items according to shared characteristics.

clustering illusion. The clustering illusion is the intuition that random events which occur in clusters are not really random events.

cognitive content. The descriptive or literal sense or reference of a word or expression.

communal reinforcement. The process by which a claim becomes a strong belief through repeated assertion by members of a community.

composition, fallacy of. Reasoning that what is true of the parts must be true of the whole.

conclusion. A statement asserted to follow (either with necessity or with some degree of probability) from another statement or set of statements.

conditional statement. A complex statement asserting that a statement--B-is true, on condition that another statement--A--is true. The form of the conditional statement is *If A, then B*.] The A statement is called the *antecedent*]; the B statement is called the *consequent*.

confabulation. A fantasy that has unconsciously replaced events in memory.

confirmation bias. A type of selective thinking whereby one tends to notice and to look for what confirms one's beliefs, and to ignore, not look for, or undervalue the relevance of what contradicts one's beliefs.

consequent. The *then* statement in a conditional statement.

consistent statements. Statements are said to be consistent with each other if they can be true simultaneously.

contradictory statements. Statements are said to contradict one another if both cannot be true and both cannot be false. If S_1 is the contradictory of S_2, then if S_1 is true, S_2 must be false, and vice-versa. E.g., The sun is round is the contradictory of The sun is not round.

contrary statements. Statements are said to be contrary to one another if both cannot be true. Contraries may both be false. E.g. The sun is square is contrary to The sun is triangular.

correlation. Mutual or reciprocal relation between two things.

counter-argument. A refutation; an argument offered against another argument.

counter-example. A refuting example; an example which shows that a claim is false.

D

deductive argument. An argument which asserts that its conclusion follows necessarily from its premises.

descriptive generalization. A generalization which ascribes a characteristic or quality only to those members of a class which have actually been observed.

division, fallacy of. Reasoning that what is true of the whole must be true of the parts.

dogmatic. Characterized by an authoritative, arrogant assertion of unproved or unprovable principles.

E

emotive meaning. The attitude or feeling expressed by a word or expression.

empirical. Originating in or tested by sense experience and observation.

empirical generalization. A generalization based on sense experience and observation..

enthymeme. A syllogism in which one of the premises is unstated. (The term is sometimes extended to refer to any argument in which a premise is unstated).

enumerative or simple inductive generalization. A generalization which ascribes a characteristic or quality to all or some of the members of a class which have not been observed, on the basis of observations made of some of the class members.

epistemology. The study of the origins, nature and extent of knowledge.

equivocation. Ambiguous use of a key term in an argument whereby a term is used in different senses in different places in the argument.

euphemism. An inoffensive or mild expression used in place of one that might offend or suggest something unpleasant.

evaluation of an argument. To determine the warrantedness of premises and the warrantedness of the inference made in the argument that a conclusion follows from the premises with necessity or some degree of probability.

explain. To render intelligible; to make clear the cause or reason for something; to account for.

F

fallacy. Incorrect or invalid reasoning; also, deceitful arguing.

false analogy. A fallacious argument in which one tries

to prove a point about an item or group of items by comparing it to something very dissimilar.

false cause. A fallacy in which one reasons that simply because two things are correlated they are causally related.

false dilemma. An argument that considers fewer than all of the relevant alternatives to a decision.

falsifiability. Term used by Karl Popper to describe the defining characteristic of scientific theories, viz., they are capable of being tested in ways which might prove them false. He opposed falsifiable theories to metaphysical ones, which cannot be tested in any empirical way to prove them false.

false implication. A statement which is true, but which implies that something is true when it is not, makes a false implication.

Forer effect. Tendency to accept vague and general personality descriptions as uniquely applicable to oneself.

G

generalization. A statement which ascribes some quality or condition to members of a class.

H

hasty conclusion. A conclusion based on relevant but insufficient evidence.

hasty generalization. A generalization based on a sample which is too small.

hypersensory perception (HSP). What some people call intuition (Schick and Vaughn 2001). A person with HSP is very observant and perceptive.

hypothesis. A proposed explanation of some phenomena.

I

ideomotor action. Unconscious muscular movements that can cause such things as dowsing rods or ouija boards to move.

implication. Something that is implied; an inference.

imply. To assert or suggest that something logically follows from something else and may therefore be inferred from it.

inattentional blindness. Not perceiving things that are right before our eyes.

inconsistent statements. Statements are said to be inconsistent with each other if both cannot be true. See contrary statements.

inductive argument. An argument which asserts that its conclusion follows with some degree of probability, rather than necessity, from its premises.

inductive generalization. Empirical generalization which ascribes a characteristic or quality not only to class members which have been observed but also to class members which have not been observed.

infer. To conclude or judge from premises or evidence.

inference. The act of inferring; or, that which is inferred.

L

loaded question. A question which, if answered directly, commits one to implying the truth of a claim which ought to be proved.

M

motive. A psychological reason which explains an action or belief.

N

necessary condition. C is a necessary condition for E if it is necessary that C occur for E to occur. Put another way, it means that *if* C had not occurred, E would not have occurred.

non sequitur. A conclusion or inference that does not follow from its premises.

238

P

pareidolia. A type of illusion or misperception involving a vague or obscure stimulus being perceived as something clear and distinct.

placebo. An inert substance used as a control in an experiment or given to a patient for its psychological effects.

placebo effect. The measurable or observable effect on a person or group that has been given a placebo rather than an active substance.

population or **target population**. A class from which a sample is taken and about which generalizations are to be made based upon the sample..

post hoc fallacy. A type of false cause reasoning in which one reasons that simply because one event preceded another even, the first event is the cause of the second.

preconception. A conception or opinion formed beforehand; a bias.

premise. A statement put forth as a reason for accepting the truth or reasonableness of another statement.

presumption. An assumption that something is true.

presupposition. Something assumed to be true, but left unstated.

Q

questionable analogy. An analogical argument in which the analogue is too dissimilar to the subject to warrant any inference about the subject based only on what is known to be true about the analogue. Also known as **false analogy** and **irrelevant comparison**.

questionable assumption. A premise which is unwarranted.

R

random sample. A sample selected in such a way that every member of the target population has an equal chance of being selected for the sample.

refutation. An argument put forth to disprove a statement, argument, theory, etc.

regressive fallacy. The failure to take into account natural and inevitable fluctuations of things when ascribing causes to them.

repressed memory. A memory of something unpleasant which has been forgotten until years later when an experience triggers the memory.

S

sample. The members of a target population which have been observed and studied.

selective thinking. The process whereby one selects out favorable evidence for remembrance and focus, while ignoring unfavorable evidence for a hypothesis.

self-deception. The process or fact of misleading ourselves to accept as true or valid what is false, invalid, or inadequately supported.

slippery slope. A fallacious form of reasoning which asserts, without providing any proof, that taking (or not taking) a particular action will lead to a series of disastrous consequences.

sound argument. An argument whose premises are warranted and whose conclusion follows from its premises with the degree of certainty asserted for it.

statistical generalization. One which asserts that a quality either does or does not belong to *some* members of a class.

stereotype. An oversimplified classification, invested with special meaning, by a group.

straw man. A distorted or weak version of an argument set forth so as to be easily refuted or defeated.

sub-argument. An argument whose conclusion serves as a premise is another argument.

sufficient condition. C is a sufficient condition for E if the presence of C is sufficient to bring about E. Put another way, it is to say that IF C occurs, E will occur-- everything else being equal.

T

target population. All of the members of a class being studied and from which a sample is taken.

tautology. A statement which is necessarily true.

traditional wisdom, appeal to. A fallacy in reasoning which assumes that because something is well-established and customarily assumed to be true, it therefore is true. The age and traditional acceptance of a belief are irrelevant to the establishment of either its wisdom or its truth.

truth-value. A statement is said to have either the value of true or the value of false; the truth-value of a true statement is true and the truth-value of a false statement is false.

U

universal generalization. One which asserts that a quality or characteristic does or does not belong to *all* the members of a class.

V

vagueness. Lack of clarity due to imprecision or indefiniteness.

validity. The quality of an argument whose conclusion follows from its premises with the degree of certainty asserted for it. A deductively valid argument is one whose conclusion follows necessarily from its premises.

verbal disagreement. An apparent disagreement due to different people using the same term differently.

W

wishful thinking. Believing something is true because one wants it to be true rather than on the basis of solid evidence.

worldview. A person's set of basic beliefs and attitudes about the world, knowledge, and experience.